Using GeoWorks Pro™

GW00726745

GREG SCHULTZ

Library of Congress Catalog No: 91-66627

ISBN: 0-88022-748-6

95 94 93 92   4 3 2 1

Interpretation of the printing code: the rightmost double-digit number is the year of the book's printing; the rightmost single-digit number, the number of the book's printing. For example, a printing code of 92-1 shows that the first printing of the book occurred in 1992.

Using GeoWorks Pro is based on GeoWorks Pro and also can be used with GeoWorks Ensemble Versions 1.2 and 1.0.

Publisher: Lloyd J. Short

Acquisitions Manager: Rick Ranucci

Project Development Manager: Thomas H. Bennett

Managing Editor: Paul Boger

Book Designer: Scott Cook

Production Team: Jeff Baker, Claudia Bell, Scott Boucher, Paula Carroll, Michelle Cleary, Keith Davenport, Mark Enochs, Brook Farling, Dennis Clay Hager, Audra Hershman, Carrie Keesling, Phil Kitchel, Laurie Lee, Anne Owen, Caroline Roop, Louise Shinault, John Sleeva, Kevin Spear, Bruce Steed, Mary Beth Wakefield, Phil Worthington, Christine Young.

CREDITS

Product Director
Timothy S. Stanley

Production Editor
Diane L. Steele

Editors
Tracy L. Barr
Robin Drake
Beth Hoger
Susan M. Shaw

Technical Editor
Marshall Kragen

Composed in **Cheltenham** and
MCP Digital by Que Corporation

DEDICATION

To Inez, for her unfailing love and support.

GREG SCHULTZ

Greg Schultz has written and edited instructional texts on a variety of microcomputer topics. He is the co-author of the second edition of Que's *Using Quicken 3 for the Mac* and has served as technical editor for Que's *Using DacEasy* and *Using MS-DOS 5*. He has taught more than two thousand hours of classroom microcomputer training and has managed training for the northwest branch of a national computer training organization.

In addition to a masters degree in adult education, Mr. Schultz brings to his work a 20-year background in publications and retail management, during which time he has been active in applying computer technology to business problems.

TRADEMARK ACKNOWLEDGMENTS

ACKNOWLEDGMENTS

I would like to thank Diane Steele and the editing team for their excellent contributions and flexibility in the face of two version changes. Thanks also to Marshall Kragen and the GWReps who were always willing to share their technical insights. My appreciation to Tim Stanley and Tim Ryan for their good advice, and particular thanks to Steve Nelson for his counsel and his confidence.

—G.S.

Que would like to thank Chris Noble, Jim Kirkpatrick, and Matt Loveless of GeoWorks for their time invested in providing us with helpful information about GeoWorks Ensemble and GeoWorks Pro. Special thanks to Brian Dougherty for his interest in this project and for contributing the Foreword for the book. Our thanks and appreciation to Kathleen Ryan, especially, and other staff members at America Online who enabled our use of their excellent communications service to transfer important information among people working on this book. Thanks also to Don Eamon of Que for his expertise and assistance with the DR DOS 6.0 task switching section of the book.

CONTENTS AT A GLANCE

TABLE OF CONTENTS

Part II Working with a Desktop

Part III Using the Applications

FOREWORD

Back in 1986, GeoWorks (then Berkeley Softworks) began looking at doing
a high performance graphical environment for Intel based PC's. We had
bootstrapped our company by doing technical consulting work. Many of our
consulting projects required very efficient programming for custom systems.
As we began developing our own products for PC's we were struck by how the
advances in hardware technology were being wasted by increasingly bloated
software. We set out to create a state-of-the-art graphical operating environment that would take maximum advantage of Intel based PC's. While other
system software companies had abandoned efficiency for ease of programming
and portability (the ability to quickly move the operating system to different
machines) we believed the enormous number of Intel based PC users deserved
an operating environment as tightly tuned to their hardware as humanly possible. Four years and over 120 man years of programming later we introduced
GeoWorks Ensemble.

PC/GEOS (PC Graphic Environment Object System), the technology at the heart
of all GeoWorks products, is the highest performance, most robust system
technology you can purchase for your PC. The efficiency and performance built
into the PC/GEOS technology will protect your existing hardware investment
and open PC technology to a much wider audience through more affordable
systems. While the initial applications included in the Ensemble package de-
liver terrific capabilities at a very affordable price, they are only the
beginning. The engine that lies beneath the Ensemble package has only begun
to demonstrate its power. In the fall of 1991, GeoWorks teamed up with Borland
to introduce GeoWorks Pro, combining GeoWorks' integrated suite of graphical
applications with Borland's award-winning Quattro Pro SE spreadsheet. Over
the next few years you will see more and more powerful applications delivered
for the PC/GEOS environment from GeoWorks and other software vendors.

We at GeoWorks appreciate how well accepted our products have become;
in its first 10 months, over 300 copies of Ensemble were shipped to end users
and over 1,000,000 copies were licensed to hardware manufacturers to include
in their PC's. One real measuring rod of success, however, is when you see

publications about your product. I know that Que is a leading, and well-respected publishing company in the computer business. Seeing Que publish a book about GeoWorks Ensemble is really gratifying. I know you will enjoy this book. *Using GeoWorks Pro* will help you get the most out of the product.

As you master GeoWorks Pro, or one of our personal office series products, with the help of this book, rest assured that we will be burning the midnight oil to come up with additional innovations for the GEOS environment. Last, but not least, thanks for using our product.

Brian P. Dougherty
CEO, GeoWorks

Introduction

Whether you are a new computer user or an experienced power-user of other programs, Using GeoWorks Pro provides a comprehensive introduction to GeoWorks Ensemble and GeoWorks Pro. This book provides short lessons, called quick starts, for key applications; a unique collection of tips, contributed by GeoWorks power users; and complete coverage of GeoWorks Ensemble 1.2, a free upgrade issued to all registered users in the fall of 1991, and GeoWorks Pro, a version that is bundled with a special edition of Borland's Quattro Pro spreadsheet. This book introduces the Intermediate Workspace, a feature in GeoWorks Pro that makes file and directory management easier for novices.

Ensemble and Pro are collections of productivity applications that run under the common PC/GEOS interface—a windowing, multitasking graphical operating system. Since its introduction in late 1990, the PC/GEOS operating system has drawn high praise for its capability of providing fast, powerful performance on almost any PC, from the original PC/XT series to the latest 386/486 machines.

Although GeoWorks Ensemble and GeoWorks Pro have had to stand in the shadow of the massively marketed Microsoft Windows interface, the GeoWorks programs have won a growing and enthusiastic following from reviewers and users. A special capability of GeoWorks Ensemble and GeoWorks Pro is that these programs can run on computers which are unable to run Windows; in addition, when these programs run head-to-head with Windows on the more powerful machines, Ensemble and Pro perform with superior speed and ease. These programs are like movies that, although not widely publicized, become word-of-mouth favorites and go on to rival the "blockbusters."

GeoWorks Ensemble and Pro are beautiful examples of the best in graphical interfaces. If you have been a user of DOS-based programs, you can benefit from switching to a graphical interface. The advantages of a graphical interface include the following:

■ All applications share a common interface, eliminating the need to learn different commands for each interface.

■ The capability of multitasking—running multiple applications at one time—places a variety of other capabilities within instant reach.

■ The capability of moving data easily from one application to another enhances the effectiveness of your work.

■ A graphical interface makes learning easier; therefore, even "computer-phobic" users are more comfortable with GeoWorks than the world of DOS commands and multiple menus.

Who Should Use This Book

Users of any version of GeoWorks Ensemble or GeoWorks Pro can benefit from this book. The coverage of all GeoWorks versions in one volume provides a single, comprehensive source for answers to your questions. The quick-start tutorial chapters provide hands-on training not available elsewhere, and tips from power users offer a unique bonus.

Every user can benefit from the collection of tips, identified by the GeoWorks WORLD icon. These tips come from GeoWorks staff members and volunteer representatives who work in the GeoWorks Forum on America Online.

How To Use This Book

This book progresses from basic skills to major applications, concluding with chapters on optimizing program performance. This book provides quick-start tutorials for five key applications in the programs and includes complete coverage of GeoWorks Ensemble 1.0 and 1.2, as well as GeoWorks Pro. (Pro version 1.1 is a minor maintenance upgrade, not widely distributed.) Ensemble users can skip Chapters 3, 14, and 15, which discuss features specific to GeoWorks Pro.

If you are a beginner, you can proceed through the book from front to back. You may find the quick-start tutorials for each major application an excellent way to learn the program. You can create your own "short course" by using only the quick-start chapters; however, after you are comfortable with the program, you can benefit from skimming the reference chapters for additional features that the quick-start tutorials do not cover. Because of the common interface shared by all applications, you can transfer the skills you learn in one application to other applications.

For the new user, the most important chapters are Chapter 3, "Learning with File Cabinet," (for Pro Users) and Chapter 4, "Mastering GeoManager," (both Ensemble and Pro users). These chapters explain the workspaces that the programs use as "control centers." You manage applications, files, and directories from the File Cabinet and GeoManager windows. To use the program's capabilities effectively, you must have a solid understanding of these features.

If you know PC's but don't yet know GeoWorks Ensemble or Pro, the quick starts are the best way to learn key concepts quickly. The reference chapters fill in the details on more complex topics. If you are using the program already, you may find the reference chapters a source of detailed information on sections of the program you have not explored fully.

Appendix C contains a list of the differences between GeoWorks versions. Experienced users may want to consult this list to locate features with which they are not yet familiar; new users may want to compare features as they upgrade or purchase a GeoWorks version.

How This Book Is Organized

Using GeoWorks Pro is divided into five parts.

Part I, "Introducing GeoWorks," includes chapters that cover the PC/GEOS interface and an introduction to the simple Appliances programs.

Chapter 1, "Understanding the PC/GEOS Interface," explains how to use a mouse and the structure of buttons and dialog boxes you use to convey information. This chapter prepares the reader for Chapter 2, which explains using the Appliances.

Chapter 2, "Learning GeoWorks Appliances," uses the six Appliances— simple, but useful applications—as teaching tools for basic skills, such as text entry, menu management, help features, and dialog boxes.

Part II, "Working with a Desktop," contains file management information. In Part II you can find a quick start on file management and two key chapters discussing the File Cabinet (GeoWorks Pro only) and GeoManager (all versions).

Chapter 3, "Learning with File Cabinet," is relevant only for users of GeoWorks Pro. The File Cabinet is the centerpiece of Pro's new Intermediate Workspace. This feature provides "point and click" directory and file management, as well as replacing complex commands with simple buttons.

Quick Start I, "GeoManager," is a hands-on tutorial that teaches the basic skills needed throughout Ensemble and Pro. Highlights of this chapter include window management, directory navigation, and file creation and duplication.

Chapter 4, "Mastering GeoManager," contains a detailed introduction to the advanced file and disk manager found in all versions of the GeoWorks program. The chapter explains window management techniques and reviews the menus and commands found in the workspace. A substantial portion of the chapter covers file and disk management, including explanations of directory trees and floppy disk management.

Part III, "Using the Applications," contains information and tutorials that cover the major GeoWorks applications: GeoDex, GeoPlanner, GeoWrite, GeoDraw, and GeoComm.

Quick Start II, "GeoDex," takes you through the process of starting GeoDex and entering information. You also learn to search, print, and maintain lists of names and addresses.

Chapter 5, "Using GeoDex," explains how to use the address book and autodialer combination. Instructions include methods for locating entries, printing lists, and maintaining files.

Quick Start III, "GeoPlanner," leads you through a hands-on exploration of GeoPlanner views, calendars, and event lists. With this tutorial, you create event entries and learn to print from GeoPlanner.

Chapter 6, "Using GeoPlanner," shows you how to use the combination calendar, scheduler, and event planner to maintain multiple schedules. You learn the procedures necessary to use the calendar, event lists, alarms, and repeating events entries.

Quick Start IV, "GeoWrite," is a practice session in using GeoWrite to edit, format, and enhance a document.

Chapter 7, "Using GeoWrite," contains a detailed list of the many features of the GeoWrite word processor. You learn to create and edit a document. You also learn the several methods of paragraph and character formatting. The document formatting section includes details on creating multiple columns, page breaks, and headers and footers. The chapter concludes with a discussion of enhancing documents with paragraph color, borders, and reverse text.

Quick Start V, "GeoDraw," leads you through drawing a logo, using all of GeoDraw's principal features. You draw, edit, assemble, and print the elements necessary to complete the project.

Chapter 8, "Using GeoDraw," begins with a tour of the drawing screen and its tools. You learn to use the drawing tools and work with graphic objects. The chapter concludes with a detailed description of managing text in the graphical GeoDraw environment.

Chapter 9, "Using GeoComm," introduces the communications application. Starting with a short communications primer, the chapter shows you how to prepare to use GeoComm and how to go on-line with another computer or information utility. This chapter provides a complete list of the components of the script language used to build automated communication sessions.

Chapter 10, "Using America Online," departs from the pattern of the quick starts. America Online is an independent information service that provides a GeoWorks Pro forum. GeoWorks includes a complete version of the American Online software with every version of GeoWorks Ensemble or GeoWorks Pro. Because America Online furnishes free trial connect time, this chapter provides instructions for preparing the necessary hardware and software settings and running a "live" session with America Online. You must have a modem to use this feature.

Part IV, "Using Advanced Features," contains information on using GeoWorks desk tools to customize and optimize program performance, enabling you to make the best use of your equipment.

Chapter 11, "Customizing with the Preferences Desk Tool," shows you how to change the look and feel of the program to make GeoWorks perform in the most efficient and convenient way. The Preferences Desk Tool controls printing, keyboard, memory management, video mode, screen background, modem, and sound option settings.

Chapter 12, "Learning Other Desk Tools," completes the survey of desk tools with an explanation of how to use the Notepad, Scrapbook, Calendar, and Banner tools. This chapter introduces the Tetris and Solitaire games, and the Banner tool found in the Advanced Workspace.

Chapter 13, "Operating DOS Programs" explains how to use nonGEOS programs from the DOS Programs Area and how to use the task-switching features of DOS 5.0 and DR DOS 6.0 to move quickly between GeoWorks Pro and DOS applications.

Part V, "Using Spreadsheets," deals with the techniques that enable you to use the Quattro Pro SE spreadsheet in conjunction with GeoWorks Pro. Part V includes chapters explaining basic spreadsheet concepts and procedures and how to use the Quattro Pro Viewer to move spreadsheets into GeoWorks Pro for editing and enhancement.

Chapter 14, "Learning about Spreadsheets," is a beginning-level tutorial on the fundamentals of using the Quattro Pro SE spreadsheet. You learn the elements of the screen display, how to enter and edit information, and the basic use of formulas and functions.

Chapter 15, "Using Quattro Pro Viewer," shows how to make the link between Quattro Pro SE and GeoWorks Pro, using the built-in Viewer utility. Using this feature, you easily can cut, copy, and paste your spreadsheet data, charts, and graphs directly into GeoWrite and GeoDraw.

Appendix A, "Installing GeoWorks Ensemble and Pro," walks you through the procedure for first-time installation. Screen shots and lists of information you need enable you to rehearse the installation procedure on paper before you proceed.

Appendix B, "Troubleshooting Tips," offers remedies for the most common problems encountered while using the program. This appendix also includes ways of reaching GeoWorks or the America Online GeoWorks Forum if you encounter a problem you cannot solve.

Appendix C, "New Features in Versions 1.2 and Pro," lists the enhancements found in GeoWorks Pro 1.2 and in GeoWorks Pro.

Appendix D, "GeoReps on Online America" lists the volunteers (many of whom contributed tips to this book) who provide support in the GeoWorks Forum.

Conventions Used in This Book

To assist you in understanding the program and to maintain consistency, this book uses the established conventions.

Variable or optional words and terms used for the first time are printed in italic typeface. Screen messages and prompts are printed in a special typeface. Words and phrases you must type appear in boldface.

NOTEs mark text that provides brief, additional information relating to the topic in the surrounding text. CAUTIONs warn you about potential negative consequences of an operation. TIPs, additionally identified with the GeoWorks WORLD icon, mark tips from expert GeoWorks users on Online America.

Using GeoWorks Pro helps you learn to use GeoWorks, regardless of the version you own; however, the text and figures represent GeoWorks Pro, the most recent version of the program.

Introducing GeoWorks

PART

I

OUTLINE

Understanding the PC/GEOS Interface

I f you can imagine the applications that comprise GeoWorks Pro as fish, PC/GEOS is the ocean in which they swim. PC/GEOS is a computer program called an *operating system*, which provides the common graphical environment that all parts of GeoWorks Pro share.

PC/GEOS administers the screens, windows, mouse pointer, screen buttons, visual activities, and hidden tasks such as opening and closing files. Applications such as GeoWrite, GeoDraw, and the other parts of GeoWorks Pro perform specialized activities, but all depend on PC/GEOS for routine activities and technical support.

The shared environment of PC/GEOS gives common features and behaviors to GeoWorks Pro applications. These features comprise the PC/GEOS graphical interface, the icons, commands, and windows that enable you interact with the program. In this chapter you learn the fundamental skills to make GeoWorks Pro run with the ease and power built into it. These skills should enable you to swim like a dolphin in the PC/GEOS ocean.

The PC/GEOS icon that appears in figure 1.1 is found only in an area of the Preferences menu that is rarely used; however, it is presented here for its symbolism. The small sphere in the center is a globe; the "world" of PC/GEOS, if you will. The icon serves as a reminder that all applications you use in GeoWorks Pro exist within the world of the PC/GEOS operating system.

Using the Mouse

GeoWorks Pro is designed to work with a *mouse*. A mouse is a hand-held device with two or three buttons that you move around on the table or desk surface next to the computer to accomplish various computing tasks. You can move through many parts of GeoWorks Pro with the keyboard, but the mouse is indispensable in activities such as graphics manipulation.

New computer users or users who have worked with the more traditional, nongraphic PC applications sometimes are frustrated when they first encounter the mouse. First tries at using the mouse are often awkward and uncomfortable. On the other hand, if you talk to a "mouser" who has been using the device with a graphical program like GeoWorks Pro, you almost are guaranteed to get an enthusiastic response. You soon may find you prefer using the mouse.

Many computer programs today have mouse capabilities because users ask for them. With a bit of practice, using the mouse becomes second nature. Often, the biggest obstacle to using the mouse is your uncertainty about this strange device, completely unlike any object you may have used earlier in your working environment. Crank up your courage and your curiosity and move on to mousing!

Understanding Mouse Anatomy

A basic understanding of how a mouse works can help you better understand how to use it.

Installation of the mouse can involve software and hardware. You plug the mouse into a connector called a *port* on your computer. You also may need to install some software programs supplied with the mouse. Part of the installation process for GeoWorks Pro involves selecting the type of mouse you have and testing the mouse software GEOS uses with your particular type. As a consequence, this section assumes that your mouse is hooked up and operative. Appendix A, "Installing GeoWorks Pro," deals with installing the *driver*, or software, not the physical handling of the mouse circuit board.

Flip the mouse over so that you can see its underside. A small ball, usually Teflon coated, protrudes from the bottom of the device. As you
move the mouse across your desk top, the ball rolls, transmitting its
motion to sensors in the mouse body and down the "tail" (its connecting
cable) to the computer. Mouse motion is translated into the matching
motion of a *pointer* on-screen.

The pointer—generally arrow-shaped—sometimes changes shape as you
move to different areas of the screen. The different pointer shapes (see
fig. 1.2) enable the mouse to give you additional information about the
action you are performing or may perform, as follows:

- *Arrow Pointer.* The normal pointer shape.

- *Circle/Slash Pointer.* The pointer shape when the pointer is in an
  inactive area of the screen.

- *Hourglass Pointer.* The pointer shape when the program is busy
  performing an operation.

- *I-beam Pointer.* The pointer shape when you can type text.

Fig. 1.2

The four mouse pointer
shapes.

The buttons on the mouse are the key to making the pointer active. Just
like a child points to a piece of candy and says, "That one," a mouse user
points to a selection and clicks a button. The most common mouse has
two buttons, left and right. Some programs also use the center button of
three-button mice, but GeoWorks Pro does not. Figure 1.3 shows a typical two-button mouse.

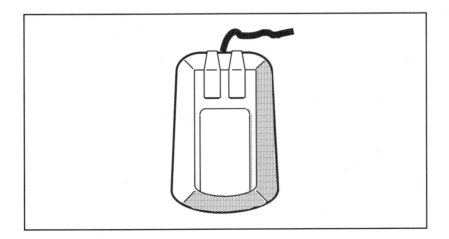

Fig. 1.3

A two-button mouse.

In GeoWorks Pro—and in most programs that use the mouse—you use the left button most often. When the right button is appropriate, the text specifically states that you should use the right button. When a button is not specified, use the left one. *Note:* Left-handed mice, on which the functions of the buttons are reversed from the preceding description, are available for left-handed users.

NOTE Try to hold the mouse between your thumb and third (ring) finger. Rest your palm lightly on the mouse, slightly toward the rear. Your index and second finger are free to operate the left and right buttons, respectively. Many people hold the mouse between thumb and second finger, awkwardly switching buttons with their index finger and sometimes hitting the wrong button. Holding the mouse between the thumb and third finger feels a bit strange when you start. Persevere.

Pointing, Clicking, and Dragging

The basics of using a mouse boil down to three words: point, click, and drag.

Pointing puts the mouse pointer at the location on-screen where you want to work. Roll the mouse on your work surface to move it in the direction you want the pointer to travel. If you run out of desk space, pick up the mouse, put it in a convenient position, and resume rolling. When the mouse ball isn't touching anything, the pointer doesn't move.

Many mouse users buy a mouse pad. Usually a square of foam-backed fabric, the pad provides a clean, slightly resilient area on which to move the mouse where the ball doesn't slip as it may on a polished surface. A pad is a convenience, not a necessity.

After pointing to the place you want to work, *click* a button to tell the computer to take some action. Mouse buttons don't take much force to activate; a light press or tap is sufficient. *Note:* Clicking or tapping is not hammering, and pressing the button too hard can move the mouse accidentally so that it isn't pointing where you expect.

A well-made mouse gives you some sort of feedback, such as a soft clicking sound, a click movement you sense through touch, or both. What happens on-screen when you click depends on the program you are using. The most common outcomes are that you choose a command or activate some type of program feature.

Besides clicking, you can double-click. Often something you can do by clicking once, moving the mouse, and then clicking again or pressing Enter, can be done with a quick double-click of the left button. This technique is one of the major shortcuts available with the mouse. After you master the technique, you can use it frequently.

The computer senses the time between clicks. If you are too slow (tap.........tap), the computer interprets your action as two separate single mouse clicks. At the right speed (tap tap), the computer correctly interprets the double-click and performs the appropriate action, usually saving you a step or two.

GeoWorks Pro carries multiple clicking to the heights. Sometimes you can use double, triple, quadruple, or even quintuple clicks. (Five successive clicks in GeoWrite selects an entire page). If you have trouble with this technique, don't worry. You always have the alternative of a series of single clicks at different locations.

The third mouse technique, *dragging*, means moving the mouse while continuously holding one of the buttons (usually the left). This technique often is used to move or resize objects across the screen.

Dragging also is used to pull a highlight across something you want to change. The process, called *selecting*, is vital when you want to apply a program command to a specific object or area. In figure 1.4, the dark area on-screen has been highlighted (or selected) by dragging the mouse pointer across it. You now can delete, copy, or otherwise change the selected area. The program looks for the selected area when a command is chosen and applies the command to that area.

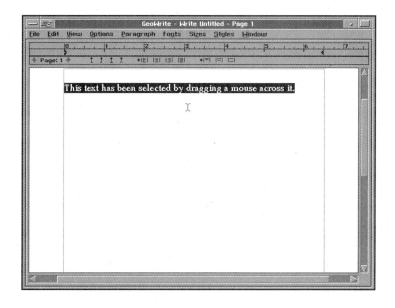

Fig. 1.4

Drag the mouse to select an area.

Using Buttons and Dialog Boxes

Among the first features you encounter in GeoWorks Pro are *buttons* and *dialog boxes*. Both features provide you with ways to communicate with GeoWorks. The three illustrations on the GeoWorks Pro Welcome screen (see fig. 1.5), for example, are large buttons you click to activate different program areas. When you are ready to leave GeoWorks Pro, the dialog box shown in figure 1.6 appears, asking you to confirm your decision.

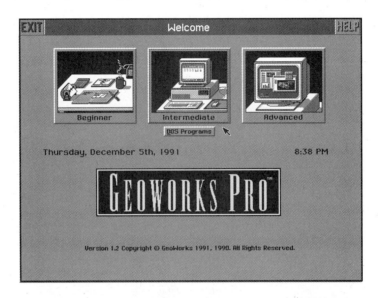

Fig. 1.5

The Welcome screen buttons.

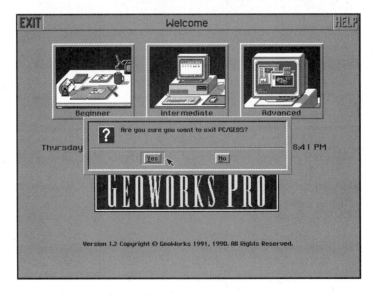

Fig. 1.6

A sample dialog box.

Which program do you want to open? Click the appropriate button. Which file do you want to save? Type its name in the dialog box. The button and dialog box features can save you considerable time in the course of a work session.

In this section you get a limited look at buttons and dialog boxes to prepare you for a comfortable encounter with the GeoWorks Pro appliances in Chapter 2, "Learning GeoWorks Appliances." Chapter 3, "Learning File Cabinet," and Chapter 4, "Mastering GeoManager," fully develop the topics of buttons and dialog boxes.

If GeoWorks Ensemble is not yet running, switch to the GEOWORKS directory by typing **cd geoworks** and start the program by typing **geos**. Normally, you see the Welcome screen shown in figure 1.5. The three buttons at the top of the window switch you to the three major parts of GeoWorks Pro: Beginner, Intermediate, and Advanced Workspaces. *Note:* If you do not see the Welcome screen, look for an EXIT button in the upper left corner of the screen. Click the button to "back up" one screen. Repeat the process until you see the Welcome screen.

The mouse usually activates buttons. After you click the button, the action programmed into the button takes place. Sometimes you use buttons to change settings instead of starting actions.

NOTE If you examine the large buttons on the Welcome screen, you find that one of them has a thin dotted line around it, just inside the button edge, indicating that this button is selected. If you press Enter, the selected button is activated and performs the action for which it is designed. Now press Tab. Notice that the dotted line moves to another button. Pressing Enter, now, "pushes" the new button. You can use this technique to activate buttons from the keyboard. Sometimes removing your hands from the keyboard to reach for the mouse is inconvenient. The keyboard way saves you the trouble.

Practicing with Buttons

To practice with buttons, take a short excursion into the Beginner section of GeoWorks Pro.

The programmers at GeoWorks called the applications in the Beginner workspace *Appliances* to emphasize their simplicity and utility. These applications are the toasters and juicers of the PC/GEOS world. In Chapter 2, "Learning GeoWorks Appliances," you take a comprehensive tour of the Beginner area. For now, make a quick stop to practice some techniques you need for a more prolonged visit. Follow these steps:

1. Click the button labeled Beginner once. The Choose an Appliance screen shown in figure 1.7 opens.

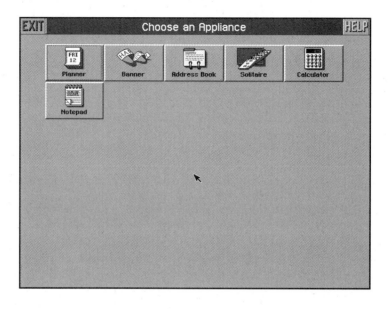

Fig. 1.7

The Choose an
Appliance screen.

2. This time use the keyboard to choose and activate a button. Press Tab until the button for Notepad has a thin dotted line around it.

3. Now press Enter. The Notepad screen (see fig. 1.8) opens exactly as it would if you had clicked the icon with the mouse pointer.

   Some buttons across the top of the Notepad are grayed out, indicating that you cannot use them in the current situation. You cannot edit with the Cut and Copy buttons, for example, because no text is in the Notepad. Paste is available because you might have cut something from elsewhere in the program to paste in the Notepad.

4. Type **This is some sample text** (see fig. 1.9).

5. Click the radio button marked **Medium**. The size of your text changes.

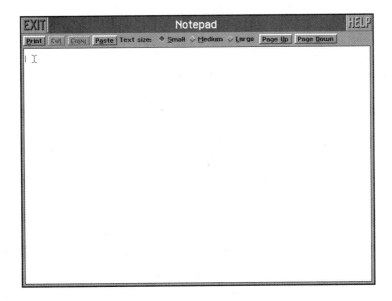

Fig. 1.8

The Notepad screen.

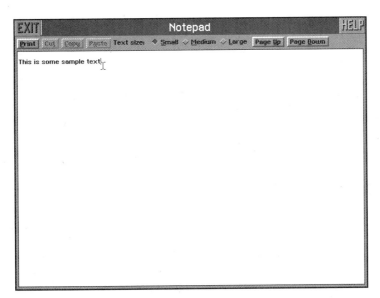

Fig. 1.9

Sample text typed in Notepad.

The three buttons at the top center of Notepad are examples of *radio buttons*, so named because of their similarity to the appearance and behavior of car radio buttons. Just as you can tune in only one station at a time on your car radio, you can activate only one computer radio button at a time. When you click the **M**edium button, the **S**mall choice turns off.

Later you see button groups where you can choose several buttons at once, but these buttons are shaped differently. In GeoWorks Pro, radio buttons are always round or diamond shaped, depending on the video monitor you use.

Using the Keyboard

Look closely at the words inside or next to the buttons. Each word has an underlined letter—often, but not always, the first letter of the command (see fig. 1.10). The underlined letters enable you to activate a command from the keyboard, without using the mouse. Hold down the Alt key while pressing the underlined letter. (Many keyboards have an Alt key at either end of the space bar.)

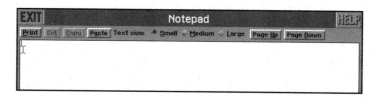

Fig. 1.10

Underlined letters run commands from the keyboard.

To practice activating a command from the keyboard, notice that the **L** in the word **Large** (next to the right radio button) is underlined, hold down the Alt key, and press **L** (upper- or lowercase). The text on-screen increases in size (see fig. 1.11).

Practice activating the other two radio buttons with the keyboard.

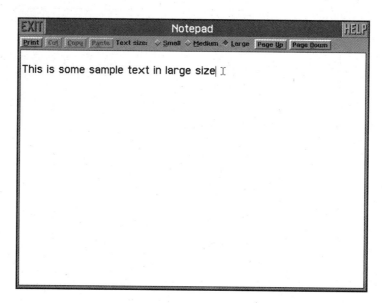

Fig. 1.11

Large text in the Notepad.

Introducing Dialog Boxes

Sometimes GeoWorks Pro cannot carry out a command without additional information. You may choose Save, for example, when you have not specified a file name; or you may choose Print, but the printer isn't ready. The dialog box is designed to solve these kinds of problems.

Examine a sample dialog box by following these steps:

1. Be sure that your printer is turned off. You do not want it on for this exercise.

2. Click the **P**rint button.

   GeoWorks Pro quickly determines that the printer is not available and displays the dialog box shown in figure 1.12.

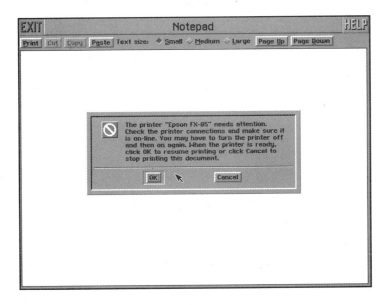

Fig. 1.12

A dialog box noting a printer error.

   The buttons at the bottom of the dialog box enable you to choose a solution. The box does not close until you correct the problem and retry or cancel the attempt to print.

3. Click Cancel to dismiss the dialog box.

You can summon another type of dialog box with the HELP button at the upper right of the different appliance screens. Follow these steps:

1. Click the HELP button in Notepad. The dialog box shown in figure 1.13 opens.

2. Use the Page **D**own and Page **U**p buttons on the dialog box to read through the text.

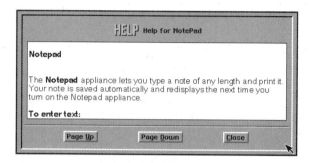

Fig. 1.13

The Help for Notepad dialog box.

3. Choose **C**lose to dismiss the dialog box.

4. Click the EXIT button in the upper left corner of the Notepad window to return to the Choose an Appliance screen.

5. Click the EXIT button again to return to the Welcome screen.

6. If you are ready to quit, click the EXIT button in the Welcome window. The dialog box shown in figure 1.14 asks you to confirm your choice.

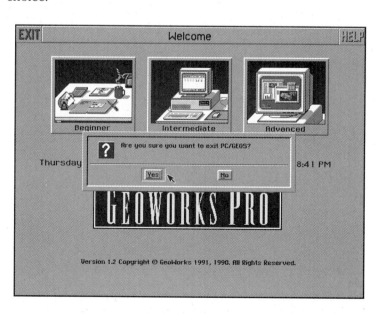

Fig. 1.14

The dialog box confirming your exit to DOS.

7. Choose **Yes** or press Enter to return to DOS.

After you move on to the Advanced Workspace, you encounter more complex dialog boxes, some with many choices and lists for you to review. However complex, the general principles of operation you learned here apply.

Finding Help

One reason for GeoWorks Pro's popularity is the intuitive quality of its interface. If you aren't quite sure what to do, you often can guess from the many visual cues and logical commands that run the program. Sometimes, however, you reach an impasse. For those circumstances, the creators of GeoWorks Pro have done their best to help you.

Inside Help

The prominent HELP buttons at the upper right of the Welcome screen and on each appliance screen lead to condensed explanations of major activities on these screens. The explanations often sufficiently clarify a procedure or get you moving again. Figure 1.15 shows a portion of the Help for Welcome.

Other sources of inside help are the dialog boxes that appear automatically when a problem occurs. The printer error dialog box shown in figure 1.12 is typical of the helpful notes that appear when you need them.

Outside Help

In your eagerness to run GeoWorks Pro, you may have raced through or even ignored a good deal of the documentation packed with the program. Several pamphlets besides the User's Guide offer help with troubleshooting, installation, and familiarization. Leave the computer off one evening and carefully review the material packed with the program.

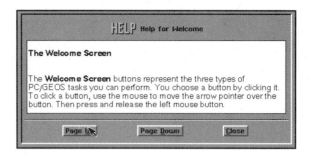

Fig. 1.15

The Help for Welcome
dialog box.

GeoWorks maintains support telephone lines. The Customer Service Hotline at (415) 644-3456 is not toll-free but is staffed by experienced technical consultants. You also can fax or write GeoWorks if your need is less urgent.

Packed with GeoWorks Pro is a trial membership offer for America Online, a telephone information resource available to computers with a modem. The service maintains a GeoWorks forum where users can exchange tips and files and ask questions. Chapter 10, "Using America Online," explains this service. The GeoWorks staff and an outstanding group of nonpaid volunteers called "GeoReps" monitor the forum and provide a valuable resource for troubleshooting and the latest tips.

Finally, look in your own community. Computer users' groups exist in cities of almost every size. In the larger metropolitan areas, computer newspapers or newsletters often contain listings of these groups and their phone numbers. Having someone with whom to talk shop adds to your pleasure and broadens your knowledge.

Chapter Summary

In this chapter you learned and practiced some of the beginning skills you need to use the GeoWorks Pro interface. You learned to point, click, and drag with the mouse—essential skills in this graphical environment. You also have been introduced to buttons and dialog boxes—basic tools used to direct GeoWorks Pro. Finally, you reviewed the internal and external help resources for GeoWorks Pro.

With these skills, you are ready to move ahead to work with the appliances in Chapter 2. More complex skills with window management are introduced in Chapter 4, "Mastering GeoManager."

Learning GeoWorks Appliances

The Appliances are six handy programs that are so easy to operate you immediately can be productive with them. Although the Appliances are found in the Beginner Workspace, some share data with other program applications and all use the same menu and command techniques used throughout GeoWorks Pro.

You can use the Appliances to gain immediate hands-on experience with GeoWorks Pro and to learn important basic skills that are useful when moving on to other workspaces.

In this chapter, you learn how easy moving through the GeoWorks Pro environment is. You can read through the examples, but you probably can learn more if you prop the book up next to your computer and run through the numbered steps as you proceed. Skills you learn with one appliance transfer easily to another—and later, to the entire program.

As you progress through this chapter, skills you already have had the opportunity to learn and practice are not repeated in detail. Later, for example, when you are asked to switch to the Choose an Appliance screen and start an appliance, you will not find a complete restatement of the steps described in the next section, "Accessing the Appliances." If you do not recall certain skills, loop back through the relevant sections in this chapter to refresh your memory.

After working with the Appliances, you will find moving on to the concepts and commands of other program elements easy. The common interface that all activities share means that when you start on a new section of GeoWorks Pro, you can move immediately to the content of the new section rather than first mastering a new menu and new commands.

An experienced computer user may move through this chapter rapidly. Even if you are familiar with other programs, spend some time with the Appliances. First, they are useful and fun to explore. Second, they introduce you to features such as automatic saving of files, which may be unfamiliar. Finally, the Appliances form a fine introduction to computing for friends and family.

The Appliances are so elegantly simple, you easily can introduce them to others who express an interest in your activities with GeoWorks Pro. After a short briefing about the mouse, your friends should be able to explore and enjoy one or all of them. Show them Solitaire or Banner, and you may have to negotiate the return of your computer! Experimenting with the Appliances may well ignite the spark of interest that starts another of the "computer-curious" on the way to becoming a computer enthusiast. By the time you complete this chapter, you will be a qualified guide for such a tour.

Accessing the Appliances

You access the appliances section of GeoWorks Pro from the Welcome screen. The three pictures across the top of the screen are large buttons you can choose to move you into the main sections of GeoWorks Pro. For this chapter, choose the Beginner button on the left (see fig. 2.1).

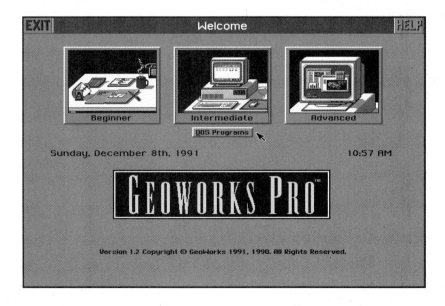

Fig. 2.1

The Welcome screen.

The Choose an Appliance screen appears (see fig. 2.2). The screen contains six buttons that take you to the various appliances: Planner, Banner, Address Book, Solitaire, Calculator, and Notepad.

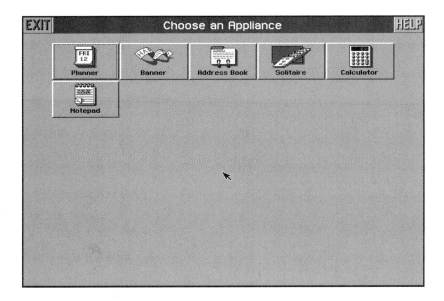

Fig. 2.2

The Choose an
Appliance screen.

The following table lists the six appliances and their descriptions:

Appliance	Description
Planner	A combination calendar and event list that automatically tracks and displays the events you enter
Banner	A simple tool to make spectacular banners using almost any printer
Address Book	An automatic card file and phone dialer
Solitaire	The famous card game in computer form; tutors the beginner and challenges the expert
Calculator	An ever-handy version of a simple pocket calculator; includes memory features
Notepad	A basic word processor with minimum complexity; excellent for memos and short notes

NOTE If you have used computers before, you may notice that you are not asked to save your work each time you finish an activity or leave Planner, Address Book, or Notepad. As you work within these three appliances, the program automatically keeps a working copy of your entries. When you leave the appliance, the program saves your work to a default data file. Banner, Solitaire, and Calculator do not save your work. Chapter 4, "Mastering GeoManager," details file management.

To open an appliance for your first exercise, choose the button labeled Notepad. The Notepad screen appears (see fig. 2.3).

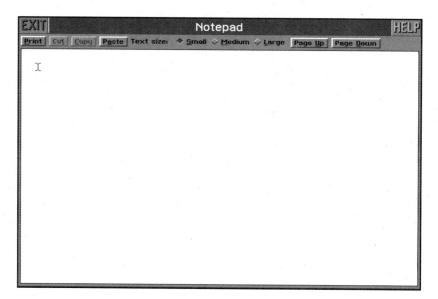

Fig. 2.3

The Notepad screen.

Using the Notepad

Entering and editing text—formally called *word processing*—is the most frequent reason people use computers. The Notepad appliance is a basic word processor, great for producing short notes or lists. For lengthy or complex text, however, you should use GeoWrite (see Chapter 7, "Using GeoWrite").

You can use Notepad to learn some fundamental text handling skills that are useful anywhere in GeoWorks Pro where text is used. Even beyond GeoWorks Pro, most current graphics word processing programs use similar techniques for handling text.

Entering Text in Notepad

To discover how easy using Notepad is, follow these steps to enter a simple list:

1. Type **To Do List** and then press Enter twice.

2. Type the following list, pressing Enter after each item to start a new line:

    Deposit paycheck
    Buy groceries
    Do laundry

3. Press Enter once to create a blank line. Then type the following sentence (do not press Enter after typing the sentence; have Notepad do the work this time):

    Steve, please be sure you stop by the Shur-Kleen dry cleaners on the way home from work tomorrow evening

    Your screen should resemble figure 2.4.Fig. 2.4

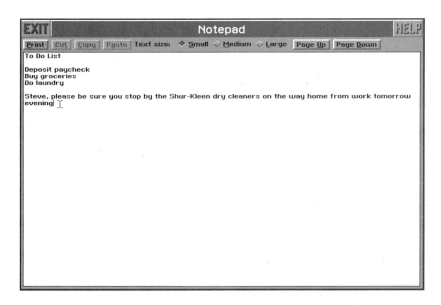

Fig. 2.4

The completed To Do List.

Observe these points in the simple list you just typed:

When you work with text, the mouse pointer changes to a shape called an *I-beam*. You use the I-beam to position a short flashing vertical bar to mark where you want your words to appear. The vertical bar is called a *text cursor.*

Think of the I-beam as a tool that moves the text cursor to different locations. By clicking the mouse to position the text cursor, you say in effect, "I want to type here." You also can move the text cursor with the arrows on the keyboard, but for larger moves using the mouse makes sense.

The Enter key plays an important role in the Notepad. Each time you press Enter, you end the current line of text and the text cursor drops to the beginning of the next line. You also can create blank lines by pressing Enter at the beginning of an empty line.

On the other hand, you do not always want to press Enter to break to a new line. The sentence you typed earlier in step 3, for example, is long enough to be more than one screen wide. When you reach the right edge of your screen, Notepad wraps your sentence to the next line. *Word wrap*, as this feature is called, saves you the trouble of watching for the right margin and pressing Enter to start a new line.

You do not want to break longer lines by pressing Enter repeatedly, because each time you press Enter, Notepad interprets your keystroke as a request to create a new paragraph. If you press Enter every time you wanted to break a sentence to a new line, you wind up with a mess of fragmentary paragraphs.

Changing Text in Notepad

In this section, you learn how to insert and remove text. You actually can accomplish this most important of word processing activities in several ways, but in this short section you deal with mouse techniques.

Actually, you want to *get* the laundry rather than *do* it, you want to deposit a *particular* paycheck (your son, Jeff's, from his fast-food job), and you want to add an item "to do." Edit your initial list by following these steps:

1. Select the word Do by dragging the I-beam sideways across the word. Do not release the mouse button until you are satisfied you have selected the word. The selected area is highlighted (see fig. 2.5).

2. If you release the mouse button but are not satisfied with the selected area, repeat step 1.

3. Type **Get**. Your typing replaces the selected text.

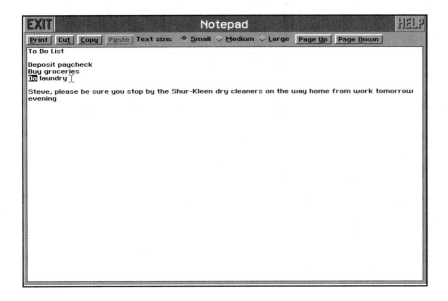

Fig. 2.5

The highlight on the
selected word.

NOTE For small changes (a few characters) you can position the
text cursor and press Del or Backspace. Del removes characters to the right of the text cursor; Backspace removes characters to the left of the text cursor. If you use the Del key on
the numeric keypad, be sure that the Num Lock key is off or
you will type a period (.).

4. To insert **Jeff's** after the word Deposit, click just before the word
   paycheck. The text cursor appears when you move the mouse
   away. Type **Jeff's**.

5. Create a new blank paragraph by placing the text cursor just after
   the y in laundry and pressing Enter once. Make up another item for
   the list and type it. Your completed document should be similar to
   figure 2.6.

Using Notepad's Command Buttons

Like the other Appliances, Notepad avoids complex menus and window
management features, but the few important command buttons you see
in the Notepad screen can help with essential tasks and demonstrate
some general points that apply throughout GeoWorks Pro.

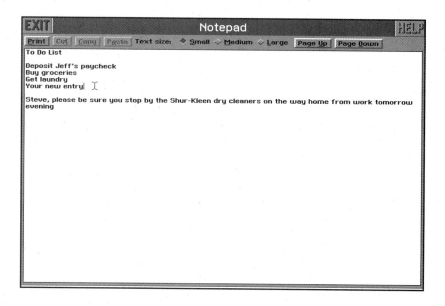

Fig. 2.6

The revised To Do List.

The Print button sends your document to the printer. If you selected the correct printer when installing GeoWorks Pro, and if that printer is properly connected and turned on, choosing Print produces a printed copy of the document on the Notepad.

The Cut, Copy, and Paste buttons introduce a new kind of text editing. They work together to remove, duplicate, or move a selected block of text.

NOTE   The program stores a cut or copied selection in a special location in memory until you cut or copy something else. You can have only one cut or copied item stored at a time. If you cut several pages and then cut a single word, your several pages are "bumped" by the single word. You cannot retrieve them.

Follow these steps to practice using the Cut, Copy, and Paste commands:

1. Jeff just called to say he will deposit his paycheck; you can remove Deposit Jeff's paycheck from the To Do List. Select Deposit Jeff's Paycheck by dragging the mouse across the text.

2. Choose Cut. The selected text disappears into a storage area in Notepad's memory.

3. Jeff just called back to say he cannot get to the bank after all; you need to restore the item to your list. The text cursor still should be on the now-empty line from which you removed the item. Choose Paste to insert the item you cut just a moment ago.

4. Test the Copy option by selecting the entire sentence Steve, please be sure ... and then choosing Copy. Nothing visible happens as the copy is put in memory.

5. Place the text cursor at the end of the long sentence; then choose Paste. A copy of the sentence appears to the right of the text cursor.

The three Text Size radio buttons in the middle of the button bar present different text sizes on-screen. Click each button in an experiment to see which one looks best on your video monitor. *Note:* The different text size is not reflected in the printed document.

The Page Up and Page Down buttons take you to other pages of the Notepad if you have created a large document. They are not used in this one-page example.

Click the HELP button at the upper right of corner of the Notepad screen to open a window containing help text. Use the Help window's Page Up and Page Down buttons to move through the text. After you are done, choose Close to return to the Notepad screen.

When you want to leave Notepad, click the EXIT button at the upper left corner of the screen to shut down the appliance, save the information, and return to the Choose an Appliance screen. Then you can choose the Planner button to begin working with that appliance.

Using the Planner

The Planner appliance, shown in figure 2.7, serves as a combined calendar and appointment list; it shares files with the GeoPlanner (discussed in Chapter 6, "Using GeoPlanner"). You do not have to reenter information you store in the Planner when you switch to the more powerful GeoPlanner.

The buttons across the top of the Planner for changing year, month, and day move you forward or back in the calendar. Notice that the upper button of each pair precedes the current setting and the lower button follows. By clicking the top button in each pair, you move back in the calendar. The bottom button of the pair takes you forward.

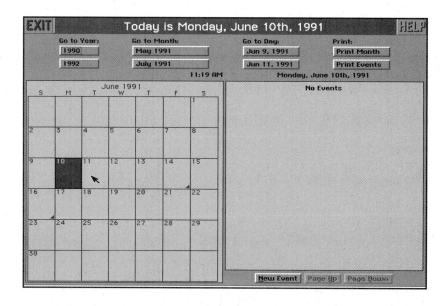

Fig. 2.7

The Planner screen.

The print buttons at the right side of the screen print a full-page sheet with the current calendar or a separate sheet with scheduled events in order by time. The more complex sibling of the Planner, GeoPlanner, is able to print several combinations and various sizes of calendars and event lists. GeoPlanner is fully covered in Chapter 6.

The text skills you learned in the preceding section are put to use with Planner. This section, however, focuses on mouse skills because Planner is a mouse-intensive application. You click for almost every purpose.

Entering Planner Date and Time

The Planner presents a calendar on the left half of the screen and an event list on the right. Buttons at the top of the screen enable you to move through the dates. The title bar at the top of the screen shows the current date, and the time appears just above the right edge of the calendar, under the buttons.

The accuracy of the current date and time depends on the clock/calendar in your computer. Many computers include battery-operated clock calendars. If you manually have to enter time and date when you boot your computer, PC/GEOS reads it properly, but you should consider adding a relatively inexpensive ($20-$40) clock/calendar chip or board to your machine.

Entering Events in the Planner

If you recently have started using GeoWorks Pro, the calendar and its associated list are empty. Add two items to your Planner by following these steps:

1. In the Planner, click the 13th day of the month that is showing—presumably, the month in which you are doing this exercise.

   Notice that on the calendar the current date has a heavy outline and the 13th has a solid highlight. Note also that the date above the blank events list is the 13th. Figure 2.8 shows a sample for June 10, 1991.

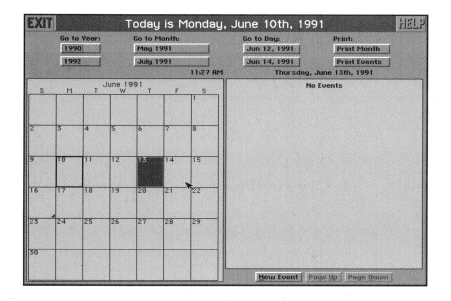

Fig. 2.8

A sample calendar.

2. Choose the **New** Event button under the blank event list. A blank event for 8:00 AM appears at the top of the event list.

   NOTE To enter a time that is out of the sequence generated by the New Event button, select the time with the mouse and type in a different time. To delete an item, drag the mouse across the item and the time and delete both. Click EXIT. When you re-start, the event will be gone.

3. Type **10:00 am**. The Planner expects that particular format, with the colon and am or pm following.

If you make a mistake in format, the program reminds you via a dialog box and corrects the error.

4. Press Tab to move to the area where you enter the event description. Type **This is a sample event**. Figure 2.9 shows the result.

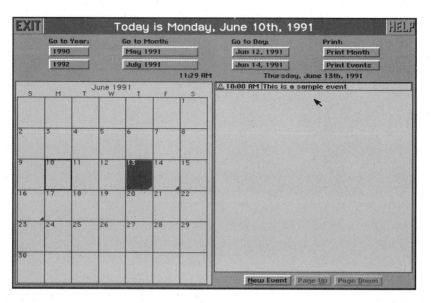

5. After you move the text cursor away from the event description by clicking elsewhere on-screen or using Tab, Planner records your event. *Note:* Pressing Enter just gives you a new blank line but does not save the event.

6. Now that you have recorded an event for the 10th, look at that square on the calendar. A small triangle appears in the lower right corner, indicating that an event has been recorded for that date.

Next, record a New Year's Day party for January of next year. Follow these steps:

1. Click the bottom of two buttons labeled Go to Year, which advances the calendar to next year.

2. Click the Go to Month buttons until January shows in the calendar window.

3. Click the calendar square for January 1 to move to the events list for that day.

4. Choose **New Event** and then type **1:00 pm** and **New Year's Party**. Remember to press Tab to move from the time area to the note area.

5. Move the text cursor away from your event entry to record it (click the calendar, for instance). Your screen looks similar to figure 2.10.

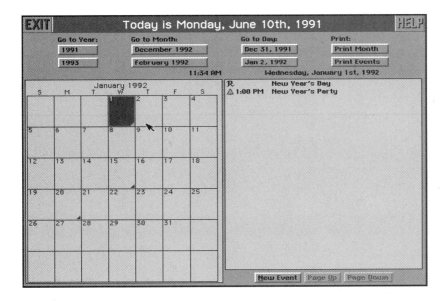

To print a particular month or list of events, use the date buttons to make the item visible on-screen, and then click the appropriate Print button to Print Month or Print Events.

To leave the Planner appliance, click the EXIT button in the upper right corner of the screen. The program returns to the Choose an Appliance screen, where you can choose the next appliance, the Address Book.

The Planner, as mentioned earlier, shares files with GeoPlanner. When you get to GeoPlanner in Chapter 6, you discover additional techniques such as searching for events or displaying multiple months.

Using the Address Book

Much like a desktop card file, the Address Book stores the names, addresses, and phone numbers you need to have handy. Like Planner events, the Address Book information is linked to the GeoDex application described in Chapter 5, "Using GeoDex."

The Address Book (see fig. 2.11) hides considerable speed and power behind its friendly exterior, which resembles a stack of index cards with alphabetic tabs. You use the text skills you learned in the Notepad section of this chapter for data entry in the Address Book.

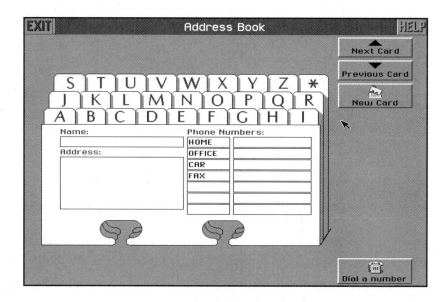

Fig. 2.11

The Address Book appliance.

Entering Data in the Address Book

Use the following steps to practice with the Address Book:

1. On the Address Book screen, enter your last name and first name. If you make a mistake, use the Del or Backspace keys.

2. Press Tab to move to the address entry area. Type your street address on the first address line. Press Enter to move to the next line and type your city, state, and zip code.

3. Press Tab or click to move to the phone number area. Tab or click through the choices, entering the appropriate numbers.

   If you plan to use the Dial a number feature, be sure to enter any prefixes or area codes needed to dial the complete number (see next section, "Using Dial a Number").

   A completed card is shown in figure 2.12.

4. Click the New Card button to present a new blank for you to complete.

5. For this exercise, repeat steps 1 through 4 to create at least two more cards for different letters of the alphabet.

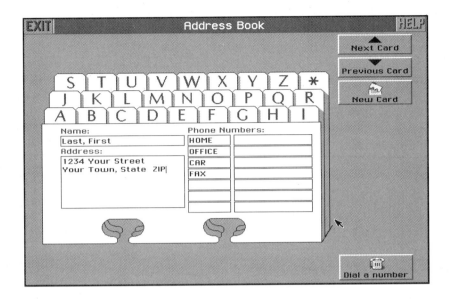

Fig. 2.12

A completed Address
Book card.

To explore the rest of the Address Book's features, click the Next Card
or Previous Card buttons to see how they rotate you through your active
cards. You can jump directly to the first card in an alphabetic section by
clicking the tab representing the letter you want.

Before ending your exploration of the Address book, click the HELP button and read through the information presented. You leave Address
Book, as you do all other appliances, by clicking the EXIT button.

Using Dial a Number

The Dial a number feature (the Dial a number button in the lower right
corner of the Address Book screen) works if you have a *modem*, a device
that translates computer signals so that they can be transmitted over
telephone lines. If you already have a modem in your system, you must
enter settings using the Modem icon found in the Preferences desk tool.
This step is described in Chapter 11, "Customizing with the Preferences
Desk Tool."

You need to enter modem settings only once, unless you change your
hardware configuration. Assuming your modem is properly set and
turned on, dialing a number automatically is simple. Bring the card containing the number you want to the front of the address book, using the

alphabetical tabs and the Next Card and Previous Card buttons. Click the Dial a number button to open a dialog box listing the number(s) on the card. Click the number you want to dial. A second dialog box opens.

Click the Dial button in the dialog box to start the call. You can hear the dialing proceed through your modem speaker. When the call is answered, click the Talk button in the dialog box. This step disconnects the modem from the call and enables you to talk. Hang up normally when you are through. If you want to interrupt the automatic dialing process and disconnect, click the Cancel button.

Using the Calculator

Calculators are everywhere today, from liquid-cooled supercomputers to 99-cent battery-powered models sold at the grocery checkout counter. The only problem with calculators lies in their mysterious capability to be somewhere else when you want them! GeoWorks Pro takes care of this problem by including a calculator in the Appliances group. When you are at your computer, the calculator is always just a few mouse clicks away.

You probably are familiar with the operation of a simple calculator such as the Calculator appliance shown in figure 2.13. This brief section points out the features of the Calculator and invites you to spend a bit of time practicing. If you are new to the mouse, the Calculator is a great practice area for pointing and clicking accurately.

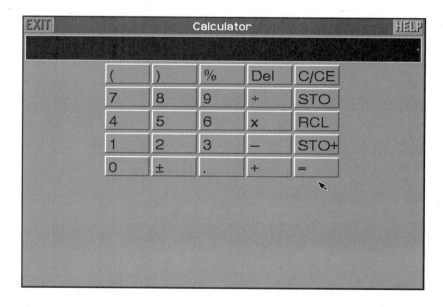

Fig. 2.13

The Calculator appliance.

Making Standard Calculations

To use the calculator with the mouse, just click the appropriate numbers and symbols with the mouse pointer. The numbers you click appear in the display window. The results appear in the display window when you click the keys for the desired operations.

To operate the calculator from the keyboard, use the numbers across the top of the keyboard or turn on the Num Lock key and use the numeric keypad at the right end of your keyboard.

In addition to using the number keys or the numeric keypad to enter numbers, you can use the keys in the following table to operate the calculator from your keyboard:

Key	Result
Del	Erase last digit in display
C	Once: Clear display Twice: Clear calculation
S	Store display in memory
R	Retrieve stored number
T	Add displayed number to memory
_+	Change sign of displayed number
/	Division operator
X or *	Multiplication operators

Performing Memory Operations

The Calculator's memory holds a single number that you can replace, recall, add to, or clear. To perform the memory operations available in the Calculator appliance use the following mouse or keyboard actions:

■ To store a number from the display, click the STO key or press **S**.

■ To recall a stored number, click the RCL key or press **R**.

■ To add the display amount to the number in memory, click the STO+ key or press **T**.

■ To clear the memory, enter a zero and click STO or press **S** to store the zero amount.

The Calculator has a more complex sibling, found among the Desk Tools described in Chapter 12, "Learning Other Desk Tools."

Using Banner and Solitaire, the Bonus Appliances

The people at GeoWorks have added two bonuses to their already brimming basket of GeoWorks Pro features: the Banner and Solitaire appliances. An early version of the GeoWorks Pro User's Guide does not list or describe these two appliances.

Banner is surprisingly useful for printing signs for work or play. Solitaire is the sort of recreation all computer users need occasionally to avoid the mental "meltdown" that comes from too many hours at the keyboard.

Printing with Banner

You can learn a good deal about GeoWorks Pro while experimenting with the Banner appliance. Although limited to one predetermined format, Banner enables you to view all the fonts (character sets) used in GeoWorks Pro and change them to produce some striking special effects.

You may have seen the output of other large-character programs where the edges of the letters have an unattractive "stairstep" appearance. Banner produces smooth, well-formed shapes.

You will find a number of uses for output from Banner. The appliance serves as a preview of the highly developed printing capabilities of GeoWorks Pro.

Follow these steps to produce a test banner:

1. Choose the Banner appliance from the Choose an Appliance screen. Your screen should look like figure 2.14.

   The appliance opens with a text cursor flashing in the Banner message box at the top of the screen.

2. Type **Big!** (You want a short message so that it prints rapidly.)

3. Click the Font button.

   GeoWorks displays a panel of font names at the top of the screen. Click the various choices and examine their appearances in the preview area, as shown in figure 2.15. Choose a font you like.

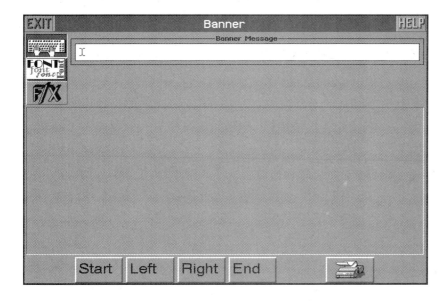

Fig. 2.14

The Banner appliance.

Fig. 2.15

The Banner Fonts panel and preview.

4. Click the button marked F/X.

Figure 2.16 shows the panel of choices for special effects that Banner can create. Click the various choices to see their effects. Note that you can choose more than one effect with a check box (underline and italic, for example); however, you can choose only one effect in each of the columns of radio buttons.

Fig. 2.16

The F/X button displays the Special Effects panel.

The buttons at the bottom of the screen marked Start, Left, Right, and End enable you to move through the preview of a long banner. The banner image may pause and flash briefly while scrolling—a normal activity when a complex image is being redrawn.

In the preview area, notice that the sample banner purposely includes the letter *g* to demonstrate the positioning of banner letters. Letters with *descenders*, or strokes that go below the baseline of letters, need space below the line along which they print. Consequently, the Banner program moves a typical line as high on the paper as possible, leaving space below for descenders.

5. After you choose the font and effects you want, click the printer button at the lower right of the screen to begin printing.

   Printing a large banner may take a long time. The printer pauses periodically for 5 or 10 seconds while the image for the next section of the banner is being computed. Theoretically, you can print a banner up to 60 pages long. You may want to go to dinner while that job prints, however.

   If you have difficulty printing, you may need to reconfigure your printer. Follow the instructions in the printer section of Chapter 11, "Customizing with the Preferences Desk Tool."

GeoWorks does not save your banner with its fonts and effects when you exit the Banner appliance. If you have laid out a banner you like, print before you click EXIT.

Relaxing with Solitaire

Taken one by one, the Appliances are surprisingly easy for even a novice to master. Exposure to all of them at once, however, may become a bit wearying. Relax with a round of Solitaire (see fig. 2.17).

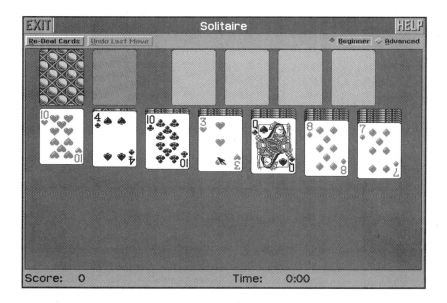

Fig. 2.17

The Solitaire appliance.

Throughout this chapter you may have been gaining an appreciation of what a graphical environment like PC/GEOS can do to make computing easier. A game of Solitaire should consolidate that appreciation. Watching the colorful cards snap into place (or snap back when you make an illegal move) convincingly shows why computer users are embracing the graphical approach to computing.

To move a card, drag the card you want to move to another stack. Release the mouse button to complete the move. If the move is illegal, the card jumps back to its original location.

If you do not know Solitaire, choose **B**eginner at the upper right of the screen. Then, when you pick up a card, the stacks to which you can move turn black. If no stacks turn black, you cannot move with that card.

If you don't like the hand Fate (or your computer) dealt you, choose **R**e-Deal Cards. Choose **U**ndo Last Move to retract your last legal move. Choosing the **A**dvanced button requires you to move the entire pile from one stack to another in order to win.

Use the skills you have gained so far to unravel the challenge of Solitaire. Click the HELP button to get a digest of game rules and hints.

Advanced Solitaire, found in the Advanced Workspace, enables you to use different scoring methods, draw three cards, and change the card back designs. Chapter 12, "Learning Other Desk Tools," describes Advanced Solitaire more fully.

Chapter Summary

In this chapter you have used the six Appliances to learn skills needed throughout GeoWorks Pro. These skills transfer to many other activities in the chapters to come. You probably want to step up from some appliances to the full-fledged parallel applications of the Advanced Workspace introduced in Part III, "Using the Ensemble," but for a quick note, a banner, or a game break for Solitaire, you can come back to the Appliances area again.

Working with a Desktop

PART

II

OUTLINE

Learning File Cabinet

The Intermediate Workspace in GeoWorks Pro provides a graduated step between the simplicity of the Appliances and the complexity of the Professional Workspace. All the major features of GeoWorks Pro are available, but you do not need to manage multiple windows or deal with operating system commands. To give you the power without complexity, GeoWorks Pro programmers created a work area called the *File Cabinet*.

The Intermediate Workspace is an excellent starting point for mastering concepts that later enable you to use every aspect of GeoWorks Pro. The Intermediate Workspace's extensive use of document templates enables you to be productive immediately and to explore the details of the programs when you are ready.

This chapter discusses using the Intermediate Workspace to manage files and directories and to access GeoWorks Pro applications. Other chapters cover each application. Although the Intermediate Workspace eases the "housekeeping" work, and the document templates get you off to a quick start, you still must study the individual applications to tap their full potential.

Understanding the File Cabinet Window

The center button in the Welcome window opens the Intermediate Workspace (see fig. 3.1).

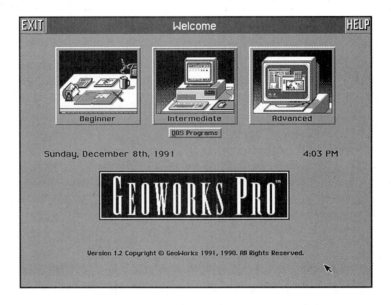

The "home" window from which you manage the Intermediate Workspace is the File Cabinet window. The documents, programs, and commands you need are gathered in this central location. When installed with the standard configuration, the File Cabinet window opens when you choose Intermediate from the Welcome window (see fig. 3.2). The window is more complex than the Appliance windows, but the principles learned from the appliances apply.

The File Cabinet window is the operating center of the Intermediate Workspace. This window contains the icons that link you to documents and programs. Command buttons, which enable you to manage your work, surround the window. The File Cabinet presents a document-centered version of GeoWorks Pro. When you select and open a document, GeoWorks Pro knows which application to start. Rather than opening a default document, as you do in the Professional Workspace, you have a choice of prepared templates on which to build. Table 3.1 gives a very brief description of the components of the File Cabinet window. The following sections explain the most important features in greater detail.

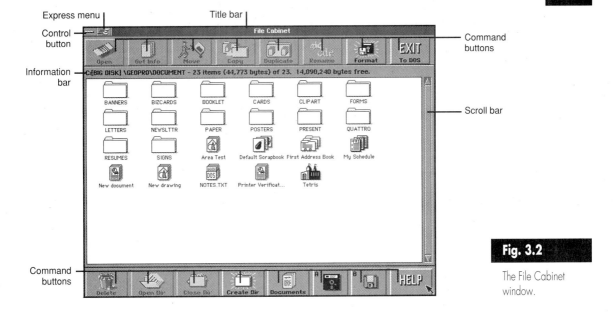

Fig. 3.2

The File Cabinet
window.

Table 3.1 Parts of the File Cabinet

Part	Purpose
Title bar	Located at the top of the window, the Title bar contains the name of the current application—in this case, the File Cabinet.
Express menu	To the left of the Title bar, this button enables you to switch rapidly to any other active application, move to the Welcome screen, or exit to DOS.
Control button	You primarily use this button, which is to the left of the Express button, to manage windows in the Professional Workspace. Double-clicking the Control button closes the File Cabinet window; otherwise, this button is largely inactive.
Information bar	Just below the top row of buttons, the information bar displays information regarding your location in the directory structure, the current directory size, and the available free space.
Scroll bar	At the right edge of the window, the scroll bar enables you to move the window display when file contents exceed the size of a single window.

continues

Table 3.1 continued

Part	Purpose
Command buttons	Command buttons surround the window. The commands and their functions are as follows:
Open	Opens the selected file or directory
Get Info	Shows statistical information about files
Move	Moves files to another location
Copy	Copies files from one folder to another
Duplicate	Creates a copy of a file at its current location
Rename	Changes the name of a file or directory
Format	Prepares new disks to store information
Exit to DOS	Shuts down GeoWorks Pro
Delete	Removes files or directories
Open Dir	Opens a selected directory to show its contents
Close Dir	Closes the current directory
Create Dir	Creates a new, empty directory folder
Documents	Switches to the default File Cabinet window
Drive buttons	Switches to floppy drive (varies with machine configuration)
Help	Opens Help for File Cabinet dialog box

Using the Express Menu

At the upper left of the File Cabinet window is a button that resembles a slanted letter E. This feature is the *Express menu*, a tool that enables you to switch quickly from one active application to another. The Express menu contains an entry for each currently active application (see fig. 3.3). These entries change, depending on which application you are using.

To switch applications, click an application name. If you are working in the word processor and must switch back to the File Cabinet window, for example, clicking the File Cabinet name in the Express menu immediately switches you to the File Cabinet window. The Welcome window always is available from the Express menu if you must move to another GeoWorks Pro workspace.

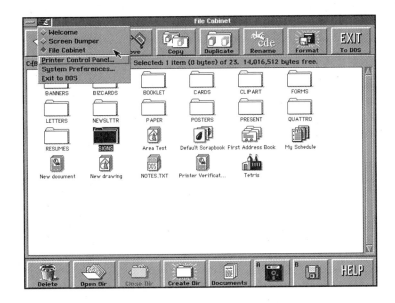

Fig. 3.3

The Express menu to
switch applications
quickly.

At the bottom of the Express menu are commands that enable you to
monitor printing and change system settings. The last command on the
Express menu enables you to quit to the DOS prompt. By using the Exit
to DOS command, you tap an extremely useful property of GeoWorks
Pro: the program saves your screen configuration.

If you are working on a letter and decide to quit, you can use the Exit to
DOS command on the Express menu without closing the letter or exiting
the word processor. When you next enter the Intermediate Workspace
from the Welcome window, GeoWorks automatically returns to the letter. You can use this feature in the Intermediate and Professional Workspaces. As you work, keep in mind that GeoWorks Pro opens with the
configuration it had when you last quit.

NOTE To avoid the Welcome screen and go directly to the Inter-
mediate Workspace, use the Look and Feel button on the
Preferences desk tool. For instructions, see Chapter 11,
"Customizing with the Preferences Desk Tool."

Understanding Command Buttons

Sixteen command buttons surround the File Cabinet window. Instead of
using complex menus and DOS commands to manage the creation, storage, and removal of directories, files, and disks, you can use these buttons. In this section, you learn to use the buttons to organize your work.

When the File Cabinet window first opens, some buttons appear *grayed*, indicating that no item in the window is selected. You must select an item and then click a command button to issue a command. The capability of selecting a file or a folder is a key to using these tools. Chapter 2, "Learning GeoWorks Appliances," fully discusses selecting items.

Selecting an item only indicates that a choice has been made. To specify what action GeoWorks takes, click a command button or choose a menu item. An important variant of the selection process is double-clicking. Clicking the left mouse button twice rapidly selects and then carries out a default (built-in) action on the double-clicked item. Usually double-clicking opens or launches a file or program. Double-clicking is the single most useful shortcut when using a graphical interface.

You also must understand that most buttons work differently on files than they do on directories. Using the Open button on a file starts the associated application; using the Open button on a selected directory opens a window showing icons for the files contained in the directory. The following discussions of individual buttons note these differences.

Directory Buttons

The following three buttons are exclusive to the management of directories in the File Cabinet:

 Open Dir. The Open Dir button opens a selected directory and displays the contents of the directory in the File Cabinet window.

 Close Dir. The Close Dir button closes the displayed directory and returns to the File Cabinet window.

 Create Dir. The Create Dir button creates a new, empty directory in the File Cabinet window. When you choose the command, a dialog box in which you can enter a name for the new directory appears. Although the dialog box suggests a name that includes a three-letter file name extension (see fig. 3.4), the standard practice is to give directories a one-word name from one to eight characters in length. This naming procedure conforms to requirements of the underlying DOS operating system. Model your directory names on the folder names in the File Cabinet. Make names meaningful and avoid using symbols and spaces.

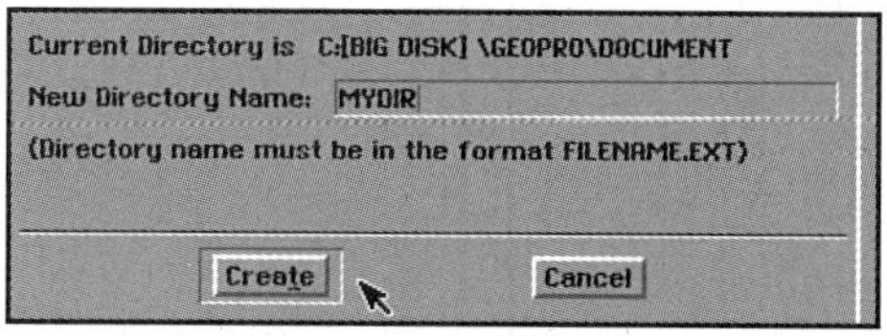

Fig. 3.4

The dialog box used to name a new directory.

Current Directory is C:[BIG DISK] \GEOPRO\DOCUMENT
New Directory Name: MYDIR
(Directory name must be in the format FILENAME.EXT)

Create   Cancel

File Management Buttons

You use the following six buttons for file and directory management. If you use these buttons for a directory, remember that you are affecting the contents of the directory in addition to the directory folder itself.

 Open. The Open button opens the selected file. Opening the file launches the associated application and enables you to modify the file, using the application menu.

 Move. The Move button enables you to remove selected items from one directory and place these items in another directory. A dialog box appears, enabling you to choose a destination for the copied material (see fig. 3.5). Use the tools in the dialog box to select and move to your destination; then click the Move button in the dialog box. You also can use this command to move files to other disks. The Change disk icon in the dialog box enables you to choose a different disk as a destination.

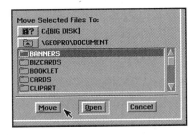

Fig. 3.5

The Move dialog box.

 Copy. The Copy button is almost identical to the Move button; however, when you use the Copy button, the program does not remove the selected items from their original directory. Instead, GeoWorks duplicates the items at their new destination *and* the items remain in their original location. You also can use Copy to copy files to different disks. The Copy dialog box is very similar to the Move dialog box.

 Duplicate. The Duplicate button creates a copy of a selected file in the same directory. Because two files in the same directory cannot have the same name, a dialog box suggesting an alternative name appears (see fig 3.6). You can accept the proposed name or enter your own. This command is useful when you want to experiment with a file and retain a backup file to return to the preceding version.

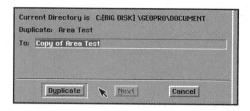

Fig. 3.6

The duplicate file name dialog box.

Rename. The Rename button enables you to give a new name to a selected item. GeoWorks Pro files can have names of up to 32 characters. Limit directory names and file names for use with DOS to eight characters plus an optional three-character extension. If you use a file name extension, you must use a period to separate the extension from the name: FILENAME.EXT.

Delete. The Delete button removes a selected item from your computer. You also can delete an item by using the right mouse button to drag an item's icon on top of the Delete button. A dialog box appears, asking for confirmation of your deletion (see fig. 3.7). Do not take this message lightly. You cannot retrieve deleted material. To continue with the deletion, choose **Yes**.

Fig. 3.7

The deletion confirmation dialog box.

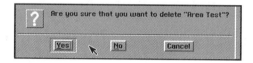

Drive Buttons

In addition to the Format button, the number of drive buttons may be two or three, depending on the drive configuration of your computer. GeoWorks Pro creates a button for each floppy disk drive (see fig. 3.8).

You can copy files and directories to floppy disks by selecting a file or directory and using the right mouse button to drag the icon onto a drive button. To move rather than copy the document, hold down the Alt key as you drag the icon. To copy files from a floppy disk to the File Cabinet window, open the floppy directory by clicking the drive button. Using the right mouse button, drag the file on top of the Document button. Holding down the Alt key as you drag the icon moves, rather than copies, the file. These techniques also work on groups of files or directories.

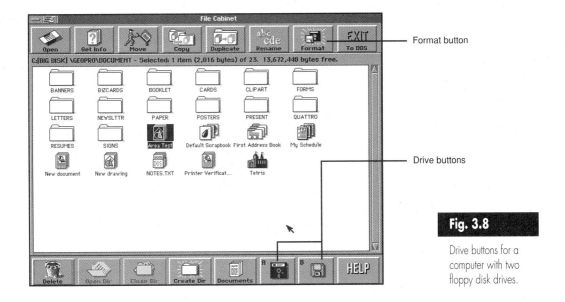

Format button

Drive buttons

Fig. 3.8

Drive buttons for a computer with two floppy disk drives.

Format Button

You use the Format button to prepare blank disks for use. Because formatting destroys all information on a disk, be sure that you do not need anything on a used disk before you reformat it. To format a disk, follow these steps:

1. Insert the disk to be formatted in the drive and click the Format button.

2. In the dialog box that appears (see fig. 3.9), choose the drive you are using and the size of the formatted disk.

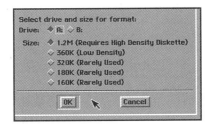

Fig. 3.9

Select drive and size dialog box.

3. Click OK. A dialog box asking for a *volume name* appears. Every time you open a directory listing of the disk, the volume name appears. *Note:* A volume name is like the title of a book, suggesting what you will find "inside." FONTS, for example, is a good volume name for a font library floppy disk.

4. Type a name and choose the Format button in the dialog box to continue.

5. If the disk contains information, you receive an additional warning telling you that formatting destroys material on the disk. Click **Yes** to proceed; click **No** or **Cancel** to abandon the format.

Special Purpose Buttons

The following four buttons serve special purposes that apply to almost all activities in the File Cabinet window.

 Help. The Help button opens a scrolling dialog box that contains short descriptions of the commands and procedures used in the File Cabinet window (see fig. 3.10).

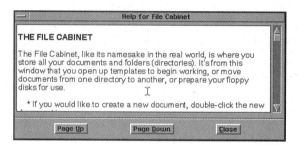

Fig. 3.10

The Help for File Cabinet window.

 Get Info. If a single file or file folder is selected, clicking the Get Info button opens a specialized dialog box that provides summary information about the selected item (see fig. 3.11).

The User Notes text field at the bottom of the dialog box accepts short notes. You can use the Get Info button as a useful way to note the purpose or contents of a file, to assist someone else who retrieves the file, or to help yourself if you forget the file's purpose.

 Documents. The Documents button is the fastest way to return to the File Cabinet window from a directory window. If you click this button when another directory window is open, GeoWorks switches immediately to the default File Cabinet view. You also can copy files or directories from a directory window to the File Cabinet window by using the right mouse button to drag the file or directory icon onto the Documents button.

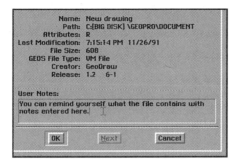

Fig. 3.11

File information in the Get Info dialog box.

 Exit to DOS. Clicking the Exit to DOS button opens a dialog box which asks you to confirm that you want to leave PC/GEOS, the operating system that runs GeoWorks Pro. Clicking **Yes** shuts down GeoWorks Pro, saving your files in their current state. You also can use the Exit to DOS command on the Express menu to leave the program. Either way, GeoWorks returns you to the DOS prompt, where you can safely shut off your computer. ***Note:*** Do not turn off your computer while GeoWorks Pro is running because you may lose files.

If, rather than exiting to DOS, you want to return to the Welcome window so that you can move to another section of the program, open the Express menu and choose a Welcome menu item. GeoWorks switches you directly to that screen.

Understanding Directories and Files

The most prominent features of the File Cabinet window are file folder images. The metaphor of a file cabinet is quite appropriate for understanding how GeoWorks Pro stores and retrieves information. This section helps you understand the organizational tools you use to manage information in GeoWorks Pro.

Electronic Files

A *computer file* is a named collection of electronically stored information. The file may be a document you created, a computer program, or other information copied to your computer. The grouping of computer information into files enables your computer to distinguish one piece of information from another. Storing and retrieving files is one of the most important functions of a computer operating system.

Although you must name the files you create and direct the computer to the location of files you want to retrieve, the process of creating, storing, and retrieving files proceeds primarily inside your computer without your intervention. The following section, "Directories and Paths," describes these procedures.

Files have an electronic signature that varies, depending on the application that creates them. GeoWorks Pro identifies the major types and represents each with a different *icon*—a small picture representing an object. In addition to file folder icons that represent directories, nine other icons occupy the opening window. Although the icons vary in appearance, eight of the nine nonfolder icons have something in common: they represent documents from GeoWorks Pro applications.

Notice that document icons look like stacked sheets of paper (see fig. 3.12). GeoWorks uses the same icons to represent document types throughout GeoWorks Pro. You come to recognize the icons as you work with the program.

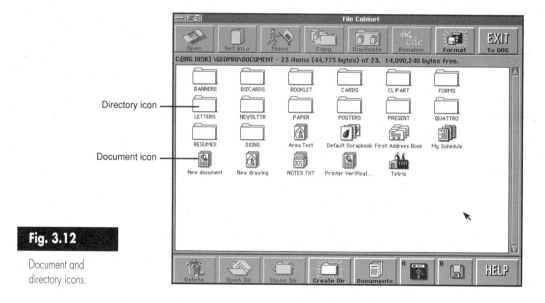

Directories and Paths

For a computer equipped with a hard disk to contain more than a thousand files is not unusual. Whether you have a hundred or a thousand files, however, you must be able to manage files effectively. Just as a file drawer crammed with a thousand unsorted documents is unmanageable, a hard disk with all its files in a single location is difficult to manage. Computers use *directories* to solve the problem of file storage.

Think of a directory as an electronic folder for storing files. You can keep your correspondence in one folder, your novel in another folder, and your budget in a third. You can create hundreds of directories on your hard disk. GeoWorks Pro uses an icon of a manila folder to represent its electronic folders (directories). The folders in the File Cabinet window separate different categories of documents (refer to fig. 3.12).

Electronic directories possess a feature their cardboard cousins do not: you can store computer directories within computer directories. A directory stored inside another directory is a *subdirectory*. You can create a directory for your correspondence, for example. Within this correspondence directory, you can create subdirectories, one for business and one for personal correspondence. To further divide your business correspondence, you can create a subdirectory for customers and one for suppliers.

The diagram of a directory structure on a typical computer hard disk resembles an upside-down tree, with directories and subdirectories being the tree's branches. In GeoWorks Pro, you can find your way through the directory structure with the assistance of a directory dialog box.

Important commands—like Move, Copy, or Save as—begin with a directory dialog box that says, in effect "What is the destination for this command?" The line just above the scrolling list in the dialog box displays your current directory. In figure 3.13 the current directory is DOCUMENT; the folders in the scrolling list are subdirectories of the DOCUMENT directory.

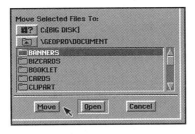

Fig. 3.13

The Move command directory dialog box.

Dialog Boxes

Dialog boxes, which are not initially visible when you open the File Cabinet window, are important components of the Intermediate Workspace. You can carry out some commands immediately; other commands require additional information—a file name, for instance. If a command requires additional information, a dialog box appears. Dialog boxes enable you to specify the details required to carry out a command.

Most dialog boxes appear in the middle of your screen. You must respond to them before you can continue. If the dialog box contains a message, your only response is to click the OK button to acknowledge you have read the message. More complex dialog boxes may require several decisions. A Cancel button is always present to enable you to close the dialog box without taking any action.

Dialog boxes throughout GeoWorks consist of standard elements. The dialog box in figure 3.14 appears when you click the Format button. This dialog box has a column of diamond-shaped *radio buttons*. The name comes from the fact that, like a car radio, you can choose only one button at a time. When you click one button, all other buttons turn off.

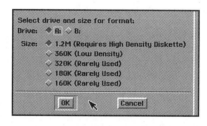

Fig. 3.14

A typical dialog box.

At the bottom of the dialog box are the OK and Cancel buttons, which appear in a majority of dialog boxes. Clicking OK accepts the current settings in the dialog box. Clicking Cancel closes the dialog box, leaving everything as it was before you opened the box.

The special border around the OK button indicates you can activate the button by pressing Enter. Although in most dialog boxes pressing Enter is equivalent to clicking OK, GeoWorks programmers try to put the thick border around the button most frequently used so that you don't have to take your hands off the keyboard to activate the button. Check the buttons in an unfamiliar dialog box to determine which button has the special border because pressing Enter is not always equivalent to clicking OK.

In another example of a dialog box, shown in figure 3.15, you can move to a directory higher up the directory structure by clicking the small button with a folder icon containing the upward pointing arrow. This Up-directory button opens a list of directories in the folder "above" the current directory. The folder above the current directory is sometimes referred to as the *parent* of the current directory. You also can switch to a floppy disk drive (or another hard drive if you have one) by clicking the Change disk button, which contains the image of a disk.

Other important features are shown in the dialog box in figure 3.15. This dialog box, which appears when you choose the Move command, has a scrolling list of directories in the center. Use the scroll bar to the right of the small window to move through the list. To select an item on the list, click the item. You use the two buttons at the upper left of the dialog box to move through the directory structure. Use the lower button with a small folder icon to move up the directory tree. Each click of the button moves you one step up the directory structure. If you click the button with the disk icon, GeoWorks presents a list of available hard disks and floppy disk drives. (Note that this dialog box does not contain an OK button. The Open and Move buttons are appropriate.)

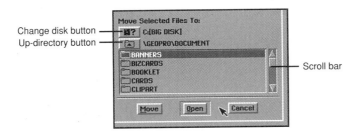

Change disk button ───
Up-directory button ───

Scroll bar

Fig. 3.15

A scrolling list dialog box.

Using the File Cabinet

The File Cabinet window is a document-centered workspace. Instead of starting an application and then creating a new document, you select an existing document to use as a template for creating a new document. This document-centered orientation enables you to concentrate on the results rather than the program you are using. With the exception of the Tetris game, every item in the File Cabinet window or its folders contains a document or document template.

Templates are models created by the GeoWorks designers that contain default settings enabling you to build your own documents. You can use blank documents that start a related application with standard settings; you also can use completed documents that contain text and images which you can adapt.

Understanding Icons and Applications

Each GeoWorks Pro application has a distinctive document type. The File Cabinet window includes icons that launch each major application. Table 3.2 lists the icon names and the programs they launch.

Table 3.2 Icons and Associated Applications

Icon Name	Application
New document	GeoWrite (word processing)
New drawing	GeoDraw (drawing and clip art)
Default Scrapbook	Scrapbook (clip art storage)
First Address Book	Address book
NOTES.TXT	Notebook (read/write DOS files)
My Schedule	GeoPlanner (calendar/scheduler)

Using Application Templates

The six icons listed in table 3.2 can be considered *triggers* that launch their associated applications. This chapter discusses only the general steps that apply to the use of any template. Other chapters in this book discuss each of the applications, and quick-start practice sessions enable you to practice the applications.

As table 3.2 shows, a template is linked to each major GeoWorks application. You can activate an application by double-clicking the application icon or by clicking the application icon once with the mouse and then clicking the Open button.

To preserve the template so that you can use it again, most templates open as *Read Only* documents. You cannot save changes to a Read Only document (see fig. 3.16). To create a document you can modify and save, use the Save as command on the File menu. The Save as command "clones" the original template, creating a copy for modification and preserving the original for re-use.

Fig. 3.16

The "New document" Read Only dialog box.

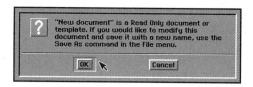

To create your own document from a Read Only document, follow these steps:

1. Select a template.

2. Click the Open button to open the application template. A Read Only message dialog box appears.

3. Click OK to close the dialog box.

4. After the application opens, select the File menu.

5. Choose the Save as command. A dialog box appears.

6. Type a new name in the text field.

7. Choose the Save button in the dialog box to store your new file.

You can work on the newly saved template.

Using Data Files

Because the GeoWorks applications that create the address book, calendar, and clip art scrapbook use only a single data file to store and index their data, you cannot use template copies when you work with these files. When you click the My Schedule, First Address Book, or Default Scrapbook document icons, you access the active file that stores information used by these applications. Do not erase or rename these files. Use the Save command from the File menu to save these files. For detailed information about managing the data files for these applications, see Chapter 5, "Using GeoDex," Chapter 6, "Using GeoPlanner," and Chapter 7, "Using GeoWrite."

Using Specialty Templates

All but one of the folders on the File Cabinet screen contain template documents. The folder names suggest their contents. The Quattro folder, a special case, is used with the Quattro spreadsheet viewer feature discussed in Chapter 15, "Using Quattro Pro Viewer." This section uses the NEWSLTTR folder as an example. The procedures that apply to NEWSLTTR apply to the other folders, but not the Quattro folder.

To open the NEWSLTTR folder, select the NEWSLTTR directory. The grayed buttons on-screen become active when you select an item. Open the folder by clicking the Open Dir button at the bottom of the screen or double-clicking the newsletter folder. (Although you can use the Open button at the upper right to open the folder, you primarily use that button to open files.) When you open the NEWSLTTR directory, the screen displays changes to show the contents of the NEWSLTTR directory (see fig. 3.17).

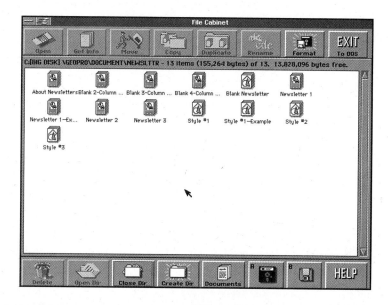

Fig. 3.17

Contents of the
NEWSLTTR directory.

The directory contains two types of icons. The icons, with lines (representing text) and a small drawing in the upper right corner, link to the GeoWrite word processor. The icons containing geometric shapes link to the GeoDraw drawing application. A directory can contain icons for more than one application. You can find more information about GeoDraw and GeoWrite in Chapter 7, "Using GeoWrite," and Chapter 8, "Using GeoDraw."

Notice that some of the file names are blank documents, some are examples, and others are templates. Typically, in the dozens of sample files provided in the File Cabinet's folders, some files are blank forms, and other files are complete models on which you can modify or build. The blank templates often include some type of preparation to save you time. In this case, 2-, 3-, and 4-column blank layouts have been prepared for you.

To build on an expert's work, you can adapt a completed template, such as Newsletter 1-Example (see fig. 3.18). The template also contains instructions for its own use. GeoWorks often provides an example of a finished product built on a template. In figure 3.19, the Newsletter 1 template has been completely developed.

GeoWorks saves these templates as Read-only documents so that you can reuse the templates. Refer to the section "Using Application Templates," in this chapter for instructions on using the Save as command to convert a read-only template to a document you can modify and save.

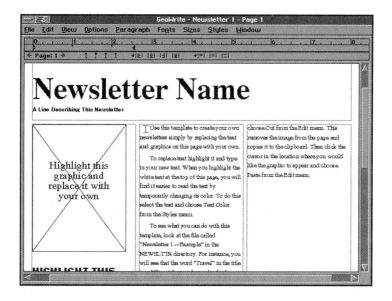

Fig. 3.18

A template with user
instructions.

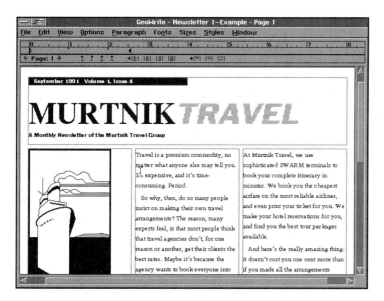

Fig. 3.19

A fully-developed
example.

Closing a Document

Closing a document removes the document from the screen but does not
shut down the application. You can open another document in the same
application and continue working.

To close a document, follow these steps:

1. Select the **F**ile menu.

2. Choose the **C**lose command. If you are closing work you have not saved, a dialog box appears.

3. Choose **Y**es to save.

Exiting an Application

When you work with a template, the Exit command shuts down the current application. What appears when you exit depends on the active applications. Think of the active application windows as a stack of papers. When you remove (exit) one, the sheet behind appears. In the same way, exiting an application window reveals the application behind it. You can exit applications until the application you want appears; however, the simpler way to jump to another application is to use the Express menu.

The current window contains an Express menu, which lists all currently active applications. To exit GeoWorks Pro, click the Express button to open the Express menu; then choose Exit to DOS. (You do not need to close a document to leave GeoWorks Pro.) Choosing Exit to DOS from the Express menu is like putting a bookmark in GeoWorks Pro. When you restart the program and enter the Intermediate Workspace, GeoWorks returns you to the document on which you were working when you exited the application.

Chapter Summary

In this chapter, you learned to use the tools of the Intermediate Workspace. The File Cabinet provides easy file and directory management. You can use the many templates found in the folders of the File Cabinet to ease the job of learning individual GeoWorks Pro applications. The Intermediate Workspace makes an excellent starting point for developing familiarity with the breadth of GeoWorks Pro. After you have explored and mastered the File Cabinet's capabilities, you should be comfortable moving to the full power of the Advanced Workspace.

GeoManager

For this and four other applications covered in this book, you find a quick-start lesson that helps you learn GeoWorks' features without doing a great deal of reading. This first quick-start lesson covers GeoManager.

GeoManager is the hub of GeoWorks Pro. This quick-start lesson teaches important GeoManager skills, such as opening, moving, and sizing windows. You learn to use scroll bars and menus. You also learn to create and remove a directory as you use multiple directory windows. This exercise takes approximately one-half hour to complete. For more extensive descriptions of GeoManager procedures, refer to Chapter 4, "Mastering GeoManager."

Starting GeoManager

In this section, you start GeoManager, learn about its principal parts, and set up the screen arrangement to use during this quick start. Your screens may look slightly different from the ones in the figures; don't worry about exactly duplicating the position and content of every window.

Working with GeoManager's rich set of tools may seem difficult at first, but you can gain confidence rapidly and master skills you can use everywhere in GeoWorks Pro. To learn about GeoManager, do the following:

1. If you installed GeoWorks Pro in the GEOWORKS directory, type **cd\geoworks** at the DOS prompt to move to the GEOWORKS directory; then type **geos** to start GeoWorks Pro. The Welcome screen appears.

2. Move the mouse pointer to the Advanced button and click the left mouse button to enter the Advanced Workspace.

3. If this is the first time you have entered the Advanced Workspace, the caution shown in figure I.1 appears. Choose **Yes** to proceed.

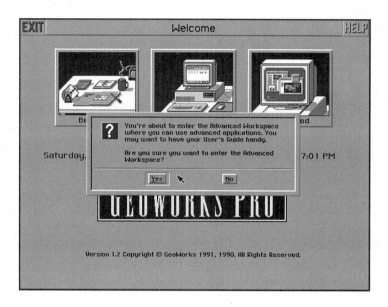

Fig. I.1

Advanced Workspace caution dialog box.

GeoManager opens, displaying the WORLD directory (see fig. I.2). The following instructions refer to the items labeled in figure I.2. Check this figure if you need to refresh your memory.

4. If you open the Advanced Workspace and GeoManager does not appear, select **S**tartup from the Express menu; then click GeoManager in the cascade menu. The GeoManager screen displaying the GeoManager icons appears.

An icon is a small graphic image that represents an item. Many icons are like buttons, which you can activate with the mouse. The row of icons along the bottom of the GeoManager window is shown in figure I.3.

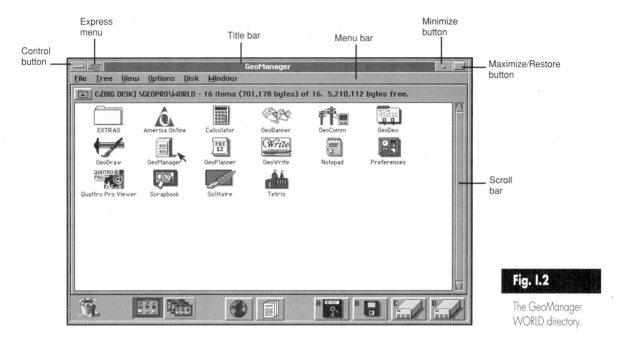

Control button

Express menu

Title bar

Menu bar

Minimize button

Maximize/Restore button

Scroll bar

Fig. I.2

The GeoManager
WORLD directory.

Using figure I.3, locate the WORLD and DOCUMENT icons. The default
GeoManager display shows the WORLD directory, which contains applications such as GeoWrite and GeoDraw. Hidden under the WORLD
directory—like one sheet of paper under another—is the DOCUMENT
directory.

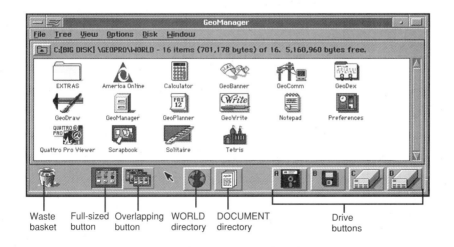

Waste
basket

Full-sized
button

Overlapping
button

WORLD
directory

DOCUMENT
directory

Drive
buttons

Fig. I.3

The GeoManager
icons.

When you work with GeoManager, you may need to shift frequently between the WORLD and DOCUMENT directory windows. To switch directory windows, do the following:

1. Click the mouse on the DOCUMENT icon. New contents appear in the GeoManager window.

   The DOCUMENT directory, shown in figure I.4 contains a display of files and directories. You learn later how to use these items.

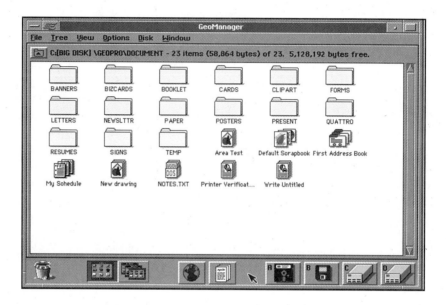

2. Click the WORLD directory icon. The original window display returns.

Manipulating Windows

Because GeoWorks Pro has the capability of running several applications at one time, you cannot use GeoWorks Pro effectively unless you are able to manipulate the program windows. The information contained in this section explains how to view multiple windows; how to move, resize, and close windows; and how to use window features, such as the scroll bars and the Maximize and Minimize buttons.

Viewing Multiple Windows

The default displays of the WORLD and DOCUMENT directories fill the entire window. In some circumstances, you will find having several windows visible at one time helpful. If you must search several directories, for example, you may want several windows open.

The Full-sized and Overlapping buttons enable you to view the contents of the GeoManager window in two ways. You can view one window at a time, or you can view several overlapping windows. The small images in the buttons indicate the arrangement that results from using each of these buttons.

Using the Overlapping and Full-sized buttons is very easy. Simply click one button or the other, and the screen display changes accordingly. If you click the Overlapping button, for example, an arrangement similar to that shown in figure I.5 appears. (If you have not opened any other applications, you see two overlapping windows: the WORLD directory and the DOCUMENT directory.) If you click the Full-sized button, the active window (the window with the dark Title bar) fills the window area.

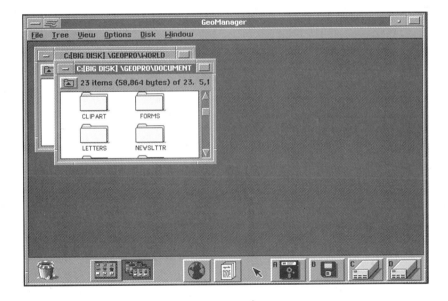

Fig. I.5

Overlapping
GeoManager
directory windows.

72

Moving and Sizing Windows

When they occupy the full GeoManager window, the WORLD and DOCU-MENT windows hide one another. In this exercise, you use these windows to learn more about window management. Do not worry about the content of the windows; you are just using them as examples to manipulate windows.

> **NOTE** One of the useful features of GeoWorks Pro is its capability for remembering its arrangement when you quit the program. GeoWorks returns you to that point when you resume the program. If you get carried away in your experimentation and create stacks of variously-sized windows, you may find getting everything back where it started a bit difficult. Following the steps in this section takes you back to a convenient starting point.

To practice moving and resizing windows, do the following:

1. Click the Overlapping button at the bottom of the window.

2. You should see a window display similar to the display shown in figure I.6. If you don't see this display, click the DOCUMENT and WORLD icons to open those windows.

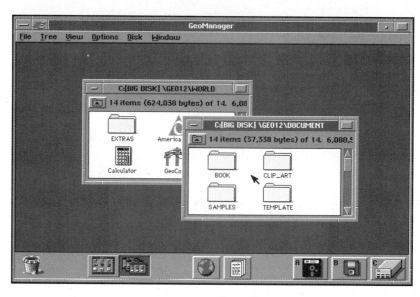

Fig. I.6

The Overlapping window view of WORLD and DOCUMENT.

3. Using the mouse pointer, click the window at the bottom of the "stack". The window you click comes to the front of the stack. You can move an overlapped window to the top of the stack by clicking any part of that window.

4. Point to the Title bar of the top window. Hold down the left mouse button and drag the window down and to the left approximately one inch; then release the mouse button. Notice the phantom outline which moves as you drag. The window fills in when you stop.

5. Drag the window to partially cover the other one. Because the window being moved is selected, it goes to the top of the stack. Notice the difference in the Title bar colors of the active and inactive windows.

6. Examine the window border, which is broken into eight segments. Move the mouse pointer over each segment and notice how the pointer changes shape.

7. Drag the lower right border segment of the window a half inch downward at a 45-degree angle to the right. Hold the mouse button down until you finish resizing. Notice that you have made the window both taller and wider with a single move (see fig. I.7).

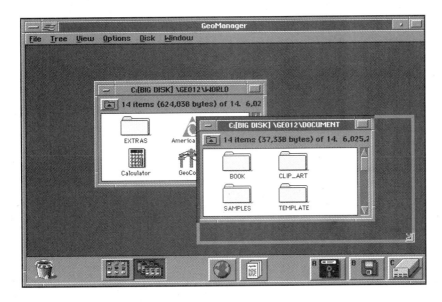

Fig. I.7

Drag the window boundary to resize.

8. Drag the center segment of the bottom and right borders to restore the window to its preceding size. Notice that you can drag only horizontally or vertically if you use the center segments.

Leave the screen arrangement as it is. You use this arrangement for the next exercise.

Using the Minimize and Maximize/Restore Buttons

You have learned how to use the mouse to control the location and size of a window. In this exercise, you use additional automatic sizing features that are built into most windows. The two buttons found in the upper right corner of GeoWorks windows control these sizing features. The button containing a large rectangle is the Maximize/Restore button. The button containing a small dot is the Minimize button (refer to fig. I.2).

For this exercise, you use the large GeoManager window, which occupies most of the screen. (Because of the special features of the WORLD and DOCUMENT windows, these windows are not appropriate for this demonstration.) To use the Maximize/Restore and Minimize buttons, do the following:

If you click the Maximize/Restore button at the upper right corner of the GeoManager window, the window expands to fill the screen. This window is *maximized*. You cannot move or resize a maximized window. If you try to drag the Title bar or the borders, you discover that you cannot move either one. Click the Maximize/Restore button again to restore the window to its default state. You can move or resize the window in this state.

If you click the Minimize button to the left of the Maximize/Restore button, the window is *iconized*—collapsed to a small image at the lower left corner of your screen. At the moment, you don't have other applications running; however, if other applications are running, you can rotate between having the application iconized and maximized as you work. To restore the window to default size, double-click the icon.

After you restore your window, click the Control button. The Control menu provides a keyboard alternative to using the mouse for window management (see fig. I.8). To the right of the commands are keyboard shortcuts, which provide another way to control windows.

As you become experienced with GeoWorks Pro, you memorize keyboard shortcuts for frequently-used commands. As a relative beginner, however, you may be more comfortable using the mouse and menus.

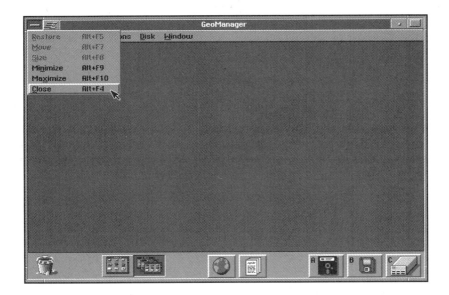

Fig. I.8

The Control menu.

Using Scroll Bars

Scroll bars, which are part of almost every window, enable you to move around in documents that are too large to fit on a single screen. You also can use a scroll bar to judge your position in a document.

To practice using a scroll bar, bring the WORLD window to the front of your GeoManager display by clicking the mouse anywhere in the WORLD window. Use the window sizing techniques you learned in the previous exercise to reduce the size of the WORLD window to fill approximately one-quarter of the screen (see fig I.9).

Because the window is too small to show all the GeoWorks Pro application items at one time, you can use the scroll bar down the right edge of the window to view the window contents. To use the scroll bar, follow these steps:

1. Identify the slider, a gray box in the scroll bar (refer to fig. I.9).

2. To view quickly the entire contents of the window, drag the slider from the top to the bottom of the scroll bar.

   The length of a slider is proportional to the amount of the window that is visible. If you can see half the window contents, the slider is half the length of the scroll bar, for example.

3. To move one full window at a time, click the gray areas on either side of the slider.

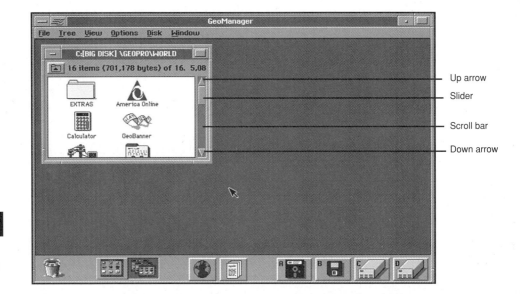

Up arrow

Slider

Scroll bar

Down arrow

Fig. I.9

The quarter-screen WORLD window with vertical scroll bar.

The size of the slider also tells you how large the document is and what your relative position in the window is. If you use the mouse pointer to drag the boundary of the WORLD window until the WORLD window is nearly as large as the GeoManager workspace, for example, all the program icons are visible in the window (see fig. I.10). Notice that the slider occupies the entire scroll bar. Scrolling is not necessary in this case because everything in the window is visible.

Fig. I.10

The full-length slider in a large window.

If you use the mouse pointer to return the window to approximately quarter-screen size, the scroll bar becomes active again.

4. Point to one of the arrows at either end of the scroll bar and single-click the mouse button. The screen scrolls a small distance in the direction the arrow points.

5. Point to an arrow and hold down the mouse button; the screen crawls slowly in the direction the arrow points.

NOTE Now you're qualified to enter one of the longest-running debates in computing history! When you click a scroll arrow that points up, should the contents of the screen move up or down? In GeoWorks Pro, the consensus favors having the page move down; however, this topic has been debated since the scroll bar was invented.

Closing a Window

One of the handiest shortcuts in GeoWorks Pro is double-clicking to close a window. Equivalent menu techniques exist, but nothing equals double-clicking for speed. Close one of the windows on-screen by double-clicking the Control button. The window immediately disappears from the screen.

Single-click the Control button of the window remaining on-screen. The Control menu appears (refer to fig. I.9). Close the window by clicking the Close command on the Control menu. Single-clicking the Control button and choosing the Close command is the menu-based equivalent of double-clicking the Control button. *Note:* You do not need to worry about inadvertently losing unsaved work when you close a window. If you double-click the Control button but have not saved changes made to a file, a dialog box appears, asking if you want to save.

Choosing Commands from the Keyboard

GeoWorks Pro is strongly oriented to the use of the mouse; however, you can use the keyboard to activate commands as you are typing. In this section, you continue to use the GeoManager window.

If GeoManager is not visible, select the **S**tartup command from the Express menu in the active window. Click GeoManager in the cascade menu that appears.

To activate the Tree command in the GeoManager window by using the keyboard, follow these steps:

1. Press Alt+T (hold down the Alt key while you press T, which is the underlined mnemonic letter for the Tree command). The menu appears.

2. To choose the Show Tree Window command, press Alt+S.

3. Leave the Tree window open (see fig. I.11). You use the Tree window in the next exercise.

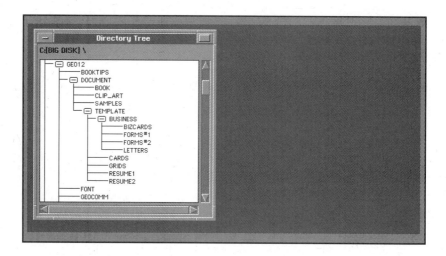

Fig. I.11

The unexpanded Tree window.

Navigating through Directories

You can use a "tree" diagram, which is a visual representation of the directories and files on your computer, to explore your computer's disk structure. Remember, your tree diagram undoubtedly looks different than the diagram shown in the illustrations. You can use the same general instructions to navigate through the structure, however. If you are not familiar with directory structure and paths, read the appropriate section in Chapter 4, "Mastering GeoManager."

1. If you are continuing from the last exercise, GeoManager should be running with the Tree window showing. If not, use steps one through three from the section, "Choosing Commands from the Keyboard," which immediately precedes this exercise.

2. From the Tree menu, choose Expand All. This command opens all directories to show any subdirectories (see fig. I.12). Depending on the complexity of your hard disk, you may want to drag the window boundaries or click the Maximize/Restore button to see more of your tree diagram.

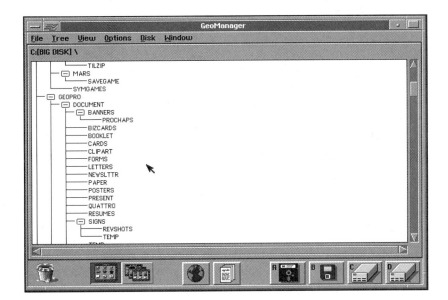

Fig. I.12

The expanded Tree diagram.

NOTE If you have multiple hard disks or floppy disks with a directory structure, you can see the tree diagrams for these disks by clicking the appropriate drive icon at the lower right corner of the GeoManager window.

3. To collapse the entire structure, click the minus sign on the root directory folder (named with a backslash). The minus changes to a plus, and you can begin unfolding the structure again by clicking or by using menu commands from the Tree menu.

4. Open the Tree menu and experiment with the commands that expand and collapse the directory tree. These commands are menu substitutes for the mouse techniques you have been learning.

5. Close the Tree window by double-clicking its Control button.

Creating a Directory

This exercise is not complex; however, to work through it you must understand the concepts behind directories and paths. If necessary, review the appropriate section in Chapter 4, "Mastering GeoManager."

You must have a specific setup to do this exercise. To create a directory, do the following:

1. Open the GeoManager window.

2. Click the icon representing drive C in the lower right corner of the GeoManager window. A directory window showing the contents of the root directory appears in GeoManager.

3. Click the Maximize/Restore button to enlarge the directory window.

   Your window should resemble figure I.13. The names and quantity of directory folders and files will vary, however, depending on the structure of your hard disk.

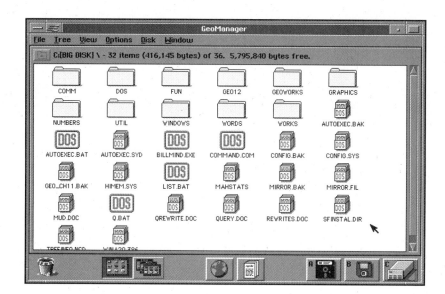

Fig. I.13

A directory window
maximized in
GeoManager.

4. Select the File menu and choose Create Directory. A dialog box appears.

5. Type **atest**; then click the Create button.

   A new directory folder icon appears in your directory window. Because its name begins with *A*, this directory appears near the upper left corner of the window.

Removing a Directory

You can remove the directory you created in the preceding exercise.

CAUTION   When you delete a directory, you also delete the directory's contents. If carelessly done, deleting a directory can be very destructive. You mistakenly may remove dozens or even hundreds of files that you cannot recover without a backup of your work.

Check your selection carefully and read the next steps completely.

To remove a directory, do the following:

1. Click the ATEST directory to select it. GeoWorks highlights the folder (see fig. I.14).

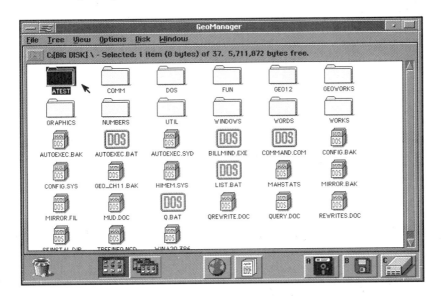

Fig. I.14

The directory window with ATEST selected for deletion.

2. Select the File menu and choose **Delete**. Carefully read the dialog box that appears. The dialog box must specify ATEST as the directory to be removed. If ATEST is not specified, click the Cancel or No button and recheck your directory selection.

3. If the dialog box verifies that you made the correct selection, choose **Yes** to delete the ATEST directory.

T I P   An alternative way to delete a directory is to select the directory and hold down the *right* mouse button as you drag the folder image onto the Wastebasket icon at the bottom on the GeoManager screen, according to GWRep MK.

Viewing Files by Name

Although useful, icons are limited in the amount of information they can convey. When you use files, you may want to see additional information, such as file size and creation date. GeoManager enables you to see this additional file information. To access additional file information, do the following:

1. Switch to the WORLD window and click the Full-sized button (to the right of the Wastebasket icon).

2. Open the **View** menu and click the **N**ames Only command. Your display should resemble figure I.15.

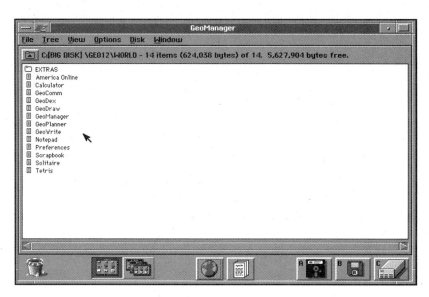

Fig. I.15

The Names Only display.

You can display dozens of files in a single window, using the Names Only command. As you accumulate files in GeoWorks, this sort of display option becomes more appealing. GeoWorks displays the files in alphabetical order. Although icons also are alphabetized, scanning a column of names is easier than jumping across a screen full of images.

3. From the **View** menu, choose the **Names and Details** command to add additional information. The result resembles figure I.16. GeoWorks adds the file size in bytes, the date and time the file was created or copied to the disk, and a letter showing the attributes of the file.

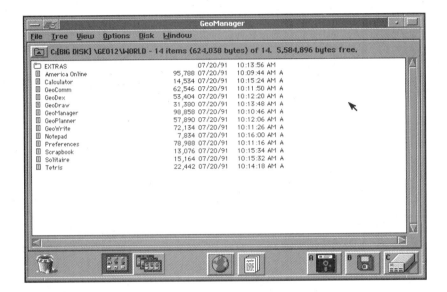

Fig. I.16

Files list using the Names and Details command.

You can sort the lists by date and time or by size, using the cascade menu attached to the **Sort by** command in the **View** menu. When you use the Sort command, directories always sort first, followed by files.

Moving through the Directories

You have confined much of your recent activity to the DOCUMENT and WORLD directories. As your skills grow, you will need to learn to move among the directories.

To move among directories, do the following:

1. Open the DOCUMENT window by clicking the DOCUMENT directory button.

2. Click the Overlapping button to see multiple windows.

3. Close any open windows other than DOCUMENT by double-clicking their Control buttons.

4. Using your mouse, move and resize the window as shown in figure I.17. You don't need to see the entire window contents for this exercise.

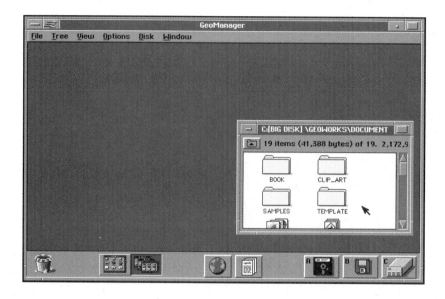

Fig. I.17

Moved and resized
DIRECTORY window.

Notice how GeoManager tells you where you are. Across the top of the DOCUMENT window, GeoWorks lists the path: C:[*DISK NAME*]\GEOWORKS\DOCUMENT. If you do not understand the meaning of a path, review the appropriate section in Chapter 4, "Mastering GeoManager."

5. Move the mouse pointer to the arrow in the file folder icon located in the upper left of the DOCUMENT window (refer to fig. I.17). This icon is the Up Directory button, which you use to move upwards in the hierarchy of directories. Click the left mouse button once. A second directory window appears as in figure I.18.

Examine the path description at the top of the new window. You have moved one step up the directory tree, into the GEOWORKS directory. The path now reads C:[*DISK NAME*]\GEOWORKS. By clicking the Up Directory button in the DOCUMENT directory window, you moved to GEOWORKS, the "parent" directory of DOCUMENT.

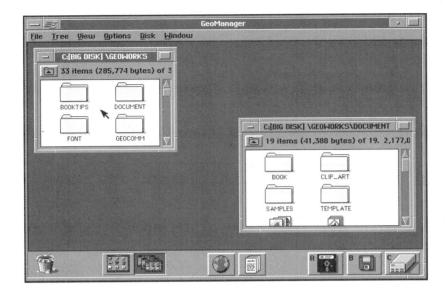

Fig. I.18

GEOWORKS
DIRECTORY window,
the "parent" directory
of DOCUMENT.

6. Again, click the Up Directory button in the second window. A third
directory window appears. Move and resize this window as shown
in figure I.19.

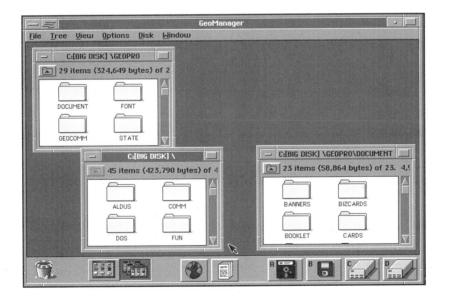

Fig. I.19

The root directory (\)
window, from which
all other directories
originate.

You have moved all the way up to the root directory, the parent of all other directories. The root directory is always named (\). The path is C:[DISK NAME]\.

Notice that each directory contains a folder with the name of the directory below it. The root directory contains GEOWORKS, which contains DOCUMENT, which contains CLIP ART, and so on, as far as a particular branch extends. For the purpose of this exercise, ignore other files and directories contained in the exercise windows.

To complete this exercise, return to the DOCUMENT directory window from the root directory, using the following steps:

1. Close the two lower directory windows (GEOWORKS and DOCU-MENT) by double-clicking the Control button in the upper left corner of each window.

2. Find the GEOWORKS folder in the root directory window. You may need to scroll through the window (see fig. I.20).

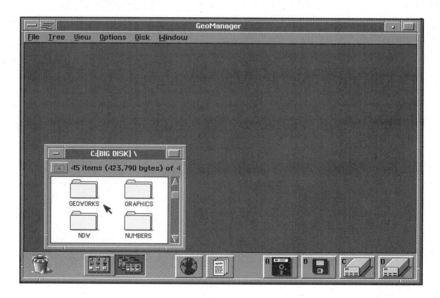

Fig. I.20

The GeoWorks directory in the root directory window.

3. Double-click the GEOWORKS folder icon to open a window showing GEOWORKS's contents, which include the DOCUMENT directory.

4. Locate and double-click the DOCUMENT directory to open its window.

5. Click the Full-sized button to expand the DOCUMENT directory to a full window.

In this exercise, you climbed up and down one branch of a typical directory tree. The same principles work with any other group of directories and subdirectories. Although GeoWorks Pro installs its directories in a standard pattern, what you see in the windows varies with your computer's setup.

If you have multiple drives on your hard disk, each one has its own root directory from which its own directory tree extends. To switch drives, click the drive icon at the bottom right of the GeoManager window. Using the techniques learned in this section, you can locate any directory or file on your computer.

Copying and Moving Files

After a directory structure is in place, you can move and copy files to various directories. In this exercise, you learn how to copy and move files with the mouse. You use the *right* mouse button to copy and move files.

To copy and move files, follow these steps:

1. Open the DOCUMENT directory by clicking the DOCUMENT directory button at the bottom of the GeoManager window.

2. Select the First Address Book file by clicking it with the left mouse button. GeoWorks highlights the file (see fig. I.21).

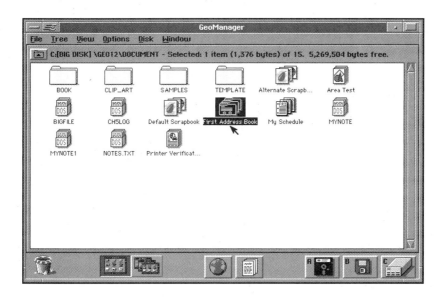

Fig. I.21

The DOCUMENT window with First Address Book highlighted.

3. Place the mouse pointer on the selected file and hold down the right (not the left) mouse button.

4. With the right button held down, drag the mouse pointer on top of the SAMPLES folder (subdirectory). A small rectangle travels with the mouse pointer as you drag the mouse pointer (see fig. I.22).

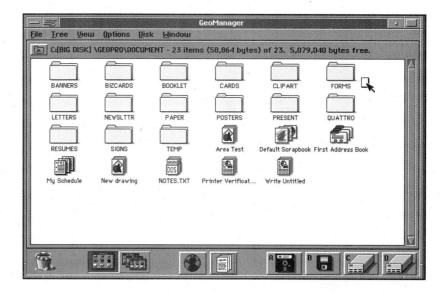

Fig. I.22

Move a file to a new directory by dragging.

5. When you release the mouse button, the First Address Book file moves to the SAMPLES folder, and the First Address Book icon disappears from the DOCUMENT screen.

6. Open the SAMPLES folder by double-clicking it. The SAMPLES directory window opens, showing the First Address Book file inside.

7. Reverse the process by dragging the First Address Book file onto the DOCUMENT icon at the bottom of the GeoManager window, using the right mouse button.

You have moved, not copied, the file. As long as the destination directory is on the same disk, the GeoWorks Pro program can move the file. You can force a copy instead of a move by holding down the Ctrl key as you drag the file icon.

NOTE The Address Book Appliance and GeoDex use the First Address Book file. If you previously have saved any names and addresses, be sure to return the First Address Book file to the DOCUMENT directory; otherwise, GeoWorks creates a new empty file with the same name when you run the Address Book Appliance or GeoDex.

Mastering GeoManager

GeoManager is the hub of GeoWorks Pro. From this software control tower, you manage applications and storage for GeoWorks Pro and DOS. The principal activities that GeoManager conducts are as follows:

- ■ Opening PC/GEOS applications
- ■ Creating, removing, and maintaining directories
- ■ Creating, deleting, and changing files
- ■ Managing floppy disks
- ■ Providing facilities for viewing files and directories

In this chapter you learn how to use the management tools that make GeoWorks Pro so effective.

Exploring the Advanced Workspace

So far in this book, you have confined your exploration of GeoWorks Pro to the Beginner and Intermediate Workspaces. Now, with the skills gained in the previous chapters, you are ready to move to the Advanced Workspace, which you access by choosing the right button on the Welcome screen (see fig. 4.1).

Fig. 4.1

The Advanced Workspace button in the Welcome window.

The Advanced Workspace is the name for the heart of GeoWorks Pro—the part managed by GeoManager. The Beginner and Intermediate Workspaces and the DOS Programs areas are the only parts of the program that exist outside the Advanced Workspace.

In the Advanced Workspace, you find most of the GeoWorks Pro applications. The "lineup" appears in the window that represents the WORLD directory (see fig. 4.2).

If you open the Advanced Workspace and GeoManager is not visible, choose the **S**tartup command from the Express menu in any visible window. (The Express menu button, detailed later in this chapter, has a blue stylized letter E on it.) Click GeoManager in the cascade menu that opens from Startup (see fig. 4.3). Then open the WORLD directory window by clicking the icon of the globe at the bottom of the window.

The first time you enter the Advanced Workspace from the Welcome screen, a dialog box appears to give you a gentle warning. This caution is intended to reduce frustration for novice users who may enter the Advanced Workspace without first acquiring the basic skills discussed in the opening chapters of this book. Coming unprepared into an environment as rich and complex as GeoManager can be frustrating for the unwary user.

Control button   Express menu   Title bar   Minimize button

Menu bar

Information
bar

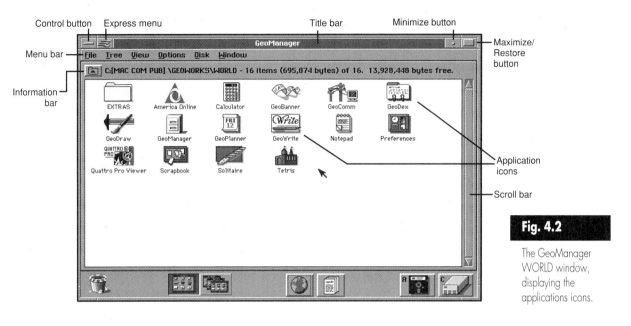

Application
icons

Scroll bar

Maximize/
Restore
button

Fig. 4.2

The GeoManager
WORLD window,
displaying the
applications icons.

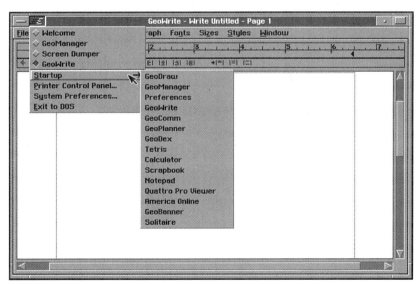

Fig. 4.3

The Startup cascade
menu to start
GeoManager.

If you have skipped the first section of this book, consider a quick review
before forging ahead. If you have some familiarity with a graphic operating environment and using the mouse, drop-down menus, and dialog
boxes, you'll do fine. If those terms are a bit confusing or mysterious,
some review may save you time as you begin to work with GeoManager.

Two important "views" of GeoWorks Pro are available only when you are working within GeoManager in the Advanced Workspace. The WORLD directory (refer to fig. 4.2) is "home port" for specialized applications such as GeoWrite and GeoDraw. The DOCUMENT directory (see fig. 4.4) is an organized presentation of the directories and files that serve the applications—a location where you can add, delete, move, and rename files and directories.

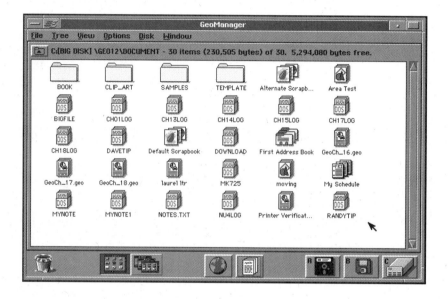

Fig. 4.4

The DOCUMENT directory holds directories and files.

With standard installation settings, the Advanced Workspace opens with GeoManager running and the WORLD window open.

Understanding the GeoManager Window

The GeoManager window—the first and most frequent to appear in GeoWorks Pro—is a good example of a typical window. It has a few distinctive features, but basically it is built from the same mixture of parts used for all windows.

If you have confined your explorations to the Beginner Workspace so far, the GeoManager window appears considerably more complex. The easiest way to dispel its mystery is to reduce it to component parts. Two important window elements may need definitions: an *icon* is a small symbolic image used to represent various elements of GeoWorks Pro; a *directory* is a named storage location for computer files.

Table 4.1 lists the elements of the window, starting at top center and moving clockwise. You learn to use these features as you move through the chapter.

Table 4.1 Parts of the GeoManager Window

Part	Purpose
Title bar	Contains name of application and any open document; turns dark when window is active
Express menu	Opens special menu containing commands to switch rapidly to another active application, launch another application, move to Welcome screen, or exit directly to DOS
Control button	Opens special menu that controls GeoManager window
Menu bar	Displays menu names
Information bar	Displays directory information
Scroll bar	Moves through window contents that are too large to display at one time; appears along bottom or right edge of window when contents are too large
Maximize/Restore button	Enlarges window to fill the full screen or restores window to normal size
Minimize button	Reduces window to icon at bottom left of screen
Application icons	Represent the programs you work with in GeoManager; double-clicking application icon launches associated program
Wastebasket icon	Deletes files and directories
Full-sized icon	Enables viewing full-size directory window on-screen
Overlapping icon	Presents open directories as overlapping multiple windows on-screen
WORLD icon	Opens WORLD directory that contains programs
DOCUMENT icon	Opens DOCUMENT directory that contains data files
Drive buttons	Enables switching among floppy and hard drives

GeoManager is an application in its own right, but one with a special purpose. Its business is to manage other GeoWorks Pro applications and their files. You use the icons on the bottom row of the WORLD directory for the following operations:

- One activity you perform most often in GeoManager is moving between the WORLD and DOCUMENT directories. To switch to the DOCUMENT directory from the WORLD directory, click the icon that looks like a stack of documents, next to the globe icon. The directory window opens, filling the entire window area.

- Windows viewed in GeoManager can be seen two ways: to view a window inside GeoManager as a full screen, click the Full-Size icon that resembles a miniature computer screen with a document on it; to view windows as smaller overlapping windows that you can move and size, click the Overlapping icon that resembles a series of overlapping windows stacked on one another.

  Alternatively, you can choose **F**ull-Sized or **O**verlapping from the **W**indow menu, or press Ctrl+F10 for full-size and Ctrl+F5 for overlapping.

Moving and Sizing Windows

The capability to move, stack, and size windows gives you various display possibilities. You can make a single window occupy the entire screen or fill the same area with a mosaic of windows that display several different programs or documents. When learning how to manage windows, try to visualize each window as a separate small environment with its own content and set of controls.

Although GeoWorks can display several windows at once, only one can be the *active window*, which responds to menu commands. You can identify the active window by its Title bar, which is darker than the inactive window Title bar (see fig. 4.5). Click inside its boundary to activate and move a window to the top of any stack of windows.

Clicking on a window to activate it is the essential first step toward moving or resizing it. The next two sets of steps show you how to manipulate an active window.

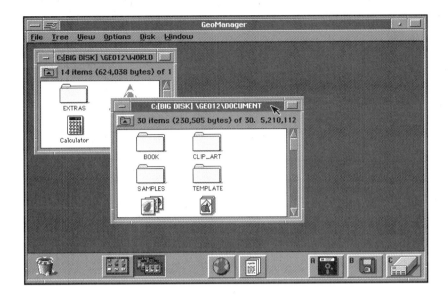

Fig. 4.5

The active window
with a dark Title bar.

To move a window, follow these steps:

1. Move the mouse pointer to the Title bar of the window you want to move.

2. Hold down the left mouse button and drag the window to its new location. An outline of the window moves with the mouse pointer.

3. Release the mouse button to redraw the window at the new location.

You easily can resize windows by dragging sections of the window border. If you examine a typical window, you notice that the border is divided into eight segments—four corners and four sides. Dragging a corner segment resizes the window vertically and horizontally at the same time. Dragging a side segment resizes in only one direction at a time.

Follow these steps to resize a window:

1. Point accurately to the window border you want to resize. Watch for the mouse pointer shape to change, as shown in figure 4.6.

2. Drag the window boundary in the appropriate direction. An outline of the new boundary appears as you drag (see fig. 4.6).

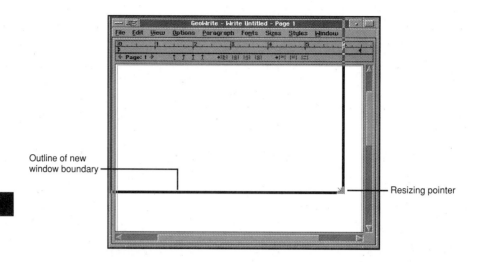

Outline of new
window boundary

Resizing pointer

3. When you release the button, the window is redrawn at its new size.

T I P Complex screen backgrounds slow down redrawing of the screen, which slows down the entire system. If you are working on something that will require the background to be redrawn (opening and closing Notepad at the bottom of the screen, for example), change to a simple background like Fullmoon.bit, advises GWRepDave.

Using Scroll Bars

When a window is small or contains a large piece of data, some of its data is hidden. The scroll bar at the right edge of each window enables you to move the window's contents so that you can see everything in the file.

A scroll bar consists of three parts: the bar itself, running vertically or horizontally at the right or bottom of a window; the slider, a box that moves in the bar; and the scroll arrows at each end of the bar. Figure 4.7 shows a window with two scroll bars.

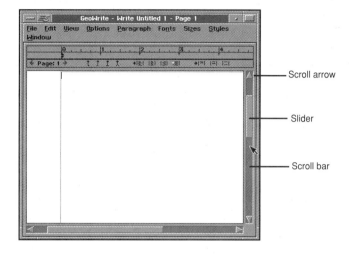

Scroll arrow

Slider

Scroll bar

Fig. 4.7

A window with scroll
bars.

To use a scroll bar, follow these procedures:

■ To view the entire contents of a window quickly, drag the slider
from the top to the bottom of the scroll bar with the mouse pointer.

The length of a slider is proportional to the amount of the window
that is visible. If you can see half the window, the slider is half the
length of the bar, and so forth.

■ To move one full window at a time, click the gray areas on either
side of the slider.

■ To move in small jumps, click the arrows at the top or bottom of
the scroll bar.

■ Pointing to one of the small arrows and holding down the left
mouse button causes the contents of the window to move continuously in the direction of the arrow.

Using the Control Button

Every window has a Control button at the extreme upper left; you click it
to open the Control menu that is devoted entirely to managing the window. If you examine the choices, you find that you have done almost all
these things using the mouse. You may want to use this menu, however,
to access the keyboard shortcuts it provides (see fig. 4.8).

Fig. 4.8

The Control menu.

You still haven't used one very useful mouse-oriented feature. Double-clicking the Control button closes the window with which it is associated. If a program is running in the window, it is shut down. This shortcut is one of the most useful in GeoWorks Pro.

To the right of the commands in the Control menu are keyboard shortcuts that provide yet another way to control windows. After you become experienced with GeoWorks Pro, you begin to memorize keyboard shortcuts to speed often-used commands. Now, as a relative beginner, you probably are more comfortable using the mouse and menus.

Using the Express Button and Menu

The useful Express button shown next to the Control button is a gypsy. It travels from window to window, appearing on the menu line of the currently active window. Clicking the Express button opens the Express menu (see fig. 4.9), which has two sections: at the top, a list of any applications now active, and at the bottom, commands called Startup, Printer Control Panel, and Exit to DOS.

After you have a good sense of GeoWorks Pro, you can start and switch applications rapidly through the Express menu. The top of the menu lists any applications now running. Clicking the button next to the application name switches you to that application. Depending on the video resolution, this button may be round or triangular.

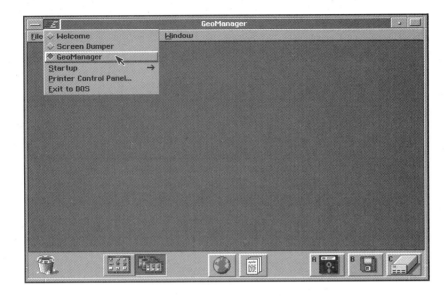

Fig. 4.9

The Express menu.

If the application you want is not running, choose **S**tartup from the Express menu. A small cascade menu opens, listing all the GeoWorks Pro applications. Click the name of the application you want to start, and it launches immediately.

Notice that the Express menu travels to the menu of the newly launched application, because this window now is active. If you have overlapping windows, as described earlier in this chapter, you can watch the Express menu jump from window to window as you click different windows to activate them.

Using the Express menu to exit GeoWorks Pro has one great advantage: The next time you restart GeoWorks Pro, it starts exactly as you left it when you chose the Exit to DOS command. In this way, you can quit in the middle of a document and start again with the same page of the same document on-screen. For some activities, opening the needed windows and loading the documents you need take time. Using Exit to DOS preserves your exact setup, so you don't have to recreate it when you return.

Maximizing, Minimizing, and Restoring Windows

Your final step to controlling windows involves the buttons at the upper right of most windows. The button with the rectangle inside is the

Maximize/Restore button. The one with the small dot is the Minimize button. Conceptually, you may say these buttons expand and collapse your window.

When GeoManager opens, the GeoManager window is in its default size. You can display the window in one of three possible sizes as follows:

■ In its *default* state, a window is smaller than the Workspace surface on which it sits. The space showing below the window is the PC/GEOS Workspace, the "surface" on which the program arranges windows (see fig. 4.10). You can move, resize, and stack a window in this state.

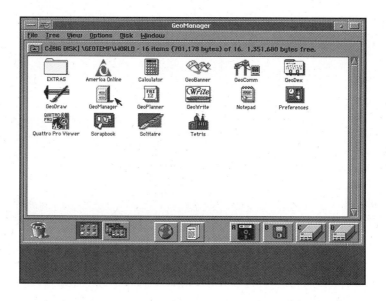

■ A *maximized* window (see fig. 4.11) has been expanded to fill the screen, enabling you to see the largest possible amount of the window's contents. You should use this setting when you are working on a single application with no need to see or move often between other windows.

■ When you *minimize* a window, you shrink it to a small icon at the lower corner of your screen (see fig. 4.12). Use this window state when you want to collapse a window temporarily to work in another window and then return to the minimized window. The file or application in a minimized window is suspended rather than shut down and returns instantly when you double-click the icon.

Fig. 4.11

The maximized
GeoManager window.

Fig. 4.12

The minimized
GeoManager
window.

To manipulate these window sizes, use the sizing buttons as follows:

- To maximize a window, click the Maximize/Restore button. The window fills the screen. Now maximized, the window cannot be moved or resized.

- To restore the window to its default size, click the Maximize/Restore button again. You can move or resize the window in this state.

- To minimize a window, click the Minimize button to the left of the Maximize/Restore button. To restore the minimized window to default size, double-click the window's icon.

- To close any open window, double-click the Control button in the upper left corner or press F3 to close the application running in the window.

In this section, you have learned skills that apply to windows in the Advanced Workspace. Because windows throughout the program share the same features, you will use this information everywhere in GeoWorks Pro.

NOTE The design principles guiding GeoWorks Pro's graphic interface also are shared by other programs that use the Motif design standards developed by the Open Software Foundation. Companies such as IBM, DEC, and Hewlett-Packard use the same approach when designing graphic interfaces for their products. Should you have occasion to use another Motif-based graphic computer interface, you will find you already know a good deal about how it operates.

Using Menus and Commands

You have absorbed many techniques using the mouse and buttons so far, but most of them apply to broad-based activities such as opening windows and switching screens. Much of the detail—and consequently the power—of GeoWorks Pro lies in the menu commands found on most windows. In this section you learn how to identify and use GeoWorks Pro's several menu types.

Choosing Commands

The Menu bar, located just below the Title bar, contains a list of menu names. GeoManager has six main menus, not counting the Control and Express menus shared by most windows. These menus are drop-down menus that you can open by clicking or by using the keyboard. Although the File menu is present in most applications because it manages the opening and closing of data files used by the application, the menus on the Menu bar and the commands on these menus differ for each application.

The menus and their general purposes follow:

Menu Name	Purpose
File	Manages program files and documents
Tree	Controls display of graphic diagram of files and directories
View	Controls display of items in windows
Options	Controls whether you are asked to confirm certain choices
Disk	Provides tools to prepare and manage disks and drives
Window	Controls arrangement and display of windows

The most frequently used commands within each GeoManager menu are discussed throughout this chapter.

Using Mouse Menu Techniques

If you are a beginner, you probably will find the point-and-click technique easier than the keyboard approach. The mouse method gives you visual confirmation of your command choice and a chance to abandon your selection before the command takes effect.

To activate a menu and choose a command with the mouse, click the menu name to open the menu; then click the command you want to use. If you want to close the menu without choosing a command, click somewhere away from the menu.

Another way to use the mouse with the menu involves dragging the mouse with the left button held down. To employ this method, point to a menu and hold down the left button. The menu you are pointing to opens. Drag the mouse horizontally across the menu names and notice the menus drop down one after another.

To choose a command by dragging, keep the left mouse button down as you drag down a menu to the command you want. Each available command is highlighted as the mouse pointer drags across it. After you highlight the command you want, release the mouse button to run the command.

A command that appears in light gray on a menu is not available under the current situation. The last four commands in the Tree menu shown in figure 4.13, for example, are initially gray, indicating that these commands are available only when you display the tree. After the tree display is active (see fig. 4.14), you can use the darkened commands. The "Understanding Directories" section later in this chapter explains the Tree menu commands.

Fig. 4.13

Commands are gray when not available.

Fig. 4.14

The open Tree window activates previously grayed commands.

Using Menus from the Keyboard

When you are new to the program or uncertain about your choice, using the mouse is appropriate. After you are familiar with GeoWorks Pro and speed becomes a concern, you begin to look for shortcuts. One major shortcut for frequently used commands is activating them from the keyboard.

Each menu name and each command name includes an underlined letter or number—often, but not always, the first letter. The programmers at GeoWorks call these letters (or, at times, numbers) *mnemonics*, an elegant name for a memory-prompting device. You press a mnemonic with the Alt key, usually found at either end of the space bar on most keyboards. While holding down Alt, press the mnemonic to activate the appropriate menu or command.

Using Cascade and Pinned Menus

An arrow at the right end of the command signals another menu variation. See the Tree menu's Drive command in figure 4.13. The arrow shows the presence of a *cascade menu*, a secondary list that opens when you select the command. Cascade menus pack several choices into a small side menu to avoid unnecessary lengthening or cluttering of the main menu. You find cascade menus throughout GeoWorks Pro.

The small symbol at the top of each menu is an image of a push pin, meant to remind you that you can pin menus to your screen. You can drag a *pinned menu* to any convenient location on-screen, where it stays open until you close it. In a specialized sense, a pinned menu is a miniature window, with some properties of a larger window.

To pin a menu, click the pin symbol at the top of the menu. The menu becomes a small independent window, with a Control button in the upper left corner and a Title bar (compare fig. 4.15 to fig. 4.13). To position the menu window, use its Title bar to drag it to the desired location. After you are through with the menu, close it as you would any window by double-clicking its Control button.

Using Dialog Boxes

An *ellipsis* (...) follows some menu commands. This symbol tells you that the command needs additional information. A dialog box opens when you choose the command. A dialog box does not have any control icons or scroll bars characteristic of windows and cannot be moved or resized.

Most dialog boxes appear in the middle of your screen. You must respond before you can continue with your activity. Sometimes, when the box contains a message, your only response is to click OK to acknowledge that you have read the message. More complex boxes may require several choices. A Cancel button is usually present to enable you to close the box without taking any action. You also can press Esc to cancel a dialog box.

Dialog boxes are made up of standard parts. Figure 4.16 shows the dialog box that opens when you choose the Print command in the GeoWrite application. It includes three buttons: Print, Cancel, and Change Options.

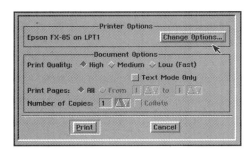

Note that an ellipsis follows the Change Options button. Clicking that button leads to another dialog box.

A row of three *radio buttons* appears in the middle of the dialog box. Radio buttons get their name from the fact that, like a car radio, you can choose only one at a time. If you click one, any other button that has been chosen turns off.

Next to the heading Number of Copies is a small *text field* in which you can type the number of copies desired; to its right is a pair of up and down arrows that you can click to increase or decrease the number of copies.

In the center is a *check box* that you check or uncheck by clicking. Unlike radio buttons, if you see multiple check boxes, you can click any number of them on or off.

GeoWrite's File Save As dialog box shown in figure 4.17 includes a scrolling list in the center—another important dialog box feature. You can use the scroll bar to move through a list that is larger than the "window" through which you view the list.

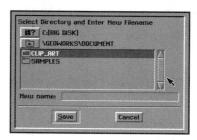

Dialog box with scrolling list and text field.

Below the list is a text field in which you can type a name for the file. In text fields, you can use standard editing techniques with mouse and keyboard—Backspace or Del to remove characters and the I-beam to select text, for example.

The keyboard can play a useful role in dialog boxes. Notice in figure 4.17 that a thin dotted rectangle surrounds the Save button. The rectangle can be moved from location to location within the dialog box by pressing Tab to advance or Shift+Tab to back up. The dotted rectangle selects the option it highlights. In a group of options, several radio buttons, for instance, you can select within the group by using arrow keys. You can activate a selected button by pressing Enter.

This rectangle surrounds the default button in most dialog boxes when they open. When a button is preselected in this way, you can press Enter to activate it. This procedure saves you from having to move your hand to the mouse just to click OK or give another routine response.

Managing Your Work

If you have been working methodically through this chapter, by now you should have several important new techniques available to you. You can manipulate windows, use the mouse and keyboard with menus, and respond to different types of dialog boxes. You have encountered most of the generic elements in the GeoWorks Pro environment.

You need to master another set of general skills, however, before you are ready to set off into the individual GeoWorks Pro applications: understanding directories and files.

An often-used analogy relates your disk drives to file cabinets, directories to file folders, and files to the documents stored in file folders. You can use this analogy to think about the storage structure of any computer. In fact, GeoWorks Pro uses icons of file folders and sheets of paper for a graphical presentation of the elements of storage. When you minimize the GeoManager window, its icon resembles a file cabinet.

In this section, you tie all these ideas together into a working model of file and program management.

Understanding Storage, Files, and Directories

Figure 4.18 shows the GeoManager window containing the Tree display on the left and the DOCUMENT window on the right. The highlight in the Tree window rests on a folder called DOCUMENT, the same one whose contents are shown in the window to the right.

To begin, take a moment to learn how your computer handles storage. Your computer stores data on magnetically coated disks of various sizes and capacities. Disks record data in much the same way as video tapes record. You insert a program disk in one of your computer's disk drives and copy the data from the portable floppy disk to the larger hard disk in your computer. Although much larger and faster than a floppy disk, a hard disk uses the same magnetic recording technique to store data.

Just as a video cassette is not very exciting until you play it back, the data stored on your computer represents only potential power until you choose to use it. To enable you to identify and retrieve data from your computer, the program stores data in files. *Files* are simply logical, named groupings of recorded information. You can store a program in one file and accounting records in another file. When you need a file, you must have an easy way to find it.

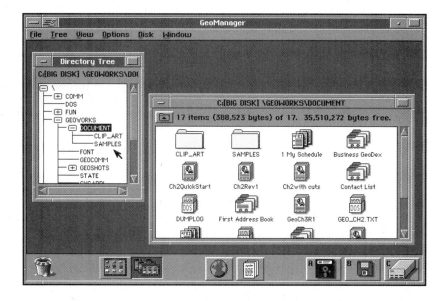

Fig. 4.18

GeoManager, showing Tree and DOCUMENT windows.

Most computers store files on an internal hard disk. Hard disks have very large storage capacities. One size, in increasingly common use, can store more than 100M (megabytes) of data. Even the smallest hard disk in common use holds around 20M. *Note:* For practical purposes, a *byte* is an amount of data roughly equal to one character of text or one numeric digit.

With so much storage space, files multiply. Without some sort of system to order them, your files soon resemble a pile of library books delivered by a dump truck—lots of potential, but tough to work with. The directory is the pivot of file management.

A *directory* is a named storage location for files. The analogy to a drawer in an office file cabinet is almost perfect. You can store files in directories and, when you leave, the files remain inside the directories as though you have closed a file drawer. When you want to retrieve a file, find and open the right directory and use your file.

If your directory becomes too complex, you can create a *subdirectory*. This action is like putting a hanging folder inside your file drawer, enabling you to separate the contents (files) of the drawer (directory) further into subcategories. You can create directories and subdirectories on floppy disks, but that method usually doesn't make sense because you can store so few files on a floppy compared to a hard disk.

GeoWorks Pro stores the tools for file and directory management in the GeoManager window. First you look at the directory features and then the file management tools.

Understanding Directories

Besides the analogy of a file cabinet, directory and subdirectory structure is often explained in terms of a *tree structure*. The directory tree is a bit more like a family tree than a pine tree, but the branching structure, growing from a root, is quite distinctive.

Figure 4.19 shows the tree display for the author's hard disk. Your display varies depending on the structure of your hard disk, but the principles are similar.

Every disk, floppy or hard, has at least one directory—the *root directory*. Created as part of the formatting process, which prepares a disk for use, the root directory is the starting point for any structure of directories, which accounts for its name.

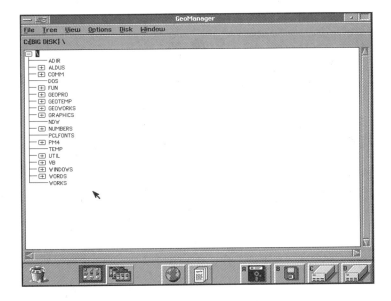

Fig. 4.19

The tree directory display.

Because you refer to the root directory when locating something on disk, every root directory has the same name, one that's easy to type and remember. A root directory is always named \. You usually find the symbol, called a *backslash*, on the keyboard, often near Enter, so that you easily can type it. Note that a backslash is not the same as the slash (/) also found on the keyboard. The slash leans to the right, whereas the backslash leans to the left.

Look again at figure 4.19. Notice the root directory at the upper left, with its name just to the right. Consider the root directory as the parent of all directories that grow from it. As you examine the tree diagram, notice that the lines connecting directories all grow out of the root directory.

Examine some other aspects of the diagram. The plus signs on many directories mean that they have subdirectories hidden inside them. A minus sign, like you see on the root directory, means that the directory is opened fully and has no more hidden subdirectories. If you click a directory icon that shows a minus sign, the directory closes again, hiding any subdirectories it contains.

Now you are ready to explore your own disk structure. Remember that your tree diagram undoubtedly looks different from the diagrams in the figures. You can use the same general instructions to navigate through the structure, however.

Use the following steps to examine the tree structure on your computer:

1. Move to the GeoManager screen. Click the Overlapping icon at the bottom of the screen to the left of the WORLD icon.

   This icon produces a display of overlapping windows.

2. If necessary, move windows to uncover their Control buttons; double-click the Control buttons on any windows *other* than the GeoManager window to close them.

3. From the **Tree** menu, choose **S**how Tree Window.

4. From the **Tree** menu choose, Expand **A**ll to open all directories to show any subdirectories.

   Depending on the complexity of your hard disk, you may want to drag the window boundaries to see more of your tree (see fig. 4.20).

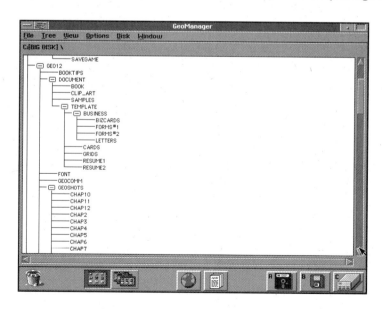

Fig. 4.20

Enlarging the window shows more of a complex tree.

NOTE If you have multiple hard disks (C, D, and so on) or floppy disks with a directory structure, you can see their tree diagrams by clicking the appropriate drive icon at the lower right corner of the GeoManager window.

5. To collapse the entire structure, click the minus sign on the root directory folder. The minus changes to a plus. You can begin unfolding the structure again by clicking the plus sign.

Alternatively, the Tree menu contains keyboard substitute commands that expand and collapse the directory tree. Quick Start I, "GeoManager," includes a short exercise that demonstrates how to use the Tree menu and its commands.

Creating and Deleting Directories

Having examined the tree structure, the next step is to learn to modify it. This straightforward process has one exception—you must be careful who your "parents" are.

When you create a directory, it becomes a child (subdirectory) of the directory that was active when you issued the command. If, for example, you have the root directory active and create a new subdirectory, it is one level below the root directory. On the other hand, if you activate a directory two levels below the root and create a subdirectory, the new subdirectory is three levels down.

Going more than two or three levels deep in directories rarely makes sense, because typing the description of the path necessary to reach the directory can fill an entire text box and more. Even clicking through three or more levels slows you down.

For this example, you create a new directory in the DOCUMENT directory. You use the same procedure from any other starting directory. To create a directory, follow these steps:

1. Click the DOCUMENT icon in GeoManager to open the DOCUMENT window.

2. Choose Create Directory from the File menu.

The dialog box shown in figure 4.21 appears. The current directory line shows whether you are in the correct parent directory.

3. Type a name for your directory in the New Directory name text field.

You must enter a directory name, using the file name pattern FILENAME.EXT. (You learn more about file names in the "Creating File Names in GeoWorks Pro" section later in this chapter.) For now, confine your directory name to no more than eight characters; do not use spaces or numbers. MYDIR, for example, is fine; MY DIR is not.

4. Select Create in the dialog box and observe the new directory folder appear alphabetically in the DOCUMENT window.

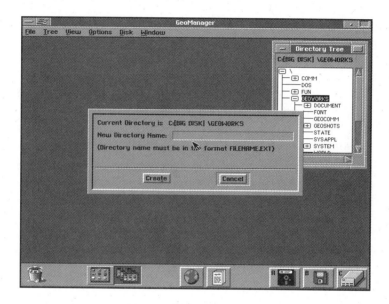

Fig. 4.21

The Create Directory dialog box.

Removing a Directory

Carelessness or confusion in removing a directory can result in the loss of important program or data files. If you are not comfortable with the process, create a practice directory and practice removing the practice directory before you remove a real directory.

CAUTION Approach this activity carefully. When you remove a directory you also delete the directory's contents. Deleting directories is potentially destructive. You may remove dozens or even hundreds of files with no way to recover them unless you have a backup of your work.

Although you use the DOCUMENT directory for this example, you can use this process in any directory. To remove a directory, carefully follow these steps:

1. Open the DOCUMENT directory so you can see the folder that represents the directory you intend to remove.

2. Double-click the folder to open the directory; ensure that it is empty. If the directory contains files and subdirectories you want to keep, move the contents of the folder to another location, using techniques described in the "Copying files" and "Moving Files" sections later in this chapter.

3. Click the Up-directory button (just above the window at the left) to return to the parent directory.

4. In the parent directory (DOCUMENT in this example), place the mouse pointer on the folder of the directory to be removed.

5. Hold down the right mouse button and drag the folder icon on top of the Wastebasket icon at the lower left corner of the GeoManager window. A dialog box appears, asking you to confirm your deletion.

6. When you are confident that you have chosen the right directory, click Yes to remove the directory.

Using Paths

One last step in the mastery of directories involves understanding what a path is. In computer terms, the word *path* describes the steps you use to move from the root directory to a subdirectory. When you want to navigate to a deeply buried subdirectory or save a file to another disk, knowing how to specify a path enables you to move confidently.

Refer to figure 4.22 as you read the following discussion.

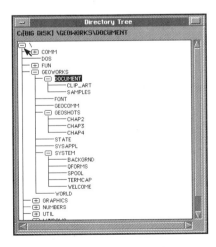

Fig. 4.22

A multilayered tree diagram.

The center of the tree diagram in figure 4.22 shows the multiple directories that GeoWorks creates when installed. In the figure, the selected subdirectory is DOCUMENT. As a result, the path at the top of the window says C:[BIG DISK]\GEOWORKS\DOCUMENT. If you study this path, you see a complete verbal description of the path from the root directory to the DOCUMENT subdirectory. The path starts on drive C, named BIG DISK, which accounts for the C:[BIG DISK] part of the path. From there it continues in the root directory (\), leads through the GEOWORKS directory, and ends in the selected DOCUMENT directory.

NOTE   Any backslash used after the first one (the root directory) is a divider, separating one directory name from another.

Notice in figure 4.22 that the DOCUMENT directory has two subdirectories. Test yourself: without looking, write the path from the root directory to the SAMPLES subdirectory.

If you have written C:[BIG DISK]\GEOWORKS\DOCUMENT\SAMPLES, you have got the idea. If the path still seems obscure, start deciphering paths displayed at the top of many windows when you select a file or a program within the window. In the graphical world of GeoWorks Pro, you can get by without a strong knowledge of paths, but even a knowledge of the general principles helps you to manage your files and directories better.

Managing Files

So far in this chapter, you have learned to manage windows, menus, and directories. In this section you move on to the items where the work gets done—the files that comprise the programs and data your computer uses to run GeoWorks Pro. The ability to manage files and disks is not particularly exciting or glamorous, but, like the ability to put oil in your car, things rapidly stop if you cannot manage the task!

You need these skills to format new unformatted diskettes before using them and to copy files you want to share. If you want to remove a directory but not its contents, you have to know how to move files. These mundane activities, done with GeoManager, are essential support for the more exciting parts of GeoWorks Pro.

Manipulating Files and Directories in Dialog Boxes

Every GeoWorks Pro application that uses files also uses dialog boxes to help you locate and specify those files. These file and directory dialog boxes have some features that make them easier to use but need a little explanation.

Figure 4.23 shows a typical dialog box opened by choosing the Open command from the File menu. The central feature of the window is the list of directories and files. Folder icons represent directories, and icons that look like small sheets of paper represent files. Double-clicking the icon you want selects and opens the associated file or directory.

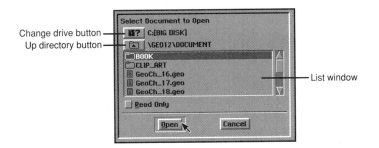

Fig. 4.23

A typical dialog box for directories and files.

Suppose that you want a file on a disk in the A drive. To switch to that drive, follow these steps:

1. Click the Change drive button. A dialog box displays a list of the drives available on your machine.

2. Double-click the drive you want in the dialog box window. GeoWorks switches to that drive and displays the files or directories on that drive.

Below the Change drive button is a button showing a file folder with an upward pointing arrow. Recall or review the earlier discussion of the tree diagram of directories in the "Managing Files" section. Clicking the Up Directory button moves your directory up one level in the tree directory structure. If you are in a directory one level below the root level, clicking the Up Directory button moves you to the root directory.

You may wonder how to move down the directory structure. Because any directories showing in the list window are below the level of the current directory, to move down to one of those directories, double-click the directory icon in the list window. You use this type of dialog box repeatedly in GeoWorks Pro. Take the time to understand its workings clearly.

Creating File Names in GeoWorks Pro

PC/GEOS interacts with DOS, the disk operating system that runs your PC. Consequently, you must name some files to follow DOS rules, but you can name others under the more liberal PC/GEOS rules.

GeoWorks Pro files can use up to 32 characters in their file names. In DOS, however, directories and files must follow DOS naming rules, such as the following:

■ A DOS file name has two parts: a one- to eight-character name and an optional three-character extension. If you use an extension, a period must separate the extension from the name.

■ DOS file names do not accept spaces.

■ A typical DOS file name is FILENAME.EXT.

You rarely create a DOS file name in GeoWorks Pro, except directory names. Directories are a special sort of file, so file naming rules apply. Directory names almost never use the three-letter extension.

Create a name from one to eight characters long. Don't start the name with a number (1MYSTUFF), although you can use numbers within the name (MYSTUFF1). Don't use symbols such as @ and #, or spaces. If you want a substitute for a space, use the underscore (_) symbol, as in A_SPACE. If these rules seem confusing, just model new directory names on existing ones. You will see an error message if you make a mistake.

Viewing Directories and Files

By now you should be familiar with the WORLD and DOCUMENT directory windows as they appear in GeoManager. To refresh your memory, take a moment to view them both, flipping between them with the two icons in the bottom center of the window.

GeoWorks Pro assigns distinctive icons to its program elements. The attractive icons for the applications in the WORLD window are preassigned. Similarly, files in the DOCUMENTS window belonging to GeoDex look like Rolodex cards, Planner files look like calendar pages, and so forth.

If you create a new file or directory, GeoWorks applies an icon based on the general type of the new element. This system helps you quickly find the type of file you are looking for. The following table gives you an idea of the icons available:

Item	Icon type
Directory	File folder with directory name below
Subdirectory	File folder with directory name below
Document file	Stack of paper
DOS file	Papers in box marked DOS

Although icons are graphic and, with the right monitor, colorful, they don't convey much detail, and if you have many icons in a window, seeing them all can be difficult. One quick solution to the quantity problem is the **Compress Display command on the View menu. This command moves the icons closer together so that more fit a given window. Compress Display, however, can cause long file names below the icons to be truncated with an ellipsis so that they do not overlap one another (see fig. 4.24).

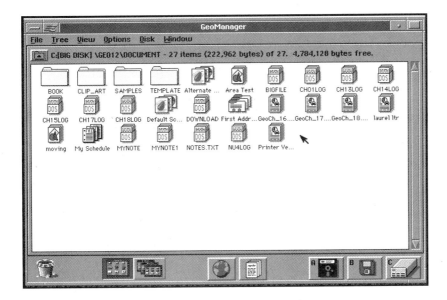

Fig. 4.24

The Compress Display command shows more information.

Try the **Compress Display command. Choose it a second time to remove the effect.

You can view a list of file names without icons. In this way room is available to include more data about the files. To view files by name, follow these steps:

1. Open a full-sized view of the window containing the files you want to view.

2. From the **View menu, choose **Names Only.

Figure 4.25 shows the DOCUMENT window displayed using the **Names** Only view, with which you can display dozens of files in a single window. As you continue using GeoWorks Pro, you steadily accumulate files, and this display option becomes more important.

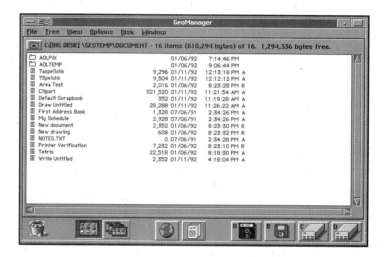

Fig. 4.25

The DOCUMENT directory viewed with Names Only.

T I P If you have a template or file you would like to have appear at the top of your menu, rename the file with a "!" as the first character. When GeoWorks sorts file names, punctuation marks are sorted first. GWRepPeter

Notice also that the files are in alphabetical order. The icons also are alphabetized, but scanning a column is easier than jumping across a screen full of images. To return to the icon display in the window, choose **Icons** in the **View** menu.

You also can sort the lists by date and time or by size using the cascade menu attached to the **S**ort By command from the **View** menu. In all sorts, directories sort first, followed by files.

The **Names** Only display can be augmented by choosing the command **Names** and Details from the **View** menu. The result looks similar to figure 4.26. In addition to the names, the file size in bytes, the date and time the file was created or copied to the disk, and a letter showing the attributes of the file appear on-screen.

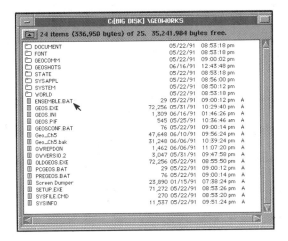

Fig. 4.26

Files list using the Names and Details command.

As mentioned earlier, a byte is an amount of computer storage sufficient to store 1 character or number. A typewritten page solidly filled with text may contain about 2,000 characters. A 3,000-byte file is needed to store the page.

Date and time may seem trivial, but when you want to find the most recent file in a directory or the file you worked on Thursday morning, these pieces of data become essential. GeoWorks stamps the date and time of the activity on a saved or copied file. The date and time data comes from the clock/calendar in your computer.

NOTE The program to set the clock usually comes with your computer or with the documentation for the board that holds the device. A long-lived battery maintains the time and date while the power is off. After four or five years, the time and date will become erratic, which means you must replace the battery. If you are reasonably handy, you can change the battery yourself. If not, take the system to a repair or maintenance shop.

The final item shown in the Names and Details view is the file attribute. *Attributes* are "switches" that give files different properties, such as making them invisible in a directory listing or enabling users to read but not change them. Most of the files in your list probably show A for Archive, indicating a conventional file.

The **View** menu has a command to Show **H**idden Files. Hidden files, usually system files you never have a reason to use, are hidden with good reason. They should not be deleted, modified, or moved unless you fully understand the consequences. Look but don't touch until you are confident in your handling of attributes in general and the hidden file attribute in particular. File attributes are primarily handy in the DOS world. Consult your DOS manual for a full discussion of the topic.

Maintaining Files

Now that you have gained a sense of how to access, create, and delete directories, your next logical step may be to plan how to build a structure that suits your working needs. File management tools are essential to the construction of any directory structure. You must copy new files, delete old ones, and move groups from one directory to another.

With the graphical interface of GeoWorks Pro, you easily can accomplish most file management options. If you have any experience working with the DOS command line, you can appreciate the ease with which you can work in GeoWorks Pro.

Selecting Files and Directories

Select a single file or directory on which to use a command by clicking it. The file or directory becomes highlighted and the command you use applies to it. This technique selects only one file at a time. Three additional techniques are available that select multiple files or directories.

The first technique involves drawing a selection box around a group of items you want to select. Follow these steps:

1. Visualize a box that surrounds the files you want to select. Point to the upper left corner of your box and drag diagonally across the area you want to enclose. Do not release the mouse button.

   You see the dotted outline of a box appear as you drag (see fig. 4.27).

2. Keep the left mouse button pressed as you adjust the box.

3. After you release the mouse button, the box outline disappears and the items inside the box are selected.

   To remove the selection, click an area away from the selected items.

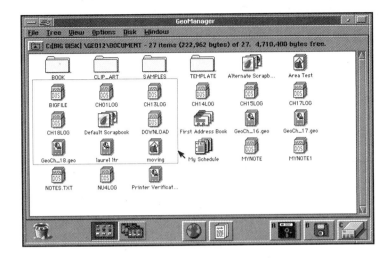

Fig. 4.27

Drag a boundary
around files to be
selected.

The second selection method enables you to add or remove items from a
group one by one. Follow these steps:

1. Click to select the first item.

2. Shift+click the second item you want selected. Repeat as often as
   needed. (You also can Shift+click to deselect a previously selected
   item.)

The third selection method uses the **File** menu command **S**elect All,
which selects every item in the active window. Remove the selection by
choosing Deselect All from the **File** menu or by clicking an unselected
area of the screen.

Moving Files

If you have been waiting for a chance to use the right mouse button, you
now have one. To copy and move files, drag them with the right mouse
button held down.

Some clever thinking went into the logic used to control copies and
moves. The program logic assumes that if you drag a file from directory
to directory on the same disk, you probably intend to move the file. The
second assumption is that if you drag a file from one disk to another you
probably intend to copy the file, leaving the original file untouched.
These rules are built into copying and moving with the mouse. You can
override them when necessary, but you will find the logic quite sound
and very convenient.

To move a file with the mouse, use the following steps:

1. Select the file you want to move.

2. Position the mouse pointer on the selected file and hold down the *right* mouse button.

3. Drag the mouse pointer on top of the folder (subdirectory) to which you want to move the file. A small rectangle travels with the mouse pointer as you move it.

4. When you release the mouse button, the file moves to the new folder; its icon disappears from the old folder. *Note:* The file has been moved, not copied. As long as the directory is on the same disk, the program moves the file.

The two other ways to move a file on the same disk are as follows:

■ Dragging the file (right mouse button down) onto the up folder icon in the upper left of a window copies it to the parent of the current directory.

■ Choosing the **Move** command from the **File** menu while a file is selected opens a dialog box listing directories to which you can move. You select a directory and then choose **Move** to move the highlighted file to the selected destination.

Copying Files

Copying is similar to moving except for the built-in assumption that if you drag a file from one disk to another, you intend to copy it. Use the following steps to copy a file from one disk to the root directory of another:

1. Click the file to highlight it.

2. While holding down the right mouse button, drag the file over the disk icon at the bottom of the GeoManager window (see fig. 4.28).

If you want to copy to a specific directory on another disk, open the directory window for the disk by double-clicking the disk icon. Use the skills you have learned to scroll to and open any subdirectories until you have reached the destination you want.

You also can use the **File** menu **Copy** command to specify a destination on another disk. Figure 4.29 shows the File Copy dialog box, which lists directories, not files. Select the destination directory you want and then choose **Copy**.

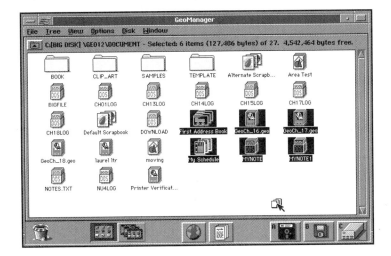

Fig. 4.28

Selected files to copy to another drive.

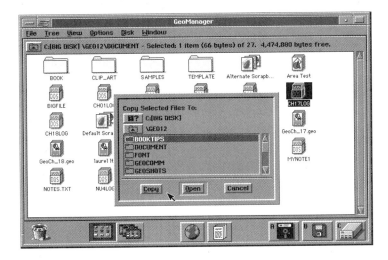

Fig. 4.29

The File Copy dialog box.

At the top left, notice the icon that you use to change drives. Clicking this icon presents you with a list of drives. After you choose a drive, you can navigate through its tree structure using the path concepts you previously learned in this chapter.

NOTE Although GeoWorks Pro assumes that dragging from one disk to another implies copying, you can force a *move* operation, instead, by holding down the Alt key while dragging with the mouse.

Duplicating a File

Suppose that you are writing the ending to a story and want to try it two different ways. Rather than deleting the first ending to make room for the second, GeoWorks Pro enables you to copy the file quickly.

The Duplicate command from the File menu creates an exact image of the selected file in the current directory. As shown in figure 4.30, the File Duplicate dialog box suggests a default file name, which precedes the original name with the words Copy of. If you prefer a different name, type one, but remember that you cannot have two identical file names in the same directory.

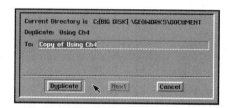

Fig. 4.30

The File Duplicate dialog box.

Deleting Files

Yes, you guessed correctly the purpose of the wastebasket icon at the bottom left. Using the wastebasket icon is another right mouse button operation.

To delete a file or directory, drag the item to the wastebasket. If Confirm Delete has been checked on the Options menu, a dialog box opens, asking you to confirm your deletion. Don't be hasty—you *cannot* retrieve items from this wastebasket.

T I P   Although we don't recommend that you remove any fonts from the FONT directory, here's the scoop on which ones you need for which applications: The only fonts that are absolutely required are UNIVERSI.FNT and BERKELEY.FNT. If you intend to use America Online, you must keep the BISON.FNT. If you intend to use GeoWrite or GeoDraw, you should keep the ROMAN.FNT. The Calculators use LED.FNT and GeoPlanner prints using SANS.FNT, according to GWRepRandy.

Using Other GeoManager File Commands

This section completes your introduction to file management by introducing three commands: Get Info, Attrib, and Rename. Although rarely used, these commands are important to know.

Get Info Command

The Get Info command on the File menu gives you detailed information about a selected file. Choosing the command opens the dialog box shown in figure 4.31.

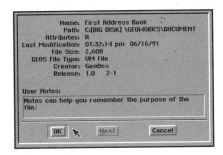

Fig. 4.31

The Get Info dialog box.

Some of the data in the dialog box is identical to that presented with the View menu's Names and Details command. Additional information like Token and Creator are of limited use. Every user, however, can take advantage of the User Notes text field. Click the box and enter a short description of the file. Even with the liberal 32-character names you can use in GeoWorks Pro, you easily can forget the purpose of a file after months have passed. These notes can be a great help in file maintenance or disk housekeeping.

Attributes Command

Only one element of the File menu's Attributes command is of day-to-day use. Applying the Read Only attribute to a file enables the file to be viewed, moved, and copied, but not changed.

Choosing the Attributes command opens a self-explanatory dialog box with check boxes for applying or removing attributes (see fig. 4.32). Do not use other attributes unless you understand them. Improperly set attributes can make files disappear from directories or cause programs to fail. If you want to learn how to manage file attributes, consult your DOS documentation.

Fig. 4.32

The File Attributes
dialog box.

Rename Command

The **R**ename command from the **F**ile menu can be of great use in organizing your work. By renaming a group of files so that they begin with the same letter, all the files sort together in a directory. You can change a file name to start with A to make a file move to the top of a list.

Use of this command is straightforward. Select the file or files you want to rename and choose **R**ename. A dialog box opens with a text field where you can type a new name (see fig. 4.33). Select **R**ename or **N**ext to skip the current item and move to the next selected item.

Fig. 4.33

The File Rename
dialog box.

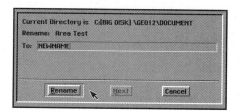

Understanding Disk Management

Despite their limited storage capacity and slow speed compared to a hard disk, floppy disks are still the portable medium of exchange in computing. GeoWorks Pro gathers its floppy disk management commands under GeoManager's **D**isk menu. The commands enable you to do the following:

- Format a disk
- Copy from disk to disk
- Rename a disk
- Scan a disk for new data

Formatting a Disk

Formatting is the process of preparing a disk so that a computer can read or write to it. Because of various computer drives, floppy disks come from the factory unformatted. The formatting process puts on the disk magnetic markings that the computer uses to locate files.

Formatting is complicated by the various types of disk capacities now on the market. Be aware that a difference exists between *double-density* and *high-density* diskettes. Although they have the same physical dimensions, they have different magnetic coatings and considerably different storage capacities. Consult your hardware documentation if you are not certain what type of drives your machine has.

Figure 4.34 shows the dialog box opened by selecting **F**ormat Disk from the **D**isk menu.

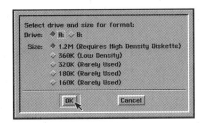

Fig. 4.34

The Format Disk dialog box.

The first floppy drive on your machine is called drive A. A second floppy drive is drive B. The first hard disk is always drive C, even if you do not have a drive B. If you have only one floppy drive, the B drive button doesn't appear. If you have 3 1/2-inch drives with different disk capacities, they also are listed properly in the dialog box.

To format a disk, follow these steps:

1. Insert a disk of the proper capacity in your drive.

2. From the **D**isk menu choose **F**ormat Disk. The dialog box in figure 4.34 opens.

3. Select the proper radio buttons for the drive and disk capacity.

4. Choose OK or press Enter. A dialog box keeping you informed of the progress of the format appears.

5. When asked, give the disk a name from 1 to 11 characters. You can use spaces.

6. Click **F**ormat. A message box keeps you advised of progress.

After the process is complete, your disk is ready to store files. Many computer users format a whole box of disks at once to eliminate the problem of needing a new, formatted disk in the middle of a complex activity.

Using Other Disk Commands

Although you will use two other commands on the **D**isk menu infrequently, you will find them indispensable when you need them.

Rename Disk enables you to change a disk name. GeoWorks' graphical interface makes this capability more useful than it is in the traditional DOS environment.

The path description in the Title bar of directory windows includes the disk name. You can create an organized naming system to identify multiple disks or otherwise clarify the content of a disk. You also can have fun by naming your hard disk after a pet or friend. You can easily change the name when you tire of it.

To rename a disk, follow these steps:

1. From the **D**isk menu choose the **R**ename Disk command. The Rename Disk dialog box opens (see fig. 4.35).

Fig. 4.35

The Rename Disk dialog box.

2. In the dialog box, click the radio button for the drive containing the disk to be renamed.

3. Type the new name in the text field.

4. Select **R**ename.

The Rescan Drives command updates the directory display. If you switch disks in a drive, the directory window continues to show the old list until you take some action that accesses the disk. The **R**escan Drives command forces PC/GEOS to reread the contents of all displayed disks and update the display.

Copying Floppy Disks

With most software programs, including GeoWorks Pro, you can make one archival copy of your master disks in case the originals are later damaged. Such a task is a perfect example of the use of the Copy Disk command, which produces a replica of a disk.

One implication of this command that you may miss, however, is that you must copy to a disk of identical size and storage capacity. In other words, you cannot copy a 3 1/2-inch, high-density floppy to a 5 1/4-inch high-density floppy, or a high density floppy to a double density floppy. If you have two floppy drives of differing size or capacity, you cannot copy a disk from one to another.

To avoid this problem, you can use the same drive for what is called the source disk and the destination disk. First, insert the disk carrying the data you want to copy—the source disk. Part of the data is read into the computer's memory, and then a message appears telling you to insert the disk to which the copy will be made—the destination disk. Depending on the number of files to be transferred, you will be prompted to swap disks a few times before the copy is complete.

To copy a floppy disk to a disk of identical size and capacity, follow these steps:

1. Choose the Copy Disk command from the **Disk** menu. The Copy Disk dialog box appears (see fig. 4.36).

Fig. 4.36

The Copy Disk dialog box.

2. In the dialog box, click the radio buttons for the source and the destination of the copy.

    Remember that you can copy only between drives and disks of the same size or capacity. You can choose the same drive for source and destination.

3. Select **C**opy and follow the instructions on-screen.

T I P GWRepJohnK suggests that even if you have only one floppy drive, you can copy files from one disk to another without going to DOS. Insert the source disk and open a window for it. Then remove the source disk and insert the target disk. Open a window for the target disk. Now you can select the file(s) you want to copy and drag them from the first window to the second window. GeoManager prompts you to switch disks as required. One caution: The two disks cannot have the same volume name (created when formatting).

Chapter Summary

This chapter describes how to use the tools available in GeoManager—window management techniques, techniques for working in windows, and general methods of using menus—for both the mouse and the keyboard.

The chapter also explains how to understand and use directories to organize your work. Techniques covered include creating, deleting, and changing directories. Finally, this chapter describes the tools for file management, including moving, copying, and deleting files, and the commands on the **F**ile and **D**isk menus.

Now you are prepared to use the GeoWorks Pro applications introduced individually in the following chapters. The techniques learned here apply to every aspect of GeoWorks Pro.

PART III

OUTLINE

Using the Applications

GeoDex

In this quick start, you get hands-on practice with the major activities of GeoDex, GeoWorks Pro's computerized address and phone directory. The exercises in this section should take about one-half hour to complete.

Starting GeoDex

By now you probably are familiar with the procedure for starting GeoWorks Pro from DOS. Typically, you start your computer, change to the GEOWORKS directory by typing **cd geoworks**, and type **geos** to launch GeoWorks Pro.

Starting from the Welcome screen, use the following steps to open GeoDex:

1. Click the button labeled Advanced.

2. The default installation opens the Advanced Workspace with GeoManager showing the WORLD directory. To start GeoDex, double-click its icon (see fig. II.1).

If you open the Advanced Workspace and GeoManager is not visible, open the Express menu in any active window and choose **S**tartup as in figure II.2. From the cascade menu, click GeoDex to open the GeoDex window (see fig. II.3).

Fig. II.1

The GeoDex icon in the WORLD directory window.

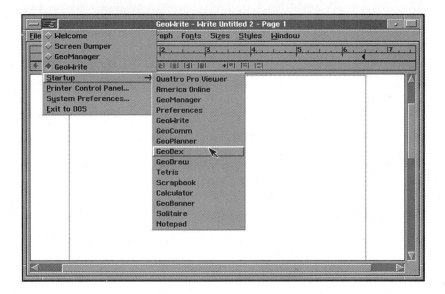

Fig. II.2

Start GeoDex from the Express menu.

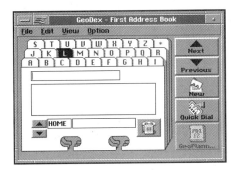

Entering Information

The following exercises will be more useful if you have enough entries in your list to follow along with the description of the features. Three or four entries are adequate; however, to try the scroll bars you should enter enough names to more than fill the browse window—about a dozen should do it. Include one card containing your own name and address.

Follow these steps to enter names in your GeoDex:

1. If GeoDex opens with a filled-in card showing, click the New button to display an empty card.

2. The flashing text cursor appears in the index text field. Type a last name, a comma, and then a first name.

3. Press Enter; GeoDex automatically copies the name to the first line of the address area in the first name/last name order.

4. Type the rest of the address, pressing Enter to start each new line and using the Backspace or Del keys to correct errors.

5. Click the down arrow next to the phone number box to choose the appropriate type of number (Home, Office, Car, Fax); then type in the number, including any prefixes or area codes.

   Figure II.4 shows a completed card, with the index entry copied in correct form in the address field.

6. Click the up and down arrows again to enter additional telephone numbers for the same address, if desired.

7. When you are ready to begin a new card, click the New button.

   Repeat steps 2 through 7 to enter additional names (remember to include your own).

Fig. II.4

The index entry copied in the address field.

8. When you have finished creating new cards, select **F**ile menu and choose **S**ave. GeoDex saves your entries to First Address Book, the default GeoDex file.

Searching in GeoDex

In GeoDex, you can search for any word or series of words on any card; you can perform a speedier search using just the index field (the top text on each card).

To search for information anywhere on the cards, follow these steps:

1. From the **V**iew menu, choose **B**oth View (see fig. II.5).

   Throughout this exercise, you will use a card that contains your name and address. If you have not entered one, please do so now, using the steps under "Entering Information" in this quick start.

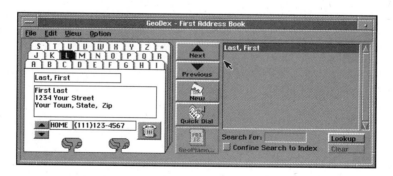

Fig. II.5

The search field options in the lower right of the Both View window.

2. Type the name of your street in the Search For text field below the list on the right side of the Both View. Because the search is case-sensitive, capitalize the name exactly as you did when you entered it on the card.

3. Click the Lookup button. The search finds and highlights your street name. Notice that the name on the Lookup button has changed to Find Next.

4. If no items on any cards match your item, a dialog box appears, giving you that message. If a match is found, click the Find Next button to locate other matches. In this example, if no other street names are identical to yours, you will keep "finding" the same entry until you click Clear.

5. When you are through searching or want to begin another search, click the Clear button to remove the search item entry from the Search For box.

6. Click any alphabet tab that is not the first letter of your last name to "hide" your index card, making the practice search more realistic.

7. To search for your name in the index field only, click the Confine Search to Index check box.

8. Enter your last name in the Search For box.

9. Click the Lookup button to begin the search. The program checks only index field items, which speeds the search.

10. When the search is complete, click the Clear button to clear both the search entry and the Confine Search to Index option.

Moving Text

Imagine you were starting a letter to a friend, but you couldn't quite remember the correct address. Using GeoDex, you can verify that the address is correct and copy the address to your letter. In this exercise, use your own name and address.

To move your address to the GeoWrite application, follow these steps:

1. Click the appropriate letter tab or the Next or Previous buttons, if necessary, to turn to your own address card.

2. Move the mouse pointer to the upper left of the address entry; then hold down the left mouse button and drag the mouse across your complete name and address in the large text field. Be sure that you highlight the *entire* name and address (see fig. II.6).

3. Select **E**dit and choose Copy. A copy of the highlighted information is placed in your computer's memory.

4. Open the Express menu in GeoDex. The menu looks like a stylized letter **E**.

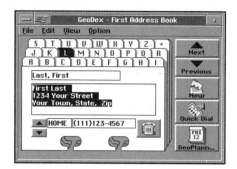

Fig. II.6

The name and address
selected.

5. Choose **S**tartup to open the cascade menu showing the GeoWorks Pro applications. Click GeoWrite (see fig. II.7). Don't worry if you are not familiar with GeoWrite—you only use it briefly in this exercise.

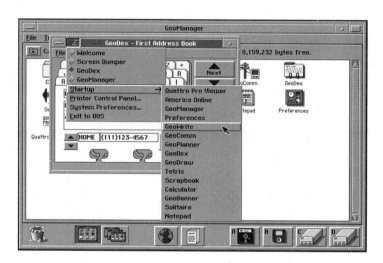

Fig. II.7

GeoWrite opened
from the Express menu
to move text from
GeoDex.

6. The GeoWrite window opens with a text cursor flashing in the upper left corner of the writing area. The text cursor indicates the location of the text you are going to paste in the document.

7. Open the **E**dit menu and choose **P**aste. The text you copied from your GeoDex card is pasted into the document (see fig. II.8).

8. Close GeoWrite by double-clicking the Control menu in the upper left corner and choosing **C**lose. For this exercise, when the dialog box appears asking whether to save changes, choose **N**o.

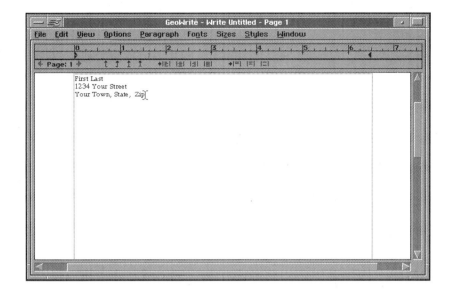

Fig. II.8

A GeoWrite document
with a pasted address
pasted from GeoDex.

Printing Your GeoDex Lists

This section assumes that you successfully installed the proper printer
when you installed GeoWorks Pro. If you have printing problems, refer to
"The Printer Option Button" section of Chapter 11.

To print from GeoDex, use the following steps:

1. Choose **P**rint from the **F**ile menu. The dialog box shown in figure
    II.9 appears.

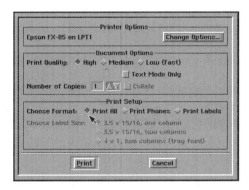

Fig. II.9

The GeoDex print
dialog box.

2. For this exercise, in the Print Setup area, choose Print All to
    produce a complete list of the names and addresses you entered.

3. Verify that your printer is on-line and properly loaded with paper.

4. Click the **P**rint button to start printing.

    The dialog box closes and you can continue.

Dialing with GeoDex

If you do not have a modem, skip this section and continue with Chapter 5, "Using GeoDex."

This short exercise assumes that you have a modem properly installed and configured. The Preferences application in GeoWorks Pro contains a modem control panel that must be set properly before dialing with GeoDex. This feature is covered in "The Modem Option Button" section of Chapter 11.

When entries are correctly made and settings are established, use the following steps for automatic dialing:

1. Turn on the modem and hang up the phone, if it is not in its cradle.

2. Choose a GeoDex address card, make sure that the card displays the number you want to call, and click the telephone icon button.

    or

    Click the Quick Dial button; then click a name on the list that appears.

3. You can hear the dialing proceed through the modem speaker. When you hear a connection or your party answers, click the Talk button in the dialog box shown in figure II.10 to disconnect the modem and switch to the phone.

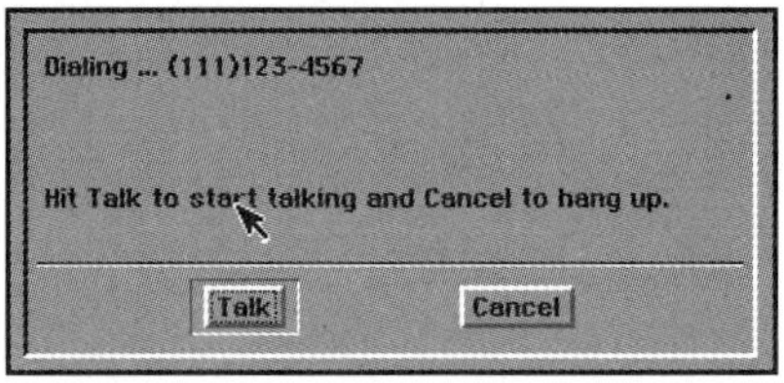

Fig. II.10

The dialing dialog box.

```
Dialing ... (111)123-4567


Hit Talk to start talking and Cancel to hang up.
                            ▸

        [ Talk ]              [ Cancel ]
```

NOTE   Don't forget to click the Talk button as soon as your party answers. A modem generates a high-pitched "squeal" when trying to connect. Your party may think you have a line problem and hang up if you forget to switch from modem to voice.

Using GeoDex

G eoDex is the computerized equivalent of the phone directories most of us compile. But far from being the haphazard pile of notes and scribbles most of us accumulate, GeoDex offers simple, accurate and powerful management of the type of information that most of us use frequently. Once you have a taste of accurately alphabetized, neatly printed name and address lists, you may just want to toss your dog-eared paper version.

To get technical for just a moment, GeoDex is a simple *flat-file* database. Its sorting abilities make GeoDex a distant relative of products like dBase and Paradox. In the case of address management, the simplicity of GeoDex is still more than enough to do a fine job with the tasks needed to keep an address book.

GeoDex is a more powerful version of the Address Book appliance you first explored in Chapter 2, "Learning GeoWorks Appliances." Not only can you store names and addresses, but you also can search for the information you entered. You can display the address cards as a list and print the list. If you have a modem, GeoDex can dial the phone number for you. Both GeoDex and the Address Book appliance share the same default data file; therefore, GeoDex can use and modify any work you do in Address Book. You also can copy information from the address book to GeoWrite, Notepad, or other applications that accept text.

Opening and Closing GeoDex

Launch GeoDex from the GeoManager WORLD directory window. Double-click the icon that resembles an address card (see fig. 5.1).

You also can start GeoDex from any active window that has the Express menu. Click the Express menu and choose **S**tartup. When the cascade menu containing all the GeoWorks Pro applications appears, click GeoDex (see fig. 5.2).

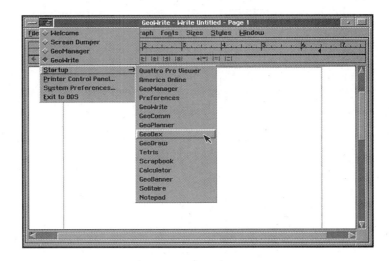

To close GeoDex, double-click the Control button, press the F3 function key, or choose **Close** from the **File** menu.

Understanding the GeoDex Window

If you worked with the Address Book appliance in Chapter 2, you may recognize many of the features of the GeoDex window. One major difference between the Address Book appliance and GeoDex is the Menu bar containing the File, Edit, View, and Option menus.

The File menu controls opening, closing, and saving GeoDex. The Edit menu contains the standard tools for cutting, pasting, and copying text. The View menu switches between the default Card View (refer to fig. 5.3) and the Browse and Both Views, explained in the next section. The Option menu modifies phone dialing for features such as dialing prefixes.

The Address Card and its icons form the focal area of GeoDex. You enter information in fields on the card, and you use the icons and their associated buttons to control the presentation of the Address Card (see fig. 5.3).

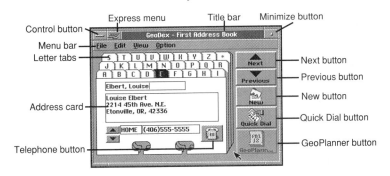

Fig. 5.3

The GeoDex window.

Table 5.1 outlines the GeoDex window features.

Table 5.1 GeoDex Window Features

Feature	Function
Title bar	Contains the name of the application and any document currently open; turns dark when the window is active

continues

Table 5.1 continued

Feature	Function
Express menu	Enables you to switch rapidly to another active application, launch another application, move to the Welcome screen, or exit directly to DOS
Control button	Opens a special menu containing commands that control the GeoDex window
Menu bar	Displays the four menu names
Letter tabs	Moves to the first card in each alphabetic section
Next button	Turns to the next card in GeoDex
Previous button	Turns to the preceding GeoDex card
New button	Presents a blank card
Quick Dial button	Opens a list of frequently called numbers
GeoPlanner button	Connects with GeoPlanner to search for a name listed in GeoDex
Telephone button	Dials the number showing in the phone number text field
Minimize button	Reduces the window to an icon at the bottom of the screen. *Note:* The window does not have a Maximize/Restore button because screen-filling size is not necessary.

The major area of the window contains the address card (see fig. 5.4).

Fig. 5.4

The address card.

The card face contains text fields and buttons. The first text field is the index field, containing the entry by which GeoDex indexes the card.

The first word you enter in this field becomes the index by which GeoDex sorts the card. If you have two or more cards with the same first word, the second word in the index field becomes a tie-breaker. You can enter numbers, such as area or ZIP codes, as well as words in the index field.

The second address card text field contains the complete name and address of an entry. If the entry is longer than five lines, the window scrolls to show the entire entry.

The third text field contains phone numbers. You can store seven different phone numbers for each entry. You can rotate through the phone numbers by using the arrows at the left side of the phone number text field. Pre-labeled entries are available for Home, Office, Car, and Fax numbers. Blank boxes enable you to enter labels of your choice.

Clicking the *alphabetic tabs* at the top of the card enables you to jump between sections. *Note:* Some buttons in GeoDex will appear grayed-out until you enter addresses and phone numbers, save the First Address Book file, and reopen it.

The Browse View

Choosing the Browse View command from the View menu opens a window showing the Browse list of GeoDex entries (see fig. 5.5). You can scroll through the phone numbers by clicking the scroll buttons. Clicking a name on the list displays the entry's phone number in the phone number text field below.

The Browse View also has a Quick Dial button that appears in all the window views. The "Dialing a Phone with GeoDex" section of this chapter describes the Quick Dial button.

The Both View

Choosing the Both View command from the View menu opens the window shown in figure 5.6. The right side of the window contains an alphabetized Browse list of the entries on your GeoWrite cards. The scroll bar at the right end enables you to move through a Browse list that is longer than the window.

The Both View window also contains search buttons. You can find information on using these buttons to search for text in the section, "Locating Entries."

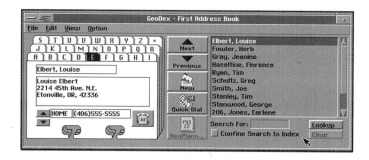

Fig. 5.6

The Both View
window.

Using GeoDex

With a knowledge of the parts of GeoDex, you can enter addresses and phone numbers. You also can use the GeoDex features to locate and retrieve numbers and automatically dial your phone.

GeoDex also can link with GeoPlanner to locate calendar and schedule entries for individuals in your address list. You can copy address information to other applications and print lists of the entries in your GeoDex.

Entering Information

An effective way to make entries into GeoDex is to gather a quantity of numbers together to enter in one session. Although you don't have to work this way, when you eliminate the need to open and close GeoDex frequently, you build your address file more efficiently. When you start GeoDex, the program displays the first card, alphabetically, in your list.

To enter names in your GeoDex file, make sure that you are in the GeoDex application (see "Opening and Closing GeoDex," if necessary); then do the following:

1. At the flashing text cursor in the first text field, type the last name and first name, separated by a comma.

2. Press Enter to copy the name to the address area. GeoDex copies the name into the second text field in first name, last name sequence (see fig. 5.7).

   If you do not want to copy the name automatically, press Tab instead of Enter to move the text cursor to the second text field.

NOTE You can use entries other than names in the first text field so that you can sort your list by something other than last name (ZIP codes, for example). (In this case, you do not want to copy the indexing entry to the address box.)

Fig. 5.7

The index name in first last order in the second field.

3. Type the rest of the address, pressing Enter to start a new line.

   Use the Delete or Backspace key to correct a mistake.

4. Tab to or click the arrows next to the phone number; then click the up or down arrow button to scroll through the numbers. Choose the appropriate label (Home, Office, Car, or Fax) for the first number.

   You can use the arrows again to enter additional telephone numbers for the same name.

5. To begin a new card, click the New button.

6. To record changes after you finish entering numbers, select the File menu and choose **S**ave.

T I P According to GWRepJohnK, to add comments to a GeoDex card, put the comments after the address. Start on the fifth line; the window scrolls to accept additional lines. When you print labels in GeoDex, GeoWorks prints the first four lines only; therefore, your comments do not print on your labels.

Locating Entries

You can search manually for entries in any view. Using the letter tabs, Next and Previous buttons, and scroll bars, you can flip through any address book. The Both View window (refer to fig. 5.6) also includes the search feature to help you locate entries.

From the Both view window, you can search for anything from a single letter to a string of words. GeoDex looks at every entry on every card and finds your search item, even if the search item is embedded in another word. If you searched for *cat*, for example, the program stops at *cat*ering, *cat*egory, s*cat*ter, and any other word that contains cat.

To search for information anywhere on the cards from the Both View window, follow these steps:

1. Click in the Search For text field to activate it; then type any portion of the information you want to search for.

NOTE The GeoDex search is case sensitive; use the same capitalization as the word you are looking for. If you enter *Large* in the Search For text field, for example, GeoDex searches for *Large* only, not *large*.

2. Click the check box labeled Confine Search to Index to search for an entry in the index field only (the top field on the card). GeoDex searches only index field items.

   Do not click the Confine Search to Index box if you want to search all entries on each card.

3. Click the Lookup button to begin the search. GeoDex finds the first occurrence of your search item. Notice that the label on the Lookup button changes to Find Next.

   If GeoDex cannot find a match with your item, a dialog box appears to indicate no match. If you are certain the item is in the list, check for different capitalization.

4. Click the Find Next button to locate other matches.

5. Click the Clear button to remove the search item entry from the Search For text field when you are through searching or want to begin another search.

   Clicking the Clear button also clears the Confine Search to Index option.

Linking Searches to GeoPlanner

You can use the GeoDex search to locate a name or piece of text in the GeoPlanner calendar. Before searching, you must start GeoPlanner. See chapter 6, "Using GeoPlanner," for more information on GeoPlanner.

To link a GeoDex search to the GeoPlanner calendar, start GeoPlanner from the Express menu and arrange the GeoDex and GeoPlanner windows vertically, using techniques explained in Chapter 4, "Mastering GeoManager." Then follow these steps:

1. In GeoDex, select the name or text to search for. You can drag the mouse to select text, or you can type the text into the Search For text field in the Browse or Both views.

2. Click the GeoPlanner button.

   GeoPlanner displays the first event containing your search item highlighted in the Event window (see fig. 5.8).

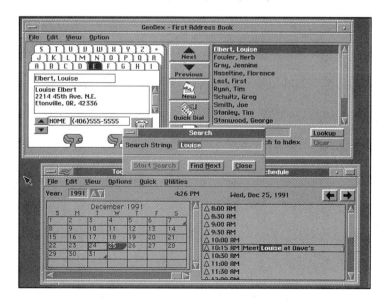

Fig. 5.8

A GeoPlanner entry matching the search specification.

3. To continue searching, click the Find Next button in the small search window that opens.

4. Click Close in the search window after you finish searching.

5. Close GeoPlanner by double-clicking the Control button in the upper left corner of the application window.

6. Return to GeoDex by clicking the GeoDex window. You can also click GeoDex from the Express menu if GeoDex is hidden behind another window.

Retrieving Information

You may want to copy a name and address from GeoDex to a letter you are working on in GeoWrite, or you may want to move information from one GeoDex card to another. The commands on the Edit menu make moving or copying information from one location to another within GeoDex easy, and because of Pro's integrated character, you easily can move or copy information from GeoDex to another application.

To move text within GeoDex or from GeoDex to another application, follow these steps:

1. If necessary, start the destination application using the Express menu.

2. Switch back to GeoDex by choosing GeoDex from the Express menu.

3. Select the text you want to move.

4. Select the Edit menu and choose Cut to remove the information from GeoDex, or choose Copy to duplicate the information.

5. Switch to the other application's window and click the mouse button to place the text cursor where you want the transferred text to appear.

6. Select the Edit menu of the receiving application and choose Paste to place the material from GeoDex at the text cursor's location (see fig. 5.9).

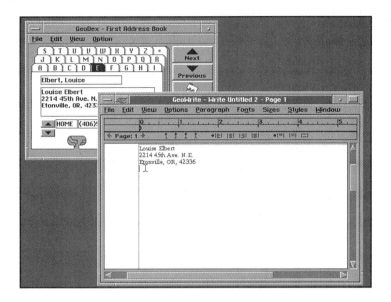

NOTE When you can make both the source and destination of a copy visible at the same time, as they are in figure 5.9, you can make effective use of the Quick Copy feature. Select the material you want to copy, point to it, and hold down the *right* mouse button. Without releasing the right button, drag the pointer to the destination. Release the pointer to copy the selected material at the destination.

Printing GeoDex Lists

Printing is another useful way to retrieve information from GeoDex. You can print a complete list of names, addresses, and phone numbers from the cards; you can print names and phone numbers only; and you can print mailing labels in two popular dot matrix and one laser printer size.

To print from GeoDex, choose the **P**rint command from the GeoDex **F**ile menu. In the Printer Options dialog box that appears (see fig. 5.10), change printer options, print quality, and number of copies, if necessary. In the Print Setup section of the dialog box, choose one of the following radio buttons:

■ *Print All.* To produce a complete list of names and addresses.

■ *Print Phones.* To create a two column list of names and phone numbers.

■ *Print Labels.* To activate buttons for printing different label sizes.

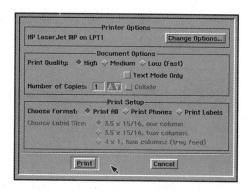

Fig. 5.10

The Printer Options dialog box.

After you set the appropriate options, verify that your printer is on-line and that the paper is aligned properly; then choose Print to begin printing.

Dialing a Phone with GeoDex

A *modem* is a device for converting computer signals to signals that can be transmitted over the telephone system. If you have a modem connected to your computer, you can use GeoDex to dial numbers. Before using automatic dialing, you must set up your modem, using the modem settings in the Preferences application. See Chapter 11, "Customizing with the Preferences Desk Tool," for information on modem settings.

If you do not have a modem, you may want to skip these instructions and continue with the section, "Maintaining GeoDex," that follows.

You must *plan* for automatic dialing when you *enter* phone numbers because you must include required area codes or prefixes in the number you enter. For long-distance calls, you typically need to enter a 1, the area code, and the number. Although not required by the program, you can use dashes and parentheses within the numbers to make the number easier to read.

If a dialing sequence requires a pause (reaching an outside line, for example), insert a comma where a one-second pause belongs.

The GeoDex Option menu contains a single command, Dialing, which can be helpful if you always (or even frequently) use the same prefix or area code for phone calls. You may need to dial the prefix "9" to access an outside line from your office, or you frequently may use a certain area code to reach your customers.

You can insert a code, prefix, or area code you always dial for every number. GeoDex uses the Prefix or Area Code entry for all automatic dialing (see fig. 5.11). Open the **O**ption menu and choose **D**ialing. In the dialog box that appears, enter the appropriate prefix or area code. Click the check box to the left of the entries to activate them. When you close the dialog box, the program remembers your settings and uses them for every call. To deactivate the settings, open the Dialing dialog box again and uncheck the appropriate box.

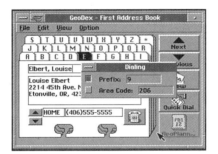

Fig. 5.11

The Dialing dialog box.

After you make the entries and establish the settings, you can dial a phone number by doing the following:

1. Turn on the modem and hang up the phone (if the receiver is not already in its cradle).

2. Click the telephone icon button in any window where it is visible.

   GeoDex dials the currently selected phone number; you can hear the dialing through the modem speaker.

3. When you hear a connection or your party answers, click the Talk button in the dialog box, shown in figure 5.12, to disconnect the modem and switch to the phone.

NOTE Don't forget to click the Talk button as soon as your party answers. A modem generates a high-pitched squeal when trying to connect. If you forget to switch from modem to voice, your party may think a line problem exists and hang up.

Fig. 5.12

The Talk button dialog box.

Using the Quick Dial Feature

Quick Dialing uses a GeoDex list. The Quick Dial button, a hand pushing a button, appears in all three views of GeoDex. When you click the Quick Dial button, GeoDex produces the display shown in figure 5.13.

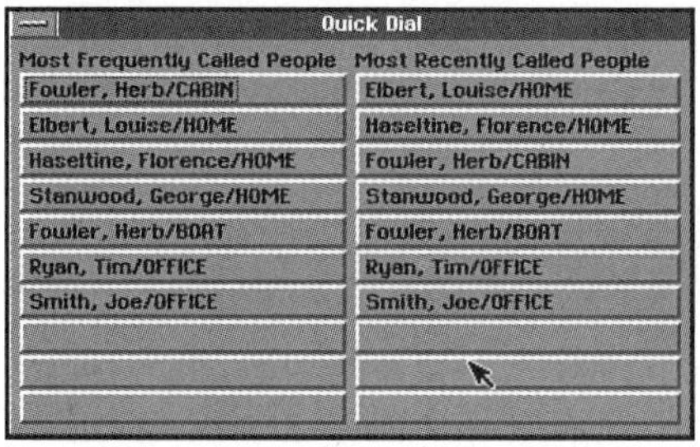

Fig. 5.13

The Quick Dial listing.

GeoDex creates and automatically maintains the two-column list. A number moves on one or the other list based on how often or how recently that number has been called. Besides furnishing an interesting profile of your phone use, the list has your most important numbers at the top.

For the fastest automatic dialing—assuming your modem is active and set up properly—click the Quick Dial button to see the Quick Dial display. When you click the name you want, dialing begins. If you entered several numbers for one person, the number that dials is the number displayed in the number window on the address card.

Maintaining GeoDex

When you build a GeoDex file, you have a powerful and useful resource available. Inevitably, you will need to change entries as your personal situation changes. GeoDex provides commands, described in the sections that follow, which make maintenance of the listing easy.

Adding Cards

Card view and Both view display the New button, which enables you to add a card to GeoDex. To add a new card, simply click the New button in either window and enter information on the empty card. After you complete the new card, click the Next, Previous, or New button as appropriate. GeoDex stores the card in the proper location.

Indexing by Number

Although you may find the standard "last name, first name" entry suitable for most purposes, don't overlook the possibility of organizing your index by some other key, such as ZIP code or area code.

Suppose that you are a salesperson with a vast territory You can group your customers by area code to make locating customers in a particular state or region easy. Figure 5.14 shows the Browse View with a group of names preceded by area codes.

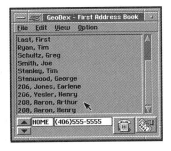

To enter information other than names into the index field, make the first entry in the index field a numeric code that is useful to you. Put a comma between each part of the field so that each segment sorts properly.

Notice the sort of the ZIP code entries in the example. Numeric entries appear at the end of the GeoDex list; in the card view you can find them under the card tab marked with an asterisk. Within the example group, the entries sort first by area code, then by last name, and then—as with the Aarons—by first name.

If you enter something other than a last name in the index field, press Tab (instead of Enter) after you type the index entry to avoid entering the index information at the top of the address panel. See the "Entering Information" section of this chapter for more information.

You can use other index entries in conjunction with saving address books with different file names to create a complex, yet highly organized, address book. You can have one GeoDex file indexed in conventional format and another indexed by ZIP code, for example. See the section, "Saving Multiple GeoDex Files," in this chapter for instructions on how to save multiple address books.

Editing Cards

An advantage of integrated programs like GeoWorks Pro is that techniques learned in one portion of the program can be used in other parts. The entries on a GeoDex card can be changed using the text editing techniques available throughout GeoWorks Pro.

The GeoDex Edit menu contains a group of commands you use to change text. Table 5.2 lists the commands and their purposes.

Table 5.2 The Edit Menu

Editing Command	Purpose
Undo	Removes all changes, if used before leaving the card
Cut	Removes highlighted text from the card and saves to Clipboard
Copy	Copies highlighted text, leaves original, and saves a copy to Clipboard
Paste	Places text from Clipboard at the text cursor
Clear(**x**)	Removes all information from the current *new* card, if used before leaving the card
Delete	Removes the entire card from GeoDex

All the commands, except Clear and Delete, have keyboard shortcuts to the right of them (see fig. 5.15). As you become familiar with the program, keyboard shortcuts become a natural way to speed your work. The keyboard equivalents for Clear and Delete do not appear on the Edit menu; they are Alt-X (Clear) and Alt-B (Delete).

Fig. 5.15

The GeoDex Edit
menu.

Deleting and Saving Cards

To make your GeoDex effective, you need to go through a periodic
housekeeping cycle, organizing and saving new material and discarding
old listings.

Deleting a card is simple. Locate the card to remove and choose **D**elete
from the **E**dit menu. The program removes the entire card from GeoDex.
If you delete a card by mistake, remember that you can use the Undo
command from the Edit menu to restore your deletion. You must use the
Undo command immediately to retrieve a deleted card, however. If you
continue to another card or leave GeoDex, Undo does not remember
your previous action.

As you add and modify entries, GeoDex automatically saves your
changes every few minutes. You control the interval by a setting you
enable in the Preferences menu, explained in Chapter 11, "Customizing
with the Preferences Desk Tool." If you have enabled this feature, you
will notice the mouse pointer or I-beam briefly turn to an hourglass as
the automatic save occurs.

This process saves only the changes you made since the last automatic
save and adds the changes to a temporary file. When you want to leave
GeoDex or make your changes permanent, use one of the two save commands on the File menu (see fig. 5.16).

If you exit to DOS without using Save or Save As, the program retains
your work up to the last automatic save. When you restart GeoDex, a
message reminding you to save your work appears.

If you ever want to discard the changes accumulated in the temporary
file maintained by GeoDex, select the **F**ile menu and choose the **R**evert
command. GeoDex displays the dialog box shown in figure 5.17. If you
choose **Y**es, GeoDex discards the temporary file and returns you to the
file as it was when you last used the Save command to make a permanent record.

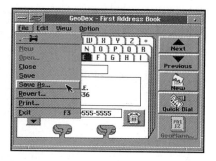

Fig. 5.16

The GeoDex File
menu.

Fig. 5.17

The Revert dialog box.

The Save command makes a permanent record of your document, using its current name and folder. The program incorporates any changes in the temporary file kept by the automatic save feature into the permanent file.

The Save As command gives you an opportunity to change the name of the file and its storage location. Choosing Save **As** opens the dialog box shown in figure 5.18. You can click the Up Directory button or directory names to move to different folders. You also can enter a new name for the file.

Fig. 5.18

The Save As dialog
box.

Saving Multiple GeoDex Files

One of the most useful reasons to use the Save As command is to create multiple GeoDex files. You may want one GeoDex file for personal numbers, another for business, and yet another entirely organized by ZIP code. The default GeoDex file is First Address Book. By typing Business Address Book or some other name in the Save As text field, you create a new GeoDex file when you click the Save button.

To create a new GeoDex file from the default GeoDex file, select the GeoDex **F**ile menu and choose Save **A**s. In the Save As dialog box, type the name for your new GeoDex file and click **S**ave to store the file. GeoDex creates and loads your new file to replace the default file. GeoDex displays the new file name in the title bar.

The contents of the two files are identical because you just saved the old file with a new name. You can now reorganize and edit your records in the new file. This process can be repeated as often as needed to produce different GeoDex files.

Before saving an active file to a new name, use the Save As command to save the current file first. If you don't save the current file, the program saves changes made during the current session to the new file, but not the old one.

You can load the original, or any other, GeoDex file by first choosing **C**lose from the GeoDex **F**ile menu to shut down the current file. Then return to the **F**ile menu and choose **O**pen. The dialog box shown in figure 5.19 appears, showing the names of the default file and the names of any new GeoDex files. Double-click the name of the file you want to load.

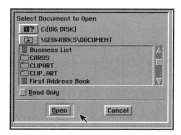

Fig. 5.19

File Open dialog box, listing First Address Book.

Because GeoDex can't access fonts, you should copy the name and address information into GeoWrite to print labels using **T I P** different fonts. Use 18-point fonts with 4-line mailing labels, and they will feed through like a charm (18 x 4 = 72 points = 1 inch). If you only need three lines, throw in a blank line to keep the spacing correct for 15/16 inch labels (which have 1/16 inch space between them). If you are adventurous, use different combinations of fonts to total 72 points. You could have, for example, a 24-point name, two 18-point address lines, and a 12-point blank line. GWRepRandy

Chapter Summary

This chapter describes the features of and procedures for working with GeoDex, the address manager. The chapter explains methods of entering, editing, and retrieving information and describes using GeoDex and a modem for automatic phone dialing. The chapter also discusses techniques for maintaining and creating GeoDex files.

With GeoDex, you can create simple and intricate automatic address books to meet your needs. Using different index choices, you can sort the same address information in different ways, making GeoDex useful for list management tasks beyond simple name and address maintenance.

GeoPlanner

Quick-start chapters emphasize hands-on practice—in this case offering the basic techniques for using GeoPlanner. After about half an hour, you will be comfortable enough to strike out on your own to refine and customize GeoPlanner for your scheduling needs. If you want more background on any topic in this tutorial, consult the companion reference Chapter 6, "Using GeoPlanner."

Before you begin this quickstart, be sure that you know the basic techniques for manipulating a GeoWorks Pro window and how to use menus and icons. If you need to review these topics, refer to Quick Start I, "GeoManager," and Chapter 4, "Mastering GeoManager."

Starting GeoPlanner

Use the following steps to start GeoPlanner:

1. Open the GeoManager WORLD window either by clicking the Advanced Workspace button in the Welcome window or by choosing GeoManager from the Express menu (the button with the stylized E in the upper left corner) of an active window.

2. If GeoManager is not displaying the WORLD view (see fig. III.1), click the globe icon at the bottom center of the window.

Fig. III.1

The GeoPlanner icon
in the WORLD
directory.

3. Double-click the GeoPlanner icon, which looks like a calendar, to
   launch GeoPlanner.

   The GeoPlanner window appears in its default Both view, showing a
   calendar on the left and an events list on the right (see fig. III.2).

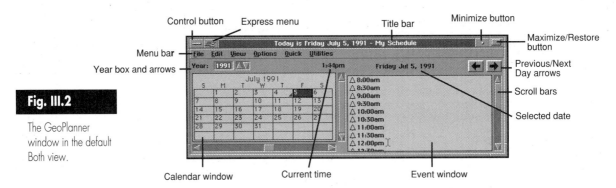

Fig. III.2

The GeoPlanner
window in the default
Both view.

Learning the GeoPlanner Window

To help you follow the directions in this quick start more easily, take a
moment to go through the following steps in getting comfortable with
the GeoPlanner window:

1. Click the Maximize button to enlarge the GeoPlanner window.

2. Use the up and down arrows next to the Year text field to change
   the year and return to the current year; use the Previous and Next

Day arrows to change the selected day and return to the current day; use the horizontal scroll bar to change the month and return to the current month.

3. Check the date in the Title bar and the current time (above the vertical scroll bar). If the current date and time are not accurate, see Chapter 6 for additional information.

4. Select the View menu and choose Events Only to change the default Both view to the display of the Event window only.

5. Select the View menu and choose Calendar Only to change the view to only the Calendar window with the default Single Month display.

6. Return to the View menu and choose Full Year to display calendars of all 12 months of the selected year; then return to the Both view with the Single Month calendar.

Entering an Event

Now that you know how to move through the calendar, you easily can enter events. The steps that follow guide you through a practice session in which you enter an event for the tenth of the current month.

1. If you have not returned to the Both view of the GeoPlanner windows, open the View menu and choose the Both command.

2. If necessary, use the scroll bar at the bottom of the Calendar window to display the current month.

3. In the Calendar window, click the 10th. The date box for the 10th is highlighted in the calendar and the date reflecting the 10th of the current month appears just above the Event window on-screen, similar to figure III.3.

   A heavy dark line outlines the current day (matches today's date in the Title bar). Unless the current date happens to be the 10th, you should see one date with a heavy outline and one date with a fill-in highlight (see fig. III.3).

4. From the Edit menu, choose New Event. A blank event entry box appears on the list in the Entry window; the time of the event is highlighted. Alternatively, you can click an existing blank event time to create an entry box; double-click to highlight the time if you want to change it.

5. Press the Tab key to move the text cursor to the description box.

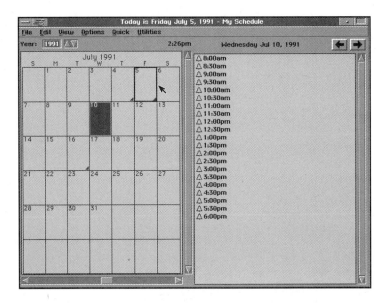

Fig. III.3

The current date outlined; the selected date highlighted.

6. Type **Staff meeting. Moved to 12th floor conference room.** When your description is longer than one line of text, the lines wrap automatically to give you more room as in figure III.4.

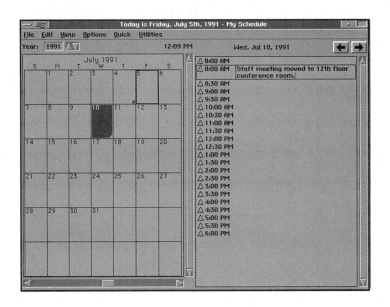

Fig. III.4

A typical event entry.

7. Leave the event box by clicking another date on the calendar. GeoPlanner makes a temporary record of your entry.

8. Open the **File** menu and choose the **S**ave command to make the record permanent.

   You do not need to save every time you enter an event. Save when you want to make several event entries permanent. If you choose the **Exit** command from the **File** menu, a dialog box appears reminding you to save your work.

9. Repeating steps 3 through 7, enter at least one event each on the 8th and the 9th of the month for use later in this quick start. Enter more events if you want additional practice.

NOTE   If you make an error in entering an event, you can use the standard technique with the mouse to select the text you want to change, and then retype the text. You can also use the **Undo** command on the **Edit** menu to restore the event to its original form—before you change another event or move to another day on the calendar.

Viewing Events for Several Days at Once

You can view a list of events for one day by selecting that date on the calendar. To view events for a range of dates, in the Calendar window, drag the mouse across the dates of the 8th, 9th, and 10th. All three dates are highlighted (see fig. III.5). The list of events for the selected days appears in the Event window.

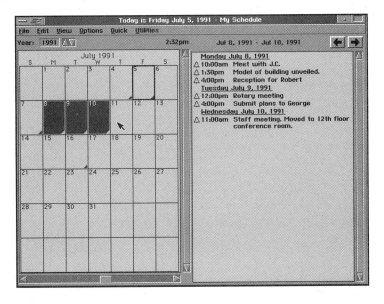

Fig. III.5

Events for the highlighted days displayed in the Event window.

Entering Repeating Events

Among the most important events you keep track of are those events that recur regularly. The monthly club meeting or a relative's birthday are difficult—but important—to remember. GeoPlanner has an excellent facility for entering recurring events. With the span of the calendar, you can log events well into the next century.

In this exercise, you enter an imaginary family picnic on every Fourth of July to come, using the following steps:

1. Open the **U**tilities menu in GeoPlanner and click **R**epeating Events.

2. In the Repeating Events dialog box click the **N**ew button. The large dialog box shown in figure III.6 appears.

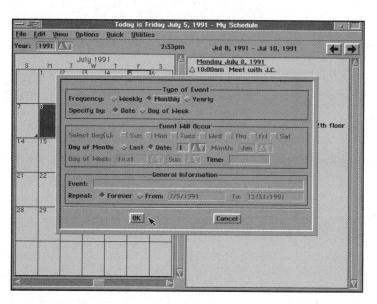

Fig. III.6

The recurring events
dialog box.

3. In the top rectangle of the dialog box click the Yearly button because this holiday occurs annually.

4. Click the Date button because the holiday falls on the same date every year.

5. In the Event Will Occur rectangle, type an entry, or use the up and down arrows to change the Date field to **4**.

6. Set the month to July, using the up or down arrows adjacent to the Month field.

7. Click in the Time field and enter **4:00 pm**.

8. In the Event field, type the description **Annual Fourth Picnic**. Capitalize the first letter of each word so that using the Search command is easier.

9. Because the event continues annually, click the Forever button in the Repeat field.

10. Click OK to record the event, which then appears in your calendar every July fourth.

11. Open the File menu and choose **S**ave to record your changes.

12. Choose **C**lose to exit the Repeating Events dialog box.

 You can edit an individual occurrence of a repeating event in the Event window, using the same editing techniques you use to edit any single event.

Setting Alarms for Events

If GeoPlanner is running—even as an icon—at the designated time, it displays a dialog box containing an entry for any item in the day's events list for which you have set an alarm. To set an alarm, follow these steps:

1. Select today's date on the calendar. Be sure that you are in the current year; if you are not, use the up or down arrows above the calendar to return to this year.

2. From the **E**dit menu choose New Event to insert a blank event in the Event window.

3. Select the time section of the blank event and type in a time about five minutes from now.

4. Tab to the text section of the event and type **Hi There!**

5. Click the small bell shape to the left of the event to turn on an alarm for that event. Take a short break or experiment with GeoPlanner for about five minutes.

   When the time expires, a dialog box, shown in figure III.7 appears, showing the event description and including buttons to turn off the alarm or make it "snooze" for five minutes and then reappear.

NOTE To see or hear GeoPlanner alarms when you are working in other applications, GeoPlanner must be running. You can minimize GeoPlanner to an icon or hide GeoPlanner behind another window. When the alarm "goes off" the alarm dialog box appears in the active window. You also hear the alarm beep on your computer's speaker.

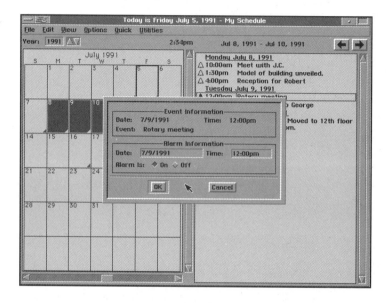

Fig. III.7

The Alarm dialog box.

6. Click the Off button in the dialog box to turn off the alarm.

Searching GeoPlanner

As you accumulate a large number of events, you have an increasingly difficult time locating them quickly. GeoPlanner anticipates this problem by providing the capability to search for information anywhere within the events list.

In this exercise, you search for your Fourth of July entry following these steps:

1. Open the **Utilities** menu and choose the **S**earch command. The Search dialog box opens as in figure III.8.

2. Type **Fourth** in the Search String text field. Because the GeoPlanner search is *case sensitive*, it checks for capitalization; the search finds Fourth but not fourth.

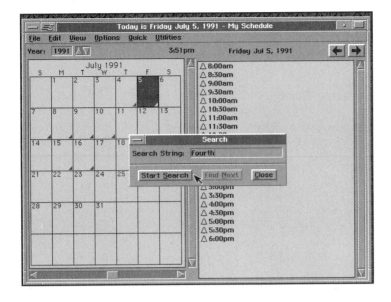

Fig. III.8

The Search dialog
box.

3. Choose the Start **S**earch button to begin.

4. GeoPlanner searches forward from the current date to find the first instance where the word Fourth appears, probably the Fourth of July picnic you have been working on.

5. To find additional instances of the search string, choose the Find **N**ext button. When you finish searching, choose **C**lose.

NOTE With repeating events that you entered *Forever*, you don't have to worry about spending an eternity searching. GeoPlanner identifies the latest nonrepeating event in the file and searches to the end of the year after that event appears. Unless you have entered a nonrepeating event beyond this year, the search ends two years from now.

Printing from GeoPlanner

With GeoPlanner, you can produce handsome calendars and event lists in several formats. To print a monthly calendar showing events in the calendar use the following steps:

1. If the current month does not appear in the Calendar window, move to the month, in this year, by using the arrows above and the scroll bar below the Calendar window.

2. Click any day to be sure that the month is selected.

3. From the **F**ile menu choose **P**rint. The dialog box shown in figure III.9 appears.

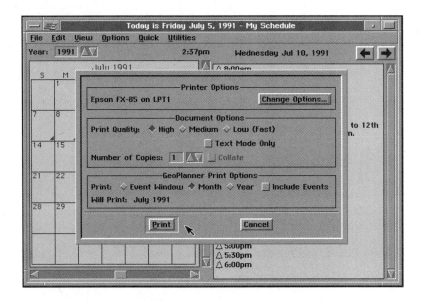

4. If you need to change printers or paper sizes, click the Change Options button and make the necessary changes.

5. Select low print quality for this exercise and select one copy. The higher the print quality, the slower your image prints. ***Note:*** If you cannot enable the Low button, click Text Mode Only and try again.

6. To select a full-page calendar for this month, click the Month button.

7. To print events on the current month calendar, click Include Events. Only seven short lines are available for printing; any excess text does not print.

8. The entry displayed after Will Print near the bottom of the dialog box indicates the month currently selected. Use this entry to double-check that you are printing the month you want to print.

9. Ensure that your printer is on and on-line and then choose the **P**rint button.

To print a list of events without the calendar for the same month follow these steps:

1. If necessary, choose File, **P**rint and move to the current month using the scroll bar at the bottom of the calendar window.

2. To compile events for the entire month, open the **Q**uick menu and choose This **M**onth. The entire month is selected and a list of the month's events appears in the Event window.

3. From the File menu choose **P**rint. The dialog box shown in figure III.9 appears.

4. If you need to change printers or paper sizes, click Change Options and make the necessary changes; select print quality and number of copies.

5. In the GeoPlanner Print Options rectangle, click Event Window; check the Will Print line to ensure that you print the events for the dates you want to print.

6. Choose the **P**rint button to begin printing a list of the month's events.

7. When printing is complete, click any date to remove the whole-month highlight.

Using GeoPlanner

GeoPlanner is an electronic calendar and appointment book with a memory to rival that of the fabled elephant. You can remember a recurring date like your anniversary or Uncle Harry's birthday from now into the next century or check what day of the week July 4th fell on in 1910. You can list an almost unlimited number of events and, optionally, link them to alarms that remind you of the events. Easy to use and automate, GeoPlanner can be an unobtrusive but powerful companion in your busy life.

Exploring GeoPlanner

This section introduces you to the principal features of GeoPlanner. The versatile display window enables you to choose a variety of calendar and events list views. You can choose to display a single month to an entire year. You also can view Calendar and Event windows together or individually. This flexibility enables you to tailor a useful tool that suits your personal style.

Because of the integrated PC/GEOS environment, you can transfer skills you learned in other GeoWorks Pro applications to GeoPlanner. Window management and the use of menus is almost identical. You use the same techniques that you use in other GeoWorks applications to open, save, and close files—one of the great benefits of an integrated program like GeoWorks Pro. You accumulate skills as you learn the program, and the skills you learn in one application can be used in other applications.

Because of the integrated PC/GEOS environment, you can transfer skills you learned in other programs to GeoPlanner. An organized effort to build and maintain your own GeoPlanner returns a rich payback of convenience. If you don't tell your friends you use GeoPlanner, they may assume you have a phenomenal memory!

Opening and Closing GeoPlanner

To start GeoPlanner, double-click the calendar icon in the WORLD directory shown in figure 6.1. GeoPlanner also is among the applications in the Express menu, the stylized letter "E" in the upper left corner of an active application window. To open GeoPlanner from the Express menu, open the menu and choose the **S**tartup command. In the cascade menu that opens, click GeoPlanner.

To close GeoPlanner, select the **F**ile menu and choose the **E**xit command. **Note:** Remember that the F3 function key is a shortcut for closing this, and any other, active application window.

Fig. 6.1

The GeoPlanner icon in the WORLD directory.

Learning the GeoPlanner Window

Figure 6.2 shows the default Both view GeoPlanner window, with the calendar on the left and an events list on the right. Table 6.1 lists the major features of the window.

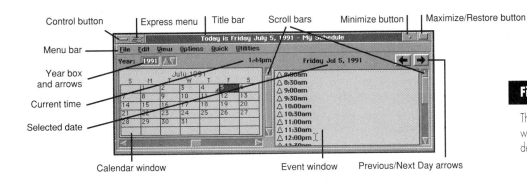

Fig. 6.2

The GeoPlanner window with the default Both view.

Table 6.1 GeoPlanner Window Features

Feature	Function
Title bar	Lists the date and GeoPlanner file in use
Express menu	Enables access to other applications when the window is active
Menu bar	Lists menu names
Year box and arrows	Selects year in calendar window
Current time	Displays the time during the work session
Selected date	Displays the date of the events list
Calendar window	Displays months of selected year
Scroll bars	Moves through calendar and events
Event window	Displays selected events for selected day
Previous/Next Day arrows	Increases or decreases selected date
Maximize/Restore button	Makes active window full-screen or normal
Minimize button	Shrinks window to icon

Using GeoPlanner Window Views

The default window for GeoPlanner presents the Both view with the Calendar and Event windows side-by-side (refer to fig. 6.2). The calendar shows the current month and day. The date highlighted on the calendar appears above the events list.

When you start GeoPlanner, the date highlighted and the time shown between the two windows represent the PC/GEOS reading of your computer's clock/calendar. If your date is not correct or the clock seems erratic, you may need to replace the clock battery. Consult your dealer or your equipment manuals for maintenance instructions.

NOTE On some older computers, you may have to enter the time manually each time you start a work session; after you set the date, the computer maintains it until you turn your computer off. Newer computers frequently have a built-in clock calendar with a long-life battery. These clocks maintain accurate time even when the computer is off. If necessary, you can reset them from the keyboard, using utility programs furnished by your computer manufacturer or the clock board maker. You also can reset the clock by opening the Preferences tool, clicking the Date and Time button, and entering the correct information. Chapter 11, "Customizing with the Preferences Desk Tool," explains this tool in more detail.

When you choose the **Events Only** command from the **View** menu, the Event window fills the entire screen (see fig. 6.3). This view makes viewing and scrolling through a large events list easier.

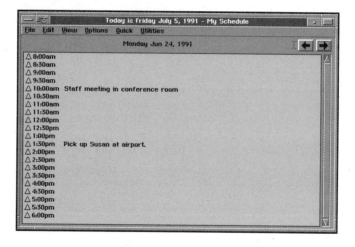

Fig. 6.3

The Events Only view of the GeoPlanner window.

The third view option shows a single month or an entire year of small calendars depending on your settings on the View menu. If you choose the **Calendar Only** command from the **View** menu, the view shows you a single month in a window about one-fourth the screen size. You can expand the window size to fill the entire screen (see fig. 6.4).

If you choose the command Full **Year** from the View menu, the window displays as much as it can fit of twelve small monthly calendars for the current year. By using the horizontal scroll bar, you can scroll the display to see a particular month or maximize the window to see the entire year on a single screen, as shown in figure 6.5.

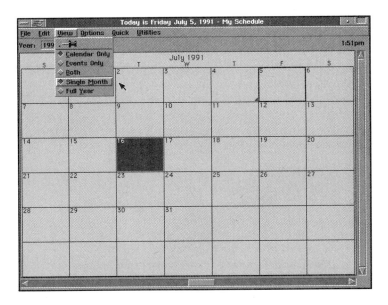

Fig. 6.4

The Calendar Only, Single Month view of the GeoPlanner window, maximized.

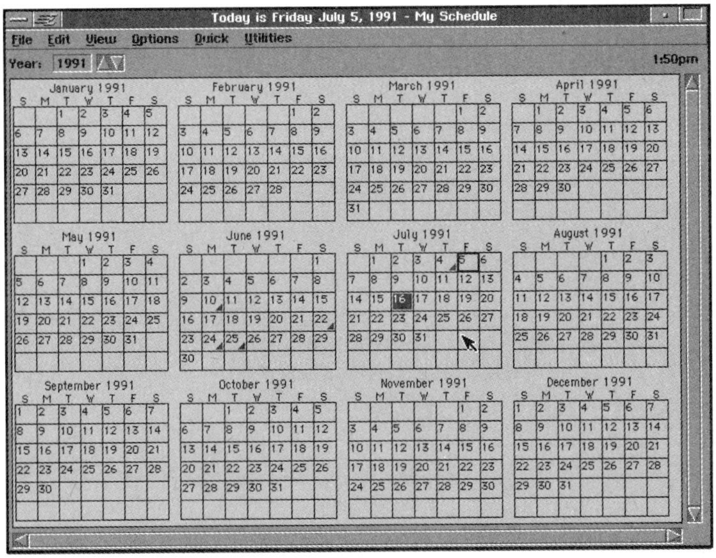

Fig. 6.5

The Calendar Only, Full Year view of the GeoPlanner window, maximized.

Managing Windows

This section provides a capsule version of the basic skills necessary to move, resize, scroll through, and close a GeoWorks Pro window. For more detailed instructions, see the section of Chapter 4 titled "The GeoManager Window."

Moving Windows

You can move a window by dragging its Title bar with the mouse. Place the mouse pointer on the Title bar and hold down the left mouse button. Then drag the mouse in the direction you want to move the window. An outline of the window moves as you drag. After you release the button, the redrawn window appears in its new location.

Resizing Windows

You can resize a window by dragging its border, which has six sections. When you place the mouse precisely on a border segment, the pointer shape changes to an arrow indicating the directions in which you can drag that segment. You can drag corner segments diagonally; you can drag vertical and horizontal side segments only left and right or up and down.

The Maximize/Restore and Minimize buttons also affect window sizes. When you activate the Maximize/Restore button, the window fills the entire screen, using the largest amount of screen area for your window. You cannot move or resize a maximized window by dragging its borders. When you click the Maximize/Restore button again GeoWorks restores the window to its previous window size, which you can move and size.

The Minimize button (the button with the small dot to the left of the Maximize/Restore button) collapses a window to a small icon at the lower left corner of the screen. When you minimize a window, it retains the contents; any program the window contains goes into suspended animation but does not close. When you double-click an icon representing a minimized window, the window resumes its previous size and shape with its contents unaltered. You then can resume whatever you were doing in the window before you minimized it.

Scrolling Through Windows

The scroll bar is another essential feature of window management. If a window is too small or a document too large for you to see everything at once, use the scroll bar to move the screen contents within the window. Depending on its size and contents, a window may show vertical or horizontal scroll bars or both. Some windows, with fixed contents, have no scroll bars.

A scroll bar has four parts: the bar itself, the slider box that moves in the bar, and the two scroll arrows at either end of the bar. You can drag the slider with the mouse to scroll rapidly to any part of the document. The length of the slider box, compared to the length of the scroll bar gives you an approximate idea how much of the window is visible. As you change window or document size, the slider length changes. If an entire document or image fits within the window, the slider box fills the entire length of the scroll bar.

Clicking the mouse in the scroll bar above or below the slider moves the window contents approximately the height of the window with each click. Clicking the arrows at either end of the scroll bar moves the window approximately one line of text with each click. Holding down the left mouse button while pointing to a scroll arrow causes the material in the window to move continuously through the window.

Closing Windows

The quickest way to close a window is to double-click the Control button in the upper left corner of the window. This action is equivalent to opening the menu and choosing the command Close. (The keyboard shortcut for window closing is Alt+F4.)

Introducing GeoPlanner Menus and Commands

GeoPlanner has six menus on the Menu bar that contain the commands that control its actions. Table 6.2 describes the menus and their general purposes.

Table 6.2 The GeoPlanner Menus

Menu Name	Purpose
File	Controls opening, closing, saving and printing files; also paper size and type
Edit	Enables editing of events and setting event alarms
View	Sets view of calendar, events, or both; sets calendar to month or year
Options	Selects desired setup for GeoPlanner
Quick	Rapidly sets time span shown in Calendar and Event window
Utilities	Controls repeating events, searches, and GeoDex link

Using GeoPlanner

Basically, GeoPlanner is easy to use. In this section of the chapter, you learn techniques for using the calendar and for entering and retrieving events. Beyond the basic skills, you also learn ways to get more powerful and customized performance from the program.

Using the Calendar

When you start GeoPlanner, if you have not changed the default view of Both, you see the window shown in figure 6.6. If your computer's clock and calendar are correct, you should see the current date in the window Title bar and above the events list. The time appears in the middle of the window to the left of the date. The current date appears highlighted on the calendar. The calendar can show dates from 1900 to 9999, a more than adequate range for most of us!

To change the year shown on the calendar, click the up or down arrows above the calendar until the year you want shows in the window; alternatively, double-click inside the year text field just above the calendar, type the year you want, and press Enter. This display changes to the specified year.

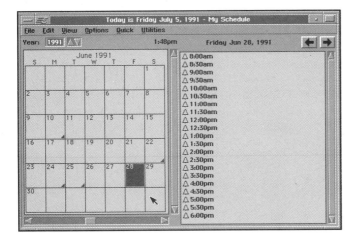

Fig. 6.6

The maximized
GeoPlanner window
with the default Both
view.

The bottom scroll bar in the Calendar window enables you to change the month that appears. To move a month at a time, click the mouse pointer to the right or left of the slider box or click the arrows at either end of the bottom scroll bar. To jump several months at once, drag the slider box left or right while holding down the left mouse button. You also can use the mouse to change dates within the displayed month.

GeoPlanner differentiates between the current date (the actual calendar date) and the selected date. The current date is always today's date, but the selected date can be any date in any year. The selected date is the date you choose for entering or retrieving event information.

The current date always appears in the Calendar window with a heavy line around it; the current date also appears in the GeoPlanner Title bar. The selected date appears just above the Event window and has a solid highlight in the Calendar window. Figure 6.7 shows a calendar in which the current and selected date are different. To select any date, simply click it with the mouse.

Viewing Events

When you enter an event, a small triangular mark appears in the calendar in the lower right of the appropriate date box. By surveying the Calendar window, you can quickly spot dates for which you have listed events. Click a date that has an event marker to see the list of events in the Event window.

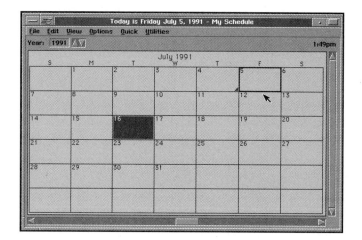

Fig. 6.7

A calendar with different current and selected dates.

If you are using the Events Only view, clicking the large arrows at the upper right moves you to the previous or next day in the calendar. The Event window shows the newly-selected date at the top and the events for that date in the window.

To use your mouse to see events for a range of dates, follow these steps:

1. Choose the **B**oth command from the **View** menu so that both the Calendar and Event windows are available.

2. In the Calendar window, drag the mouse across the dates for which you want to view events. The selected dates are highlighted, and the range of selected dates appears above the Event window (see fig. 6.8).

3. View a list of events for the selected days in the Event window. Click the arrows above the Event window to move the selection forward or back a number of days equal to the number of currently selected dates. With five days selected, for example, clicking the Previous Day arrow moves five days toward the beginning of the month.

The Quick menu (see fig. 6.9) automates the process of selecting and viewing events for a series of days. You can quickly select the day, week, weekend, or month by choosing the appropriate command. Events for the selected time period automatically appear in the Event window.

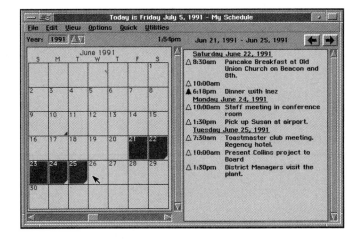

Fig. 6.8

The highlighted days appear in the list window.

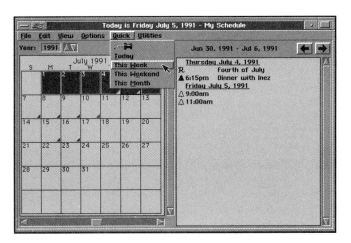

Fig. 6.9

The Quick Menu selects date groups.

Entering Events

The calendar is a convenience, but GeoPlanner's real power is in the automatic tracking of events. In the next four sections of this chapter, you learn how to enter, edit, and retrieve events. The procedures are not difficult, and the rewards of a well-built GeoPlanner are considerable.

Entering an event connects a calendar date with a particular activity. You choose the appropriate date from the calendar to open an Event window for that date. When you enter an event, you can make it a repeating event or give it an alarm setting. Although you can enter events using the Events Only view, the steps that follow assume that you have chosen the Both view for convenience in selecting the date. To enter a new event, use these steps:

1. In the Calendar window, click the day of the event. The selected date appears highlighted on the calendar and also appears just above the Event window.

2. From the **Edit** menu, choose the command New Event. A blank event entry box appears at the top of the list.

3. The time of the event is highlighted. To replace it with another time, type in the new time. Press the Tab key to move to the description box.

4. Type the event description. If your description requires additional space, the lines wrap automatically to give you more room. Figure 6.10 shows a typical entry.

5. When you leave the event box, by clicking elsewhere on the screen or starting a new event, PC/GEOS makes a temporary record of your entry. You can use the **S**ave command from the **F**ile menu to make the record permanent or, if you use the Exit command to leave GeoPlanner, a dialog box appears reminding you to save your work (see fig. 6.11).

You also can select and edit any of the empty events that appear as a list down the left edge of the Event window. You can edit an empty event to show a new time, but the program does not replace the deleted time in the list when the edited event sorts to its new chronological position.

Editing and Deleting Events

You can change events by editing them directly in the Event window, using standard GeoWorks Pro text-editing techniques. The mouse pointer changes to an I-beam in the Event window, and you can drag it to select text for editing. The Edit menu in GeoPlanner includes four commands for editing events (shortcut keys appear to the right of the commands in the menu box).

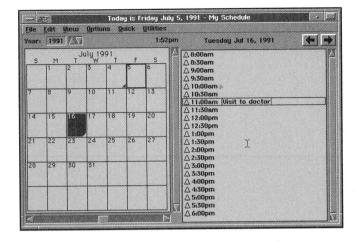

Fig. 6.10

A typical event entry.

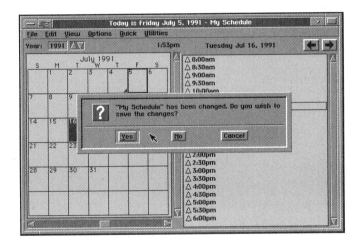

Fig. 6.11

The dialog box to remind you to save your work.

GeoPlanner does not automatically remove an event from your schedule file when its date or time has passed. To remove an event, you must use the Delete command on the Edit menu. Deleting an event removes it completely from the Event window. To delete an event, click the event you want to delete; a box appears around the event. Open the Edit menu and choose the Delete Event command, removing the entire event.

If you delete by mistake, to restore your deletion, immediately choose the Undo command from the Edit menu. Undo does not work, however, if you have begun to edit another event or if you have moved to another date.

Searching for Events

Over time you can accumulate a large number of events in GeoPlanner. You may find that it is impractical to locate a particular event by paging through the calendar, or perhaps you have forgotten the date completely and simply want to find Uncle George's birthday or your anniversary.

The Search command on the Utilities menu looks for a *string*, which is simply a group of letters and/or numbers. A string does not need to be a complete grammatical unit like a word or a sentence.

 NOTE When searching in GeoWorks Pro, you need to be specific about capitalization. Searches are case sensitive. To the computer, *Cat* is not identical to *cat*. If the computer does not find something you are certain is in the events list, check both spelling and capitalization. The computer looks for a literal replica of what you type in the search field.

To search in GeoPlanner, follow these steps:

1. Select the **Utilities** menu and choose the **S**earch command. The Search dialog box opens (see fig. 6.12).

2. In the Search String text field, type what you want to search for. Be exact about spelling and capitalization.

   The Search command finds the string you type, whether it is a whole word or part of a word. If you type *cat*, for example, GeoWorks finds s*cat*ter, *cat*egory, and so on.

3. Click the Start **S**earch button to begin the search.

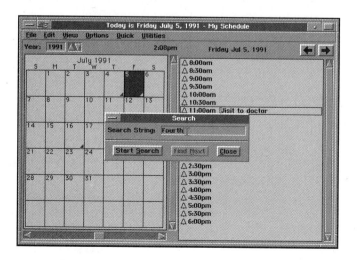

Fig. 6.12

The GeoPlanner
Search dialog box.

GeoPlanner searches forward from the current date through the last year for which you have entered an event. If the search does not find the string, a dialog box appears asking if you want to search through events you entered prior to this year. After the search is complete, click **Close** to dismiss the Search dialog box.

Linking to GeoDex

If you have read Quick Start II and Chapter 5 about GeoDex, the automated directory and telephone dialer, you have learned how to search GeoPlanner for a name or text string found in your address book. In GeoPlanner, you can search GeoDex for a string found in GeoPlanner. As with other searches, capitalization and spelling must be correct for the search to work. To search GeoDex use the following procedure:

1. Start GeoDex. Consult Chapter 5 if you are unfamiliar with the procedure.

2. In GeoPlanner, highlight the string for which you want to search.

3. Open the **Utilities** menu and choose the command **GeoDex** Lookup. The GeoDex window appears, displaying the first card that shows the text selected in GeoPlanner.

   To copy information you located in GeoDex to GeoPlanner (or another application), select the information and use the GeoDex **Copy** command to store the information in memory. Switch to the receiving application and **Paste** the copied material.

4. After you finish the search, click the GeoPlanner window or choose GeoPlanner from the Express menu to return to GeoPlanner.

Repeating Events

You can enter into GeoPlanner each occurrence of an event that occurs regularly—every month, every April 15th, twice a year. Even if you forget each occurrence of the event, it appears in the Event window as required by your repeating event entry. An R to the left of the event in the Event window marks a repeating event. Attaching an alarm to the event makes the event especially difficult to overlook.

To master the technique for scheduling repeating events, open the Utilities menu in GeoPlanner and click **Repeating** Events. In the Repeating Events box that appears, click the **New** button. The large dialog box shown in figure 6.13 appears.

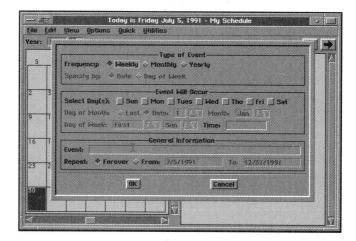

Fig. 6.13

The new repeating
events dialog box.

The key to scheduling a repeating event lies in understanding the Type of Event area in the dialog box. Ask yourself two questions: "How often does the event occur?" "Is it always the same day of the week?" If the event frequency is more than once a month, click the Weekly button; if the event occurs more than once a year, click the Monthly button; if the event happens only once a year, click the Yearly button. For the Specify by choices, if the event occurs the same day of the week on every occasion, click the Day of Week button; if the day of the week varies, click the Date button.

The buttons you choose in the Type of Event area activate the appropriate buttons for the type of event in the Event Will Occur area of the dialog box. The options you have in this area include the following:

■ *Select Day(s):* Click the day or days when the event occurs.

■ *Day of Month:* Click Last if the event always occurs on the last day of the month; for any other date, click Date and then either click the I-beam in the text field and type the date (1 through 31), or use the up and down arrows to enter the date in the text field.

■ *Month:* Click the up and down arrows to enter the month in the text field.

■ *Day of Week:* Use this option to indicate the First Tuesday of the month, the Second Saturday, and so on. Click the up and down arrows to enter which occurrence of the day in the month (First, Second, Third, Fourth, Fifth, or Last) in the first text field; click the up and down arrows to enter the name of the day in the second text field.

■ *Time:* Click the I-beam in the text field and type the appropriate time of the event.

You use the General Information area of the dialog box for any type of event you enter. In the Event text field, click the I-beam in the box and type a short description of the event. On the Repeat line, click Forever for events that occur without an ending date; for repeating events with a beginning and ending date, click From and enter the beginning and ending dates in the text fields.

After you enter all the information for a repeating event, click OK to enter the event in GeoPlanner and return to the main GeoPlanner window.

After you enter the information for a repeating event, click the OK button to store the event in GeoPlanner and return to the main GeoPlanner window.

After you create repeating events, you can change them easily, using the information in the previous section, "Editing Events." To change one occurrence of a repeating event without altering the rest of the event chain, edit that specific event in the Event window. Unless you specifically want to separate a repeating event from the event chain, use the following steps to edit the repeating event:

1. From the Utilities menu, choose the Repeating Events command. The Repeating Events dialog box lists the names of all repeating events.

2. Use the scroll bar at the left end of the list to locate the entry you want to change.

3. Click the entry to highlight it.

4. To change the event, click the Change button. The repeating events information dialog box appears.

5. Change any settings in the dialog box as needed.

6. Click OK to verify the changes.

7. Choose Close in the Repeating Events dialog box to complete the change.

To remove all instances of a repeating event from a list, follow the preceding steps 1 through 3 as you would to edit an event. After you highlight the event in the Repeating Events dialog box, choose the Delete button.

Setting Alarms for Events

The small bell shape to the left of each event entry switches on or off an alarm that you can see and hear at the event time. GeoWorks displays a dialog box showing the event description and buttons that turn the alarm off or make the alarm "snooze" for five minutes before reappearing (see fig. 6.14). At the same time the dialog box appears, your computer speaker "beeps."

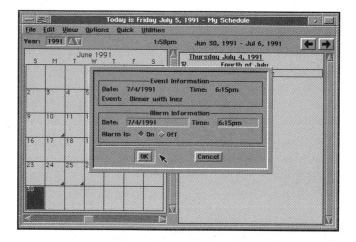

Fig. 6.14

The Alarm dialog box.

To set an alarm, click the small bell symbol to the left of an event. When the bell turns dark, the bell activates; an alarm dialog box appears, and your computer beeps at the event time. You can turn off an alarm by clicking the bell shape again.

To get an advance notice of an event, you can modify the alarm time. To edit an event alarm, select the event in the events list; then open the Edit menu and choose Alarm Settings. By double-clicking the Date or Time text fields, you can enter new values. When you click OK to set the new alarm, the time listed in the events list does not change, but the alarm appears at the date and time you specify with the Alarm Settings. You also can turn the alarm on or off in the Alarm Settings dialog box.

To learn how to set all alarms so that they appear at a specific time before the event, see "Setting Preferences" in the following section.

Fine-Tuning GeoPlanner

To be useful and reliable, GeoPlanner needs periodic maintenance beyond adding, editing, and deleting items. This section shows you how to print events lists and calendars, change GeoPlanner's appearance, and create multiple GeoPlanner files.

Printing with GeoPlanner

The GeoPlanner Print command enables you to print a list of events or print calendars for the month or the year. One useful feature enables you to print events on a monthly calendar. With the excellent printing capabilities of GeoWorks Pro, you can produce professional-looking output with almost any type of printer.

GeoPlanner prints the contents of the Event window in list form. You can print a single day's events or the events from a series of selected days.

To print an events list follow these steps:

1. Move to the appropriate month and day so that the correct events list is visible in the Event window.

2. From the File menu choose Print. The dialog box in figure 6.15 appears.

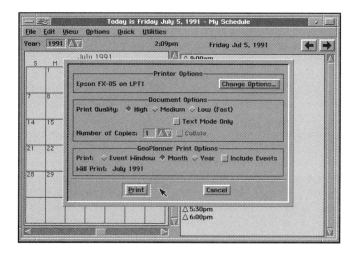

3. If you need to change printers or paper sizes, click the Change Options button in the top area of the dialog box and make the necessary changes.

4. Select Print Quality and Number of Copies in the Document Options area of the dialog box.

5. In the GeoPlanner Print Options area, click the Event Window button.

6. Be sure that your printer is on and on-line, and then choose Print.

To print calendars, follow the preceding steps 1 through 4. In the GeoPlanner Print Options area, click the Month button to print a full-page calendar for one month; click the Year button to print a full page with twelve small monthly calendars. If you want the events listed on the calendar, click Include Events. After you have made your selections, choose Print.

The Will Print field at the bottom of the dialog box confirms the month that will print. The program prints the highlighted month, whether or not the highlighted month is the same month displayed in the calendar window.

With a full-page calendar, only seven lines are available to print events. When these lines fill up, any remaining entries do not print. If you plan to use the Include Events feature, keep your event entries short and remember that some events might be dropped because of space restrictions.

Setting Preferences

Although the designers of GeoWorks Pro did a very good job of creating built-in settings that meet most users' needs, they also realized the need for flexibility. The Change Preferences command on the Options menu opens the dialog box in which you can customize your choices (see fig. 6.16).

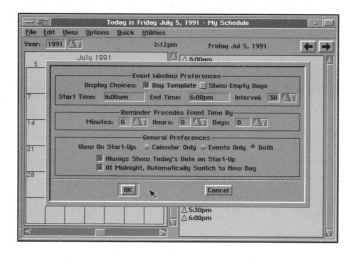

Fig. 6.16

The GeoPlanner Preferences dialog box.

You use these options to change the appearance of events lists, modify the settings to activate all alarms, and control the initial appearance of the display. The following table lists the customizing options and their effects:

Table 6.3 Preference Options

Option	Effect
Day Template	On: Shows Event window divided in blocks of time controlled by Day Template Criteria; Off: Shows only times with scheduled events
Show Empty Days	On: Lists days with no events in the Event window; Off: Does not list days with no events
Start Time	Sets the first time that appears in the Event window when the Day Template is on
End Time	Sets the last time that appears in the Event window when the Day Template is on
Interval	Controls the time between Day Template entries
Reminder Precedes Event Time By	Sets the number of minutes, hours, or days before all alarmed events when the alarm goes off
Startup As	Sets Startup to open GeoPlanner to Calendar view, Event view or Both view
Always Show Today's Date	On: Opens to the calendar for the current month with today's date highlighted; Off: Opens to the date selected when you last quit GeoPlanner
Automatically Switch to New Day	On: Moves the opening selection ahead at midnight; Off: Leaves the date selected as it was when you last quit GeoPlanner

Saving GeoPlanner Files

Figure 6.17 shows the DOCUMENT directory with the My Schedule document icon that appears as a group of calendar pages. My Schedule is the default events list for GeoPlanner.

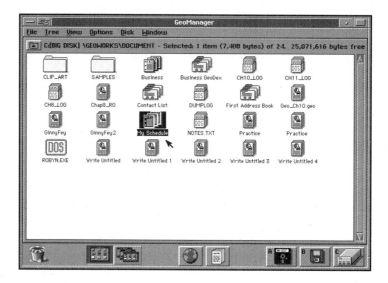

Fig. 6.17

The DOCUMENT directory showing My Schedule.

While you work with GeoPlanner, a temporary file keeps track of your changes. When you close GeoPlanner or leave GeoWorks Pro, a dialog box reminds you to save your changes permanently. When you acknowledge the message, GeoWorks saves your file in the My Schedule file. Use the Save command any time you have made major changes to GeoPlanner.

When you work with GeoPlanner, but before you use the Save command, you can use the Revert command to discard the changes that the program automatically has saved to a temporary file. Choosing **R**evert from the **F**ile menu returns to the last version you saved with the Save or Close commands.

The Save As command enables you to change a file's name or location. You may often use this command to save the file to a floppy disk instead of its normal location in the DOCUMENTS directory. You also can use Save As to create separate events lists, for example, one GeoDex list for business and another for personal activities.

To create a separate events list, follow these steps:

1. Open the **F**ile menu and choose **C**lose to shut down the current file.

2. Open the **F**ile menu and choose **N**ew to create a new, empty schedule file named Untitled Schedule.

3. Open the **F**ile menu again. Choose Save **A**s and type a name for your new schedule file. Choose the **S**ave button to complete the process.

When opened from GeoManager or the Express Menu, GeoPlanner looks for and loads its default file, My Schedule. After GeoPlanner has started, use the **O**pen command on the **F**ile menu to open additional schedule files you may have created.

Chapter Summary

This chapter gives you the tools to manage and customize GeoPlanner and its events lists. You can now recognize the parts of the program and its three screen views, and you can use the Calendar connected with the events list.

This chapter also explains the link between GeoDex and GeoPlanner, and concludes with detailed discussions of printing from GeoPlanner, setting preferences for the program and ways of creating multiple event files.

With accurate maintenance and creative use, GeoPlanner can become an effective and infallible "appointments secretary" for your home or business.

GeoWrite

This quick-start session teaches you basic GeoWrite techniques. After working through this quick start, you can create, edit, and format a basic document. Full coverage of GeoWrite is available in Chapter 7, "Using GeoWrite."

To follow the instructions for using GeoWrite, you must know the basic techniques for manipulating a GeoWorks Pro window and using menus and icons. See Chapter 4, "Mastering GeoManager," to review these topics.

Starting GeoWrite

To start GeoWrite from GeoManager, do the following:

1. Start GeoManager by clicking the Advanced button in the Welcome window. Alternatively, open the Express menu in any active application window, choose the **S**tartup command, and click GeoManager in the cascade menu that appears.

2. If the WORLD directory is not visible in GeoManager, click the globe icon at the bottom of the window to display the WORLD directory.

3. Double-click the GeoWrite icon, which resembles a fountain pen lying on a piece of paper that contains the word *Write*, to open the GeoWrite window.

When you start GeoWrite, a single, blank document appears in the GeoWrite window. Notice the name `Write Untitled` in the Title bar of the window (see fig. IV.1).

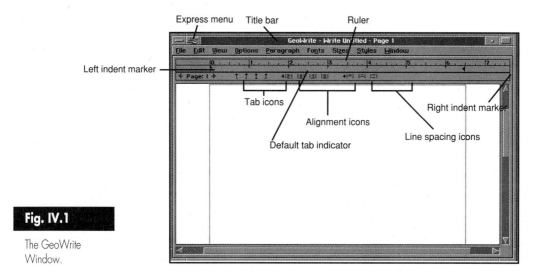

Express menu   Title bar   Ruler

Left indent marker

Tab icons

Alignment icons

Default tab indicator

Right indent marker

Line spacing icons

The GeoWrite
Window.

Entering Text

Entering text in GeoWrite is easy: place the text cursor in the location you want to begin and type. When you reach the right margin, GeoWrite wraps the text to the next line. To insert a blank line, press the Enter key. To delete characters, press the Backspace key to delete one character to the left; you also can press Del to delete one character to the right. You learn other editing techniques later in this quick-start tutorial.

To create your document, begin by pressing Enter to move the text cursor down one line; then type the following text (see fig. IV.2):

Important Notice!

GeoWrite Classes at ABC Center

A series of three-hour classes on using GeoWrite will be offered during the coming two months at the ABC Community Center located at Webster and Burnaby Streets.

Instructor Steve Nelson will lead both lecture and hands-on sessions. Nelson has taught GeoWrite for two years at the University of the North. Course topics and dates are listed below.

Class Date
July 8 Creating a Document

July 22 Editing Your Document

August 5 Enhancing Your Document

Advance registration is required.

Call Mary Bednarek at 445-1234 to register.

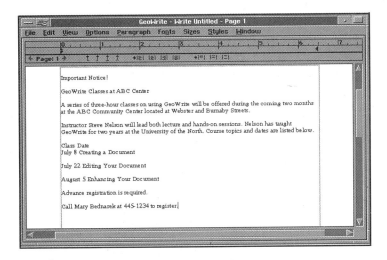

Fig. IV.2

The completed
practice document.

Formatting Your Document

Under the general term *formatting* you learn all the activities you use to change the appearance of your document. You use formatting commands to change fonts and font sizes. Changing margins, paragraph alignment, and line spacing are also formatting activities. Your practice document will look dramatically different after you complete the formatting activities in this section.

Changing Fonts

You can dramatically change your document by choosing from the nine fonts that come with GeoWorks Pro. To apply new fonts in two different ways, follow these steps:

1. Triple-click `Important Notice!` to select it.

2. Open the Fonts menu and click the Superb font to apply it to the selected sentence.

3. Select `GeoWrite Classes at ABC Center`.

4. Open the Fonts menu and choose the **More Fonts** command. The dialog box listing available fonts appears (see fig. IV.3).

5. Choose the Cooperstown font (or another available font) and pre-view its appearance by clicking the font name. A sample of the font appears at the bottom of the dialog box.

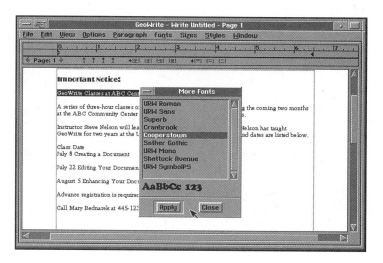

Fig. IV.3

The More Fonts dialog box.

6. Click the Apply button to apply the font to the selected text.

7. To exit the dialog box, click the Close button.

Changing Text Size

With GeoWorks you can produce an amazing range of type sizes—from tiny to page-filling. In this section, you change the type size of `Important Notice!` and `GeoWrite Classes at ABC Center`.

To make the first line in your document as large as possible while fitting it on one line, follow these steps:

1. Select Important Notice!

2. Select the Sizes menu and choose **C**ustom Size. The dialog box in figure IV.4 appears.

3. Click the up arrow to increase the point size (see fig. IV.5). Click the Apply button to check your progress. This document uses 48-point font size; however, this size may vary depending on your monitor.

4. Click Close after you finish.

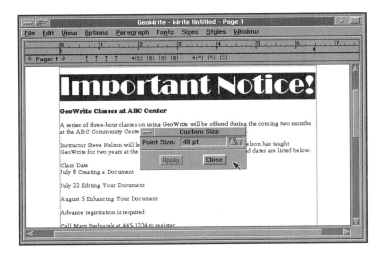

The Custom Size dialog box.

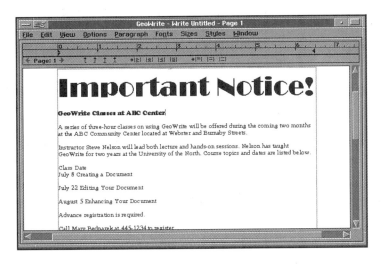

The headline after changing font style and size.

Selecting Character Styles

Bold, italic, and underline are the most common examples of character styles. You can apply these styles to selected characters. To emphasize the second paragraph in your practice document, do the following:

1. Select GeoWrite Classes at ABC Center, choose Sizes and then **4** to increase the size to 18 points.

2. Select the **St**yles menu and choose the **It**alic check box. GeoWorks adds the italic style to the text (see fig. IV.6).

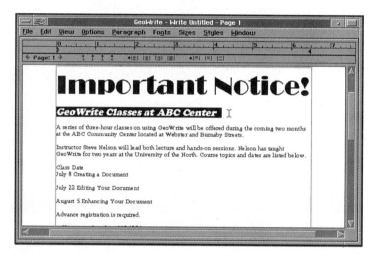

Italic added to the second paragraph.

Aligning Paragraphs

Below the Ruler are four icons that resemble text aligned in different ways (refer to fig. IV.1). To apply an alignment, select a paragraph or group of paragraphs and click the appropriate icon.

To center GeoWrite Classes at ABC Center, use the following steps:

1. Place the text cursor anywhere in the text GeoWrite Classes at ABC Center.

2. Under the Ruler, click the icon that resembles a small document with centered lines.

Setting Paragraph Margins

To change margins for the schedule of classes, follow these steps:

1. Hold down the left mouse button and drag the mouse pointer from the beginning of the Class Date paragraph to the end of the August 5 Enhancing Your Document paragraph to select these four paragraphs.

2. Drag both halves of the left triangular indent marker on the Ruler (refer to fig. IV.1) to the Ruler's one inch mark. The left margins of the selected paragraphs shift accordingly.

Setting and Customizing Tabs

In this exercise, you align the schedule of class dates and topics by inserting tabs and then changing the Ruler to control them.

To insert tabs, place the text cursor in the location you intend to place the tab and press the Tab key. (Tab characters are not visible on the GeoWrite screen.)

In your document, place a tab after Class and after each date in the schedule of classes. After you set your tabs, observe the results (see fig. IV.7). Because the default tab is a left-aligned tab, the left edge of each word following a tab character aligns with one of the default tab settings (indicated by the small upward arrow heads just below the measurement line on the Ruler).

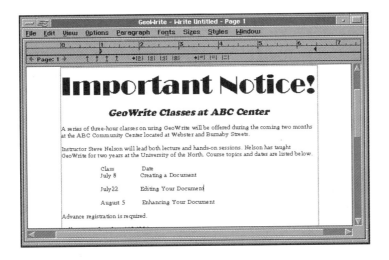

Fig. IV.7

The table aligned with default Ruler tabs.

If the default settings are not satisfactory, you can set tabs wherever you want them. In this exercise, you use only a left-aligned tab. Refer to Chapter 7, "Using GeoWrite," for a complete explanation of the tab types.

To create customized tab settings, follow these steps:

1. Hold down the left mouse button and drag the mouse from the beginning of the `Class Date` paragraph to the end of the `August 5 Enhancing Your Document` paragraph to select these paragraphs.

2. Drag a left tab icon (the leftmost arrow icon) to the 2 1/2-inch position on the Ruler (see fig. IV.8).

3. Release the mouse button to set the tab. If you miss the setting, drag the tab again to reset its position.

You can delete the custom tab by dragging it off the Ruler. The default tabs take over again.

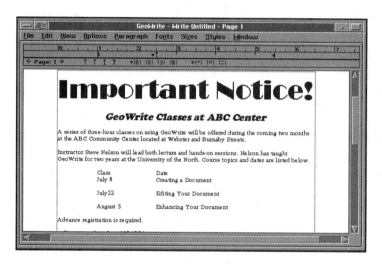

Fig. IV.8

The dates aligned with a custom left tab.

Enhancing Your Document

Your document has come a long way from the plain text with which you started. Font changes and paragraph enhancements have made the document much more effective. You also can place borders around selected paragraphs and use the color features by producing a block of reversed text.

Creating Reversed Text

GeoWrite has the capability, unusual among word processors, to change text, paragraph, and border colors. At this point color printer drivers are not available, but forthcoming upgrades will enable owners of color printers to produce colorful documents. For now, you can use the black and white features and enjoy on-screen colors; you also can create reversed text.

Text is *reversed* if white letters appear on a black background. You control the size of the background by setting paragraph dimensions. Change the lettering color with the Text Color command on the Styles menu.

To create a reversed text block, follow these steps:

1. Select the second paragraph (GeoWrite Classes...).

2. Open the **St**yles menu and choose **T**ext Color.

3. Click the white box in the dialog box color squares; then click the Apply button.

4. Click Close. Because your text is now the color of the background, it seems to disappear.

5. Open the **P**aragraph menu and choose **P**aragraph Color.

6. In the dialog box, click the black square; then click Apply.

7. Click Close. Click the mouse pointer away from the paragraph to remove the selection highlight.

Applying Paragraph Borders

The final enhancement you add to this document is the paragraph border. Outlining a paragraph or group of paragraphs draws attention to them. In this section, you place a border around the schedule of class dates.

To apply a border, follow these steps:

1. Select the three paragraphs that begin with dates.

2. Select the **P**aragraph menu and choose the **B**order command. A cascade menu with a choice of border styles appears.

3. Choose the **S**hadow Top Left choice. The border extends to the right page margin because the paragraphs have that width.

4. To bring the border in, drag the right triangular margin marker to the 5 1/2-inch mark (see fig. IV.9).

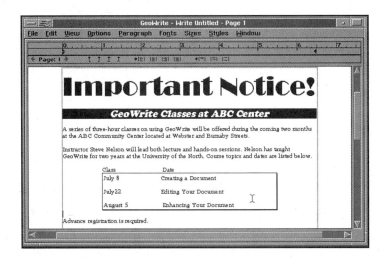

The reversed text block and border.

Because you chose a group of paragraphs, the border surrounds the entire group. You can modify borders by using the **Custom Border** command that cascades from the **Border** command in the **Paragraph** menu. See Chapter 7, "Using GeoWrite," for a detailed discussion of the Custom Border command.

Saving Your Document

After you complete your document, you should save it. Even though GeoWrite keeps an automatic backup file, use the Save command every time you change your document significantly.

To save your practice document, follow these steps:

1. Open the **File** menu and choose the **Save** command.

2. Because you have not saved the file previously, the save as dialog box—in which you name the file and choose a location where the file will be saved—appears (see fig IV.10).

3. Do not change the directory. Type **Practice** in the name text field and choose **Save** to store the file. The name `Practice` replaces the default name `Write Untitled` in the Title bar.

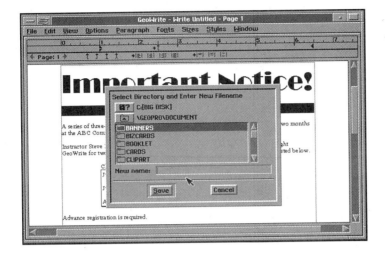

Fig. IV.10

The save as dialog box.

Printing Your Document

Chapter 7, "Using GeoWrite," contains a detailed discussion of printing with GeoWrite, including explanations of each item in the print and print options dialog boxes. For this exercise, your printer must be properly installed. For printer troubleshooting, refer to Chapter 11, "Customizing with the Preferences Desk Tool."

To print your document, do the following:

1. Select the **File** menu and choose the **Print** command. The dialog box shown in figure IV.11 opens.

2. Click High print quality for the best reproduction of your practice document.

3. Choose the **Print** button. Five minutes or more may be required to print the document at high quality on a dot matrix printer.

With GeoWrite's powerful capabilities, you quickly can add a professional look to your publication. In this quick start, you have sampled the possibilities. Chapter 7, "Using GeoWrite," gives a full description of the program's capabilities.

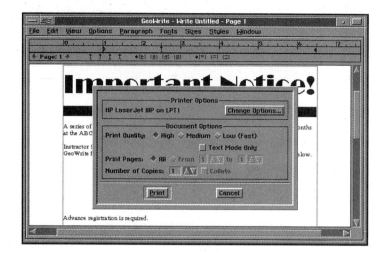

Fig. IV.11

The Printer Options
dialog box.

Using GeoWrite

G eoWrite is a powerful and capable word processor. In addition to
the full set of standard features, GeoWrite holds some surprises:
like a standard array of ten fonts and the capability to use color and
halftone—features often found only in desktop publishing packages.
Many of the following editing features are the equal of those features
found in the most advanced graphically based word processors:

- Eight different screen view sizes
- Headers, footers, and automatic page numbering
- Variable line spacing and leading
- Reverse (white on black) printing
- Automatic title page
- Graphics import

GeoWrite's close integration with other GeoWorks Pro applications enables you to move text and graphics among the applications. You also
can cut, copy, and paste information between multiple GeoWrite documents. If you are new to graphically based word processing you will
enjoy the capability of having several documents open at once, each in
its own window. Although you cannot move fully-formatted GeoWrite
documents directly into DOS-based word processors, you can move text
and basic formatting using an intermediate text file.

Because GeoWrite uses the same menu and window conventions used throughout GeoWorks Pro, skills mastered in other applications are useful in GeoWrite. You need to learn some new commands, but you do not have to learn a different way to move and size windows, or use menus and commands.

As you move through this chapter, you learn the GeoWrite workspace and review the major elements of a typical document and how to create one. You learn all the details of changing your document's appearance with commands for the character, paragraph and document levels. The third section of the chapter shows you how to enhance your document with color, halftones, and graphics. The chapter concludes with a discussion of file management and printing.

Touring GeoWrite

Each time you encounter a new GeoWorks Pro application, "touring" the program is a useful first step. Familiarity with the general structure of the program enables you to assess quickly what is familiar and what is new. In this section, you start the program and review some of its principal features such as the document window and the various reduced and enlarged views of your document found on the View menu. The section concludes with an explanation of methods for moving through the documents and selecting text.

Starting GeoWrite

GeoWrite is visible as an icon in the GeoManager WORLD view. You also can launch GeoWrite from the Express menu available in any active window or you can double-click a GeoWrite document. Each of these techniques is useful at different times, depending on where you are in a work session.

Launching GeoWrite from GeoManager is appropriate if you typically start your GeoWorks Pro work session there. Open GeoManager, displaying the WORLD directory window. Double-click the GeoWrite icon, which looks like a fountain pen lying on a piece of paper with the word Write on it (see fig. 7.1).

The Express menu is available in any active application window. It furnishes a handy way to start GeoWrite if the WORLD window is not open or if you are using another GeoWorks Pro application and want to switch to GeoWrite.

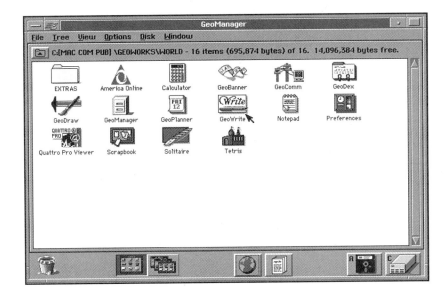

Fig. 7.1

The GeoWrite icon in the WORLD directory.

To open GeoWrite from the Express menu, click the stylized E in the upper left of the window. Choose **S**tartup to open the cascade menu that lists the GeoWorks Pro applications. On the cascade menu, click GeoWrite to launch the program (see fig. 7.2).

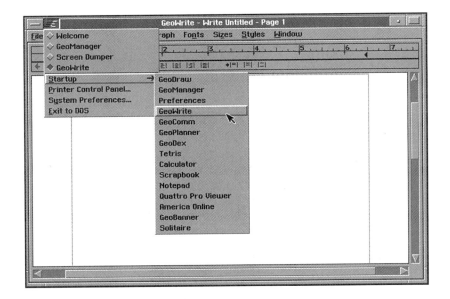

Fig. 7.2

The Startup cascade menu.

The third method of launching GeoWrite involves using a GeoWrite document. The icon for a GeoWrite document looks like a stack of papers; the top sheet has lines and a graphic on it.

To start GeoWrite using a document icon, double-click the document icon. GeoWrite starts with that document loaded.

Opening Documents

Methods for starting GeoWrite also influence which document appears on-screen. You can open a GeoWrite document in the following four ways depending on whether you are starting a new document or using an existing one:

- When you start GeoWrite from the WORLD directory or the Express menu, the program opens with an untitled, empty document on the screen.

- If you are working on a document in GeoWrite and close GeoWorks Pro without closing the document, the document is present when you restart GeoWorks Pro. Generally, GeoWorks restarts with the exact configuration you had when you last quit.

- If you start GeoWrite by double-clicking a document icon, GeoWorks opens the document in the GeoWrite window, saving you the trouble of separate operations for opening GeoWrite and the document.

- You can open a document with commands from the **F**ile menu. The New command opens a blank document in GeoWrite. If another document is present, the New command opens a blank window on top of the previous document. Don't be startled by this overlapping when your original document apparently disappears—working with multiple documents is covered in this chapter's discussion of windows and menus.

  With the **O**pen command, also on the **F**ile menu, you can open an existing document. In the file open dialog box that appears, you can double-click the file name to open the document in GeoWrite (see fig. 7.3). You also can click a name to highlight it and then choose the **O**pen button. Chapter 4, "Mastering GeoManager," details this file opening method.

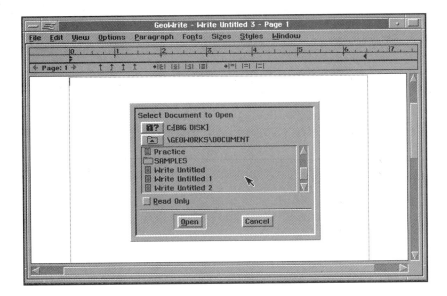

Fig. 7.3

The file open dialog box.

Getting Acquainted with the GeoWrite Window

The GeoWrite window is similar to other GeoWorks Pro application windows (see fig. 7.4).

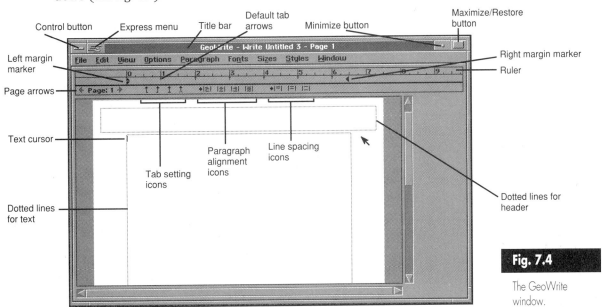

Fig. 7.4

The GeoWrite window.

The Title Bar at top center shows the application name and the name of the open file. The Express menu enables you to open other applications or exit to DOS. The Control button at the upper left provides commands for moving and sizing the window.

Scroll bars at the bottom and right sides enable you to view documents larger than the window. The Maximize/Restore button at the upper right switches between a maximized window, which fills the entire screen, and ·a standard window, which you can move and resize. The Minimize button reduces the window to an icon at the lower left corner of the screen.

New in the GeoWrite window is the assembly called the Ruler. Fitting in below the Menu bar, the Ruler contains measurements for guiding page formatting and icons for changing pages, margins, tabs, line spacing, and paragraph alignment. Later in this chapter you can find detailed discussions of these features.

The main portion of the window shows the document. Dotted outlines define areas for the text and for headers and footers—items like page numbers and document titles that appear at the bottom or top of each page. The text cursor is the I-beam shape in the document window.

Learning the GeoWrite Menus

GeoWrite has an extensive command system, reached through nine menus. Table 7.1 briefly describes GeoWrite's menus. This chapter discusses in detail the commands in each menu.

Table 7.1 The GeoWrite Menus

Menu Name	Purpose
File	Create, open, close, and save files; access Print and Setup dialog boxes; save to DOS formats
Edit	Cut, copy, and paste text; manage styles and insert page breaks and page numbers; use spelling checker
View	Reduce or enlarge page image; manage aspect ratio on older monitors
Options	Control display of Ruler and Ruler units, graphics, and scroll bars; use spelling checker options
Paragraph	Set paragraph alignment and spacing, tabs, color, and borders

Menu Name	Purpose
Fonts	Choose type styles
Sizes	Choose type sizes and character spacing
Styles	Set character formats (like bold and italic)
Window	List and switch between open documents; change page display

Many commands have keyboard shortcuts so that you can use the command without removing your hands from the keyboard. GeoWorks displays the shortcuts to the right of the command names in a menu. If you are a new user, you may want to stick to menu commands until you are comfortable with the application. Then you can introduce keyboard shortcuts for commands you use frequently.

Learning View Sizes and Aspect Ratio

The GeoWrite View menu offers a wide range of image enlargement and reduction to enable you to see both the micro and macro views of your document. Figure 7.5 shows the window reduced to 25% of its actual size. In this view, turning pages with the Next and Previous page arrows on the Ruler gives a rough preview of how the document will print. The greatest enlargement, 200%, enables you to view detailed adjustments of both inter-character and inter-line spacing (see fig. 7.6).

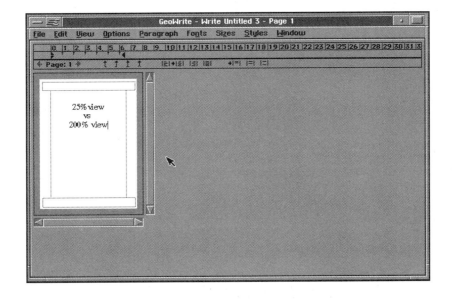

Fig. 7.5

The 25% view displays an entire page.

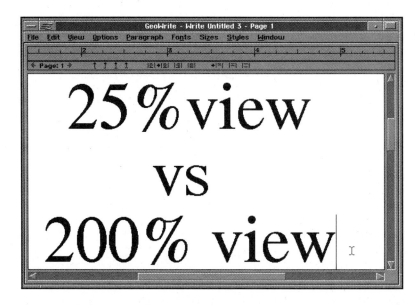

Fig. 7.6

The 200% view details fine points of spacing.

The dots that make up the image on your video screen are *pixels*. Some older PC's, notably those PC's with CGA and Hercules graphics, use rectangular pixels rather than the square ones used in more recent systems. GeoWorks Pro can compensate for rectangular pixels by adjusting the *aspect ratio* of your screen.

The aspect ratio is the ratio of height to width. If your screen image looks squashed or stretched, open the View menu and choose Correct for Aspect Ratio. Characters are legible in either mode with or without this command, but without it, characters appear different on-screen than they appear when you print them. You can use the screen either way; however, you get a better sense of the appearance of the document by turning on the command. To turn the command off, click the box again. *Note:* If the command is grayed out, the type of display you have installed has no aspect ratio problem.

Moving through a Document

The Window menu (see fig. 7.7) contains commands for moving from page to page within your current document. The following list describes the commands and their purposes.

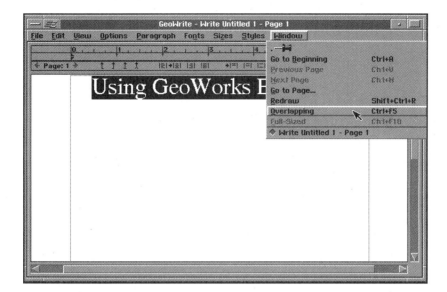

Fig. 7.7

The Window menu.

- *Previous Page and Next Page.* You can usually bypass the Previous Page and Next Page commands in favor of the paging arrows always visible at the left end of the Ruler. Clicking a paging arrow moves you forward or backward one page. The current page number appears between the arrows. If no page precedes or follows your current page, the arrows are gray.

- *Go to Page.* The Go to Page command opens the dialog box in which you can enter a number in the preselected text box by typing it, or by clicking the up or down arrows. Clicking OK takes you directly to the specified page. The Title Page button is active if you created an automatic title page for your document.

- *Redraw.* You can use the Redraw command in the special situation in which changing the document has caused the screen image to draw incorrectly. The command causes the program to redraw the screen image, usually eliminating any "garbage" left from an incorrect image.

- *Overlapping and Full-Sized.* These commands complement one another. If more than one document is open or if multiple pages in one document are open, you can display the pages as a *stack* (see fig. 7.8) with the Overlapping command. You can move and resize windows to see pages side-by-side and you can cut and paste material from window to window. To activate a window so that you can move or resize it, place the mouse pointer inside the window boundary and click.

To return the overlapping view to a view of the active window, choose the Full-Sized command.

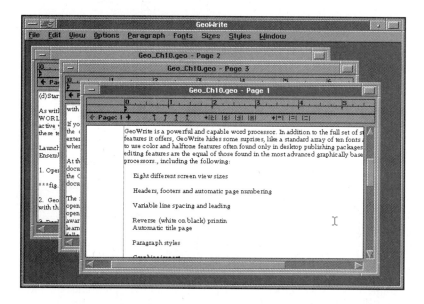

■ *Document List.* The page list at the bottom of the Window menu enables you to move quickly to an open window by clicking its name.

Creating a Document

Although you will use GeoWrite's many features to enhance text, you first need to learn how to get the words on paper. In this section, you create a basic document, examine the default formatting for the document, and learn basic editing techniques.

Entering Text

The following four steps are the heart of word processing. You can use GeoWorks' many enhancements to work faster or make your result look more sophisticated, but these four basic steps are part of every document:

1. Open the File menu and choose New. An empty page appears on the screen. The short vertical bar at the upper left corner of the typing area is the *text cursor*. The text cursor indicates the location where the text you type will appear.

2. Begin typing. You do not have to press Enter at the end of each line. GeoWrite wraps your text to the next line.

3. When you reach the end of a paragraph, press Enter to end the paragraph. Press Enter again to create a blank line between paragraphs.

4. To correct errors, press the Backspace key to delete one character to the left of the text cursor. Press the Del key to delete a single character to the right of the text cursor.

Selecting Text

Throughout GeoWorks Pro, you have learned that selecting an item tells the program where to apply an action or command. The same principle applies to GeoWrite. Using selection techniques, you can move beyond deleting single characters with Backspace or Del. You can work much more effectively with the following techniques designed to select (highlight) groups of characters for editing:

- Drag the mouse pointer across the text with the left button held down.

- Point to a word and double-click to select it.

- Triple-click a line to select the entire line.

- Quadruple-click to select the paragraph that the mouse pointer indicates.

- Quintuple-click to select an entire page.

With any of these techniques, you can keep the left mouse button down after your final click and drag the mouse to select additional text in the same quantity you made the first selection—word, line, paragraph, or page.

If you have trouble keeping track of the clicks, try the following technique that works for any quantity of text:

1. Click the left mouse button at the beginning of a block of text you want to select. A text cursor appears.

2. While holding down the Shift key, point to the end of the block you want to select and click the left mouse button. The area between the first and last clicks is highlighted.

3. To remove a selection highlight, click the mouse pointer in an area away from the highlight.

Learning Basic Editing Techniques

Now that you know some selection techniques, you can delete more text than single characters. Select an area of any size, using any of the techniques described in the previous section, and press Backspace or Del. GeoWorks removes the entire selected area.

Another important editing technique also involves selection: if you want to replace a block of text with new text, select the block and begin to type. The selected block disappears with your first keystroke, and the new text replaces the selection.

Using Insert and Overtype

When you position the text cursor in a block of text and begin to type, the new text normally moves the existing text to the right. This default situation is called the *insert* mode—GeoWorks inserts into the document what you type. At times, you may want to *overtype* over existing text rather than moving it to the right. The Ins key toggles between insert and overtype modes. You can identify the mode by the text cursor shape. In insert mode, the text cursor is the familiar vertical bar, but in overtype mode, the text cursor becomes a one-character-wide rectangle.

Moving and Copying Text

You can move any block of text to a new location. Begin by selecting the text you want to move. Use the Cut command from the Edit menu to remove the selection from the screen and store it in computer memory.

 CAUTION Because the memory storage location holds only one item at a time, while your block of text is in memory, do not use Cut to remove some other item; the most recently cut item displaces the current item and you cannot retrieve it.

To place your text in its new location, move to the new page and position the text cursor where you want the cut text to appear. Open the **E**dit menu and choose the **P**aste command. The text will appear, starting at the position of the text cursor and moving existing text to the right.

Although copying text is similar to moving text, when you copy the original text, GeoWorks does not remove the original text from the screen.

Select the text you want to copy, open the **E**dit menu, and choose **C**opy. Move the text cursor to the point where you want to insert the copied text, choose **E**dit, **P**aste. The text appears, starting at the position of the text cursor and moving existing text to the right.

GeoWorks stores copied text in the same memory location as text that has been cut. Copied text also is subject to the same vulnerability of being bumped by the next piece of text that you cut or copy.

NOTE Because you will probably use the Cut, Copy, and Paste commands frequently, you may want to memorize their keyboard shortcut keys. The keys for Cut are Shift+Del; the keys for Paste are Shift+Ins; the keys for Copy are Ctrl+Ins.

Using Quick Copy and Quick Move

GeoWorks Pro has a feature that can quickly move text from location to location, bypassing the storage area where GeoWorks stores cut or copied material.

To use Quick Copy, follow these steps:

1. Select the text you want to copy.

2. Point to the selected text with the mouse pointer and hold down the *right* mouse button. The shape of the mouse pointer changes to an arrow with a small square attached.

3. Keeping the right mouse button down, move the pointer to where you want to copy the text.

4. When you release the pointer, a copy of the selected text appears at the position of the pointer.

Quick Move is similar to Quick Copy. According to GWRep MK, follow the Quick Copy steps exactly, but in steps 3 and 4, press and hold down the Alt key before you press and hold the right mouse button. **T I P**

NOTE As you become more proficient with GeoWrite, you will want to gain speed. Keyboard shortcuts for a number of editing actions are faster because you don't have to reach for the mouse or open a menu. Consult your GeoWorks Pro documentation for a complete description of the available keyboard shortcuts.

Changing a Document's Appearance

In the previous sections you learned how to enter and edit a document with GeoWrite. These skills may be all you need for many letters, memoranda, and informal items. On the other hand, this era of desktop publishing prompts a greater awareness of a document's appearance as well as its content. Elaborate formatting cannot rescue poorly chosen words, but a polished appearance can highlight well-written material.

In this section, you explore *formatting* techniques for changing the appearance of your documents. Apply formatting to the building blocks of a document, beginning with characters and extending to paragraphs and the entire document. You learn how to change character fonts and sizes, how to control paragraph breaks, indents and spacing, and how to change page breaks, margins, columns, and other whole-document features.

Character Formatting

The characters that make up the words in your GeoWrite document have three properties that you can alter: font, size, and style. The GeoWrite window Menu bar displays menus for each of these formatting changes.

Character Fonts

Fonts are *families* of type styles that share a basic design. Figure 7.9 shows the font menu opened with a screen of font samples in GeoWrite. You can use the **More Fonts** cascade menu to preview a sample of each font before choosing one.

With its excellent printing abilities, GeoWrite can reproduce a variety of fonts. You can print an excellent replica of the text that appears on the screen.

You can change fonts before or after you type your text, and you can do so in one of two ways through the Fonts menu. The first method is simple: open the Fonts menu, and click your choice of Font. To use the second method of choosing a font, follow these steps:

1. From the Fonts menu choose the **More Fonts** command.

   A dialog box opens, listing the available fonts. You can preview the font appearance by clicking the font name.

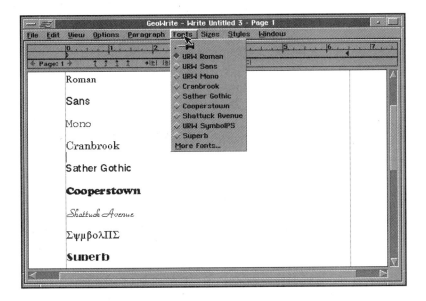

Fig. 7.9

The Fonts menu and a
screen of sample fonts.

2. To apply a font, click the Apply button in the dialog box.

3. To exit the dialog box, click the Close button.

You can use the same two methods to change the font on existing text; however, make sure that you select the text before you open the Fonts menu to choose a new font.

Character Sizes

You also can change font size. The measurement for font sizes, the *point*, comes to the computer from the printing industry—72 points equals an inch and 36-point type is 1/2-inch tall. You are not likely to run out of sizes in GeoWrite; you can size text from an almost invisible four points to a page-filling 792 points! The default selection for text in GeoWrite is 12-point type.

To choose a font size, open the Sizes menu and click your choice; or you can choose the **C**ustom Size command and use the up and down arrows or type field in the Custom Size dialog box to specify a size in points. Then click the Apply button to change the size of the selected text, and click Close to exit the dialog box. On the Sizes menu, you can choose the **S**maller and **L**arger commands to change font size incrementally.

Character Spacing

Character spacing is a sophisticated typographic control, not usually found outside of complex desktop publishing packages. GeoWrite provides a simple, effective application of this powerful tool. You can use character spacing to close up inter-character space in large type, and to *tighten* or *loosen* lines that don't quite fit their space in a layout. If you study contemporary graphics and advertising, you frequently see unusual character spacing used as a design element.

The Character Spacing command on the Sizes menu controls the space between individual characters. The best way to apply character spacing is by eye. The default spacing is considered to be zero. You can enter positive numbers up to 500 to increase the space between characters and negative numbers down to –150 to reduce the space between characters. Figure 7.10 shows an example of the effect of character spacing.

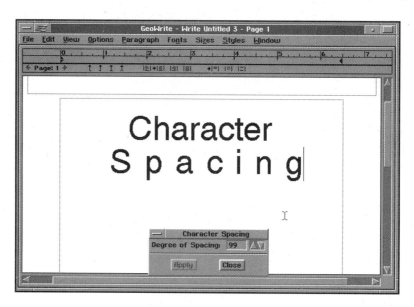

Fig. 7.10

The effects of character spacing.

Use these steps to apply character spacing:

1. Select the text you want to respace.

2. Open the Sizes menu and choose the Character Spacing command.

3. Type a number or use the up and down arrows to specify the Degree of Spacing. Positive numbers increase spacing. Negative numbers decrease spacing.

4. Click Apply to see the effect of your change. If you are not satisfied, change the number and click Apply again.

5. When you are satisfied with the result, click the Close button.

If the screen image becomes garbled while you respace text, choose the **R**edraw command from the **W**indow menu.

Character Styles

Now that you can control font type, size, and spacing, you are ready to control character style. *Style* refers to variations of the basic font. Bold, Italic, and Underline are common style variations. The Styles menu contains commands for applying text styles to selected text.

To apply a character style, select the text you want to change. Open the **S**tyles menu and click the check box for the style you want. You can choose multiple styles such as Bold and Italic. GeoWorks applies the style to the selected text.

The "Using Color" section of this chapter describes the Text Color command.

Paragraph Formatting

In GeoWrite, you create a new paragraph every time you press the Enter key. Even the blank lines you create by pressing Enter are empty paragraphs. Important and useful commands for line spacing, borders, and margins are paragraph formatting, applied to entire paragraphs. Paragraph formatting also includes features like tabs.

In this section you learn how to use the Ruler, how to control line spacing and leading, and how to set tabs. This section also explains borders and styles. With these tools, you can manage paragraphs, the major building blocks of your document.

Paragraph Alignment

Although the default setting automatically aligns the text in paragraphs along the left margin of the page, GeoWrite enables you to change the alignment to three other positions: centered, right aligned, and full (also called justified). Figure 7.11 shows samples of the four types of alignment.

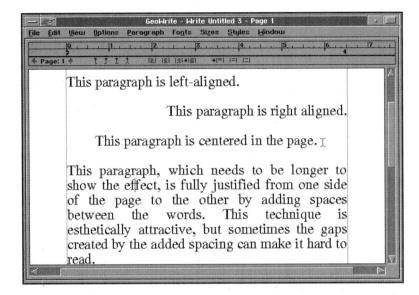

Fig. 7.11

Paragraph alignment
samples.

To change alignment using the Paragraph menu, follow these steps:

1. If you are aligning only one paragraph, position the insertion point anywhere inside the paragraph. To align more than one paragraph, select all the paragraphs you want to change.

2. Open the **P**aragraph menu and choose **L**eft, **C**enter, **R**ight or **F**ull.

   GeoWorks applies the new alignment to the paragraph(s).

You also can change paragraph alignment with the Ruler; see section "Indents and Margins" in the chapter.

Line Spacing

The lines in paragraphs are normally single-spaced. You also can choose 1 1/2- or double-spaced lines. Commands in the Paragraph menu make this process easy. Follow these steps:

1. Select the paragraphs you want to space. If you want to change only one paragraph, place the text cursor anywhere within the paragraph.

2. Open the **P**aragraph menu and choose the Single (**1**), One and a Half, or Double (**2**) command. The selected paragraphs then reflect the new spacing.

You also can control spacing with the Ruler at the top of the GeoWrite window. See the section, "The Ruler," for instructions.

Space above or below Paragraphs

As a carryover from the days of fixed typewriter line spacing, it has become customary to put one line between paragraphs by pressing the Enter key. In GeoWrite, you can change the space above (most common) or below paragraphs for improved appearance. You might alter the space below if you were trying to keep a paragraph away from a heading that follows it.

This feature also eliminates the need to create a blank line between paragraphs. If you use space above or below your paragraph, pressing Enter to complete a paragraph automatically includes the specified amount of space. To set space above or below a paragraph, follow these steps:

1. Place the text cursor inside the paragraph you want to alter, or select multiple paragraphs by dragging the mouse across them.

2. Open the **P**aragraph menu and choose Paragraph **S**pacing. The dialog box shown in figure 7.12 opens.

3. Use the arrows or type a value for Space on Top or Space on Bottom.

NOTE You should not use the Space on Top and Space on Bottom on the same paragraph. The settings interact with the paragraphs preceding and following and become confusing to manage.

4. Click Apply; then click Close.

The Ruler

The Ruler is located between the Menu bar and the text entry area (see fig. 7.13). With the mouse, you can control tabs, indentation, margins, and line spacing. Although having the Ruler visible is frequently useful, you can turn it off by clicking off the **O**ptions menu commands, Show Ruler **T**op and Show Ruler **B**ottom.

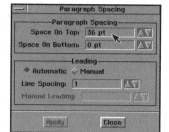

Fig. 7.12

The Paragraph
Spacing dialog box.

The Ruler reflects formatting as you set it with Ruler icons or menu commands. If you put the text cursor in a centered paragraph, for example, the arrow next to the four alignment icons points to the centered icon. If you shift to a left-aligned paragraph, the arrow shifts to the left icon.

The Ruler provides the following features (see fig. 7.13):

- A Ruler with inch markings

- Black triangles used to set paragraph indents

- Small arrows marking the default tab settings

- Four tab arrow icons for setting left, right, centered, and decimal tabs

- Four icons for setting paragraph text alignment

- Three icons for setting Single-spacing, 1 1/2-spacing, and double-spacing

Paragraph Alignment with the Ruler

Earlier in this section you learned to use the four commands from the Paragraph menu to set paragraph alignment Left, Right, Center, or Full (justified). In its lower half, the Ruler includes four icons that resemble small lines of text aligned four different ways. Selecting a paragraph or group of paragraphs and clicking the icon that resembles the alignment you want, aligns the selected paragraphs.

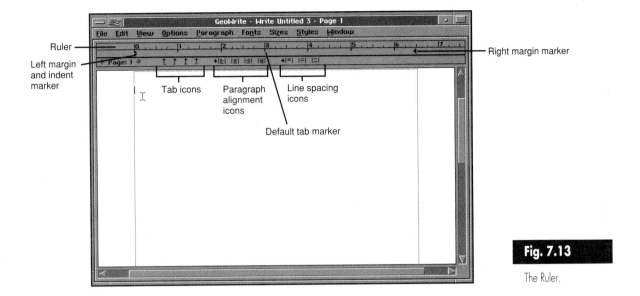

Fig. 7.13

The Ruler.

Indents and Margins

You can use indents and margins to regulate the distance between the left or right edge of a paragraph and the margins of the page. You can set margins for the entire page by using the Page Setup command from the File menu. The margin controls on the Ruler affect only paragraphs you have selected.

To change the margins for a paragraph follow these steps:

1. Place the text cursor inside the paragraph you want to alter or select multiple paragraphs by dragging the mouse across them.

2. Drag either of the triangular indent markers on the Ruler to the position where you want the left and right margins of the paragraph.

   The left triangle is made up of two sections. When setting margins, drag both parts to the left margin location.

To change the first line indent for a paragraph follow these steps:

1. Place the text cursor inside the paragraph you want to alter or select multiple paragraphs by dragging the mouse across them.

2. Drag the top half of the left margin marker to the right an amount equal to the first line indent you want.

A useful variation of a first line indent is called a *hanging indent*, often used with numbered or bulleted lists. In this case, drag the top half of the split triangle that marks the left margin to the *left*; the program *outdents* the first line to the left of the body of the paragraph.

Line Spacing

From the days of the typewriter, single-spacing, 1 1/2-line spacing, and double-spacing have been standard options for the space between lines of text. The capability to mix different type sizes and styles in a document and the need for greater graphic sophistication have introduced the need for the typographic technique, *leading* (pronounced "ledding") to give more choice for the spaces between paragraphs and between lines of text. The term leading comes from the days when cast metal type was set by hand. Because lead strips were used to separate one line of text from the next, the inter-line space came to be known as leading.

GeoWrite offers either the simplicity of standard spacing or the sophistication of customized leading; you can mix both features.

You can set standard spacing between the lines of a paragraph with the Ruler. First, place the text cursor inside the paragraph you want to alter, or select multiple paragraphs by dragging the mouse across them. On the Ruler, click the icon that represents the spacing you want: Single, 1 1/2, or Double. Remember that you can also set spacing by choosing the appropriate command on the Paragraph menu.

To set nonstandard spacing between lines, follow these steps:

1. Place the text cursor inside the paragraph you want to alter or select multiple paragraphs by dragging the mouse across them.

2. Open the **P**aragraph menu and choose Paragraph **S**pacing to open the Paragraph Spacing dialog box (refer to fig. 7.13).

3. Enter a number in the Line Spacing box. GeoWorks sets the space between lines to the size of the largest type in the line multiplied by the number you enter. If you use 14-point text and specify a line spacing of 2, for example, GeoWrite puts 28 points between the lines.

You can specify a precise amount of leading between lines regardless of their text size. This feature enables you to take control of unusual situations where automatic leading does not give you the desired result.

To customize leading, follow these steps:

1. Place the text cursor inside the paragraph you want to alter or select multiple paragraphs by dragging the mouse across them.

2. Open the **P**aragraph menu and choose Paragraph **S**pacing.

3. In the Paragraph Spacing dialog box, click the check box for Manual leading.

4. Enter a fixed value in points in the Manual Leading text field.

5. Click Apply; then click Close.

Tabs

GeoWrite has two levels of tabs. The default tabs, all left aligned, appear as small arrows just below the Ruler line. They represent settings that apply to any paragraph you create unless you customize tabs for that paragraph.

The four arrow icons at the bottom of the Ruler indicate customized tabs. You use the customizing tabs for a paragraph or group of paragraphs, and they apply only to that location in the document. When you select a paragraph to which you have applied customized tabs, the tab icons appear on the Ruler.

The icons on the Ruler represent four types of tab. From left to right they are the following:

Tab	Effect
Left	Tab is at left end of the text
Right	Tab is at right end of text
Center	Text is centered on the tab
Decimal	Text aligns to right and left of decimal point

To change the default tab settings, follow these steps:

1. Open the **P**aragraph menu and choose the command **D**efault Tabs.

2. Click the default distance you want in the cascade menu. Small arrows on the Ruler show where the default tabs are positioned.

To create customized tab settings, use these steps:

1. Place the text cursor inside the paragraph you want to alter or select multiple paragraphs by dragging the mouse across them.

2. Use the mouse pointer with the left button held down to drag a tab icon to the Ruler in the position you want. Release the mouse button to set the tab.

3. Set additional tabs as needed.

234

To reposition a tab, drag it along the Ruler; to delete a tab, drag it off the Ruler.

Tab Leader Characters

Leader characters are symbols that fill any empty space in a tab. Figure 7.14, a segment of a table of contents, shows a typical use of leader characters. The leader characters stretch between the text entry and the page number. In GeoWrite, you can choose a row of dots or a line as leader characters.

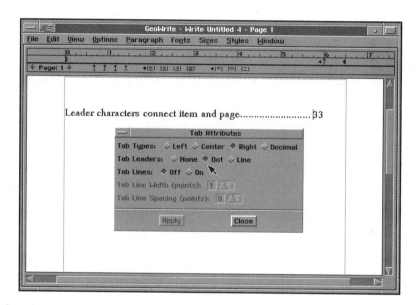

Fig. 7.14

The Tab Attributes dialog box to set leader dots for a table of contents entry.

To set tab leader characters, use these steps:

1. Place the text cursor inside the paragraph you want to alter or select multiple paragraphs by dragging the mouse across them.

2. On the Ruler, click the tab to which you want to apply leader characters. A small arrow indicates your selection.

3. Open the **Paragraph** menu and choose the **Tab** Attributes command to open the dialog box shown in figure 7.15.

4. In the Tab Leaders field, click Dot or Line.

5. In the Tab Lines field, click On.

6. Click Apply; then click Close.

The Store Style Command

When you have put time and thought into complex formatting, you often want to use the same settings for other paragraphs in your document. The Store Style command located on the Edit menu enables you to transfer formatting from one paragraph to another.

In word processing, the word "style" refers to all the formatting features applied to a paragraph. A style can include information on font, character size, styles (bold, italic, and so on), and settings applied with the Ruler (tabs, indentation, and line spacing, for example). To transfer a style from one paragraph to another, follow these steps:

1. Locate the text cursor in a paragraph that contains the formatting you want to transfer.

2. Open the **E**dit menu and choose the command **S**tore Style.

3. Select the text you want to restyle. You can select a single paragraph or group of paragraphs.

4. Open the **E**dit menu again and choose **R**ecall Style. The program applies the formatting you stored with the Store Style command to the selected text.

GeoWrite stores information on the last style you "memorized," using the Store Style command. When you use the command again, you replace the previous information with new information.

Document Formatting

You have been working your way up the ladder of formatting, from commands that affect single words and characters to the paragraph commands. You are ready for document formatting commands like margin settings, headers and footers, columns, and page breaks.

Page Setup

The Page Setup command on the File menu opens the Page Setup dialog box, which controls the structure of your document (see fig. 7.15). Settings for page size and orientation, number of columns, and margins apply to every page of the document.

To change the page setup, follow these steps:

1. Open the **F**ile menu and choose P**a**ge Setup.

2. In the Page Size scrolling list, highlight the document size you want to use.

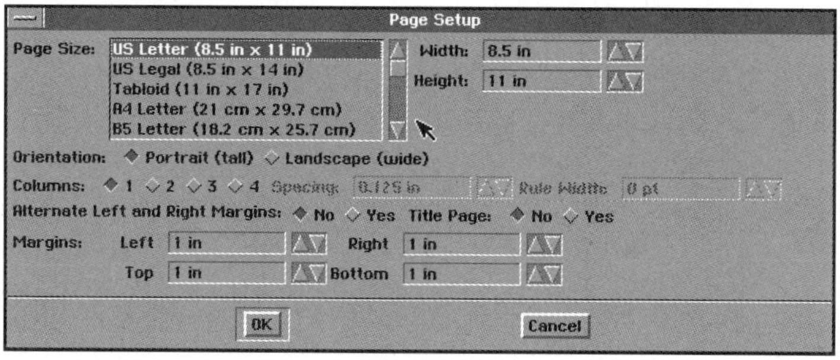

236

Fig. 7.15

The Page Setup dialog box.

3. Select a Portrait (tall) or Landscape (wide) orientation for your pages.

4. If you want to use columns, click the button for 1, 2, 3, or 4. You can change the default 1/8-inch spacing between columns from .125 inch to 1 inch. If you enter a rule width, a vertical rule separates your columns.

5. With alternate left and right margins, sometimes called *mirror* margins, you can create a wider margin that alternates from left to right page. If you activate this feature, the Left and Right margin text fields at the bottom of the dialog box change to Inside and Outside text fields. You want a wider margin, for example, if you print pages on three-hole punch paper. The inside margin must be wider to make room for the punch.

6. In GeoWrite, a title page is a page with no header, footer, or page number. If you want a title page at the front of your document, click the Yes button following Title Page. GeoWorks automatically inserts a title page at the front of your document.

7. Type a measurement or choose a margin with the arrow keys to set each of the four margins for all pages.

8. Click OK to accept your settings or Cancel to return to the default settings.

Headers and Footers

A header is information that appears at the top of every page. A footer appears at the bottom of every page. You commonly use headers and footers to display information, such as page numbers and chapter titles. If you scroll to the top or bottom of a page, you see the dotted outline of a 3/4-inch tall box reserved for the header or footer (see fig. 7.16).

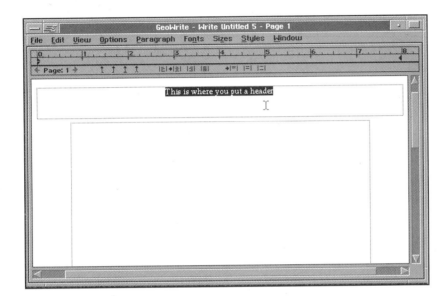

Fig. 7.16

The space reserved for a header.

When you enter the header or footer (usually on the first page) the header or footer appears on all pages except the title page. Enter text in headers and footers using standard GeoWrite techniques. You can cut, copy, and paste material into the header or footer. You can remove the header/footer areas by reducing the top and bottom margins so that no room for the header and footer exists.

To create or modify a header or footer, scroll to the top or bottom of the page and enter the text as you would normally.

If you have set up different right and left pages, you need to enter a header or footer on both a right page and a left page. If your printed copy shows a header and footer on only one page, you forgot to enter the header or footer on the mirror page.

Page Numbers

Headers and footers usually contain page numbers. GeoWrite includes a feature that, when inserted in a header or footer, automatically inserts page numbers on the printed pages.

To insert an automatic page number in a header or footer, follow these steps:

1. Place the text cursor in the header or footer where you want the page number to appear.

2. From the Fonts, Sizes, and Styles menus choose the commands to give the page number the appearance you want.

3. Open the Edit menu and choose the command Insert Page Number.

4. The automatic feature inserts only a number. If you want the word *Page* or other text to appear, enter it in the appropriate location.

The space for a header or footer is equal to the height of the top or bottom margin minus a 1/4-inch printing edge allowance. To increase or decrease the height of the header/footer area, increase or decrease the top and bottom margin by using the Page Setup command from the File menu.

Page Breaks

After you have created your document, you may find that automatic page breaks occur at awkward locations. Use the Reduced to 25% View on the View menu to preview breaks, so that you can see an entire page at once. Although the text is not legible, you can see the location of paragraph breaks and headings (see fig. 7.17).

To insert a page break, place the text cursor before the first word of the line you want at the top of the new page. Open the Edit menu and choose the command Insert Page Break to place a break just above the line containing the text cursor.

To delete a page break, position the text cursor before the first character at the top of the page created by the page break you want to remove and press the Backspace key.

Columns

You can create from one to four columns from the Page Setup menu. You can control the space between them and separate them with a vertical rule. The columns used in GeoWrite are called *snaking* columns because the text they contain goes to the bottom of one column and then *snakes* back to the top of the next column in a serpentine sequence, similar to a newspaper column (see fig. 7.18).

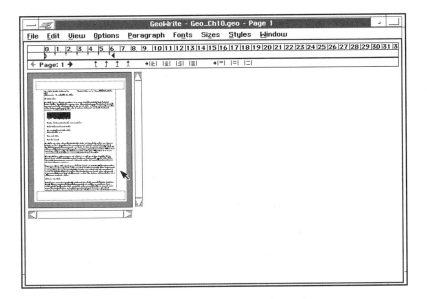

Fig. 7.17

Preview page breaks with the 25% view.

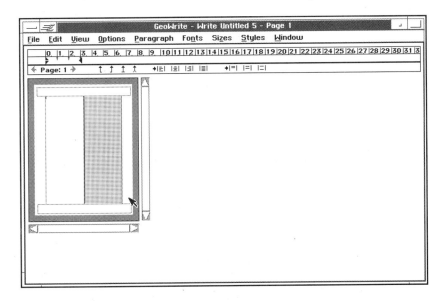

Fig. 7.18

A two-column page setup in 25% view.

To create multiple columns, use these steps:

1. Open the File menu and choose Page Setup.

2. In the Columns field of the Page Setup dialog box, click the number of columns you want to use. Choosing more than one column activates the Spacing and Rule Width text fields.

3. If you want to change the default 0.125-inch spacing between columns, enter a new measurement in the Spacing field.

4. If you want a vertical rule to appear between the columns type in a width between one and nine points. Setting the width to zero eliminates the rule.

5. Click OK to record your settings or Cancel to return to the default settings.

Column Breaks

A column break is simply a specialized page break. When you place a column break, the text below the break moves to the top of the next column.

To create a column break, position the text cursor before the first word on the line you want at the top of the next column. Open the Edit menu and choose the command Insert Page Break. GeoWorks inserts the break above the line that contains the text cursor.

To delete a column break, place the text cursor before the first letter at the top of the column that follows the break you want to remove. Press the Backspace key to delete the break.

T I P WordPerfect users might want to prepare their text in that program, save it as a DOS file, and then import the file to GeoWrite to take advantage of the terrific fonts, GeoDraw features, and printer capabilities. After using the Insert from text file command in GeoWrite, however, all the carriage returns and other tabs and indents inserted for formatting by WordPerfect still have to be deleted.

Instead of saving the text as a DOS file in WordPerfect, save it as a Generic File (CTRL-F5, 3-Save as, 1-Generic). All WordPerfect codes except tabs and indents are removed. The tabs and indents are recognized by GeoWrite. Remember, also, to set up the default font, size, tabs, margins, and so on, before using the Insert from text file command. Formatting will be much easier using this method, advises GWRepRandy.

Using the Spelling Checker

GeoWorks Pro and GeoWorks Ensemble, Version 1.2, include the new GeoWrite Spelling checker. This sophisticated tool contains a dictionary of over 100,000 words, as well as a user dictionary for words you may add. You can check whole documents, selected text, or individual words. The spelling checker suggests replacements for unknown words. You can set the spelling checker to skip correctly spelled words not found in its dictionaries. The spelling checker is a powerful and flexible writing assistant.

Starting a Spelling Check

The GeoWrite Edit menu contains the Check Spelling command. Choosing the command opens the Check spelling dialog box, shown in figure 7.19. You also can press the F5 function key, which is a shortcut to the same dialog box. Three buttons at the bottom of the dialog box control the quantity of text checked.

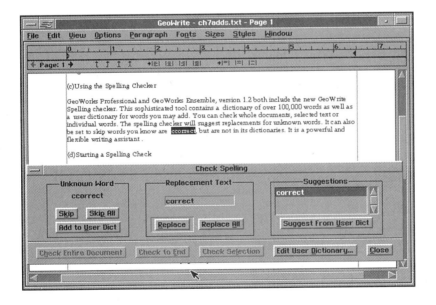

Fig. 7.19

The Check Spelling dialog box.

The Check Entire Document button checks all text. If you have text selected when you choose this command, the spelling checker checks the highlighted text only. The Check to End button checks spelling from the position of the text cursor to the end of the document. The Check Selection button checks any quantity of selected text.

Responding to Unknown Words

The spelling checker flags as an unknown word any word not found in the standard dictionary or user dictionary. A flagged word does not necessarily mean that you misspelled the word; it simply means that the spelling checker cannot find the word in its dictionaries. The program highlights the word and places it in the Unknown Word box for your response.

You can use one of the following three choices for handling the unknown word:

■ *Skip the word.* To skip the unknown word, choose the Skip or Skip All button. Skip jumps over the highlighted occurrence of the word but flags the word again if it appears elsewhere in the document. Skip All ignores any other occurrences of the word.

■ *Add the word to the dictionary.* To put the word in the user dictionary so that it will be checked in the future, choose the Add to User Dict button.

■ *Replace the word.* To replace the unknown word, you can type replacement text into the text box, or you can ask for suggested replacements by clicking the Suggest Spellings button. If you choose Suggest Spellings, the spelling checker prepares a list of words similar to the unknown word and puts the list in the scrolling suggestions box. When you highlight your choice, it appears in the replacement text box.

After you enter replacement text, choose Replace to replace the highlighted unknown word. To replace all instances of the unknown word, choose Replace All.

Customizing the Spelling Checker

The Add to User Dict button is a quick way to add a word to your user dictionary. To review or modify the contents of the user dictionary, choose the Edit User Dictionary button at the bottom of the Check Spelling dialog box. The dialog box shown in figure 7.20 appears. In the scrolling window, you can scroll through the list of User Dictionary entries and add or delete entries.

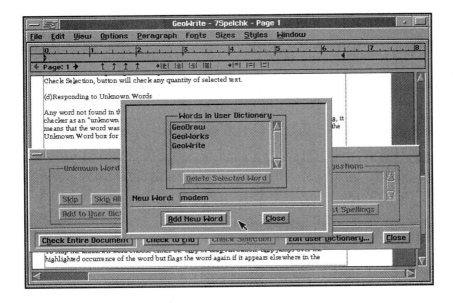

Fig. 7.20

The edit the User
Dictionary dialog box.

By opening the GeoWrite Options menu, you can find more commands
for customizing the spelling checker. Clicking the Spell Check Options
command opens the cascade menu shown in figure 7.21.

The three choices enable you to control the behavior of the spelling
checker as follows:

- *Automatically Suggest Spellings.* When turned on, this option displays a list of suggestions in the Suggestions list box each time the
  program finds an unknown word. You must weigh the convenience
  of an automatic display of suggestions needs against the short wait
  required while the program prepares a list. If you spell well, you
  may want to forego the list and enter your own replacements, using
  the Suggestions list only when needed.

- *Automatically Start Checking Selections.* This feature is the
  program's default. When you make a selection on the screen and
  start the spelling checker, the program immediately checks the
  selection. If you couple this speedy process with use of the F5 function key to start the spell checker, you can achieve rapid checking
  of selections.

- *Reset Skipped Words List When Spell Check Complete.* This command is on by default. When this command is on and you use the
  Skip All button, the program skips the unknown words until the
  current spelling check is complete. At this point, the spelling
  checker discards the list of words to skip. If you turn this command
  off, the program keeps the list of words to skip until you close
  GeoWrite, enabling you to check additional documents without
  having to manually skip the words in the list.

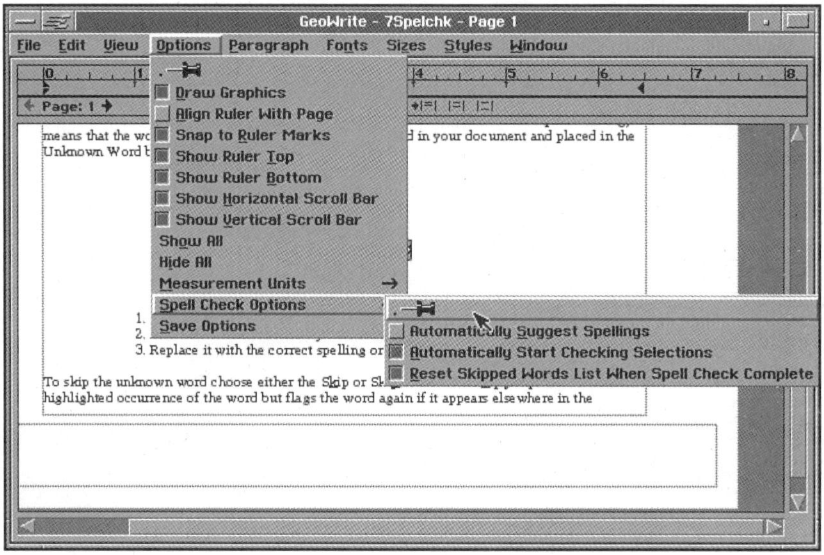

Fig. 7.21

The Spell Check
Options cascade
menu.

As you learn to use it, you will soon see why the spelling checker was the
most requested addition to early versions of GeoWorks Ensemble.

T I P

While fiddling with the spelling checker at 3 a.m. one morning,
I realized it could be used as a mini mail merge. Create and
save a basic merge document with the following text:

Name1
Address1
Address2

Dear Name2,

You owe me Amount1. Please mail it to me no later than Date1.

To begin "merging," use Save As to create a new document; then start
the spelling checker. As it encounters each of the unknown words,
type in your replacement. Filling in the blanks moves along quickly.
GWRep Rose suggests her mom would have loved this for her "generic" letters to the kids living away from home!

Completing Your Document

GeoWrite has some features not often found in word processors; it provides capabilities for applying color to text and creating halftone patterns for text, borders, and backgrounds. Although you can find the creation of reversed text (white on black) and the importing of graphics in some other word processors, GeoWrite handles these features with its characteristic elegance and simplicity.

Using Color

If you have a color printer, you can produce documents that accurately reflect colors on your screen. If you are confined to black and white printing, you can use color as a specialized annotation on your screen to help you locate important sections or to highlight editing changes.

You can apply color to text, to a paragraph background, and to a border. Although you apply color through different menu commands, the dialog box in figure 7.22 is identical from every menu, except for its title bar.

Place the text cursor in the paragraph where you want the border or background to change color, or select the text you want to color. To color a paragraph, open the **P**aragraph menu and choose the **P**aragraph Color command. To color a border, open the Paragraph menu, choose **B**order, and choose **B**order Color from the cascade menu that opens. To color text, select the text you want to color, open the **S**tyles menu and choose **T**ext Color.

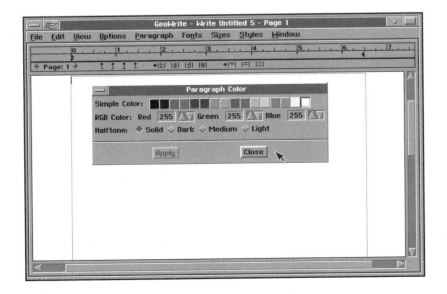

Fig. 7.22

The Paragraph Color dialog box.

The processes for applying color to paragraphs, borders, and text are identical. With the color dialog box open, apply color using these steps:

1. Click your color choice in the Simple Color field.

2. Click Apply to see the effect of the color. You can change and reapply colors until you are satisfied.

3. To modify a color, use the up and down arrows to vary the amount of red, green, and blue. You see the result in the document when you click Apply, but the Simple Color box in the dialog box does not change.

4. To lighten a color, click one of the four buttons in the Halftone field.

5. At any time during the coloring process, click Apply to see the current status of your color.

6. Click Close to exit the dialog box.

Using Reversed Text

If used with restraint, reversed text can be very effective. White text against a black background gets attention. Be careful that you don't get the text too small because it can be hard to read. Legibility depends on your printer. Reversed text uses GeoWrite's capability to change the paragraph background and text color (see fig. 7.23).

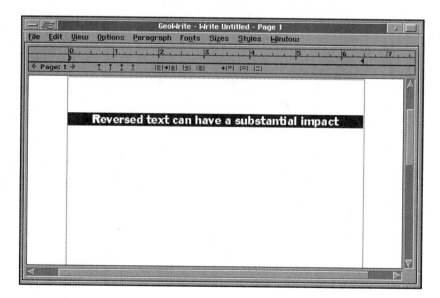

Fig. 7.23

A reversed text example.

To create reversed text follow these steps:

1. Drag the mouse to select the text you want reversed.

2. Open the **S**tyles menu and choose **T**ext Color.

3. Click the white color square in the Text Color dialog box, click the Apply button, and then click Close.

4. Open the **P**aragraph menu and choose the **P**aragraph Color command.

5. In the Paragraph Color dialog box, click the black color square, click Apply, and then click Close.

6. Click away from the paragraph to remove the initial selection.

Creating Paragraph Borders

Paragraph borders are a useful enhancement, easily applied with the Border command on the Paragraph menu. To apply a border, select one or more paragraphs to enclose with a border. Open the **P**aragraph menu, choose **B**order, and click your choice of border styles from the cascade menu. To remove a border, select **N**one.

With the Custom Borders selection, you can exercise more control over the border appearance. You can border only certain sides of a paragraph or control the border type or shadow location.

To customize a border use these steps:

1. Open the **P**aragraph menu and choose the **B**order command.

2. From the cascade menu that opens, choose **C**ustom Border. The dialog box shown in figure 7.24 appears.

Fig. 7.24

The Custom Border dialog box.

3. To change the sides of the paragraph on which a border appears, click the appropriate Sides to Border boxes.

4. To change the border width or the spacing between the border and text, type an entry or use the up and down arrows in the Border Width or Border Spacing text fields.

5. If you choose a shadow border by clicking the Shadow button, you can select the corner from which the shadow is cast by clicking one of the Shadow Anchor buttons.

6. If you choose a Double Line border by clicking its button, you can specify the space between the lines (in points) by typing an entry or using the up and down arrows.

7. Use the Apply button to inspect the effect of your choices. If the dialog box overlaps your border, use its Title bar to drag the box to a new location on the screen. When you are satisfied with the border, click Close to exit the dialog box.

Importing Graphics from GeoDraw

The compatibility of GeoWrite and GeoDraw enables the easy transfer of graphics into your documents. A copied graphic becomes, essentially, a large character. It moves with other text as you edit and you can cut, copy, and paste it within the document. You need to have both GeoWrite and GeoDraw open to transfer graphics (see fig. 7.25). If you are uncertain about using multiple application windows, consult Chapter 4, "Mastering GeoManager," for additional information.

Use these steps to transfer graphics from GeoDraw to GeoWrite:

1. Start GeoDraw by opening the Express menu, choosing Startup and clicking GeoDraw.

2. In GeoDraw, create or select a graphic, resize it if necessary, and use the Copy command to store it in memory.

   You must edit your graphic to the proper size in GeoDraw because you can not resize it in GeoWrite. See Chapter 8, "Using GeoDraw," for instructions.

3. Minimize the GeoDraw window to reveal the GeoWrite window behind it.

4. Position the text cursor in the GeoWrite window at the location where you want the graphic to appear.

5. Choose Paste to insert the graphic.

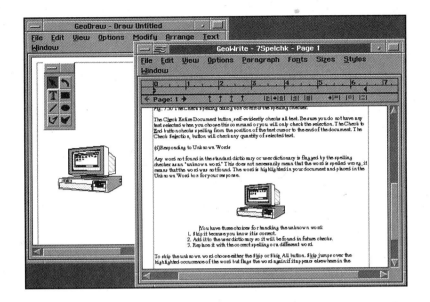

Fig. 7.25

GeoDraw and
GeoWrite windows
open to transfer a
graphic.

Printing With GeoWrite

Printing in GeoWrite is similar to printing throughout GeoWorks Pro. The
Printer Options dialog box shared by other applications makes printing
techniques easy to learn. The dialog box has option sets for the printer
and for the document (see fig. 7.26).

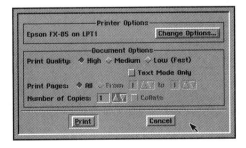

Fig. 7.26

The Printer Options
dialog box.

To set printer options for use with GeoWrite follow these steps:

1. Open the File menu and choose Print.

2. Click the Change Options button to open the dialog box shown in
   figure 7.27. The content may be different, depending on the printer
   you choose.

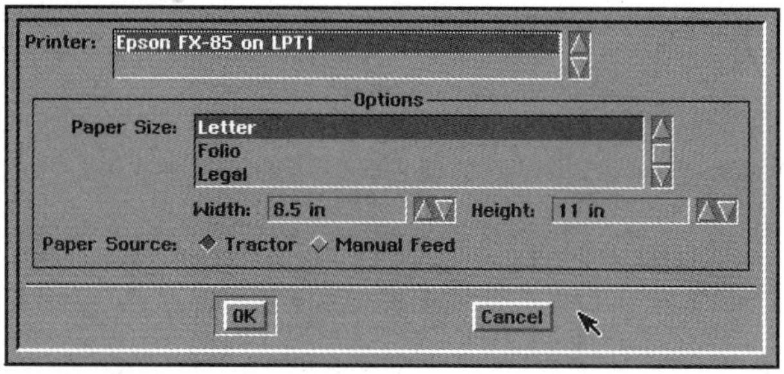

Fig. 7.27

The printer change
options dialog box.

3. To see the list of installed printers, click the up or down arrow to the right of the Printer list box.

4. To select a printer, click its name.

5. To select a paper size, scroll through the list of sizes in the Options rectangle and click your choice.

6. To specify a custom paper size, type the dimensions in the Width and Height fields.

7. Specify Tractor or Manual paper feed depending on your printer.

8. Click OK to save your settings and return to the Print dialog box.

After you have changed printer options, use the following steps to set printing options for your document.

1. In the Print dialog box, click the print quality you prefer. Higher quality means longer print times.

2. To use the fonts built into your printer, click Text Mode Only. Because this command uses your printer's internal fonts, your printed output may not look like your screen image. You may want to limit its use to draft printing, which is faster.

3. If you want to print selected pages, click the From button to activate the two text fields in which you can specify page numbers by typing them or clicking the up and down arrows.

4. Enter the number of copies you want.

5. Click the Collate command to print multiple copies of your document one copy at a time. This process slows down printing on laser printers.

6. Choose **P**rint to begin printing.

> **T I P** GeoWrite printing problems often have to do with mismatched page size designations. The two places to designate the page size must match. One is in the GeoWrite Page Setup dialog box and the other is when you choose the Change Options button at the top of the Print dialog box.
>
> If strange things happen while printing, check to see that the two settings match. If they mismatch, not-so-funny things happen. If the printer page is set smaller than the word processor page size setting, the print spooler will break the word processor page into multiple printer pages. If the printer page is larger than the word processor page, then the print spooler will center the document on the printed page, according to GWRepRandy.

Managing Files

The File menu contains commands for saving your GeoWrite files. You may notice that your mouse pointer periodically takes on the shape of an hourglass for a moment without your bidding, and then returns to the arrow shape. During those moments GeoWorks is saving automatically while you are creating a GeoWrite file. If you suffer a power failure or some other computer problem, you can retrieve a copy of your work as it was up to the last automatic save.

Use the **Revert** command on the **File** to jettison the temporary backup file created by the automatic save feature and revert to the last version created using the **Save** or Save **As** command.

To save a GeoWrite document, use these steps:

1. Open the **File** menu and choose **Save.**

2. If you have previously saved this file, GeoWorks saves it immediately, presenting no dialog box.

3. If you have not previously saved the file, the save as dialog box (see fig. 7.28) appears.

4. Move to the directory where you want to save the document.

5. Type the document name in the New name text box.

6. Choose **S**ave to save the file.

You can use the preceding "save as" steps to change the name or location of a GeoWrite file that you have previously saved.

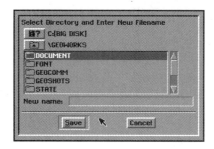

Exporting and Importing Documents

Non-GEOS applications cannot read GeoWorks Pro files in their *native* form. GeoWrite has a command that you can use to export your file in a simple, unformatted style known by the acronym *ASCII* (pronounced "askey"). A wide variety of DOS programs can read an ASCII file. You lose some of the fonts and formatting in your GeoWrite file, but the text comes through accurately.

To export a file in ASCII form, follow these steps:

1. Open the File menu and choose Save as Text File.

2. Specify the desired drive or directory.

3. Give the file a DOS file name (from one to eight characters) and the extension TXT, which typically identifies the file as an ASCII file.

4. Click the Save button.

To import a file in ASCII form, follow these steps:

1. Open a new file in GeoWrite.

2. Open the File menu and choose Insert from Text File.

3. Locate the ASCII file, using the scrolling list and drive/directory buttons.

4. Highlight the file name and click the Insert button to load the file.

> **T I P**
>
> If you hate the way imported ASCII text looks in GeoWrite because columns don't line up correctly, there's an easy solution, advises GWRepRandy. Select the URW Mono font before using the Insert from text file command. In this monospaced font, every character takes the same width. Your imported lines will align beautifully.

Chapter Summary

Chapter 7 explores the range of GeoWrite, its components, and basic techniques for entering and editing text. After the basics, you learned the various commands for formatting characters, paragraphs, and whole documents. The chapter concludes with short sections on printing, file management, and exporting and importing documents.

GeoDraw

I n this quick-start tutorial, you create a logo for an imaginary company using the tools in GeoDraw. After spending approximately 45 minutes learning the basics of GeoDraw, you should be able to use the program for basic drawing and to develop your skills to the degree that your interest and talent warrant.

The instructions in this session assume that you know the basic techniques for manipulating a GeoWorks Pro window and how to use menus and icons. If you need a review of these topics, refer to Chapter 4, "Mastering GeoManager," and Quick Start I, "GeoManager."

Quickstarts like this one emphasize hands-on practice and do not cover every feature of an application. Full coverage of GeoDraw is in Chapter 8, "Using GeoDraw."

Starting GeoDraw

To begin the lesson, start GeoDraw from GeoManager. Use these steps to open the program:

1. Start GeoManager and display the WORLD directory window (see fig. V.1).

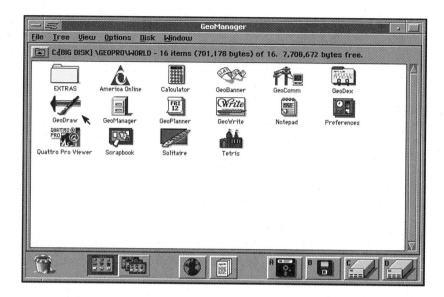

Fig. V.1

GeoDraw started from
the WORLD directory.

2. Double-click the GeoDraw icon, which looks like a paint brush
   crossing a T-square, to open the GeoDraw window (see fig. V.2).

   Generally, GeoDraw opens displaying a blank document. The Title
   bar reads GeoDraw-Draw Untitled. ***Note:*** If you need to open
   a blank document, select the **F**ile Menu and choose the **N**ew
   command.

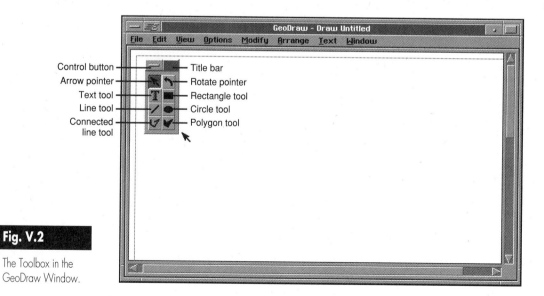

Fig. V.2

The Toolbox in the
GeoDraw Window.

Starting the Logo

In this quickstart, you create a logo for Apex Air, an imaginary commuter airline. Figure V.3 shows the completed logo. You start with basic shapes, add text, and enhance the logo with colored fills.

Fig. V.3

The Apex Air logo.

If you do not have a color monitor, you can use GeoDraw's palette of patterns instead of the palette of colors. If you have a monochrome system, when the instructions for creating the logo call for you to apply color, choose a pattern instead.

Because of the variation in displays, precise measurements for each element of the logo are impossible. Use your eyeball and the step-by-step illustrations to approximate the logo. Don't worry, that's what "artistic license" is for!

Drawing a Rectangle

You draw the elements of the logo on different parts of the page and then bring them together. Your first step is to draw the rectangle that forms the background for the logo. Create the rectangle in the lower right area of the screen (see fig. V.4) using the following steps:

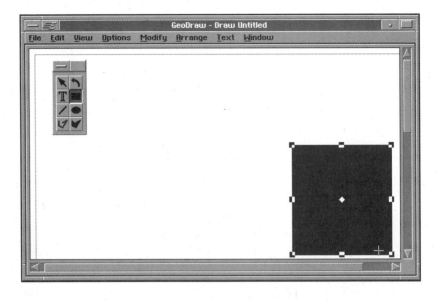

Fig. V.4

The background rectangle.

1. Click the Rectangle tool in the Toolbox. The pointer changes to a cross hair drawing tool.

2. Open the **View** menu; if **A**ctual Size is not selected, click it.

3. Visualize the rectangle you want to draw. Position the cross hairs at the top left corner of your undrawn rectangle.

4. Holding down the left mouse button, drag the cross hairs diagonally toward the lower right corner of the rectangle you envision. A dotted outline shows you the rectangle you are creating.

5. When the rectangle is the proper size, release the mouse button. The program draws the rectangle with its "handles," small squares you will use later for manipulating the drawing.

6. If the rectangle does not satisfy you, press the Del key; then redraw the rectangle. Don't worry about the fill color at this point.

7. When the rectangle is correct, click a clear area to remove the handles from the rectangle.

Drawing the Circle

Next, you draw the circle that represents the sun in your Apex Air logo. The Circle tool works like the Rectangle tool. You hold down the mouse button while dragging the cross hairs. A dotted outline of the circle forms. When you release the button, the program draws the circle. Follow these steps to draw the circle:

1. Open the **O**ptions menu and click Drag as **O**utline if it is not selected already. This feature enables you to see the actual shape of
   your circle.

2. Click the Circle tool in the Toolbox. The pointer changes to the
   cross hairs drawing tool.

3. Place the circle in the lower left of the page. You will move the
   circle into position later. Visualize the circle you want to draw and
   position the cross hairs at one edge.

4. Holding down the left mouse button, drag the cross hairs diagonally toward the opposite side of the circle you envision. A dotted
   outline shows you the shape you are creating. Refer to figure V.5
   for guidance.

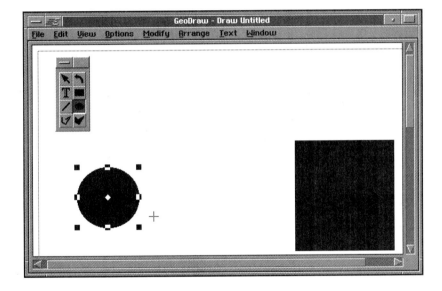

Fig. V.5

The logo circle.

5. When the circle is the proper size, release the mouse button. The
   circle appears with its handles (see fig. V.5).

6. If you need to resize or reshape the circle, click the Arrow pointer
   tool and then drag one of the corner handles of the circle to reshape or resize it.

Drawing the Logo Line

The straight line below the Apex Airline name provides emphasis. You
change the thickness and color of the line later; for now, to draw a line
follow these steps:

1. Click the Line tool in the Toolbox. The pointer changes to a cross hair drawing tool.

2. You want to draw a line about three-quarters of the width of the rectangle. Position the cross hairs in the unused area of the screen above the rectangle.

3. Holding down the left mouse button, drag the mouse to draw the line.

4. When the line is complete, release the mouse button. The line, with handles, appears (see fig. V.6).

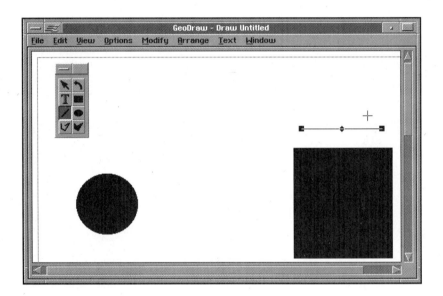

Fig. V.6

The Line tool to draw the logo line.

Creating the Triangle

You use the Polygon tool to create the triangle for the logo, making use of the fact that the figure automatically closes when you double-click the last point. The triangle should have sides of equal length and should be about two-thirds the width of the logo rectangle.

To create the triangle, follow these steps:

1. Click the Polygon tool in the Toolbox. The pointer changes to the drawing cross hairs.

2. Starting in an empty screen area big enough to contain your triangle, click the cross hairs to anchor the top of the triangle.

3. Move the cross hairs down and to the right at about sixty degrees to create the first side of the triangle. Check figure V.3 if you need a reference. Click once to anchor the first side.

4. Move the cross hairs horizontally to create a second side of the triangle, which is the same length as the first. Do not click the mouse button yet.

5. The Polygon tool closes and fills your triangle when you double-click. Double-click now to complete the second and third sides of the rectangle and fill the shape.

Entering the Text

For a completed logo, you need only to create the name *Apex Air*. The words you type will not be the final font or size, because this tutorial quickstart treats the enhancement of the font properties as separate steps.

To enter the logo text, follow these steps:

1. Click the Text tool in the Toolbox. The mouse pointer changes to an I-beam shape.

2. To create a standard three-inch long text block, move the I-beam to a vacant area of the screen and click the left mouse button one time.

3. Type **Apex Air**. Use the Backspace or Del key to correct errors.

Figure V.7 shows all the parts of the logo on the screen ready for assembling.

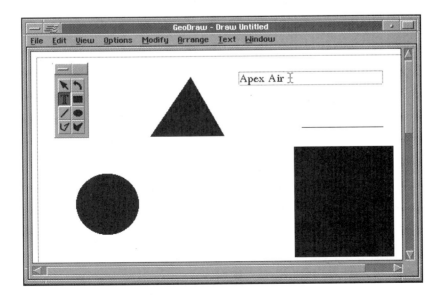

Fig. V.7

All the elements of the Apex Air logo.

Saving the Logo

You have a lot of work invested in your Apex Air logo. The time is right to save, ensuring that if you have a computer failure or a power interruption, your work on the logo will be safe.

To save the logo, use these steps:

1. Open the **File** menu and choose the **S**ave command.

2. Because you have not previously saved the file, the save as dialog box (see fig. V.8) appears.

3. Save the document in the default directory suggested in the dialog box.

4. Type the name **apexlogo** in the New name text field.

5. Click **S**ave to save the file.

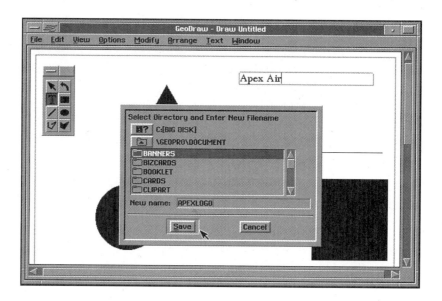

Fig. V.8

The save as dialog box.

Editing the Logo

Now you begin to modify the properties of the various logo elements in preparation for assembling them in the final section. As you gain more experience with GeoDraw, you will combine several techniques in creating an illustration. In the last step, for example, where you typed the words Apex Air, you could choose a font, size, and color in advance and then type the text in position on the logo box. Here, the steps are separate to make them easier to learn and practice.

GeoWorks has three separate properties boxes for lines, areas, and text. You work with them individually for this exercise, although you will find the boxes are similar in their content and behavior.

Changing Line Properties

In this section, you put some weight and color into the line that goes below the Apex Air name. Although you won't make use of the fact in this exercise, remember that line properties are not the only objects drawn with the Line tool or the Connected Line tool. Circles, rectangles, and polygons all have lines at their edges. You can change these lines independently of the interior fill. In other words, you can have a red circle with a blue line as its border.

To use the Line Properties tools, follow these steps:

1. Click the Arrow pointer in the Toolbox.

2. Click the line you drew so that its handles appear.

3. Open the **Modify** menu and choose the **Line** Properties command. The Line Properties dialog box appears (see fig. V.9).

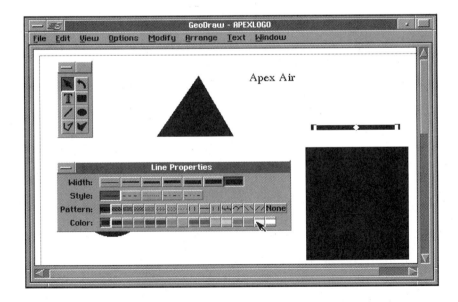

Fig. V.9

The Line Properties dialog box.

4. On the Width line, click the button with the widest line.

5. Because you do not change the style or pattern, skip the next two lines in the dialog box.

6. Click the color button for yellow.

   You should see a thick yellow line on-screen.

7. Double-click the control button in the upper left corner of the Line Properties box and choose **C**lose.

Applying Area Properties

The logo has three objects with fills (circle, triangle, and rectangle). You change them using the Area Properties box. In this case, you are applying fill properties after you draw the objects; however, you can apply properties before you start drawing. If, for example, you choose a red fill before you start drawing a rectangle, the rectangle fills with red as you draw it.

To change the area properties of the logo objects, use these steps:

1. Click the Arrow pointer in the Toolbox.

2. Click the triangle to select it.

3. Select the **M**odify menu and choose the **A**rea Properties command. The dialog box shown in figure V.10 opens.

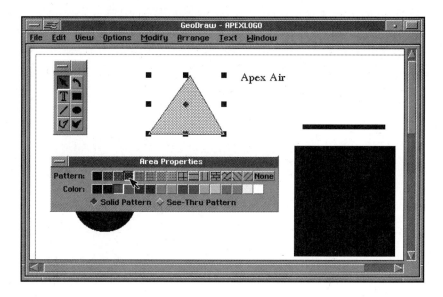

4. Click the dark green square to change the triangle fill to green.

5. Click a medium pattern (fourth from the left) in the pattern list.

6. If Solid Pattern is not selected, click its button.

Repeat steps two through six with the following changes:

1. Select the circle instead of the rectangle.

2. Fill the circle with solid red. Use the solid pattern at the far left of the pattern buttons.

3. Leave the rectangle filled with solid black.

4. Double-click the control button in the upper left of the Area Properties box and choose **Close**.

Modifying the Text

Next, you prepare the text by changing its font, size, and color. The process is similar to those steps you have taken for the shapes and lines, but be prepared for one unexpected effect: you are going to make the text white, and when you create white text on a white background, the text becomes invisible.

First, change the font and font size.

1. Click the text block to select the words Apex Air.

2. From the **Text** menu choose the **Fonts** command.

3. Click the Superb button in the cascade menu.

4. Select **Text** and choose **Sizes**.

5. In the menu that opens, click 24 points. If the size does not fit the logo you have drawn, choose another size to produce a text line approximately the length of one side of the triangle.

6. Drag the handle at the right end of the text block toward the left to eliminate the unused space in the box. Do not go too far, or Apex Air will become two lines. If you get two lines, widen the block a bit.

Now that the text is the right font and size, you are ready to color it white.

To apply text properties, use these steps:

1. If necessary, click the Arrow pointer in the Toolbox.

2. Click the text so that its handles show.

3. Open the **Modify** menu and choose the **Text Properties** command to open the Text Properties dialog box (see fig. V.11).

4. Click the properties box showing white text. The text on-screen seems to disappear.

266

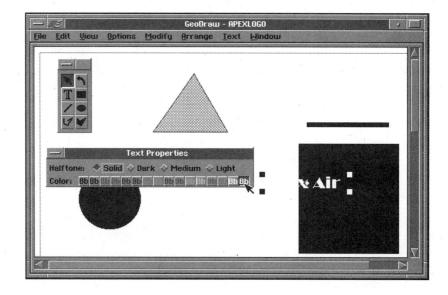

Fig. V.11

The Text Properties
dialog box.

5. Double-click the control button in the upper left of the Text Properties box and choose **C**lose.

You can locate the text by clicking in its vicinity with the pointer or
by drawing a selection rectangle around the area (drag the pointer
tool with the left button down). The handles for the "invisible" object should appear so that you can drag it onto a contrasting background where you can see it again.

Completing the Logo

In this section, you bring all the parts together and stack them as necessary to produce the logo. When you have the parts assembled, you fuse
them into a single object that you can handle without displacing the
individual parts.

Assembling the Parts

1. Click the Arrow pointer in the Toolbox.

2. Click the circle to display its handles.

3. Click the diamond-shaped move handle in the center of the shape
and, holding down the left mouse button drag the circle into the
upper part of the black rectangle (refer to fig. V.12).

4. Drag the triangle, text, and line into place using the same technique described in step 3.

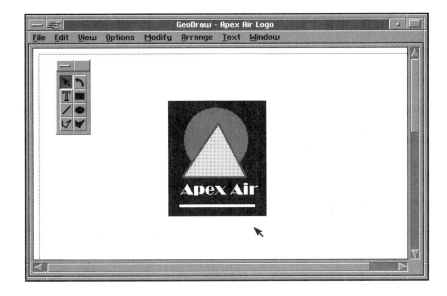

Fig. V.12

The logo pieces in place.

Fusing Objects

Five carefully aligned objects currently comprise the logo. If you wanted to move the logo, you would have to use care to select every item and to avoid displacing any part of the assembly. You can avoid this problem by fusing the logo into a single object that stays together unless you purposely defuse it.

To fuse the logo into a single object, use these steps:

1. If necessary, click the Toolbox to select the Arrow pointer.

2. Select the objects you want to fuse by opening the **E**dit menu and choosing **S**elect All.

3. If all objects are not selected, your selection rectangle was not large enough. Draw the rectangle again (see step 2), large enough to include all the objects and their handles.

4. Open the **E**dit menu and chose the command **F**use Objects. The multiple handles become one set of handles.

The individual elements of a fused object cannot be edited unless you defuse the object. You then can make changes and fuse the object again.

Printing the Logo

Your final step is to print your logo. The colors will be interpreted as shades of gray. Use the highest quality printing available so that you can get a feeling for the quality that GeoDraw can produce. The printing procedure is quite similar to other printing in GeoWorks Pro.

To print your document, use these steps:

1. Save the document to protect it if any problem develops during printing.

2. Open the **File** menu and choose the **Print** command. The print dialog box opens (see fig. V.13).

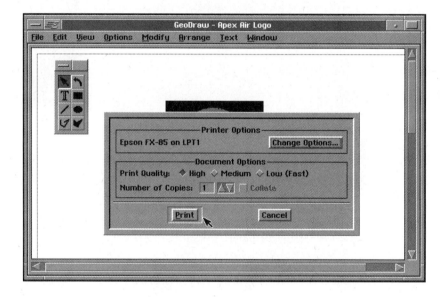

3. If you need to change printer or paper size, click the Change Options button and make the necessary changes in the dialog box that appears.

4. Click the High button for best quality printing. **Note:** Be prepared to wait five or ten minutes for a dot matrix printer to produce the image.

5. Choose **Print** to proceed.

Congratulations! You have used most of the major tools and techniques needed to work with GeoDraw. Chapter 8, "Using GeoDraw," fills in the remaining details. You also may enjoy and learn from working with the GeoDraw templates furnished with GeoWorks Pro. Open the folders in the DOCUMENT directory and look for the GeoDraw document icon to identify these files.

Using GeoDraw

GeoDraw is an important part of GeoWorks Pro. With GeoDraw, you can enhance documents created with a variety of applications. The shared "umbrella" of PC/GEOS enables you easily to cut and paste between documents. You can use illustrations created with or imported through GeoDraw wherever a bit of visual interest can make a document more effective.

GeoDraw is also fun to use. All of us have a creative streak, and the shapes and colors of GeoDraw can help us express some of that creativity, whether for personal pleasure or for business communication. GeoDraw's capability to manipulate text and illustrations is equal to some simpler desktop publishing packages. With patience you can create remarkably sophisticated documents.

You have the potential to enhance, with GeoDraw, whatever work you do with GeoWorks Pro. The power of pictures to communicate is well known, and the business of GeoDraw is pictures. Like other GeoWorks Pro applications, GeoDraw hides formidable power beneath an approachable exterior that shares features with other parts of the GeoWorks package. If you have begun to work with GeoDraw you already know how to use many of its text-handling features. The File, Edit, and Window menus are similar to those same menus in other GeoWorks Pro applications.

Basic drawing with GeoDraw is simple and enjoyable. The drawing tools enable you to create and modify any image your drawing skill can handle. If you aren't the world's best artist, you can import or modify clip art from a huge variety of sources. When you use GeoDraw, your letters, reports, and memos have the added impact that even small graphic touches can provide.

Some of the major features you discover in GeoDraw include the following:

- A toolbox with five different drawing tools
- Powerful features to add and manipulate text
- Techniques to move, rotate, flip, and stack objects
- Specialized dialog boxes for changing the properties of areas, lines, and text
- Full use of color (if your system supports it)

Touring GeoDraw

Think of GeoDraw as your artist's tool kit. In this section, you open the kit and—before plunging into your first masterpiece—look at the pieces included. You learn how to start the program, examine the main features (including the Toolbox) of the GeoDraw window, and explore the structure of the menu. You also learn about commands that control your view of the screen. At the end of this section, you will be ready to begin an illustration.

Starting GeoDraw

As with all GeoWorks Pro applications, GeoDraw appears as an icon in the GeoManager WORLD view. You can start GeoDraw from the Express menu, available in any active window. You also can double-click a GeoDraw document to start the application. Each of these techniques can be useful at different times.

Launching GeoDraw from GeoManager is appropriate if you typically start your GeoWorks Pro work session from GeoManager. When you open GeoManager, GeoWorks displays the WORLD directory window. Within this window, the GeoDraw icon looks like a paint brush crossing a T-square, as shown in figure 8.1. Double-click the GeoDraw icon to open the GeoDraw window shown in figure 8.2.

Fig. 8.1

The GeoDraw icon in
the WORLD directory.

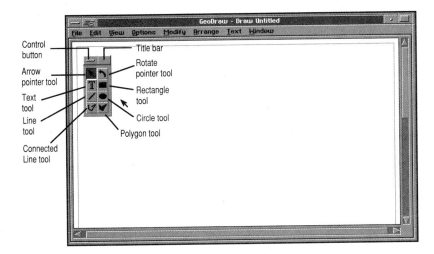

Control
button

Arrow
pointer tool

Text
tool

Line
tool

Connected
Line tool

Title bar

Rotate
pointer tool

Rectangle
tool

Circle tool

Polygon tool

Fig. 8.2

The GeoDraw
Window.

If the WORLD window is not open or if you are using another GeoWorks
Pro application and want to switch to GeoDraw, you must use the Express menu, which looks like a stylized letter E. This menu is available in
the upper left corner of any active application window and provides a
handy way to start GeoDraw.

To start GeoDraw from the Express menu, click the stylized E. When the
Express menu opens, choose the Startup menu command. The cascade
menu that lists the GeoWorks Pro applications opens (see fig. 8.3). From
the cascade menu, click GeoDraw to launch the program.

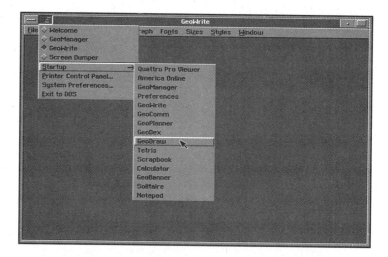

Fig. 8.3

The Startup cascade menu.

The third method of launching GeoDraw involves starting with a GeoDraw document. A distinctive icon represents each type of GeoWorks Pro file. Figure 8.4 shows the DOCUMENT directory window, for example. Three of the icons that represent files resemble a stack of papers with geometric shapes on the top sheet. The names of the files in this example are Area Test, Draw Untitled, and New Drawing. Anytime you open a window containing GeoDraw files, this icon represents the files.

If you double-click the icon representing a GeoDraw file, the GeoDraw application loads the document represented by the icon you double-clicked.

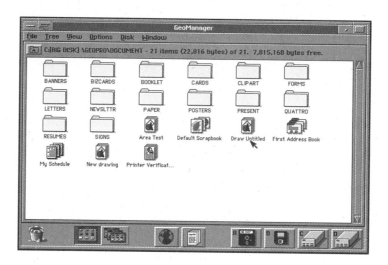

Fig. 8.4

A GeoDraw icon in the DOCUMENT window.

Understanding GeoDraw Window and Menus

The GeoDraw window is similar to other GeoWorks Pro application windows. The Title bar at the top center shows the application name and the name of the open file. The Express menu enables you to open other applications or exit to DOS. The Control button at the upper left contains commands that enable you to move and size the window.

Scroll bars at the bottom and right sides enable you to view documents larger than the window. The *Maximize/Restore* button at the upper right switches between a *maximized* window that fills the entire screen, and a *standard* window that can be moved and resized. The *Minimize* button reduces the window to an icon at the lower left corner of the screen.

New in the GeoDraw window is the Toolbox (see fig. 8.5). This small floating menu contains tools for drawing and for selecting and manipulating existing objects—tools that enable you to draw lines, connected lines, rectangles, circles, and polygons. The two arrow tools at the top of the Toolbox enable you to choose and rotate objects.

The Toolbox also has a Control button in its upper right corner. You can double-click the button to remove the Toolbox from the GeoDraw window. The **S**how Tool Box command from the **O**ptions menu returns the Toolbox to the screen. You also can place the mouse pointer in the Toolbox's Title bar and drag the Toolbox to any convenient on-screen location.

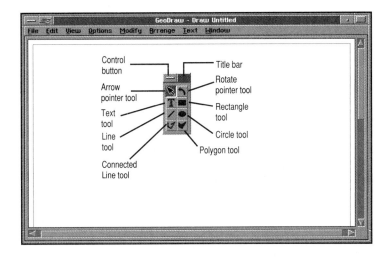

Fig. 8.5

The GeoDraw Toolbox.

The main portion of the GeoDraw window shows the document. Dotted lines define areas for illustration. Four predefined sizes are available in both portrait (vertical) and landscape (horizontal) positions. You frequently may use the scroll bars to move your field of view and the differing view sizes to zoom in and out on various parts of your document as you work.

GeoDraw has an extensive command system containing eight menus. Table 8.1 describes the menus. A later section in this chapter discusses the commands in each menu.

Table 8.1 The GeoDraw Menus

Menu Name	General Purpose
File	Controls creating, opening, and saving files; accesses Print and Import dialog boxes
Edit	Contains Cut, Copy, and Paste commands; *fuses* (joins) and *defuses* objects
View	Reduces or enlarges page image; manages aspect ratio on some computers
Options	Controls presence of Toolbox and appearance of dragged objects
Modify	Contains Nudge, Rotate, and Flip commands; gives access to properties dialog boxes
Arrange	Modifies stacking of objects
Text	Contains cascade menus for fonts, sizes, styles, and justification
Window	Switches between open documents; provides multiple or single-page display

Understanding Screen Controls

When you are drawing, sometimes you need to step back and get the big picture; other times you need to get right on top of the details. GeoDraw anticipates this need by providing an exceptionally wide range of screen reduction and magnification options. Using controls on the View menu, you can move from 12 1/2 percent of normal size to 400 percent normal size, with four stops in between (see fig. 8.6).

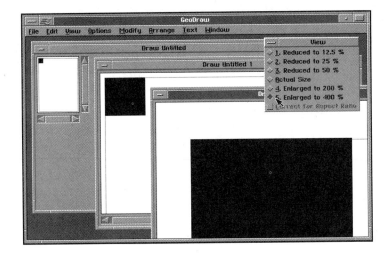

Fig. 8.6

The View menu.

Figure 8.6 gives you an idea of the range of possible view sizes, display-ing three views of a square, with an actual size of about one inch, in the upper left corner of a document. The back view, at 12 1/2 percent, shows a tiny rectangle and the entire 8 1/2-by-11-inch page behind the rect-angle. The middle view is at actual size, and the top view is at 400% magnification.

Understanding Full-Sized and Overlapping Windows

GeoWorks enables you to have several windows open at one time, and you use the Window menu to choose a view of the windows. The Win-dow menu has just two commands: Overlapping and Full-Sized.

The *Full-Sized* command produces the default presentation in which the stacked windows are on top of one another. Although you can have sev-eral windows open at one time, you see only the top window of the stack in Full-Sized view. To determine what other windows are in the stack, open the Window menu, which contains a list of the documents that are open. To bring a window to the top of the stack, click the button next to the window's name.

When you choose the *Overlapping* command, GeoDraw presents all ac-tive windows in an overlapping display similar to figure 8.6. You can resize and drag the overlapping windows so that you can cut and paste from one window to another or compare two windows.

Although you can cut, paste, and compare with the windows stacked via the Full-Sized command, flipping back and forth through the Windows menu is much less convenient than seeing several windows simultaneously, as you do with the Overlapping command.

Understanding Aspect Ratio Control

NOTE   You may not need to read these paragraphs. Open the View menu and look at the Correct for Aspect Ratio command at the bottom. If the command is grayed, your monitor does not have an aspect ratio problem. You can skip to the next section. If the command is available, read on.

Small dots called *pixels* make up the on-screen image. Some older computers, with CGA and Hercules displays particularly, have rectangular pixels instead of the square pixels that the more recent EGA and VGA screen displays use. If you display an image designed for square pixels on a screen that uses rectangular pixels, the image is elongated vertically and does not resemble its printed version.

The Correct for Aspect Ratio command on the View menu compensates for rectangular pixels. *Aspect ratio*, a term that describes the distortion caused by rectangular pixels, is the relationship of height to width.

To use the Correct for Aspect Ratio command, click the check box for the command and see if the screen more closely resembles printed output. To turn off the command, choose Correct for Aspect Ratio again. Using the command slows down screen drawing. You may want to turn on the Correct for Aspect Ratio command only when precisely judging the proportions of the screen image is important.

Starting an Illustration

Drawing programs can be intimidating to people who aren't professional artists. That empty white space on-screen seems so promising until you take the first steps. If you feel discouraged by your first clumsy attempts, you have a great deal of company. The following list offers some solutions that enable you to create impressive designs without a great deal of expertise:

■ *Let an artist do the drawing.* Clip art illustrations that you can buy and use for your own purposes are widely available. GeoDraw comes with a Clip Art folder that has samples for use or practice. Figure 8.7 shows some samples from the Clip Art folder.

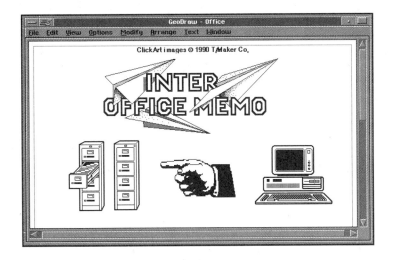

Fig. 8.7

Clip art samples.

- *Use a scanner. Scanners* are devices that convert pictures into electronic files that can be used on your computer. Scanners are moderately expensive, but you also can rent scanner time at a local typographic service bureau. You can scan any sort of picture or photograph, import it into GeoDraw, and modify it to suit your needs.

  Scanned images often are saved in a format called TIFF. Because the files can become quite large, you need a substantial amount of storage space and memory in your computer to work with scanned images. In addition, you must learn a fair amount about the scanner before you can use it effectively; however, if you need to convert existing art to electronic art, no substitute for the scanner exists.

- *Draw with simple shapes.* Confine your early illustrations to basic geometric shapes. GeoDraw provides tools that help you create and apply color and texture to rectangles, circles, and polygons (*polygon* means many-sided). You can make very effective drawings by sticking to simple, yet powerful, shapes, textures, and colors.

NOTE If you use art from other sources, be it clip art or scanned images, be sure that you do not violate copyright laws.

Opening an Existing GeoDraw Illustration

Bringing one of the GeoDraw templates furnished with GeoWorks Pro into GeoDraw is often the most effective way to start a complex project.

GeoDraw recognizes files in its own format and lists these files when you open the File Open dialog box.

To open an existing GeoDraw document, choose **O**pen from the **F**ile menu. The dialog box shown in figure 8.8 appears. Within the dialog box, only GeoDraw files appear on the filtered list of available files. Figure 8.8 shows the GeoDraw files Draw Untitled and New Drawing, which are in the DOCUMENT directory, for example.

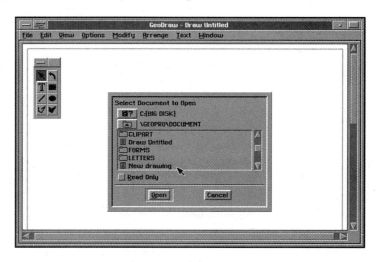

Fig. 8.8

The open document dialog box.

To view the files in other directories, move up the directory tree by clicking the folder icon containing an upward-pointing arrow symbol. You can open a directory by double-clicking the directory name. You open a file by double-clicking the file name. The file opens in its own window.

If you need instruction or a refresher on using directories, review the directories section of Chapter 4, "Mastering GeoManager."

Importing TIFF or PCX Images

TIFF and *PCX* are acronyms used to identify two major DOS file types that store images. GeoDraw recognizes both types of files. By using TIFF and PCX, you have access to a very wide range of images from a large number of DOS graphics programs. Importing a Quattro Pro EPS image is a special case covered in Chapter 15, "Using Quattro Pro Viewer."

To import a TIFF or PCX file, follow these steps:

1. Choose the **Import** command from the **File** menu.

   The dialog box shown in figure 8.9 opens.

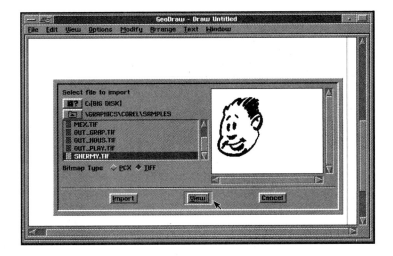

Fig. 8.9

The import dialog box.

2. Choose the **TIFF** or **PCX** button to indicate which type of file you want to locate.

   The choice sets a filter enabling you to see only the selected type of file in the directory box.

3. Locate the TIFF or PCX file you want to import. Be sure that you have clicked the filter button for the right file type (TIFF or PCX).

   Use the button with the icon of a disk to change drives if necessary. Use the button showing a folder with an up arrow to move up the directory tree.

4. To preview the file, choose the **View** button.

   The image appears in the small window to the right of the dialog box. Use the scroll bars to see hidden portions of the image. Previewing the file is optional.

5. Double-click the file name or click the **Import** button to import the file into the current GeoDraw document.

282

Opening New GeoDraw Files

Opening a new GeoDraw file when you need a blank canvas for your work is easy. Start GeoDraw from the Express menu, open the **F**ile menu, and choose **N**ew. Because opening new files is so easy, you may want to experiment with a feature available with most GeoWorks Pro applications, but particularly useful in GeoDraw: opening multiple windows. To open another window, select the **F**ile menu and choose **N**ew. Unless you have drawn something, the screen looks the same as it did before you opened the new window; however, when you inspect the Title bar you can see the change: if you haven't given the file a name, you see the name Draw Untitled 1.

Open the **W**indow menu and notice the two windows listed at the bottom of the menu. Choose the **O**verlapping command to move and resize your two windows so that you can cut and paste between them as shown in figure 8.10.

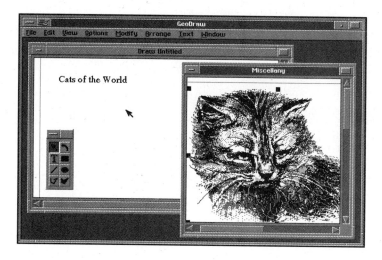

Fig. 8.10

Working between windows.

To move a window, drag the window by its Title bar. To resize the window, place your mouse pointer at the window border; the pointer changes shape to an arrow above a bar. While holding down the left mouse button, drag the border to resize the window.

Using GeoDraw Tools

The GeoDraw tools are the equivalent of a painter's brushes. You use the tools to create and revise your illustrations (see fig. 8.11). When you start to work with the tools, you may feel awkward, particularly if you are new to the mouse. If you get frustrated, ask yourself if you would expect to pick up real paints and brushes and be immediately productive. Be kind to yourself. Enjoy experimenting with GeoDraw. Before long, you may find yourself depending regularly on GeoDraw to enhance your documents.

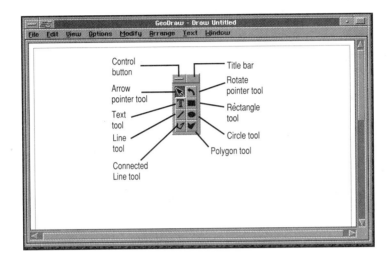

Fig. 8.11

The GeoDraw Toolbox.

The GeoDraw Toolbox has eight items in it, but only five of the items are drawing tools. Of the other three tools, the two arrows are for selecting and rotating graphics items and the Text tool places and manages text. Starting at the top left and moving right to left, the toolbox items are presented in the following table:

Tool	Function
The Arrow pointer tool	Used for selecting objects
The Rotate pointer tool	Used to select and rotate objects
The Text tool	Used to create and manipulate text
The Rectangle tool	Used to draw rectangular shapes
The Line tool	Used to draw straight lines
The Circle tool	Used to draw circles and ovals
The Connected Line tool	Used to draw a series of connected lines
The Polygon tool	Used to draw filled shapes comprised of straight lines

You use the drawing tools to create what GeoDraw refers to collectively as *objects*. Squares, circles, lines, and squiggles are all objects. Whatever tool you use, the object has shared properties with other objects in your drawing.

After you finish drawing, the objects have small squares on or adjacent to their borders. These small squares are *handles* that you use to move and reshape the objects. If you click away from the object, the handles disappear. To make the handles reappear, click the object again. The "Working with Objects" section of this chapter discusses the use of handles.

The Rectangle Tool

To use the Rectangle tool to draw squares and rectangles, you first must choose the Rectangle tool from the Toolbox; the pointer changes to a crosshairs drawing tool.

Move the crosshairs anywhere on the drawing area. Click the starting point of the rectangle you intend to draw. Hold down the mouse button and drag the crosshairs. The dotted line that follows the crosshairs shows the rectangle being drawn. When you release the mouse button, the rectangle, with its handles, appears. Figure 8.12 shows one complete rectangle and one partially complete rectangle.

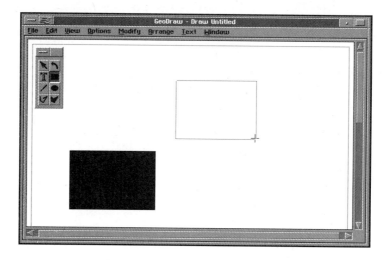

Fig. 8.12

One complete and one unfinished rectangle.

The Circle Tool

The Circle tool works like the Rectangle tool. As you create the circle, it may appear initially as a dotted rectangle if you have enabled the Drag as **R**ect(angle) option in the **O**ptions menu. The "Working with Objects" section of this chapter explains the Drag as Rectangle setting.

To draw a circle, follow these steps:

1. Click the circle icon in the Toolbox. The pointer changes to a crosshairs drawing tool.

2. Position the crosshairs at the location where you want to draw of the circle.

3. Holding down the left mouse button, drag the crosshairs diagonally toward the location where you want to place the opposite side of the circle. A dotted outline shows you the shape you are creating. (The shape of the dotted outline depends on the "drag" option you have selected in the Options menu.)

4. When the circle is the proper size, release the mouse button. The circle appears (see fig. 8.13). On your screen, before you select another option, the circle has handles.

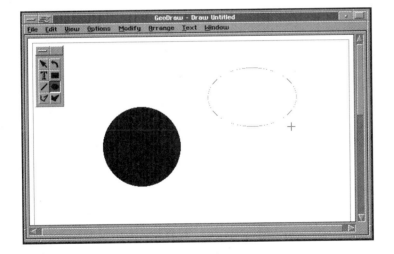

Fig. 8.13

One complete and one unfinished circle.

The Line Tool

To draw a single straight line, follow these steps:

1. Click the Line icon in the Toolbox. The pointer changes to a crosshairs drawing tool.

2. Position the crosshairs at the location where you want the line to begin.

3. Holding down the left mouse button, drag the mouse to the location where you want the line to end.

   You can move the pointer to end the line anywhere in the window as long as you have not released the left button.

4. When the line is complete, release the mouse button. The line appears (see fig. 8.14). Before you select another option, the circle on your screen has handles.

To draw a single straight line, choose the Line tool from the Toolbox. The pointer changes to a crosshairs drawing tool. Position the crosshairs at one end of the line you want to draw. Holding down the left mouse button, drag the mouse to the other end of the line. Before you release the mouse button, you can pivot the line around its starting point to draw at any angle. When the line is complete, release the mouse button. The line appears (see fig. 8.14).

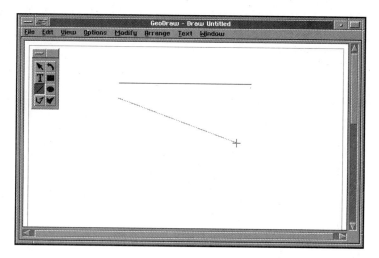

Fig. 8.14

Lines drawn with the Line tool.

The Connected Line Tool

To draw a continuous series of connected straight lines, choose the Connected Line icon from the Toolbox. The pointer changes to a crosshairs drawing tool. Then do the following:

1. Position the crosshairs at the location you want the first line to begin and click to *anchor* the line.

2. Move the crosshairs to the location where you want the first line to end (you do not have to hold the mouse button down) and click to anchor the other end of the segment.

3. Continue drawing, clicking each time you want to end a line segment. *Note:* A series of short connected lines can be used as a curved line.

4. When you complete the object, double-click at the end of the last segment to stop drawing.

   You also can quit drawing by pressing Escape or clicking the right mouse button; however, the final *unanchored* segment disappears.

Figure 8.15 shows an object drawn with the Connected Line tool.

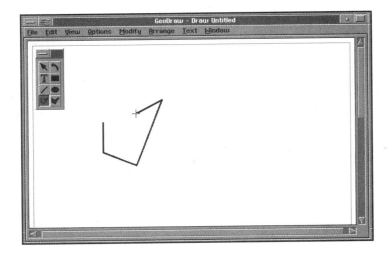

Fig. 8.15

Object drawn with the
Connected Line tool.

The Polygon Tool

The Polygon tool works like the Connected Line tool, but you use the Polygon tool to draw closed shapes that can be filled with color or texture. When you double-click to complete the polygon, the polygon automatically closes back to the first point you clicked and fills with the currently selected color. You learn how to control fill pattern and color in the "Changing Properties" section of this chapter.

To create a filled polygon, choose the Polygon tool from the Toolbox, and then do the following:

1. Click the crosshairs at the locations where you want to anchor the first segment of the object.

2. Move, then click, to draw additional segments.

3. Complete the polygon by double-clicking. The figure closes from your double-click point to the starting point.

4. You can end by pressing Esc or the right mouse button, but your last unanchored segment does not appear, and the polygon closes from the last anchored point to the first point.

Figure 8.16 shows a filled figure drawn with the Polygon tool.

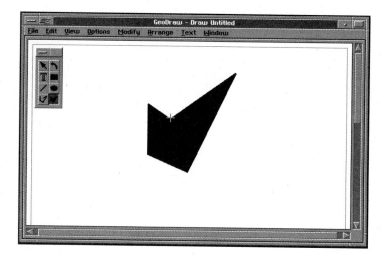

The Text Tool

Thinking of text as a decorative item takes time and some experimentation. Before the advent of desktop publishing and programs like GeoDraw, text was "plain vanilla" unless you could afford custom typography or a calligrapher.

In GeoDraw, however, text is more than just words on a page. You can drag, nudge, stretch, rotate, and flip text. After you become accustomed to the several ways of manipulating text, your biggest challenge is probably restraint. Too many sizes and too many fonts become wearying to the eyes.

The key to managing text in GeoDraw is to think of a block of text as an object like the objects you create with the drawing tools. You can enter and edit text as you do in GeoWrite, but you also can turn the block of text into an object to which you can apply all of GeoDraw's enhancements.

Before you do amazing things with text, however, you first must enter text into your GeoDraw document.

To enter text, follow these steps:

1. Click on the Text tool in the Toolbox. The mouse pointer changes to an I-beam shape.

2. To create a standard, three-inch long text block, click the I-beam where you want the block to start.

   To create a block of any other length, "draw" the block by positioning the I-beam at one end, holding down the left mouse button, and dragging the I-beam. The dotted line that follows the I-beam shows the text box being drawn. When you release the mouse button, the text box appears.

3. Begin typing to enter text. Sentences wrap at the end of the block. Although the blocks are initially only one line high, they expand as you type, and the text wraps to another line. The current selection determines the text size and font.

4. To edit the text, select it with the I-beam and apply the appropriate menu commands.

Figure 8.17 shows both a standard width and a custom width text block. The wider block has been selected by clicking with the pointer. Using the small square handles on the block, you can manipulate the entire block of text as a single object.

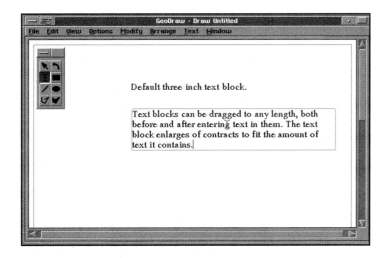

Fig. 8.17

Text blocks.

Working with Objects

In the previous sections you learned to create different types of objects, using the tools in the Toolbox. In this section, you learn techniques for selecting, moving, grouping, resizing, and deleting objects. In most cases, the techniques apply to all types of objects: circles, rectangles, polygons, text blocks, and so on. Objects that you handle differently are mentioned as exceptions.

Selecting Objects

All the objects in Figure 8.18 are selected. The small squares surrounding the objects are the handles you use to reshape and rotate the object. You use the diamond shaped *move handle* in the center of the object to drag the object to a new location.

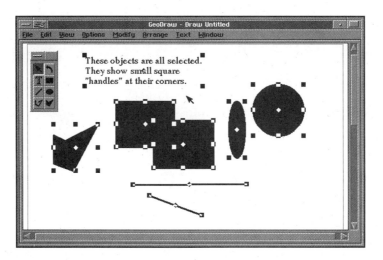

Fig. 8.18

Selected objects show handles.

You can select an object in two ways: by clicking the object and by dragging a selection rectangle around the object. Both methods use the Arrow pointer tool.

To select an object by clicking, click the Arrow pointer tool or the Rotate pointer tool in the Toolbox. Point to any visible part of the object and click the left mouse button. If you have successfully selected the object, handles appear. You can select additional objects without removing the selection on the first object by holding down the Ctrl key while clicking other objects.

You also can select a single object or a group of objects by dragging a selection rectangle around them. This method enables you to select multiple objects rapidly.

To select an object by dragging, click the Arrow pointer tool or the Rotate pointer tool from the Toolbox. Create a rectangle large enough to surround all the objects you want to select. Create the rectangle by beginning at one corner, holding down the left mouse button, and dragging the mouse diagonally to the other corner of your selection rectangle so that all objects are inside. A dotted rectangle follows your pointer and objects inside the rectangle are selected. Release the left mouse button.

Dragging to select objects is very useful for cleaning up an area. Select all the objects you want to remove, and then press Del or choose **D**elete from the **E**dit menu.

Selecting Text

Text has a dual nature in GeoDraw. A block of text can be entered and edited as you enter and edit text in a word processor. In GeoDraw, however, text also can be dragged, stretched, and flipped like an object.

If you intend to use standard word processor features to edit text, choose the Text tool. The pointer changes to an I-beam. Place the I-beam in the text you want to edit.

You can also select text for editing by dragging. Hold down the left mouse button and drag the I-beam across the text. A reverse highlight appears. You can apply any command from the Text and Edit menus to the selected text.

The following selection shortcuts used elsewhere in GeoWorks Pro also work here:

Action	Result
Double-clicking	Selects a word
Triple-clicking	Selects a line
Quadruple-clicking	Selects a paragraph
Quintuple-clicking	Selects the text block

To select text as an object, a *text block*, you must choose the Arrow pointer tool or the Rotate pointer tool. Click the pointer in the text block. Handles appear on the block. When the handles appear, you can manipulate a block of text the same way you manipulate any other object. You can move a text block by using the central diamond shape, and you can stretch it with the other handles, for example.

You can edit the entire block of text after you select it as an object. Commands to change fonts, sizes, and so on, apply to everything in the block.

Moving Objects

A dotted outline of the object follows the mouse pointer while you move a selected object. When you release the mouse button, the program redraws the object in its new location. Computing the position of a moving shape takes a great deal of computer horsepower and can result in slow and jerky progress across the screen. If you have this problem, activate the command Drag As **R**ect from the **O**ption menu (see fig. 8.19). This command shows the moving object as a simple rectangle that can be drawn more rapidly.

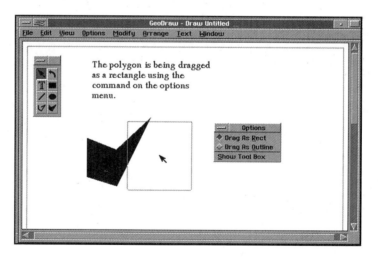

Fig. 8.19

The Options menu.

You can move objects in two ways: by dragging the move handle (the diamond in the object's center) or by using the right mouse button.

To move an object with its move handle, click the Arrow pointer tool or the Rotate pointer tool. Point to the diamond-shaped move handle in the middle of the object and drag to a new location.

To move an object with the right mouse button, click the Arrow pointer tool or the Rotate pointer tool. Point to any area of the object, hold down the *right* mouse button, and drag the object to a new location.

Other ways in which to move objects exist. You also can nudge, rotate, or flip an object to create a graphic or document that meets your needs.

Nudging an Object

Aligning an object perfectly the first time is difficult because tiny movements are almost impossible with the mouse. You can use the Nudge command on the Modify menu to move an object up, down, left, or right one pixel at a time. A *pixel* is one of the tiny dots that makes up your screen image.

To nudge an object, you first must select the object. Then choose the **N**udge command from the **M**odify menu. A small cascade menu opens. Nudge the object one pixel at a time by clicking the **U**p, **D**own, **R**ight, or **L**eft menu options.

To nudge the object repeatedly, click the push pin image on the cascade menu to *pin* the Nudge menu to the screen. When pinned, the menu does not close each time you use it. To close the pinned menu, double-click its Control button (see fig. 8.20).

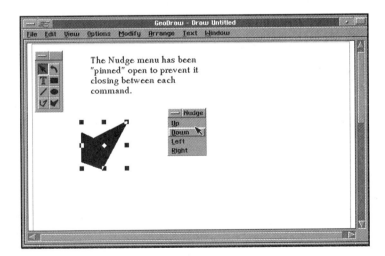

Fig. 8.20

Pin the Nudge menu to reuse it.

Rotating Objects

Graphic artists highly prize the capability of rotating objects, particularly text blocks. If you examine quality advertising, you see examples of effective use of object rotation. Some of the most powerful desktop packages are capable of rotating text in 90-degree increments only. You easily can rotate objects, including text blocks, to any angle with GeoWorks.

Some objects, however, cannot be rotated. You cannot rotate imported illustrations or circles, for example. In addition, you cannot edit a text block that is rotated away from its original position. You must return text to its original orientation for editing.

You can rotate objects in 45 degree increments by selecting the Modify menu, and you can use the Rotate pointer tool to rotate an object by any amount in freehand. To rotate an object using menu commands, select the object and choose the Rotate 45° **L**eft or Rotate 45° **R**ight command from the **M**odify menu. By choosing the command repeatedly you can rotate the object through a full circle in 45 degree increments. Remember that you can *pin* the menu open by clicking the push pin icon. Pinning the menu open enables you to use the command repeatedly without reopening the menu each time.

To rotate an object manually, click the Rotate pointer tool; then select the object. Place the pointer on one of the corner handles of the selected object. Hold down the left mouse button and drag to rotate the object in either direction.

Figure 8.21 shows examples of rotated objects and text.

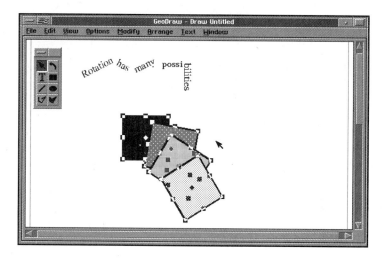

Fig. 8.21

Rotated objects and text.

Flipping Objects

Flipping means rotating the object 180 degrees around its horizontal or vertical axis. The technique can be used when you need a left-hand and right-hand version of an object or to produce reflected effects like figure 8.22, which was produced by flipping and rotating an identical text block.

Fig. 8.22

The mirror text, flipped and rotated.

To flip an object, click the Arrow pointer tool; then select the object. Choose Flip **V**ertical or Flip **H**orizontal from the **M**odify menu.

Stacking Objects

To understand the concept of stacking, imagine that each GeoDraw object you create is on a separate sheet of transparent plastic. The new objects you create are added to the top of the stack. Depending on the sequence in which you create your objects, the objects may end up stacked in an order that hides one object behind another. You can change the order of stacking, using commands from the Arrange menu.

To change stacking order, you first must choose the Arrow pointer tool from the Toolbox and select the object you want move. Then you can use the following commands from the **A**rrange menu to rearrange the placement of the objects.

Command	Result
Bring to **F**ront	Moves the selected object to the front of the stack
Send to **B**ack	Moves the selected text to the back of the stack
Move B**a**ckward	Moves the selected text one layer toward the back
Move F**o**rward	Moves the selected text one layer toward the front

Figure 8.23 shows the effect of rearranging stack order.

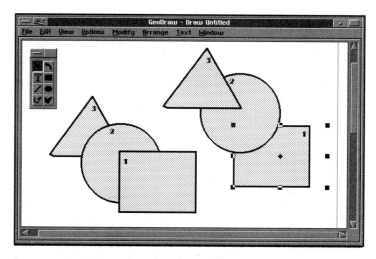

Fig. 8.23

A rearranged stack.

Fusing and Defusing Objects

Suppose that you create a complex drawing made up of many objects. How do you move the drawing without dragging the objects apart and reassembling them again? One approach is to *fuse* the objects together into a single object. You can move the fused object as a unit with no fear of leaving a part behind. If you need to edit the object, a Defuse command reduces it to component parts again.

To fuse objects, click the Arrow pointer tool in the Toolbox and select the objects you want to fuse. You can select the objects by Ctrl-clicking to add objects or by drawing a selection rectangle around the entire group.

After you select these objects, choose the **Fuse Objects** command from the **E**dit menu. (Notice that the multiple handles become one set.)

Fused text can be stretched in height and width in a way that a normal text block cannot. Just select the text block (or blocks) and choose the command **F**use Objects; then use the handles to stretch the text.

Because you cannot edit fused text or objects, you must defuse the text or objects before editing them. To defuse objects, select the object you want to defuse. Choose the **D**efuse Objects command from the **E**dit menu. (Notice that each object regains its set of handles.) If you have modified the fused object, the components return to their original state when you defuse them.

Resizing Objects

The handles around the edges of an object can be dragged to make an object larger or smaller. The handles also can be used to change the object's proportions by changing the object in one direction, but not another.

Whatever their shape, the handles of an object appear in a rectangular configuration. Larger objects show eight handles, and smaller or narrower objects show four. The exception is a line, which shows a handle at each end only. **Note:** Disregard the diamond-shaped *move handle*, in the center of the object; its sole purpose is to move the object.

Corner handles are different than the handles at the midpoint of the sides. A *corner handle* can be dragged in two directions at one time. Handles on the sides can be dragged only at a 90 degree angle to the side. The handle on the vertical side of a rectangle, for example, can be dragged to the left or right, not up and down.

You can resize text blocks by dragging their handles, but the text inside the block does not stretch; it re-wraps to fit the new boundaries of the block. If you widen the block, the lines of text widen, and the block gets shorter. To stretch text by changing its text box, see the preceding section, "Fusing and Defusing Objects."

To resize an object, choose the Arrow pointer tool and select an object. Place the pointer on one of the handles of the selected object and, while holding down the left mouse button, drag the handle in the direction you want to resize.

T I P

You can reduce the size of a bitmap object. Because of hardware limitations, however, you get only an approximation of the graphic information on-screen, even though all the graphic information is present. Although the on-screen results may appear ugly, the printed results can be stunning.

To resize, GWRepBobby uses Susan Lamb's technique of drawing a diagonal line from corner to corner, then dragging one of the corners of the picture along the line. Using this technique, the resized picture always is proportional to the original. This technique works especially well with line art.

Copying and Pasting Objects

The capability to duplicate objects is very helpful when you are creating an illustration. Repeated patterns or duplicate items may appear in your work more often than you expect. The Copy and Paste commands make *cloning* useful elements of your work easy.

To duplicate objects in your illustration, follow these steps:

1. Choose the Arrow pointer tool from the Toolbox.

2. Select the object you want to copy.

3. Choose **C**opy from the **E**dit menu.

4. Choose **P**aste from the **E**dit menu.

   A duplicate of the object you copied appears in the center of the screen.

5. Drag the copy to its new position, using its move handle or the right mouse button.

Deleting Objects

When you create artwork, you may find that you use the eraser more than the other drawing features. To delete an object, choose the Arrow pointer tool from the Toolbox; then select the objects you want to delete. Press Del or choose **D**elete from the **E**dit menu; the program deletes all the selected items.

 **CAUTION**   You cannot retrieve deleted material. If you think you may want your material back, remove the object from the screen by using the Cut command, which temporarily stores a copy. If you realize the deletion was a mistake, immediately Paste your material back before you begin another operation.

Changing Properties

Properties is the term the creators of GeoDraw chose to encompass the colors, patterns, and styles you can apply to GeoDraw objects. The three properties dialog boxes, shown in figure 8.24, are small independent windows that stay on-screen until you double-click the Control button in the upper left corner. Because the dialog boxes remain on-screen, you can use them repeatedly without constantly reopening the Modify menu. You can drag the boxes by their Title bars to a convenient location.

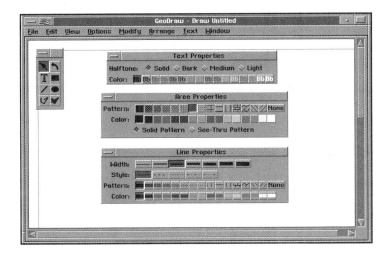

Fig. 8.24

The Properties dialog boxes.

Buttons represent the rows of colors, textures, and lines that apply your choices to the selected object. You can apply properties before or after you create an object. If you choose a red fill and a dotted line before you start drawing a rectangle, for example, the rectangle fills with red and has a dotted border line as you draw it. If you select an object you have already drawn, any changes in properties alter the original choices.

You can choose from 16 colors (with a monochrome system, 16 patterns) to apply to the lines and filled areas of your objects. Colors also can be applied to text. At this writing, however, because GeoWorks does not have printer drivers for color printers, the color is only on-screen—but textures do print.

Applying Line Properties

Objects drawn with the Line tool or the Connected Line tool are not the only objects with line properties. Circles, rectangles, and polygons have lines at their edges. These lines can be changed independently from the interior fill. You can have a red circle with a blue line as its border, for example.

You can choose four properties from the Line Properties dialog box: Width, Style, Pattern, and Color. (With a monochrome system, you have two color choices only, black and white.) You can apply any or all of the line properties. When you click a button in the dialog box, you can see the effect on the selected object. Figure 8.25 shows a selection of line effects.

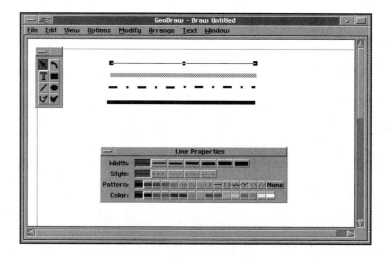

Fig. 8.25

The Line Properties dialog box with properties applied to drawn lines.

To use the Line Properties tools, choose the Arrow pointer tool from the Toolbox and select the object. Choose the **L**ine Properties command from the **M**odify menu. In the dialog box that appears, click your choices for width, style, pattern, and color. The effects are visible as you work.

Applying Area Properties

The Area Properties features are sometimes called *fills*. Any object created with the Rectangle, Circle, or Polygon tools automatically fills with the pattern currently selected in the Area Properties dialog box. The default selection is solid black.

You can choose solid or transparent patterns. A solid pattern is opaque by definition, but the other patterns are made up of dots or lines. If you choose Solid Pattern, any pattern has an opaque background. If you choose See-Thru Pattern, you can see the color of anything behind the object.

To apply area properties, choose the Arrow pointer tool from the Toolbox and select the object you intend to modify. Choose the **A**rea Properties command from the **M**odify menu. In the dialog box that appears, click your choices for pattern and color. Choose the Solid Pattern or See-Thru Pattern by clicking the corresponding button. The effects are visible as you work.

Applying Text Properties

The Text Properties dialog box enables you to apply color to text and to lighten the color by choosing a halftone effect. A *halftone* is a lighter color created by reducing the number of colored dots in an area. The eye visually mixes the color and the white areas to produce the effect of a lighter color. The halftone settings (Solid, Dark, Medium, and Light) correspond to a 100%, 75%, 25% and 15% saturation of the color.

You can apply text color to an entire text block or to individual words. If you choose a color before you begin typing, the text appears in color. The default setting is for solid black text. You may want to review the "Selecting Text" section of this chapter. The techniques described apply to selection for applying text colors.

To apply text properties, choose the Arrow pointer tool and select the text you want to modify; then choose **T**ext Properties from the **M**odify menu. In the Text Properties dialog box, choose a color; to create a halftone effect, click one of the halftone buttons other than Solid.

Using the Text Menu

The GeoDraw Text menu gives you access to cascade menus for controlling fonts, sizes, and styles. With the exception of the Text Properties command, these menus give you access to the same commands that are available in GeoWrite. If you have worked with GeoWrite, you may be familiar with the options.

Changing Fonts

Fonts are *families* of type styles that share a basic design. Figure 8.26 shows the Fonts cascade menu and a screen of GeoDraw font samples. With its excellent printing capabilities, GeoDraw can reproduce a variety of fonts. You can print an excellent replica of the text that appears on-screen.

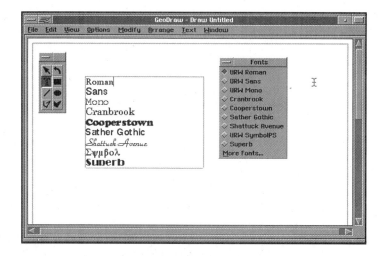

Fig. 8.26

The Fonts menu.

You can change fonts before or after you type your text. To change the font of existing text, select the text; then choose a font from the **F**onts menu. The program applies the font to the selected text. You also can choose the **M**ore Fonts command. The dialog box shown in figure 8.27 appears.

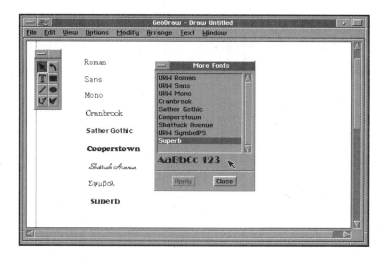

Fig. 8.27

The More fonts dialog box.

The dialog box lists available fonts. You can preview the font appearance by clicking the font name. To use the font, click the Apply button in the dialog box. The program applies the font to the selected text.

Changing Text Sizes

To work with text sizes, you must know a bit about *points*. The printing industry universally uses this text size measurement; the term has migrated to desktop publishing and drawing programs like GeoDraw. A point is one seventy-second of an inch. Two useful benchmarks for point sizes are the facts that an inch equals 72 points and that the type commonly used for text in newspapers and books is about 12 points high.

As you use the excellent text handling capabilities of GeoDraw, you may want to purchase a pica ruler from a stationer or art supply store so that you can measure point sizes directly on your sketches or samples instead of using trial-and-error methods.

You can change text size in several ways. Regardless of the method you use, however, you first must select the text. After you select the text, open the Sizes cascade menu. The first way to change text size is simply to click one of the sizes listed in the cascade menu.

Another way to change text size is to choose **S**maller or **L**arger from the Sizes cascade menu. Clicking Smaller decreases the point size of selected text in increments. Clicking Larger increases the point size of selected text.

The final way to change text size is to choose the **C**ustom Size command from the Sizes cascade menu and use the up and down arrows to increase or decrease point size. You also can type in a specific point size. After you enter a specific size, click the Apply button to change the size of the selected text. Click Close to close the dialog box.

Changing Text Styles

Not only can you control font and text size, you also can control the character style. *Style* refers to variations on the basic font; Bold, Italic, and Underline are common style variations. The Styles menu contains buttons for applying text styles to selected text. Figure 8.28 shows the Styles menu and samples of the available styles.

Apply a character style by selecting the text you want to change. Then choose a style by clicking the style's check box in the **S**tyle menu. You can choose multiple styles, such as **B**old and **I**talic.

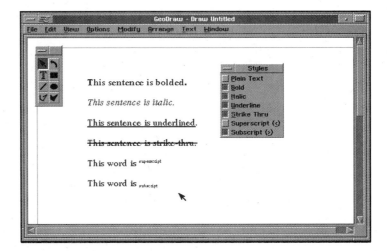

Fig. 8.28

The Styles menu with samples.

Justifying Text

Justification in GeoDraw is the alignment of a paragraph relative to its text block. Text can be aligned flush with the left or right edges or centered between the edges of the block. *Full alignment* means that both the left and right edges of the paragraph are aligned flush. The program accomplishes full alignment by adding space between words to fill out the line. Although full alignment looks good, the gaps between words can sometimes make full alignment difficult to read.

To justify text, select parts of a text block with the Text tool or select the entire block by clicking it with the Arrow pointer tool. After you select the text, choose the **J**ustification command from the **T**ext Menu. The cascade menu, shown in figure 8.29, appears. Choose the justification (**L**eft, **R**ight, **C**enter, **F**ull) to apply it to the selected text.

The Text Properties command on the Text menu opens the same dialog box as the Text Properties command on the Modify menu. Refer to the section "Changing Properties" for information on the Text Properties command.

Saving GeoDraw Documents

The File Menu contains commands for saving your GeoDraw files. Saving actually proceeds automatically while you create a GeoDraw file. You may notice periodically that your mouse pointer becomes an hour glass for a moment and then returns to the pointer. This change in the shape of the pointer indicates the automatic process that creates a temporary file of your changes is running. If a power failure or other computer problem occurs, you can retrieve a copy of your work, up to the last automatic save. The Revert command enables you to jettison the temporary file and revert to the last version created using the Save or Save As command.

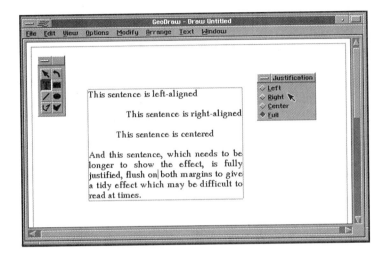

Fig. 8.29

The Justification cascade menu.

To save a GeoDraw document, choose **S**ave from the **F**ile menu. In the save as dialog box that appears (see fig. 8.30), move to the directory in which you want to save the document. Type the document name in the New Name text field and choose **S**ave to save the file.

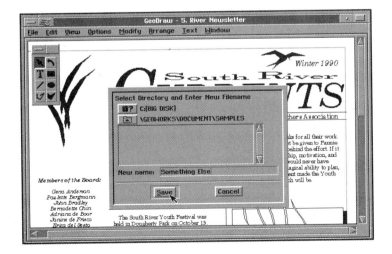

Fig. 8.30

The save as dialog box.

If you saved the file earlier, when you choose **S**ave again, the save command performs immediately with no dialog box presented; however, you can change the name or location of an existing GeoDraw file by choosing the Save **A**s command from the **F**ile menu. In the save as dialog box that appears, you can change the directory to change the file's location; you also can type a new name for the file in the New Name text field. When you choose the **S**ave button, the program saves the document to the new location and name you specified.

Printing GeoDraw Documents

Printing in GeoDraw is similar to printing throughout GeoWorks Pro. The print dialog box, shown in figure 8.31 and shared by other applications, makes printing techniques easy to learn. The dialog box has two parts: Printer Options (which enables you to choose a different printer) and Document Options (which sets print quality, pages printed, and number of copies).

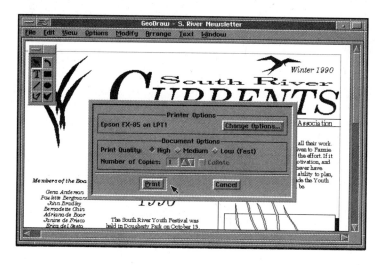

Fig. 8.31

The print dialog box.

To set printer options for use with GeoDraw, choose the **P**rint command from the **F**ile Menu. In the print dialog box that appears, click the Change Options button. When you click the Change Options button, the dialog box shown in figure 8.32 appears.

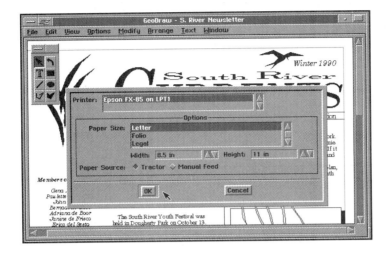

Fig. 8.32

The print options
dialog box.

From the Options dialog box, you can set the specifications for the following:

- *To see the list of installed printers.* Click the up or down arrow to the right of the Printer list box.

- *To select a printer.* Click the printer's name.

- *To select a paper size.* Scroll through the list of sizes in the Options rectangle and click your choice.

- *To specify a custom paper size.* Type the dimensions in the Width and Height fields.

- *To indicate paper source.* Specify Tractor or Manual paper feed depending on your printer.

After you set the specifications, save these changes and exit the print options dialog box by clicking the OK button.

The print dialog box reappears. From this dialog box, you can set options for printing a document. You can select the print quality: High, Medium, or Low. (Higher quality means longer print times.) Select the number of copies and click OK to begin printing.

T   I   P   If your laser printer does not have enough memory to print a full page of graphics, two ways to solve this problem exist. According to GWRepJohnK, you can create a full 8 1/2-by-11-inch page or you can print a full-page graphic as a smaller image.

To create a full 8 1/2-by-11-inch page, use the Cut command on the Edit menu to remove some of the objects on the page. Store these objects in memory and print the page with the missing material. Return the printed page to the printer paper tray. Paste on the page the images you previously cut; then cut the objects you already printed. When you print again, you have a full-page graphic.

To print a full-page graphic as a smaller image, use the **Fuse Objects** command to fuse the full page; then drag the corners of the fused page to shrink it. Rotate the fused page 90 degrees (to landscape orientation) and print it. This technique is also useful for producing single-sheet flyers.

Chapter Summary

In this chapter you became familiar with GeoDraw by learning how the program starts and how the windows and menus match or vary from other GeoWorks Pro applications. You learned that you can import TIFF or PCX files to serve as a starting point for your work and that you can build on other GeoDraw illustrations.

You learned how to put the GeoDraw tools to work creating and modifying objects. You learned how the Properties boxes can modify objects and discovered the unusually large range of text effects that are available in GeoDraw. The chapter concludes with instructions on how to save and print your GeoDraw illustrations.

Using GeoComm

C omputer communications has a reputation of being one of the most complex areas of personal computing. With concepts such as baud rates, protocols, and stop bits being tossed at you, you easily can see where the reputation has come from.

Truthfully, *telecommunications*, as the activity often is called, is not the easiest computing activity to master, but the rewards are remarkable. You can connect to an extraordinary network of individuals and information. You can swap files with a friend across town or be part of a live roundtable with participants from Europe and Asia. News flashes, stock quotes, and computer tips can be brought to your desktop. True, the telephone bill may increase, but what hobby doesn't have some related expenses?

GeoComm, the communications element of GeoWorks Pro, is an excellent place to begin learning about computer communications. GeoComm has the easy-to-use features of the rest of GeoWorks Pro.

In this chapter, you learn about GeoComm's capabilities. If you have the necessary equipment, you can use GeoComm after reading this chapter, but computer communications involves so much more that you may want to look into some books devoted to the topic, such as Que's *Introduction to PC Communications*.

Understanding Basic Communications

This section provides you with a general overview of telecommunications and a framework for understanding telecommunication elements. It introduces some terms necessary to understand the process of communicating with GeoComm and clarifies why you follow certain procedures while using GeoComm.

To get an overview of the process, use this walk-through of a typical computer-to-computer communications session:

1. Before starting, get the necessary communications settings from the person at the other end. Computers don't have to use the same software package on both ends, but they do need to have the same settings for transfer speed and certain *handshaking* signals that you will learn about later in this chapter.

2. Start GeoComm from GeoManager or the Express menu and use the Options menu to adjust any settings you need to match the remote computer. Using the Dial menu, dial the remote computer that, by prearrangement, is waiting, connected to the phone line, to answer your call.

   If your settings agree, you see a series of messages confirming the connection.

3. Use your keyboard to conduct a real-time conversation with the person at the other end. You also may decide to send a file (*upload*) or receive a file (*download*).

4. If you want to download a file, get the file name from the remote computer and tell GeoComm to begin the downloading process by using an error-checking protocol. The two computers transfer the file, exchanging signals to keep track of the process.

   GeoComm notifies you when the process is complete, at which point you can resume live communication, exchange more files, or sign off.

5. End your communications session and break the telephone connection before you review the files you received so that no further phone charges accumulate.

The design of many strategies in communication reduces the amount of expensive on-line time. GeoComm, for example, enables you to prepare a message before you go on-line. After you store the message as a file, you can upload it much more rapidly than you can type it. In a similar vein, downloaded messages can be maintained in a storage area called a buffer so that you can scroll back and read them after you disconnect.

Information Services

One reason steadily increasing numbers of computer users are using telecommunications is the growth of on-line information services.

An *information service* is a commercial venture that creates and manages a network of information and communication services you can reach from your computer. Many have local phone numbers in the larger metropolitan areas of the U.S. Although the service charges you for your minutes of connect-time (typically between $5 and $12 per hour), it does not charge you for a long-distance call from many locations. Some of the best-known services are CompuServe, GEnie, Prodigy, and America Online.

GeoWorks Pro users find America Online of particular interest for two reasons: the service maintains an area of its service specifically dedicated to GeoWorks Pro and provides a trial software package along with each GeoWorks Pro package. Chapter 10, "Using America Online," takes you through getting started with this service.

Communications Equipment

Computer signals cannot travel over telephone wires without being changed. The device used to change computer signals to phone signals is a *modem*. If you have picked up a phone when a modem is in use, you know the distinctive high-pitched squeal that data makes when moving over the phone lines.

To use GeoComm, you need a modem and the cable that connects it to your computer. You do not need an additional phone line, because most modems have a jack where you can plug in your telephone.

Modems are rated by transmission speed. The unit of measurement is the *baud*, which you can think of as a measurement of how many characters of information can be transmitted in a second. In other words, a 1200 baud modem can transmit or receive 1200 characters per second.

The faster you can move information, the less on-line time you pay for. Currently, the most popular modem speed is 2400 baud. You can buy economy models at 1200 baud or high-speed screamers that run at 9600 baud. Remember, though, that you cannot communicate any faster than the system on the other end can communicate.

The modem must be Hayes-compatible. The Hayes brand modem has established a set of commands that have become an industry standard. You don't have to buy the Hayes brand (although the company makes fine modems), but you must know that the modem you buy understands the Hayes command set. The modem's literature or packaging almost always includes this information. If the compatibility isn't clear, be sure to ask.

Your computer talks to the modem through a *serial port*, a plug on the back of the computer. You must buy a serial cable that matches the ports on your computer and modem. The connections are fairly well standardized, but check your documentation to be sure. The modem port is often labeled COM 1.

Touring GeoComm

Before digging into the details of GeoComm, tour the general features of the application. Its appearance is simple, but you must be ready to learn some new concepts as you move into the area of communications. GeoComm goes as far as possible to make communications painless for you, but you must intervene to make choices several times.

Starting and Quitting GeoComm

As with all GeoWorks Pro applications, GeoComm has its own icon in the GeoManager WORLD view. You also can launch GeoComm from the Express menu available in any active window. Each technique can be useful at different times.

Launching GeoComm from GeoManager is appropriate if you typically start your GeoWorks Pro work session from GeoManager. To open the program from the GeoManager WORLD directory window, double-click the GeoComm icon, which resembles a computer connected to telephone wires (see fig. 9.1).

The Express menu button, which looks like a stylized letter E, is available in any active application window. The Express menu provides a handy way to start GeoComm if the WORLD window is not open or if you are using another GeoWorks Pro application and want to switch to GeoComm. To open GeoComm, click the Express menu button, choose **S**tartup, and click GeoComm in the cascade menu that opens.

To quit GeoComm, open the **F**ile menu and choose **E**xit. You also can press F3, double-click the Control button, or choose **E**xit to DOS from the Express menu.

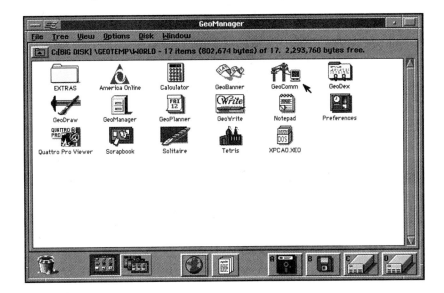

Fig. 9.1

The GeoComm icon in
the WORLD directory.

Using the GeoComm Window and Menus

The GeoComm window is similar to other GeoWorks Pro application
windows (see fig. 9.2). The Title bar at top center shows the application
name. With the Express menu, you can open other applications or exit to
DOS. The Control button at the upper left has commands for minimizing
and closing the window.

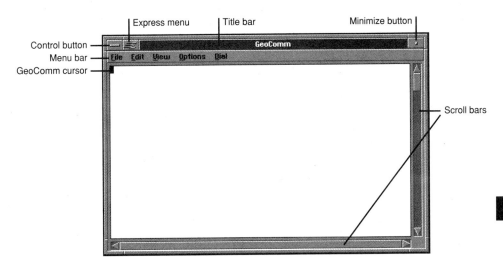

Fig. 9.2

The GeoComm
window.

Scroll bars at the bottom and right sides enable you to view documents larger than the window. The Minimize button at the upper right reduces the window to an icon at the lower left corner of the screen. The window cannot be maximized to fill the screen. Although you can reduce the height and width by dragging, the **W**indow Size command on the **V**iew menu provides a precise method of defining the numbers of columns and lines. You also can change the text size in the window by choosing **S**mall Font or **L**arge Font from the **V**iew menu.

The main portion of the window displays any text you are sending or receiving directly, along with commands to and acknowledgments from the modem. GeoComm's small square cursor moves down the screen as a marker for where data is being sent or received. When you are on-line, the cursor is solid black; when the window is not active, the cursor is hollow.

You can reach the GeoComm command system through five menus. Table 9.1 describes each menus and its general purpose. The later sections of this chapter discuss these commands in more detail.

Table 9.1 The GeoComm Menus

Menu	Purpose
File	Enables sending or receiving text or binary files and saving buffer
Edit	Enables copying from and pasting to screen and composing short messages off-line
View	Offers options for changing window size and font set
Options	Offers protocol, terminal, and modem settings
Dial	Enables direct dialing and hang up and running scripts

Preparing to Use GeoComm

To achieve successful communications, both computers involved must have the same settings. Because of the variables, setting up can be one of the more frustrating areas of communications. After you get the settings correct, communication proceeds easily, but getting that first setup can involve considerable experimentation.

In this section, the settings have been divided into three groups: modem, terminal, and protocol settings. *Modem settings* tell the modem what type of phone (tone or rotary) to deal with and how to manage the modem speaker. *Terminal settings* tell GeoComm the keyboard commands and text wrap to which your computer and the remote computer respond. *Protocol settings* tell GeoComm what method of file transfer and error checking to use.

The following sections describe the settings groups in detail.

Modem Settings

The Modem dialog box (see fig. 9.3) is the easiest dialog box to set. You must tell GeoComm whether you have a tone or rotary phone and how you want the modem speaker managed.

Fig. 9.3

The Modem dialog box.

To set the modem options, follow these steps:

1. Choose **M**odem from the **O**ptions menu.

2. In the Modem dialog box, click the button for the phone type you have.

   Most current phones are the TouchTone type that produce different sound frequencies for each button. GeoComm also can work with older rotary dial phones.

3. Click the button to indicate when the modem speaker should become active.

   For the On Until Connect option, for example, you can hear the rings and modem connect sounds until you are sure you have the settings correct. Then the speaker turns off.

4. Set the speaker volume to suit your surroundings.

5. Click OK to save the settings.

Terminal Settings

A *terminal* is a generic term for a keyboard and monitor combination, whether connected to a PC or a larger mini or mainframe computer. Sometimes, the remote computer or information service you want to talk to expects your computer to respond to a specific set of screen or keyboard instructions. To do so, your computer must pretend to be a specific terminal. You can specify the terminal in the Terminal dialog box (see fig. 9.4).

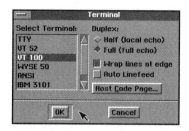

Fig. 9.4

The Terminal dialog box.

The Terminal dialog box offers the following settings:

■ In the Select Terminal section, GeoComm enables you to choose from seven different terminal types. Your choice depends on your knowledge of what the remote computer expects. The most generic choice is TTY, which should get you started with most other systems. Try to learn which setting works best with the remote computer; you may be able to use more convenient keystrokes or shortcut keys.

■ You also have Duplex choices. Many remote computers echo back what you send as a way of verifying transmission. This *full duplex* is the default setting. The *half duplex* setting, used when the remote computer does not echo what you send, tells GeoComm to echo what you type. If you see two sets of letters on-screen (lliikkee tthhiiss), switch to full duplex to get rid of the local echo.

■ You normally choose the Wrap lines at edge option to break long lines so that you can see all the text on your GeoComm screen. Otherwise, GeoComm discards the text that is wider than the screen. If you want to preserve the layout of a document wider than the screen, click off the Wrap lines at edge check box and capture the document to a file. You then can view the file in a program capable of showing the full width of the lines.

■ Auto Linefeed adds a space after each incoming line. If text being received writes on top of the preceding lines, turn on Auto Linefeed. If all lines are double-spaced, turn off the option.

To change the terminal settings, choose the **T**erminal command from the **O**ptions menu. In the Terminal dialog box, choose the appropriate settings for your computer, and then click OK to save the settings.

Protocol Settings

Just as different countries must negotiate diplomatic protocols to regulate their relationship, so must different computers. The Protocol dialog box (see fig. 9.5) enables you to specify settings to match those of the other computer. Some of the terms used may be new, but the underlying concepts are understandable and necessary for successful communications.

Fig. 9.5

The Protocol dialog box.

The following settings can be made in the Protocol dialog box:

■ You must specify to which port your modem connects so that GeoComm knows where to send the signal. The most common computer port used for connecting a modem is COM1.

■ The Baud Rate (transmission speed) on the two computers must match; otherwise, the program transmits only gibberish. (The "Communications Equipment" section discusses baud rates.)

■ You do not need to understand technically the Data Bits, Parity, and Stop Bits settings to use them. Two numbers and a letter, most frequently 8N1, often follow a number for a bulletin board or an on-line service. These digits are the settings for data bits, parity, and stop bits. Sometimes the order is different (N81), but you cannot confuse them if you remember that a letter represents parity, data bits can range between 5 and 8, and stop bits can range from 1 to 2.

■ The Handshake item establishes how one computer tells another to wait while placing a transmission. The software handshake (XON/XOFF) is most common. You use a hardware handshake for "hard-wired" connections, for example a modem connected to a minicomputer.

The dialog box is set by default for the most common situation. Unless you have specific information that one of them should be changed, try your first contact using the defaults discussed after these steps.

To change the protocol settings, do the following:

1. Choose the **P**rotocol command from the **O**ptions menu.

   The Protocol dialog box opens.

2. Change the options to match those used by the remote computer.

3. Choose Apply to use the settings. (Choose Reset to cancel all changes and return to the previous settings.)

4. Choose Close to close the dialog box.

If you had a modem when you installed GeoWorks Pro, you may have entered default modem settings. You use these settings—established in the Preferences utility—for features such as GeoDex Quick Dial phone dialing.

Every time you start GeoComm, the program uses the default settings from the Preferences utility. To change the default protocol settings, see Chapter 11, "Customizing with the Preferences Desk Tool."

Going On-line with GeoComm

So far you have learned about the GeoComm window and menus and about settings in the Modem, Terminal, and Protocol dialog boxes. Now you are ready to go on-line using GeoComm.

This section divides communications activities into two types (sending and receiving) and two content groups (text and binary data). Although general principles apply to both types and both groups, important differences must be observed.

In the first part of this section you learn how to send and receive text, and then how to send and receive binary data.

Sending Text

After you connect with the remote computer by using the Quick dial dialog box, the program sends anything you type. You can conduct a two-way conversation if someone is at the other end or tap into an information service by typing commands it understands.

After the initial novelty wears off, you become aware of the clock as you wait for someone to type a reply or try to compose a memo inside an information service that may cost 50 cents a minute of "connect" time. The answer to the time dilemma is to prepare information off-line. You can compose and edit your material, and then pop on-line just long enough to connect and send the material.

With GeoComm, you can choose one of three ways to prepare a message: you can compose a message in the Message window while you are off-line; cut or copy text from anywhere in GeoWorks Pro and paste it into the GeoComm window; or enter a DOS text file for transmission.

Using GeoComm's Message Window

The method you use in the Message window depends on the complexity of the message. If your message contains only a few lines, type the message directly. If the message or data currently exists in another file, store the file in memory and paste it into the Message window. To create your own complex message, create a DOS file off-line, using a word processor such as Notepad. The following section details these three methods.

To use the Message window, follow these steps:

1. Choose **M**essage from the **E**dit menu.

   The Message window shown in figure 9.6 opens.

2. Type your message in the window.

   You can edit the message using Del, Backspace, and other editing techniques involving selecting with the mouse. (For more details on editing, see Chapter 7, "Using GeoWrite.")

Fig. 9.6

The Message window.

3. Go on-line by using the Quick dial command or a script (discussed later in the "Using Scripts" section).

4. After your connection has been made, choose **S**end. The program sends the entire message.

5. Choose **C**lose to remove the Message dialog box.

Sending Text from Another Document

To transmit text from another document, follow these steps:

1. Open a GeoWorks application document that contains the text you want to send and highlight the text.

2. Use the application's Cu**t** or **C**opy command to store the text in memory.

3. Switch to the GeoComm window by using the Express menu.

4. Choose **P**aste from the GeoComm **E**dit menu to insert the text from memory onto the GeoComm screen. If you are on-line, the text is transmitted as it is pasted.

Sending DOS Text Files

The third method for transmitting text involves transmitting from a DOS text file. This method does not work for text files formatted for GeoWorks or with DOS files that contain formatting or graphics. You use this command to send simple ASCII text files prepared without using formatting.

You can turn a GeoWorks file into a text file by saving it from GeoWrite using the command Save as Text File on the GeoWrite File menu. See Chapter 7, "Using GeoWrite," for details.

To transmit a DOS-format text file, use the following steps:

1. Open GeoComm's **F**ile menu and choose the command **T**ype From Text File. The dialog box shown in figure 9.7 appears.

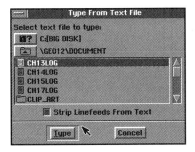

Fig. 9.7

The Type from Text File dialog box.

2. Use the icons and lists in the dialog box to select the file.

3. Choose **Type**. A status box appears to keep you advised of the transmission.

By default, GeoComm sends the text file without line feeds. Line feeds produce the space between lines. If the receiving computer needs line feeds and the word processor that created the files produces line feeds, you can toggle off the Strip Linefeeds From Text check box at the bottom of the Type From Text File dialog box. If the receiving software requires line feeds, leave the box unchecked.

You may need to send a sample file and consult with someone at the receiving end to determine which line feed setting works best. Lines written on top of one another (add line feeds) or unwanted double-spacing of lines (remove line feeds) indicate line feed problems.

Receiving Text

If your communications settings are correct, text transmissions scroll smoothly across your screen as the person or computer at the other end transmits. If the transmission is slow-paced and casual, you may be able to read the screen and then have the information move into limbo as it scrolls off screen.

More rapid or more important transmissions call for some effective way to preserve them. Even if you don't intend to keep the message, capturing the transmission rapidly as it arrives and then reading it after you sign off may be more economical.

GeoComm provides three ways to capture text. You can copy it to memory, move to another application, and then paste in the information. You can use the **Capture to Text File** command on the **File** menu to save incoming material directly to a file, or use the **File** menu's Save **Buffer** command to preserve all or part of what has scrolled across your screen.

To copy text to another GeoWorks Pro document, follow these steps:

1. Use the mouse to select the data you want to put in memory.

2. Open GeoComm's Edit menu and choose the Copy command. GeoWorks places a copy of the selected text in memory.

3. Switch to the GeoWorks Pro destination where you want to paste the copied information.

4. Use the Paste command from the destination's Edit menu to paste the material in place.

If you want to capture everything on-screen to a file for later review and editing, GeoComm makes the task possible with the Capture to Text File command on the File menu. Choosing the command opens a dialog box that enables you to choose a directory and a file name for an empty capture file. After you create the file and choose Capture, the program sends anything that appears on-screen to the capture file—a text file that you can load into Notepad or GeoWrite for later review and editing.

Because this text file is unformatted, if you want to load it into GeoWrite, use the application's Insert From Text File command on the File menu to locate and paste the file into a blank document. You don't need to do this operation unless you want to apply GeoWrite's formatting features to the text. The Notepad appliance, described in Chapter 12, "Learning Other Desk Tools," is perfectly adequate for routine text editing and printing of a captured document.

To capture a session to a text file, follow these steps:

1. In GeoComm, choose Capture to Text File from the File menu.

   The dialog box shown in figure 9.8 opens.

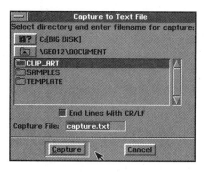

Fig. 9.8

The Capture to Text File dialog box.

2. Use the buttons and lists in the dialog box to move to the location where you want to store the file.

3. Enter a DOS file name (one to eight characters) for the file in the Capture File text box, or accept the default name CAPTURE.TXT.

4. Choose Capture to begin recording everything that crosses your screen. The small Capture Status dialog box keeps you informed of the progress of the transmission.

5. To end recording, click the Done button in the Capture Status dialog box.

The third way to save text on-screen is by using the scroll-back buffer. A *buffer* is a temporary storage area in computer memory. The GeoComm buffer can hold 175 lines of text. As the buffer fills, the program jettisons the oldest material that the latest material replaces. By using the Save **B**uffer command from the **F**ile menu, you can save the contents of the screen, the buffer, or both.

To save data in the scroll-back buffer, follow these steps:

1. From the **F**ile menu choose Save **B**uffer.

   The dialog box shown in figure 9.9 opens.

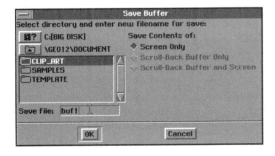

The Save Buffer dialog box.

2. Click the appropriate buttons and list items in the dialog box to move to the location where you want to store the file.

3. Enter a DOS file name (one to eight characters) in the Save File text box.

4. Click a radio button to save the screen, the buffer, or both.

5. Click OK to write the file.

Using XMODEM Error Correction

If the text transmission garbles a word or two, you usually can work out the missing word or do without knowing the word. What if an instruction is unreadable in a program transferred via modem? Computers are absolutely literal-minded. If an instruction that should say *save* actually says *rbgnf*, the computer faithfully tries to *rbgnf* and, in all probability, locks up.

Files that contain computer instructions must be transferred with 100 percent accuracy. To achieve this accuracy, GeoComm uses error-checking protocols such as XMODEM. The program sends a packet of data and then checks it for accuracy. If an error exists, the program sends the packet again and then rechecks until the accuracy is perfect. You don't need to know how the process works to use it. GeoComm has the built-in capability to use XMODEM.

NOTE   You can use XMODEM to ensure absolutely accurate transfer of text files also, but most users don't want to pay the time penalty involved in the error-checking activity. Basically, you want to use XMODEM when you are sending and receiving program files that must be absolutely accurate.

Both sending and receiving computers must be capable of using XMODEM and detecting its use or be set to expect XMODEM before the transfer begins. Both computers participate in the error-checking routines—they must be playing by the same set of rules.

To send a file using XMODEM, follow these steps:

1. From the **F**ile menu choose **S**end XMODEM. The dialog box shown in figure 9.10 opens.

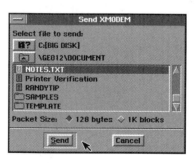

Fig. 9.10

The Send XMODEM dialog box.

2. Use the buttons and lists in the dialog box to locate the file.

3. Choose a packet size. The "lowest common denominator" is 128 bytes for XMODEM. If you know that the remote system can handle 1K (1,024-byte) blocks, that option is faster.

4. Choose **S**end to begin. The Send Status dialog box shows the progress of the transfer.

Receiving XMODEM transfers is a similar process. Follow these steps:

1. Choose **R**eceive XMODEM from the **F**ile menu.

2. Use the buttons and lists in the dialog box to move to the location where you want to store the file.

3. Enter a DOS file name (one to eight characters) and three-character extension in the Receive file text box.

4. Choose the Text button to receive a DOS text file. Choose Binary for any type of program file.

5. Choose the Checksum button for any instance where you are not certain that the more advanced CRC error checking is available.

6. Choose Receive. The Receive Status dialog box (see fig. 9.11) appears, showing the status of the transfer.

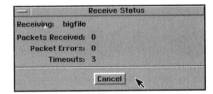

Fig. 9.11

The Receive Status dialog box.

Using Scripts

Scripts are saved sequences of GeoComm commands that you can play back to provide an automatic sequence of actions. With a script, for example, the computer can dial another computer, locate a particular file on your machine, prepare for an XMODEM transfer, send the file, and then beep to tell you that the job is complete.

Creating a script is a type of programming. Scripts use branching and conditional logic to create a series of IF...THEN steps. Teaching script programming is beyond the scope of this book, but in this section you examine a script furnished with GeoWorks and learn how to adapt it for your use. Table 9.2 lists the commands in the scripting language.

Understanding a Sample Script

This section reproduces a script that comes with GeoWorks Pro. The script contains a series of commands that calls the CompuServe information service and signs you on. To use CompuServe, you must set up an account and obtain a password. Most major computer magazines carry ads for CompuServe, containing instructions for signing on.

Read through the script to get a sense of its flow and then continue with the comments that appear after the script. If you encounter a command word you do not know, turn to the listing in "Using GeoComm Script Language" at the end of this chapter. Note that lines preceded by a semicolon are comments that clarify the script. The program does not act on them.

NOTE If you plan to use this script (found in the GeoComm directory), you must insert the correct settings for PORT, COMM, TERM, PHONE NUMBER, ACCOUNT NAME, and PASSWORD fields. Otherwise, the file cannot run correctly. Use Notepad to make these changes.

```
;
; CompuServe automated logon
; $Id: compu.mac,v 1.7.7.1 91/05/03 00:19:16 adam Exp $
;
; CompuServe is a registered trademark of CompuServe
Incorporated.
;
; We assume the modem is COM 1. If otherwise, change this
to 2, 3, or 4.
;
PORT      1
;
; As of 11/1/90, CompuServe recommends "1200-7-E-1-FULL"
for communication.
;
COMM      1200-7-E-1-FULL
;
; If the above settings do not work, use the following
line instead:
; (Remove the semi-colon from the beginning of the line,
and insert
; a semi-colon on the beginning of the COMM line above.
;
;COMM      1200-8-N-1-FULL
;
; set the terminal type
;
TERM      VT100
;
; clear the script display
;
CLEAR
```

```
:retry
PAUSE
PRINT     "This is a sample", CR
PRINT     "script for signing ", CR
PRINT     "on to CompuServe.", CR
PRINT     "You will need to edit", CR
PRINT     "the port, comm, term,", CR
PRINT     "phone number, account name", CR
PRINT     "and password fields.", CR
PRINT     "DIALING", CR
DIAL      "531-1820"
MATCH     "BUSY"        GOTO   retry
MATCH     "CARRIER"     GOTO   retry
MATCH     "CONNECT"     GOTO   connect
PROMPT    1800
PRINT     "TIMEOUT ON DIALING", CR
GOTO      done
:connect
PAUSE
SEND      ^C
MATCH     "Hostname:"   GOTO   host
MATCH     "ID:"         GOTO   id
PROMPT    600
PRINT     "TIMEOUT ON PROMPT", CR
GOTO      done
:id
PAUSE
SEND      "ACCOUNT_NAME",CR
MATCH     "word:"                GOTO    password
PROMPT    600
PRINT     "TIMEOUT ON PASSWORD", CR
GOTO      done
:password
PAUSE
SEND      "PASSWORD",CR
GOTO      done
:host
PAUSE
SEND      "CIS",CR
GOTO      id
:done
PRINT     "DONE",CR
BELL
END
```

continues

```
:ABORT
PRINT      "HANGUP PHONE?",CR
SEND       "+++"
MATCH      "OK"           GOTO   dohup
PROMPT     300
PRINT      "Couldn't disconnect the modem",CR
GOTO       end
;
; Hangup the connection
;
:dohup
SEND       "ATH0",CR
MATCH      "OK"   GOTO    hangup
PROMPT     300
PRINT      "TIMEOUT ON hangup",CR
GOTO       end
:hangup
PRINT      "HUNG UP",CR
:end
BELL
END
```

If you find the script bewildering, maybe a bit of explanation can clear up some puzzles.

The MATCH and PROMPT commands are the heart of the script. The MATCH command looks through the incoming text to find an instance of the text in quotation marks. Look at the sequence that begins just below the :dohup label at the end of the script, for example. The SEND command sends ATH0 to the modem. The ATH0 command tells the modem to hang up.

Next, the MATCH command waits for the OK, which the modem sends when it hangs up. If OK is received, the script goes to the label :hangup, which tells GeoComm to print the message HUNG UP and sound a beep (BELL).

If the OK is not received, the PROMPT command comes into play. The number 300 is the number of 60ths of a second to wait before taking action. Dividing 300 by 60 means a 5-second wait before the PROMPT command passes control to the PRINT command, which puts the message Timeout on Hangup on-screen.

All this may make you want to take up programming or vow never to touch it. Even if you never write a single script, you can learn how to change an existing one. After you begin telecommunicating, you will find others who have written scripts you can download and use on your computer.

Changing a Script

A GeoComm script is an unformatted text file, saved with any first name (one to eight characters) and a MAC extension. The CompuServe script reprinted in the preceding section, for example, is called COMPU.MAC. You can edit scripts most easily in Notepad, which you start from the Express menu. Figure 9.12 shows Notepad running with the COMPU.MAC script.

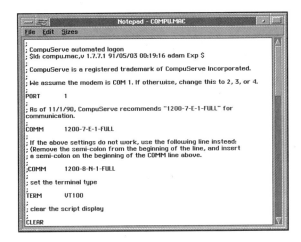

Fig. 9.12

A script displayed in Notepad.

In figure 9.12, the phone number has been selected with the mouse. You edit the script in the same way that you edit other GeoComm text. In this case, typing a new number replaces the old number. You then use the File menu to save the revised script.

Running a Script

For convenience, when you create or edit a script, you should save the script in the GeoComm directory. To run a script, follow these steps:

1. From the **Dial** menu choose **Scripts**.

2. From the Scripts dialog box that appears, select the script you want to run and then choose **Run**.

3. Execution begins and a Script Display dialog box shows you the steps as they are being carried out (see fig. 9.13).

Fig. 9.13

The Script Display
dialog box.

4. If you must intervene to end the script, click the Stop button.

Using GeoComm Script Language

The general rules for reading GeoComm Script Language are as follows:

- Angle brackets(<>) indicate where you must replace a general word with a specific name or instruction.
- All command words must be typed in capital letters.
- A line preceded by a semicolon (;) is not read as part of the script.
- A name preceded by a colon (:) is interpreted as a label.
- The GOTO instructions look for labels.

Table 9.2 contains the 14 commands that comprise the script language. Use the sample scripts as guides to their use.

Table 9.2 The Command Language for Scripts

Command	Action
:ABORT	Special label used if you select Stop in Script Display dialog box
BELL	Directs computer to beep
CLEAR	Clears Script Display dialog box
COMM <*baud-databits-parity-stopbits-duplex*>	Sets communication settings

Command	Action
DIAL *<number>*	Dials specified phone number
END	Ends script
GOTO *<label>*	Jumps to label (see notes in preceding table)
MATCH *<text>* GOTO*<label>* PROMPT*<number>*	If text string matches, jumps to label; if no match after time specified in PROMPT (60ths of a second), falls through to next instruction
PAUSE*<number>*	Pause for number of 60ths of a second equal to number
PORT*<port>*	Specifies which port number to use
PRINT *<text>*	Prints text in Script Display dialog box
PULSE	Specifies pulse phone dialing
SEND *<text>*	Sends text to other computer
TERM *<type>*	Makes GeoComm emulate specified terminal (see list in Terminal command on Options menu)

Chapter Summary

This chapter, devoted to the GeoComm communications application, includes a short primer describing information services and communications equipment, a quick tour of the elements of GeoComm, and a walk-through communications session that gave you a sense of how to conduct on-line communication. You learned how to send and receive DOS text files and binary files using XMODEM. The chapter concludes with an introduction to GeoComm scripts.

Using America Online

Perhaps in your rush to get GeoWorks Pro installed and running, you missed a very important item in the box: the booklet and accompanying card containing all the information necessary to sign-up for the America Online information service. If you have a modem or are thinking about getting one, America Online is an offer that you should consider carefully.

NOTE Because America Online is evolving constantly, some of the screens or menus you see may differ from the figures shown in this book. The general structure and procedures remain stable, however. Taking into consideration the small differences, you can get a successful start using America Online by following the instructions provided in this chapter.

Information services, sometimes called information utilities, are commercial ventures that provide the centralized computers, telephone network, and specialized software to enable computer users with a modem to connect to the resources of the system. Information services, however, are not free.

America Online is an information service like CompuServe, GEnie, or Prodigy; however, America Online has an unique appeal for GeoWorks Pro users. The software is built into your program. If you open GeoManager and look in the upper left corner of the WORLD directory window, you can see an icon for America Online (see fig. 10.1). America Online has been blended almost seamlessly into GeoWorks Pro. The screens look the same and the commands are similar. Best of all,

America Online devotes a section specifically to GeoWorks Pro, which is supervised by GeoWorks personnel and enthusiastic volunteer assistants. You can get any question about GeoWorks Pro answered quickly and accurately.

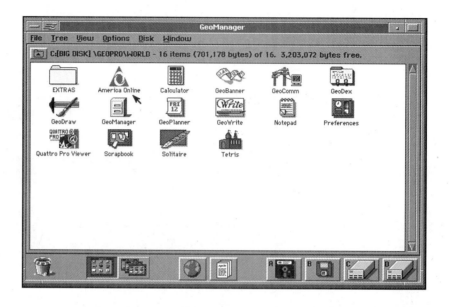

Fig. 10.1

WORLD directory with America Online icon.

This chapter takes you through the procedure necessary to make your first connection with America Online. You must have a modem, and you must give a VISA, MasterCard, or checking account number so that you can be charged for your on-line time. Local phone numbers connect you to the America Online network in most major cities, but if the network cannot be reached by a local call, you also incur long distance charges for your on-line time.

Because the data networks experience heavy use during business hours, you typically find a rate incentive for evening use. In the case of America Online, daytime rate in the Continental U.S. is $10.00 per hour. After 6 p.m., the rate drops to $5.00 per hour. You also must pay a monthly membership fee of $5.95.

Getting Ready

To get started with America Online, you need certain equipment and information. The sign-up process is not complicated; the design of the actual on-screen sign-up anticipates your needs and questions. If you do not yet have a modem, choosing and installing the modem is probably the most complex part of the entire process.

The following list explains what you need to use America Online:

- *Standard phone line.* You should get a modem that is capable of working with both rotary and TouchTone phone lines. You don't need a second phone line. Most modems have phone jacks in the back that enable you to plug in and use a phone when the modem is not active. If you begin to make extensive use of the modem, however, you may want to consider a dedicated line. Friends trying to call you may get exasperated at the constant busy signal.

- *Hayes-compatible modem.* A modem is a device that translates signals from your computer into signals that can be transmitted over telephone lines. The word modem is a contraction of the term *modulator-demodulator,* a reference to how the signals are changed (modulated) at the transmitting end and returned to their original state (demodulated) at the receiving end.

  Hayes Microcomputer Products, Inc. has been an early and consistent leader in the manufacture of modems. The instruction set to which a Hayes modem responds has become a standard in the PC industry. Almost all communication software, including the software in GeoWorks Pro, uses the Hayes instruction set. A modem that responds to the Hayes instruction set is *Hayes-compatible.* A modem you purchase for use with GeoComm or America Online does not have to be Hayes brand, but it must be compatible with the Hayes command set.

  To you, the most important feature of a modem is its transmission speed. The faster you can send and receive, the less connect time you use, and, hence, the less expense you incur. A *baud* is a measurement of modem speed equivalent to the number of characters per second that the modem can send or receive. Today, 1200 baud is considered a minimum, 2400 baud has become the norm, and 9600 baud is the leading edge.

  Modem price is directly related to speed. But don't overbuy. You cannot transmit any faster than the other end can receive, and you cannot receive any faster than the other end can transmit. Although America Online works well with both 1200 or 2400 baud modems, the 2400 baud modem is the recommended choice. This modem costs somewhat more that the 1200 baud modem, but you save money in the long run because the 2400 baud modem moves twice as much material per minute of connect time.

- *The America Online certificate.* You can find this certificate in the GeoWorks Pro box. The certificate outlines the sign-up process and contains the serial number and password you use to get on-line initially.

■ *A credit card or checking account number.* You need one of these items to pay for your on-line time. You can use MasterCard or VISA. America Online asks for this information during the course of your sign-on.

Signing On

The America Online sign-on procedure integrates smoothly into GeoWorks Pro. The first time you double-click the America Online icon, windows asking for the necessary hardware, software, and personal information appear. *Note:* Although you won't see a figure for every step in the sign-on process, the figures included cover the main "milestones."

If you have a standard setup—a 2400 baud modem connected to the COM1 port—you can move straight through the procedure. If you have a different modem or connection, or if you need to dial a prefix before phone numbers (like a 9 to get an outside line), be sure to click the Other Options button (explained in step 3).

To sign-on to America Online, do the following:

1. Start GeoManager and open the WORLD view. If you have not already turned on your modem, do so now.

2. Locate the America Online icon in the WORLD window. Double-click the icon to start America Online. The screen shown in figure 10.2 appears automatically if you have not signed up.

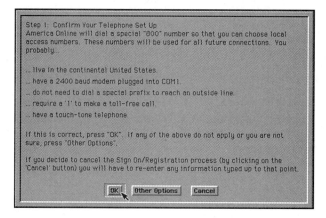

The opening sign-up screen.

3. If you have a standard number (no dialing prefixes) and a 2400 baud modem attached to the COM1 port (the sign-on sequence is geared to this combination), click OK.

If you do not have the standard setup, click the Other Options button and refer to "Using Other Options" at the end of these instructions. You need additional information before you can proceed with these steps.

If your settings are OK, the program dials a built-in 800 number. The number connects you to a database of phone numbers that connect with America Online.

4. Type your phone number in the dialog box shown in figure 10.3. Based on that information, the database presents a list of possible numbers for your local access number.

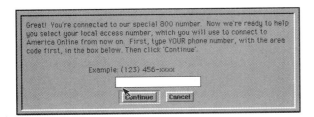

Fig. 10.3

The enter phone number screen.

5. Scroll through the list (see fig. 10.4) to find the nearest America Online number and an alternate number. Click the buttons at the bottom of the window to pick a number or continue searching. Notice that particular modem speeds require certain numbers. Pick a speed that matches your modem's capabilities.

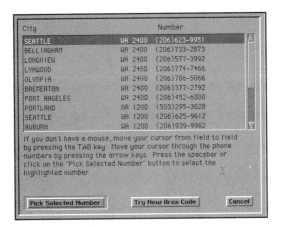

Fig. 10.4

The list of America Online numbers available for local access, based on your phone number.

When you pick a number, the first Welcome to America Online! dialog box appears (see fig. 10.5).

6. Enter the certificate number and code words found on the card in your GeoWorks Pro package and click the Continue button.

7. Enter your name, address, and home phone number on the screen that follows the code screen (see fig. 10.6).

8. You must choose a screen name to use when you are on-line (see fig. 10.7). The dialog box suggests a screen name (alias), but you can enter any name.

   One fundamental purpose of an alias is to deal with duplicate names on the system. The other purpose is to inject a bit of fun into the process. People behave more freely when wearing their network identities, however, this alias isn't a license to be a jerk. Network administrators know users' real names; if any out-of-line behavior occurs, the offender quite probably will be booted from the system.

9. The next screen asks you to make up a password and type the password twice for verification (see fig. 10.8). GeoWorks echoes your typing with asterisks so that someone looking over your shoulder cannot read the password you enter. Guard your password with care. Anyone who knows the password can run up on-line charges in your name. Store a copy of the password in a safe place in case you forget the password you use.

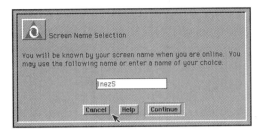

Fig. 10.7

The screen name
(alias) dialog box.

NOTE Sophisticated programs run the dictionary against known
account names to detect passwords. To avoid this problem,
use a combination—such as a # in the middle or a symbol—
that is not in the dictionary.

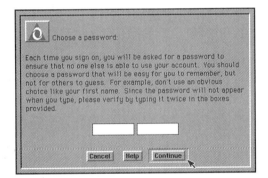

Fig. 10.8

The password dialog
box.

10. On the next screen, choose a payment method: MasterCard, VISA,
    or a debit to your checking account.

11. After you complete all the steps, the America Online Welcome
    screen appears. This screen is the on-line equivalent of the
    GeoWorks Pro Welcome screen. (see fig. 10.9)

Fig. 10.9

The America Online
Welcome screen.

12. To sign-off, select the File menu and choose Exit. A dialog box appears, asking if you want to sign-off. If you choose **Yes**, the connection is broken. Even though you see the sign-on screen, you are no longer connected. Press F3 to close the America Online screen.

Using Other Options

NOTE You need to read this section only if step 3 of the sign-on procedure in this book referred you here. Otherwise, you can continue to the next section, "Exploring Online."

If you don't have the standard setup for the automatic installation program design (2400 baud modem connected to COM1) or if you dial a prefix before the main number, you need to enter more information. Clicking the Other Options button at the bottom of the first registration screen takes you through a little "loop" of windows that guide you to entering the necessary additional information.

To enter information under Other Options, follow these steps:

1. On the first automatic registration screen, click the Other Options button. The window shown in figure 10.10 appears.

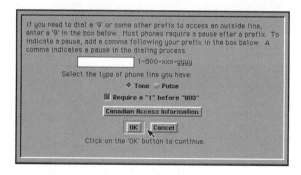

If you need to dial a '9' or some other prefix to access an outside line, enter a '9' in the box below. Most phones require a pause after a prefix. To indicate a pause, add a comma following your prefix in the box below. A comma indicates a pause in the dialing process.

[_____] 1-800-xxx-yyyy

Select the type of phone line you have:

◆ Tone ◇ Pulse

☐ Require a "1" before "800"

[Canadian Access Information]

[OK] [Cancel]

Click on the 'OK' button to continue.

Fig. 10.10

The Other Options settings dialog box.

2. If you use a dialing prefix, enter the prefix in the text field. If the number requires a pause after the prefix, type a comma to indicate the pause.

3. Specify whether you use tone or pulse dialing by clicking the appropriate button.

4. Click the box if you need to dial 1 before an 800 number. This rather odd request enables the program to know how to dial the 800 number that is part of the automatic sign-on procedure.

5. Click OK to record the settings and continue.

   A second settings box appears, in which you record nonstandard modem settings (see fig. 10.11).

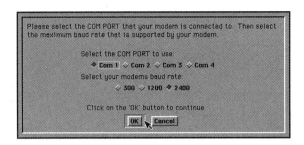

Fig. 10.11

The second Other Options dialog box.

6. Click the name of the serial port that your modem uses. If you are not sure, consult your hardware information or look for a label on your computer where the modem cable attaches. Usually, the modem attaches to the ports marked COM1 or COM2.

7. Click the proper baud rate for your modem.

8. Click OK to complete and record your input. GeoWorks returns you to the remainder of the sign-on process. ***Note:*** If you jumped to this section from step 3 of the Signing On section, return to the "Signing On" section and continue steps 4 through 12.

If you cannot get things running, contact the GeoWorks support staff who assist with first time installation. At the time of this writing, the support number is 1-800-227-6364.

Exploring Online

You have to go through the sign-on process only once. The program remembers for subsequent sessions the information you entered in the initial process. To enter America Online again, you only have to turn on your modem, double-click the America Online icon, and enter your password. The Welcome screen for America Online appears.

Your familiarity with GeoWorks Pro can help you use America Online. Because of the design and integration, the built-in America Online software presents an interface that blends right into the GeoWorks Pro structure. Commands work the same way and windows management is the same so that as soon as you get the "lay of the land" in America Online, you can use America Online with ease.

Browsing America Online

Later in this chapter, you find a full description of the menus at the top of the America Online window. The next section highlights the major departments of the service. If you are like a majority of users, you are dying to get on-line and see what this America Online is all about.

This section includes quick tips that enable you to get right to exploring America Online; however, continue reading after you satisfy your initial burst of curiosity. America Online contains much more "good stuff" than meets the eye.

To connect to America Online, follow these steps:

1. Turn on your modem.

2. Open the GeoManager WORLD directory and double-click the America Online icon. The sign-on status screen shown in figure 10.12 appears.

Fig. 10.12

The sign-on status box.

3. The sign-on process proceeds automatically until you see the prompt `Please enter your password:` (see fig. 10.13). Enter your password.

Fig. 10.13

The password dialog box.

GeoWorks connects you to America Online, and the America Online Welcome screen appears (see fig. 10.14).

Fig. 10.14

The America Online
welcome screen.

At the bottom the welcome screen is a tempting button, the Browse the
Service button. Don't fight the temptation, click the button! The Browse
the Service screen appears (see fig. 10.15). This screen has a row of buttons across the top representing the departments of America Online.
Refer to table 10.2 for a brief explanation of the contents of each
department.

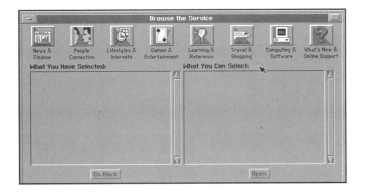

Fig. 10.15

The Browse the
Service screen.

For this session, limit your exploration to the What's New & Online Support area. If you are calling after 6:00 p.m. or on a weekend, this section
of the service is free. Follow these steps:

1. Click the What's New & Online Support button at the far right of the
    Browse the Service screen. You see a message explaining that text
    which enters this free section shuts down others. Click Yes to
    continue.

    The two list windows, which fill the lower two-thirds of the browse
    screen, display the listings you see in figure 10.16.

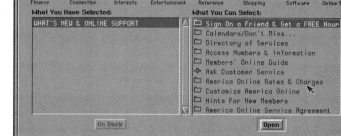

Fig. 10.16

The Browse the Service screen with What's New & Online Support selected.

The What You Have Selected list keeps track of how many "layers" deep you have progressed. Right now, you are at the top level for What's New & Online Support. Each time you open a folder in the What You Can Select window, the "layer" you enter adds to the What You Have Selected list on the right. By clicking any entry on the right, you can return quickly to that level.

2. Double-click the folder icon beside Member's Online Guide from the What You Can Select list.

You open a folder that contains sub-folders, each one a *chapter* of the Online Guide displayed on the What You Can Select side of the screen. Notice that the left-hand list shows you are two layers deep in the What's New & Online Support department (see fig. 10.17).

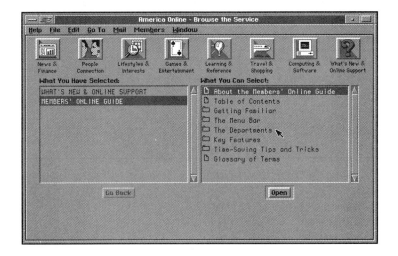

Fig. 10.17

Two levels deep in
What's New & Online
Support.

3. Select a folder that interests you and open the folder by double-clicking the folder name. (Examine the left-hand list; you are three layers deep.)

4. Browse the contents of the folder with the scroll bar (see fig. 10.18).

   Later in this chapter, you learn how to save this kind of information to your hard disk so that you can read or print it at another time.

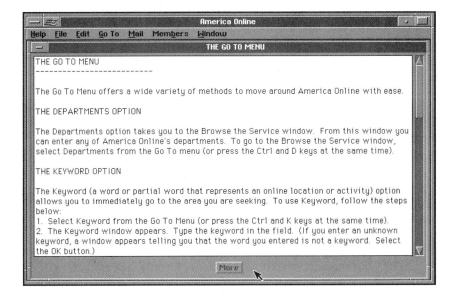

Fig. 10.18

Scroll to read folder
information.

346

5. To close the window, double-click the Control button in the upper left corner of the window. You move up one layer in the left-hand list on the Browse the Service screen.

6. Return to the top layer by double-clicking the top entry in the left-hand list.

These steps cover the rudiments of navigating through the America Online departments and windows. From here, you can experiment on your own, read more of the on-line guide, or sign-off and return later.

To sign-off from any location, do the following:

1. Open the File menu at the top of the America Online window.

2. Choose Exit. A dialog box asks you to confirm your choice to leave. Choose Yes to leave America Online.

   You also can exit by clicking the Exit Application button. Clicking the Exit Application button shuts down both the on-line and GeoWorks Pro parts of America Online. The GeoManager screen appears.

3. Press F3 to sign-off and return to the GeoWorks WORLD directory.

Understanding America Online Departments

America Online has a rich resource of instructional and help features. The following brief explanation of the service can serve as a planning guide for your on-line excursions. You can save time and money by planning your visit, choosing places you most want to explore, and saving others for later visits. You soon learn that the excitement generated by the on-line experience can lead to unexpectedly high on-line fees and possibly long-distance charges.

Table 10.2 briefly describes the main areas of America Online and some of the features you can find in each section. This limited listing can only suggest the depth and interest of this electronic crossroads. This kind of listing becomes outdated rapidly as interests ebb and flow. Although you may not find some of the listed items, you will find something new.

Table 10.2 America Online Departments

Department	Features
News & Finance	*USA Today* on-line and *Fight Back with David Horowitz*; news sections covering business, stocks, sports, technology, and entertainment
People Connection	Live conferencing and chatting with other America Online members; continuing conferences on items like teen topics, romance novels, word games, and more; major conferences at Center Stage; public and private chatting CB-style
Lifestyles & Interests	Arts and entertainment activities, career interests, hobbies, family development, special interests, sports stories, and fantasy sports leagues
Games & Entertainment	LaPub fun events; RabbitJack's Casino, MasterWord, Bulls and Bears game, Trivia Club, and entertainment news
Learning & Reference	Academic American Encyclopedia, Dictionary of Computer Terms, Interactive Education Service, Teachers' Information Network, College Board Online
Travel & Shopping	Comp-u-store Online, AutoVantage, Travel Services, Bose Express Music, Flower Shop, LaserDirect Printing Service, classified ads
Computing & Software	Computing forums, software libraries, Industry Connection, news and reference, message board
What's New & Online Support	Members Guide, rates and charges, calendars, member directory, Town Hall, create/delete screen names

Using GeoWorks Forum

One of your first stops after you master the basics of America Online should be the GeoWorks Forum. The Forum is an outstanding resource for support, services, software, and friendship. Staffed by several employees of GeoWorks and a crew of dedicated volunteers, the Forum is an on-line world where you can turn for help, information, or a chat with a fellow GeoWorks Pro user.

If you want to find your way to the GeoWorks forum from the Browse the Service window, you must go down four layers. You also can enter Forum by selecting the **G**o To menu at the top of the Browse window and choosing **K**eywords. In the dialog box that appears, type the keyword **geoworks** and click OK (see fig. 10.19). You are at the front door of the GeoWorks Forum (see fig. 10.20).

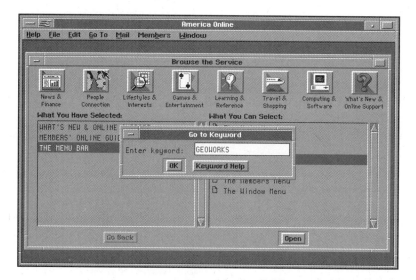

Fig. 10.19

The Go To Keyword dialog box.

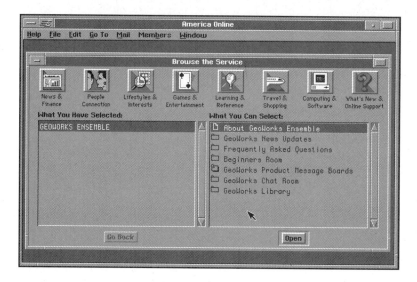

Fig. 10.20

The Geo Works Forum screen.

The main sections of the forum list in the right hand window in the GeoWorks Forum screen. The following list briefly describes the Forum sections:

- *GeoWorks News Updates.* Provides current messages describing newsworthy activities concerning the company, the software, or events of interest to GeoWorks Pro users.

- *Frequently Asked Questions.* Contains a distillation of wisdom, which can benefit new users, from the technical support staff at GeoWorks.

- *Beginners Room.* Provides a safe haven if you are embarrassed or uncertain about asking questions. You get a quick personal reply and useful references to individuals or other areas in the Forum that can help. Setting up mini-tutorials if you are having unusual difficulty with a topic is also possible.

- *GeoWorks Product Message Boards.* Provides a lively give and take between a variety of participants, including all levels of GeoWorks Pro users and company experts. Here is the place to post an opinion or a question or to prowl through the chain of responses on a variety of topics.

- *GeoWorks Chat Room.* A location for organized communication among GeoWorks Pro users, which posts a list of planned activities. If you are in the Chat Room at the right time and date, you can participate live in a variety of program-related discussions.

- *GeoWorks Library.* Contains a treasure-house of material ranging from indispensable to trivial and updates of major sections of the program (an improved GEOS.EXE, for example). You can also find art for every taste, games, articles, photo backgrounds for your screen—in short, lots of the stuff that makes computing so interesting.

Downloading Software

After you find the Library, you probably want to get your hands on some of the excellent files available for downloading.

The process of transferring a file from a remote service to your computer is *downloading*. Conversely, if you send a file to a remote location, you have *uploaded* the file. Giving full instructions on downloading and uploading is beyond the scope of this chapter, but the instructions that follow explain how to save text files that explain how to accomplish many of the activities on America Online.

A text file explaining the downloading process serves as an example. The file names and locations are correct at the time of writing, but on-line libraries are dynamic. As new files arrive, the program removes or relocates old ones. If you have trouble locating a file, post a message in the Beginners Room.

The example deals with small text files because most program and image files, as well as larger text files, have been compressed, using a program called PKZIP. *Compression* reduces file size to shorten the time and cost of transmission. To use *zipped* (compressed) files, you must download PKZIP and its companion PKUNZIP. The file containing the programs also includes instructions for using the programs.

In this section, you learn how to save the file that explains downloading. You can apply the same technique to any text file on America Online that is not a *zipped* file. The instructions provided in the downloaded files tell you how to deal with these types of files.

To save a text file for later reading off-line, sign-on to America Online, and then do the following:

1. Select the **Go** To menu, choose **K**eywords, and in the dialog box that opens, type **geoworks**.

2. When the GeoWorks window opens, double-click the Beginners Room. The window shown in figure 10.21 appears. Double-click the "How To" Answers item to open it.

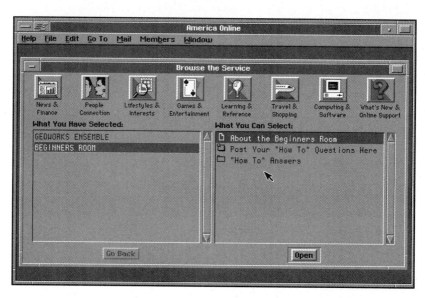

The GeoWorks Forum "Beginners Room" area.

3. Examine the list of messages for a file called How to Download a File. If you cannot see this file, click the More button at the bottom of the list. Continue paging through the messages until you find the file on downloading.

4. Double-click the file name in the list to open it on-screen (see fig. 10.22). Although you can read through the file now, you should save the file for off-line viewing.

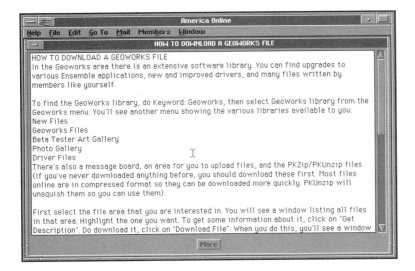

Fig. 10.22

An open file on-line.

5. Select the File menu and choose Save. The dialog box shown in figure 10.23 appears, enabling you to select the directory in which you want to save the file. For this example, choose the DOCUMENT directory.

6. After you choose the directory, click OK. If the file is short, you may barely notice any activity on your computer, but the program saves the message to the destination you specified.

7. Press F3 to sign-off America Online and click OK to confirm your sign-off. Clicking the Exit Application button shuts down America Online completely.

You can use this method to capture any sort of uncompressed text file from America Online. The program copies the entire text of a message, including any part that does not appear on-screen.

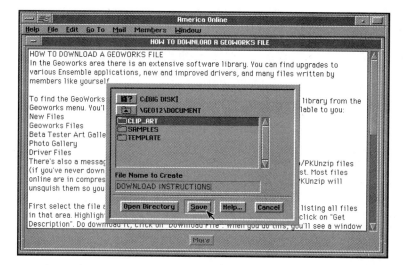

Fig. 10.23

The save as dialog box.

Because the transfer procedure uses a DOS file system, the files you save appear in your GeoWorks Pro directory display as DOS document icons.

Because these files are DOS files, you cannot read them in GeoWrite without opening them as text files; however, you can read the files by using the Open command from the File menu in the America Online window. You also can use the Notepad desk tool, which is capable of reading DOS files.

Use these steps to read your saved text files:

1. Choose the **O**pen command from the America Online window **F**ile menu. A file list dialog box appears.

2. In the dialog, locate the text file you want to view.

3. Double-click the file name to open the file (see fig. 10.24). You can scroll through the file, as well as edit and print the file, using commands from the File and Edit menus.

Fig. 10.24

A text file opened in America Online.

4. To exit the window, double-click the Control button in the upper left corner of the text window.

Using the saving and viewing techniques in this section, you can collect a specialized manual of America Online information and tips, which serve as excellent references. The techniques described here, in connection with the GeoWorks Forum, can be used in any other area of America Online where text messages are available.

Understanding America Online Menus and Commands

Your America Online activity proceeds within a window that has many of the same features as other GeoWorks Pro windows. Table 10.3 describes the menus and their commands.

Table 10.3 The America Online Menus

Menu or Command	Action
Help Menu	Obtains help information and modifies setup and viewing options
Get Help	Opens window with list of help topics
About America Online	Presents dialog box showing America Online version
File Menu	Enables you to create, save, modify, get information about, and print files
New	Opens a new blank text document
Open	Presents a list of text files you can read in the America Online window; opens the files
Save	Saves a file
Save **As**	Saves to a different location with a different file name
Disk Utilities	Presents tools for modifying files, renaming files, and so on
Print	Prints active document

continues

Table 10.3 continued

Menu or Command	Action
Logging	Saves a record of your on-line session to a file
Cancel Action(**x**)	Clears current changes
Exit	Leaves America Online
Edit Menu	Enables you to Cu**t**, **C**opy, or **P**aste text to edit documents saved from America Online
Go To Menu	Enables you to move to various areas of America Online
Setup & Sign On	Enables you to go on-line from GeoWorks
Departments	Opens the Browse the Service window from which you can move to any department, using icons
Keyword	Enables you to enter keywords that take you directly to a destination; contains lists of keywords in Directory of Services under What's New/Online Support
Directory of Services	Takes you to a searchable database of all America Online offerings
Lobby	Moves you to a public *chat* area where you can talk with other America Online members
What's New & Online Support	Jumps you to the support area for questions, calendars, and on-line manuals
Network News	Presents short news items
Edit Go To Menu	Changes items chosen with Ctrl+number key. *Note:* Remainder of this menu shows locations assigned to Ctrl+number keys, which can be edited with this command
Mail Menu	Enables you to read, write, and send electronic mail

Menu or Command	Action
Compose mail	Opens a window in which you can write a message
Read New Mail	Presents unread mail for you to read
Check Mail You've Read	Presents a list of old mail
Check Mail You've Sent	Reviews recently sent messages
Fax/Paper mail	Originates a fax or letter via AOL
Edit Address Book	Keeps your list of on-line addresses
Members Menu	Contains information about and communication with America Online members
Send Instant Message	Sends an unsavable private note to someone currently on-line
Get a Member's Profile	Presents a profile of an America Online member
Locate Member Online	Locates members currently on-line
Search Member Directory	Displays searchable directory of current America Online members
Edit Your Online Profile	Creates a short biography for others to view
Preferences	Sets text appearance in on-line windows
Edit Screen Names	Changes your "alias"
Window Menu	Lists open windows and provides commands for managing them. *Note:* The menu lists open windows at the bottom
Hide	Conceals, but does not close, current window
Close	Shuts down the current window
Close All Windows	Shuts down all windows
Overlapping	Shows multiple windows, including Browse the Service
Full-Sized	Enlarges Browse the Service to fill entire screen

T I P For those who travel and still want to keep in touch on-line, GWRepJohn provides this reminder: you will have to change your local access numbers in order to avoid long distance charges. Before you leave, sign on to America Online. Click the What's New and Online Support icon; then open Access Numbers and Information. Open the Local Access Numbers folder and locate the folder with the correct state. Select the closest city to your travel destination and choose the access number that matches your modem speed. Write the information down.

Sign off; then click Setup in the America Online dialog box. *Write down the current numbers for use when you return.* Edit the information for primary and secondary numbers and the correct service (Tymenet or Telenet). Don't enter the area code since the access numbers will be local for you. Click OK to save the changes.

Sign on to America Online when you arrive at your destination and enter your password. If you are presented with a dialog box that asks for the certificate information, just enter your screen name and then your password and you should be set. Have a good trip!

Chapter Summary

This chapter serves as a capsule introduction to America Online, the information service that is built into GeoWorks Pro. This chapter also discusses the necessary equipment, describes sign-on procedures step by step, and explains provisions for nonstandard equipment and modem problems. In addition, the chapter provides specific guidance for your first time on-line and teaches you how to download a text file from GeoWorks Forum, as well as providing information on the departments within America Online and the contents of the service window menus.

If you spend any time in the GeoWorks Forum, be sure to converse with some of the excellent GeoWorks employees and volunteers who staff the service—not only is their knowledge of GeoWorks Pro extraordinary, but they are nice people also. Drop by and say hello!

Using Advanced Features

Customizing with the Preferences Desk Tool

When you install GeoWorks Pro, GeoWorks analyzes your hardware and asks questions that help the program make choices for installation. Usually, GeoWorks does a remarkably good job of fitting itself to your equipment. As good as the results are, however, GeoWorks cannot read your mind. (Although the folks at GeoWorks haven't developed a mind-reading module yet, they are probably working on one now.) A number of choices are matters of pure personal preference.

The Preferences desk tool enables you to tailor your GeoWorks environment (see fig. 11.1). You can change screen appearance, date and time formats, and screen backgrounds, as well as printer, computer, and video types. You also can alter the mouse type, enter modem settings, and modify internal GEOS options. You can find support for a variety of keyboards, international date and time settings, and sound control.

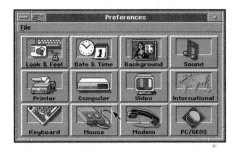

Fig. 11.1

The Preferences desk tool.

This chapter takes you through the possibilities presented by the option buttons in the Preferences window. Using these options, you can customize GeoWorks Pro to your personal working style.

The Look & Feel Option Button

The Look & Feel option button opens the Look & Feel dialog box (see fig. 11.2). In this box, you can alter settings for screen font size, automatic document saves (*safeguarding*), the screen with which GeoWorks opens, and enable overstrike mode. (Version 1.0 includes a button in the Look & Feel selections to turn sound off and on.)

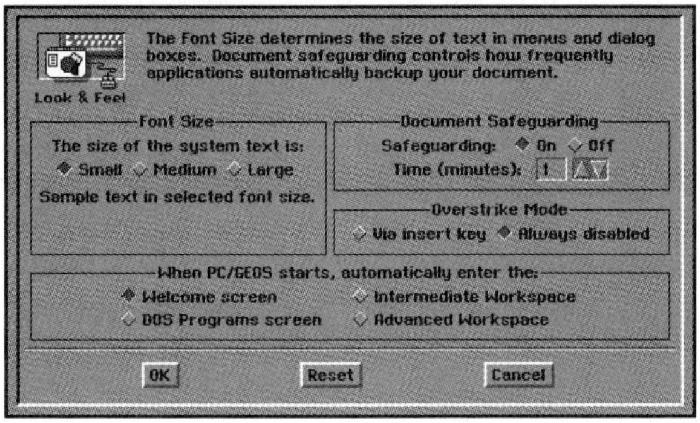

Fig. 11.2

The Look & Feel dialog box.

In this section, you learn the options in the Look & Feel dialog box. To open the Look & Feel dialog box, click the Look & Feel button from the Preferences menu. All the descriptions in this section involve sections of the Look & Feel dialog box.

Changing Font Size

In the Font Size area of the Look & Feel dialog box you can use the radio buttons to choose the default system text size you want for all standard screen text in menus and dialog boxes. You still, however, can change fonts and font sizes in applications that have controls for that purpose. The default text size when you install GeoWorks is Small.

To change the size of system text, follow these steps:

1. Click the Small, Medium, or Large radio button.

   The message Sample text in selected font size. changes in size to represent the text size you choose.

2. Click OK.

   When you change the size, a dialog box appears telling you the program must be restarted to put the new font in place.

3. Choose **Yes** to restart and use the new font. You can choose **No** to return to the Look & Feel dialog box. Click Reset or the radio button for the original size setting to restore the original font.

Using Document Safeguarding

Document safeguarding saves a temporary copy of your document at specified intervals. If the power is interrupted or another problem occurs, you can retrieve the temporary copy. You lose only the work you did since the last time GeoWorks safeguarded your document. Safeguarding takes only a moment; if you place any value on your work, you should activate this feature.

To safeguard your documents, do the following:

1. In the Document Safeguarding section of the Look & Feel dialog box, click On to activate safeguarding.

2. Enter the time between saves by typing the number of minutes in the Time (minutes) text field or clicking the increase and decrease arrows until the number of minutes appears in the text field.

3. Click OK to enter the new options (after making all the changes you require in the Look & Feel dialog box); or click Reset to return to the preceding settings.

Changing the Start-up Screen

The Look & Feel settings enable you to specify what screen appears when you start GeoWorks Pro. You can choose the default Welcome screen, the Intermediate Workspace screen (in GeoWorks Pro), the Advanced Workspace screen, or the DOS Programs screen. For the beginner, the Welcome screen provides easy and predictable entry to the main GeoWorks Pro areas. When you are more familiar with the program you may want automatically to open the Advanced or Intermediate Workspaces or the DOS Programs area.

The Intermediate Workspace focuses on the File Cabinet, a screen that enables you to manage files and directories without learning complex DOS commands. Chapter 3, "Learning File Cabinet," contains complete information on the Intermediate Workspace.

The Advanced Workspace contains thirteen applications. Depending on your purpose and the available memory in your computer, you can have several applications active at the same time. You can, for example, be writing a letter in GeoWrite and, without closing GeoWrite, open GeoDraw to retrieve an illustration for use in the letter.

If you are called away, and you shut down GeoWorks Pro with GeoWrite and GeoDraw in use, you will find when re-entering the Advanced Workspace that both applications are active with the documents you were working on when you quit. In this sense, the Advanced Workspace is chameleon-like, presenting a display that depends on what you did in the last session. See Chapter 4, "Mastering GeoManager," for further examples of configuring the Advanced Workspace.

From the DOS Programs screen, you create program buttons to start DOS programs in GeoWorks Pro. Chapter 13, "Operating DOS Programs," is devoted to this topic. You may want the DOS Programs screen as your start-up screen if you use GeoWorks Pro as a control tower from which you hop in and out of DOS applications.

To choose a different start-up screen follow these steps:

1. At the bottom of the Look & Feel dialog box, click the button for the starting screen you choose.

2. Click OK to record your choice (after making all the changes you require in the Look & Feel dialog box); or click Reset to return to the preceding setting.

   The next time you start GeoWorks Pro, it opens to the selected screen.

Enabling Overstrike

Overstriking (also called overtyping) occurs when the text you type replaces the existing text instead of pushing the existing text to the right. Using this feature is a matter of personal preference; however, the default setting of GeoWorks Pro is Always disabled. When activated, you can toggle overstrike on and off by pressing Ins. When you activate overstrike, the text cursor becomes noticeably wider. ***Note:*** Overstrike is available anywhere in GeoWorks Pro where text is used.

To enable the overstrike feature, do the following:

1. In the Overstrike mode area of the Look & Feel dialog box, click the Via Insert key.

2. Click OK to record your choice (after making all your changes in the dialog box); or click Reset to return to Always disabled.

    To use the overstrike feature, press Ins. The text cursor appears wider (see fig. 11.3). To turn overstrike off, press Ins again.

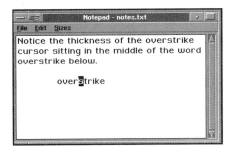

Fig. 11.3

The wider overstrike text cursor.

The Printer Option Button

GeoWorks Pro supports an unusually wide range of printers. From a list that contains much more than just a few generic printer drivers, you can probably find a driver that is not only specifically tailored to your printer, but also capable of using special features and managing the eccentricities of your particular printer brand. The Printer option button in the Preferences window opens a dialog box containing several buttons for modifying your printer setup (see fig. 11.4).

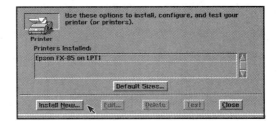

Fig. 11.4

The Printer dialog box.

The scrolling list in the Printer dialog box shows printers you have installed. If you installed a dot-matrix printer for high speed drafts, a laser printer for finished work, or you use network printers in your office, these printers are listed in the Printer dialog box.

In this section, you work within the Printer dialog box. You don't have to exit the dialog box until you complete the following guided tour. Click the Printer option button in the Preferences screen to open the Printer dialog box.

Using Default Paper and Document Sizes

Click the Default Sizes button in the Printer dialog box to open the dialog box shown in figure 11.5. Although the lists in the two windows are identical, a moment's thought reveals some situations in which paper size and document size might not be the same. You may want to draft correspondence for an executive size letterhead (7 1/2-by-10-inch paper) and print the correspondence on 8 1/2-by-11-inch paper, for example. Various envelope sizes are also included at the end of the lists.

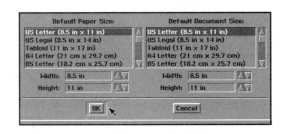

Fig. 11.5

The Default Paper and Document Size dialog box.

Because GeoWorks Pro is distributed internationally, popular metric paper sizes are available as well. You also can find some large sizes that your printer can output by printing multiple sheets.

To set default paper and document sizes, follow these steps:

1. In the Default Paper and Document Size dialog box, select the desired sizes using the lists and scroll bars.

   To change paper or document width and height in half-inch increments, use the increase and decrease arrows under the windows.

2. Click OK to record your setting, or click Cancel to return to the original settings and exit the dialog box.

Changing Printers

GeoWorks asks you to install a printer during the course of your first GeoWorks Pro installation, but if you *add* another printer, you must use the Install New option in the Printer dialog box..

To install or change a printer, follow these steps:

1. Choose Install **N**ew in the Printer dialog box.

   The dialog box shown in figure 11.6 opens.

Fig. 11.6

The dialog box used to install a new printer.

2. In the Printer section of the dialog box, use the scroll bars or type the first letter of the printer name to move to the appropriate section of the list.

3. Choose the name of the printer you want to install.

4. In the Port section of the dialog box, choose the port to which the printer attaches. ***Note:*** The most common connection is *LPT1* for parallel printers and *COM1* for serial printers. Consult the printer literature if you are unsure about the connection your printer requires.

5. If you choose a serial printer, the Serial Port Options button becomes available. Click this button to open a dialog box for port settings (see fig. 11.7).

   Consult your printer literature for guidance on the appropriate settings.

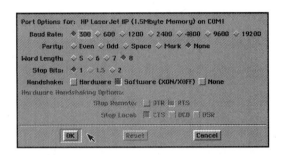

6. Edit the printer name. You can edit the printer name box to say anything. If you want to call the printer another name for convenience or fun, the program remembers the settings associated with the original name. Make a note of the original printer description in case you need to restore it.

7. Click OK to complete the printer selection and return to the Printer dialog box.

8. Choose Close to exit the Printer dialog box (after making all your changes in the dialog box).

Editing Printer Information

If you change your printer arrangement, you may need to alter information about printer brand, connections, or printer name. To change printer information, follow these steps:

1. Click the name of the printer for which you want to change information.

2. Choose Edit in the Printer dialog box.

   The dialog box used for installing a new printer opens (refer to fig. 11.6).

3. Change the printer type, printer port, or printer name.

4. Click OK to close the list of printers and return to the Printer dialog box.

5. Choose **C**lose to exit the Printer dialog box and record your changes (after making all your changes in the dialog box).

Testing a Printer

A test page is provided to ensure that your printer is installed correctly. To check your printer, use the following steps:

1. In the Printer dialog box, click the name of the printer you want to test.

2. Inspect your printer to determine that it is switched on and the on-line indicator shows that the printer is connected to your computer.

3. Choose **T**est at the bottom of the dialog box.

4. After the test page prints, choose **C**lose to exit the Printer dialog box (after making all your choices in the dialog box).

Deleting a Printer

If you need to remove a printer from the list of installed printers, follow these steps:

1. In the Printer dialog box, click the name of the printer you want to remove.

2. Choose **D**elete. GeoWorks removes the printer from the list.

3. Choose **C**lose to close the Printer dialog box (after making all your changes in the dialog box).

The Keyboard Option Button

Users of GeoWorks Pro can get an appreciation for what is required to support a program internationally by scrolling through the list of possible keyboard choices. You probably never knew that so many possibilities existed. Even though you cannot change the basic keyboard type, you can find other options helpful.

Keyboard Delay changes how long you must hold down a key before it repeats. Keyboard Repeat Rate sets the speed of the repeat. In addition to changing keyboard delay and repeat rates, you can make some useful alterations in the way certain keys respond. The power typists in the group may especially appreciate these nuances.

Changing Keyboard Delay and Repeat Rates

To reset the keyboard delay or repeat rate, follow these steps:

1. In the Preferences window, click the Keyboard option button to open the Keyboard dialog box (see fig. 11.8).

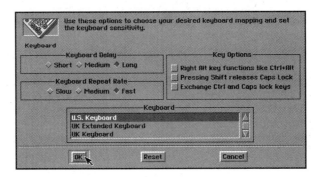

Fig. 11.8

The Keyboard dialog box.

2. In the Keyboard Delay or Keyboard Repeat Rate areas of the window, click the radio button for the speed you choose. The options for delay and repeat can be different from one another.

3. Click OK to confirm your choice, or click Reset to restore the original settings.

    If you choose OK, a dialog box appears, indicating that the program must be restarted for the change to take effect.

4. Choose **Yes** to restart and implement the change.

Changing Key Options

In the Key Options box, GeoWorks displays three options to change a key's behavior:

- *Right Alt key functions like Ctrl+Alt.* Because of the frequent use of Ctrl-Alt keystroke combinations in some applications, you can make the right Alt key function like the combination of Ctrl+Alt.

- *Pressing Shift releases Caps Lock.* This change enables you to re-lease the Caps Lock key by pressing the Shift key. Using this option may be useful if Caps Lock is in an awkward location on your keyboard.

- *Exchange Ctrl and Caps Lock keys.* The third key change enables you to exchange the function of the Ctrl and Caps Lock keys. If you make frequent use of keyboard shortcuts involving the Ctrl key, you may find placing the Ctrl function at the more easily reached Caps Lock key location beneficial.

To implement any of the preceding key options, follow these steps:

1. In the Key Options section of the Keyboard dialog box, click any or all of the options to make key changes.

2. Click OK to confirm your choice, or click Reset to restore the original settings.

   If you choose OK, a dialog box appears, indicating that the program must be restarted for the change to take effect.

3. Choose **Yes** to restart and implement the change and return to the Preferences desk tool.

The Date and Time Option Button

Whether your system has a built-in clock/calendar or you enter the time each time you start the computer, GeoWorks Pro can reset your system clock from the Date and Time option button in the Preferences desk tool.

To reset the system date and time, follow these steps:

1. Click the Date and Time button in the Preferences window to open the Date & Time dialog box (see fig. 11.9).

2. To change the date, in the Date text field, type the correct date in this format:

   1/1/92

3. To change the time, in the Time text field, type the correct time in the following format:

   5:35 pm

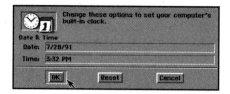

4. Click OK to update the clock and calendar, or click Reset to return
   to the preceding settings.

The Computer Option Button

During installation, GeoWorks Pro determines the presence of extra
memory and the current interrupt levels. You should change these settings only if you clearly know that the memory configuration of your
computer is different than the configuration originally detected by
GeoWorks. Installing new memory chips or adding an expanded memory
board, for example, can change the memory configuration of your computer.

The preceding warning is even more relevant if you intend to change the
serial port interrupt levels. Don't alter the settings unless you know what
an interrupt level (IRQ) is and which interrupt is used by a given port.

If you choose to change any settings, make note of the starting settings
so that you can restore them if the changes don't work. The Reset button
doesn't return you to your original settings after you restart
GeoWorks Pro.

CAUTION Do not change the memory or interrupt level settings in
the Preferences Computer dialog box unless you clearly
understand memory types and interrupt settings.

To make memory changes and to change interrupt levels for ports, follow these steps:

1. In the Preferences window, click the Computer option button.

   The Computer dialog box appears (see fig. 11.10).

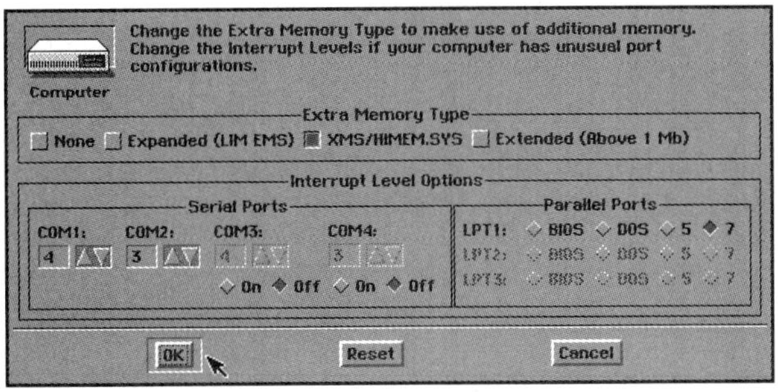

Fig. 11.10

The Computer dialog box.

2. Indicate the changed memory configuration in your computer by clicking the check boxes in the Extra Memory Type box.

3. To activate COM3 or COM4, in the Serial Ports box, click the On buttons below the boxes.

4. In the Serial Ports box, click the increase or decrease arrows to alter serial port interrupt levels.

5. To change parallel port interrupt levels, in the Parallel Ports box, click the buttons to the right of the port listings.

6. Click OK to implement the changes, or click Reset to return to the original settings.

   If you choose OK, a dialog box appears, indicating that the program must be restarted for the changes to take effect.

7. Choose **Yes** to restart and implement the changes.

The Mouse Option Button

The Mouse option button enables you to change mouse types, the port to which the mouse is attached, and the port interrupt level, as well as the acceleration and double-click characteristics of the mouse.

Changing the Mouse Type

To change the mouse type, follow these steps:

1. In the Preferences window, click the Mouse option button to open the Mouse dialog box (see fig. 11.11).

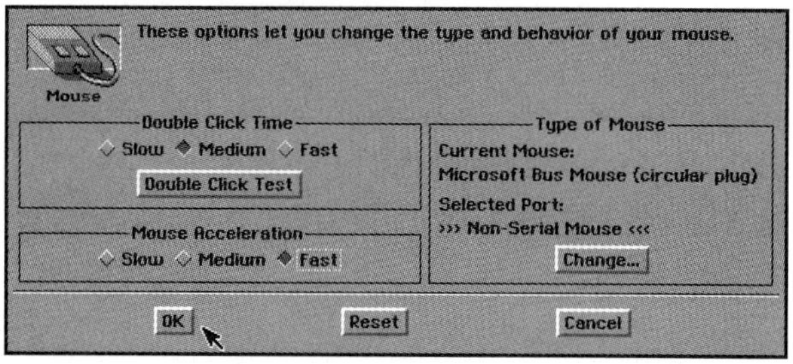

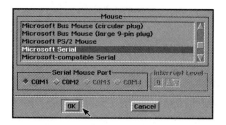

Fig. 11.11

The Mouse dialog box.

2. In the Type of Mouse section, click the Change button to open a second dialog box (see fig. 11.12).

Fig. 11.12

The Mouse dialog box to select the mouse type.

3. Scroll through the list of mice until you find your brand; choose the name.

4. If the Serial Mouse Port section of the dialog box activates when you choose the mouse, click the port setting to indicate where the mouse is connected.

5. If you must change the interrupt level of the serial port you have chosen for the mouse, use the Interrupt Level section of the Mouse dialog box to enter the correct value. Consult the literature that comes with the mouse or contact your hardware dealer for recommendations.

6. Click OK to change the mouse settings, or click Cancel to leave the dialog box unchanged.

   GeoWorks returns to the Mouse dialog box.

Changing Double-Click Time and Mouse Acceleration

The Double-Click Time setting in the Mouse dialog box is a matter of personal preference and coordination. This setting establishes the threshold speed at which two taps on the mouse button are recognized as a double-click. To alter the setting, click Slow, Medium, or Fast. You can use the Double-Click Test button to test the setting. When you double-click the button at the set speed or faster, your computer beeps.

The Mouse Acceleration setting varies the behavior of the mouse depending on how fast you move the mouse. This setting is also a matter of personal preference.

- If you choose *Slow* and move the mouse across the mouse pad one inch, for example, the pointer on-screen moves the same distance whether you move the mouse slowly or rapidly.

- If you choose *Fast* and slowly move the mouse a given distance (one inch, for example), the pointer on-screen moves a short distance. If you quickly move the mouse over the same distance, the pointer on-screen travels much farther, almost from one side of the screen to the other.

- Choose *Medium* to provide limited acceleration response from the mouse. Although some people adapt readily to the "ballistic" mouse, others prefer consistent performance at any speed.

The Background Option Button

The Background option button can be great fun. GeoWorks provides several interesting background patterns. You also can turn anything you create in GeoDraw into a potential background. If you have a modem and use America Online (see Chapter 10, "Using America Online"), you can find backgrounds ranging from spaceships to cartoons in the GeoWorks Forum Library.

Changing Screen Background

To change your screen background, follow these steps:

1. Click the Background button in the Preferences desk tool.

The Background dialog box appears (see fig. 11.13).

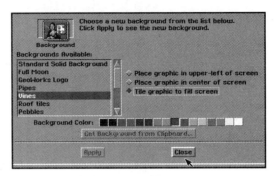

2. Scroll through the Backgrounds Available list and select an image name.

3. Click the Apply button to see the selected picture in the background.

4. Click one of the radio buttons on the right of the window to select where the image appears on the screen.

   GeoWorks offers the following display options:

   ■ *Place graphic in upper-left of screen.* The graphic appears in the upper-left corner of the screen.

   ■ *Place graphic in center of screen.* The graphic appears in the center of the screen.

   ■ *Tile graphic to fill screen.* The graphic is repeated (*tiled*) to fill the entire screen.

5. To select a background color, click a colored square at the bottom of the dialog box; then click Apply to change the background color to your choice. The background color only affects the area of the screen not occupied by the graphic.

Importing Items to Background List

In GeoWorks Pro, you can import items from GeoDraw by copying the items into a reserved section of memory called the *Clipboard* and then importing the items into the Backgrounds Available list.

To import a new background from the Clipboard, follow these steps:

1. Open the image in GeoDraw. Refer to Chapter 8, "Using GeoDraw," for more information on obtaining and preparing images.

2. Select, then copy the image into the Clipboard area of memory, using GeoDraw's Copy command.

3. Switch to the Preferences window and click the Background option button.

4. Click the Get Background from Clipboard button in the Background dialog box.

   A small dialog box appears, prompting you to Enter filename for background (see fig. 11.14).

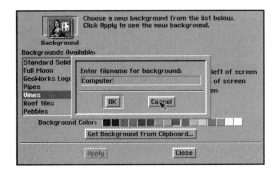

Fig. 11.14

Dialog box to name imported background image.

5. In the text field, type a name for the background you are importing and click OK to return to the Background dialog box.

   The name appears in the Backgrounds Available list.

   You can install the image as a background, using the steps described in "Changing Screen Background."

The Video Option Button

GeoWorks Pro is noted for the number of different computers on which it can run. A related strength is GeoWork's capability to run on almost any PC monitor, from the earliest CGA to the latest Super VGA. The Video options button in the Preferences window enables you to change adapters and control a built-in screen-saver utility.

Changing the Video Adapter

An appropriate video mode is selected when you first install GeoWorks Pro, but if you alter your video system, you must change the settings.

To change the video adapter, follow these steps:

1. In the Preferences window, click the Video option button.

   The Video dialog box appears (see fig. 11.15).

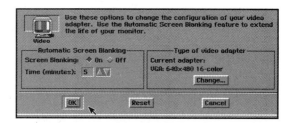

2. Click the Change button in the Type of video adapter section of the dialog box.

   A dialog box listing video types appears.

3. Scroll through the list and click the video setting that represents your new configuration.

4. Click OK to return to the Video dialog box.

   The new choice appears in the Type of video adapter section.

5. Click OK to install the new video driver.

   A dialog box appears, advising you to reboot to activate the changes. Choose **Yes**.

   When you reboot, GeoWorks presents a series of special video test windows to check the new video settings. If the new setting is not working properly, press F10 to return to the old video driver.

Activating the Screen Blanker

A built in screen saver (*blanker*) can be activated and regulated from the Video dialog box by clicking the On button in the Automatic Screen Blanking box. Screen blanking temporarily removes the image from your monitor after no activity has occurred for a specified length of time. This blanking protects your monitor from having an image permanently burned into the screen if the monitor is unused for hours. Any use of keyboard or mouse instantly restores the image.

When you activate the screen blanking feature, you must set the time your computer is idle before GeoWorks activates this feature. To set the interval, click the increase or decrease arrows or type a number of minutes in the Time (minutes) text field.

The Modem Option Button

If you use a modem with GeoWorks Pro, you must establish the basic settings, using the Modem option button in the Preferences window. Although you can change modem settings in other programs, such as GeoComm or America Online, the changes return to the default settings established in the Preferences area when you restart GeoWorks. To change the settings permanently (at least until you change the settings again), you must make the changes in GeoWorks Preferences.

To establish default modem settings, follow these steps:

1. In the Preferences window, click the Modem option button.

   The Modem dialog box appears (see fig. 11.16).

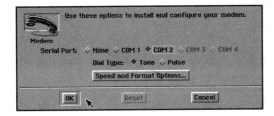

Fig. 11.16

The Modem dialog box.

2. Click the COM port name to which the modem is connected.

3. Click the Speed and Format Options button.

   GeoWorks displays the Port Options for My Modem dialog box (see fig. 11.17).

4. Click the baud rate for your modem.

5. Unless you know specifically that the other settings must be altered, leave these settings as they are initially set. The default settings (Parity: none; Word Length: eight bits; Stop Bits: one) are widely used for telecommunications. The Hardware Handshake is also the most frequent selection.

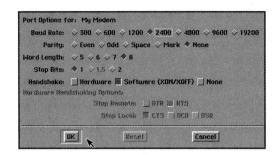

Fig. 11.17

The Port Options for
My Modem dialog
box.

6. Click OK to confirm your settings, or click Reset to return to the
   original settings.

   GeoWorks redisplays the Modem dialog box.

7. Click OK to record your settings, or click Cancel to abandon your
   changes and return to the default settings.

The Sound Option Button

The Sound option button is the least complicated option you have yet
encountered in the Preferences window. Clicking the Sound option button opens a dialog box with only two choices: On or Off (see fig. 11.18).

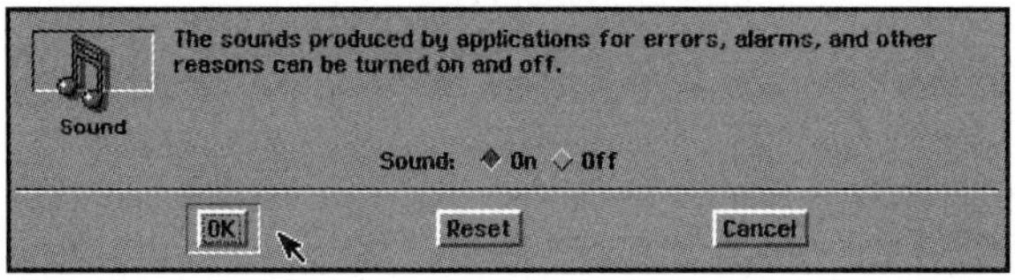

Fig. 11.18

The Sound dialog box.

By default, sounds are on. Choose Off to mute any beeps or other warning sounds your computer makes while you use GeoWorks Pro. Choosing
Off does not disable dialing sounds while using the modem.

The International Option Button

Although this section is primarily important to international users of
GeoWorks Pro, U.S. users should not overlook it. You can find useful,
and even essential, settings in the International option. You can set the

number of default decimal places in a number and the appearance of date entries. You also can choose Metric and English rulers.

The layered dialog boxes in the International option contain dozens of settings. The most important features are described in the following summary:

- *Currency.* Controls number of decimal places in currency; change currency symbol

- *Number.* English or Metric measurement; default number of decimal places

- *Quotation.* Enable true typographic quotation marks (" ")

- *Long and Short Dates.* Remarkably flexible formats for any country or personal taste

- *Time.* Varied formats, as with dates

The general procedures for using the International settings dialog box are as follows:

1. In the Preferences window, click the International option button.

   The International dialog box appears (see fig. 11.19).

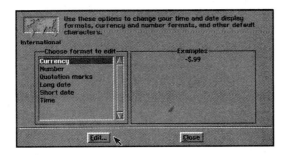

Fig. 11.19

The International dialog box.

2. From the Choose format to edit box, choose the setting you want to change.

   An example of the current default setting appears in the Examples box.

3. Choose the Edit button to open a secondary dialog box containing the settings for the chosen item.

   The secondary dialog boxes contain text fields with or without associated increase/decrease arrows. Place the text I-beam in the plain text fields to type characters or numbers.

The boxes with associated arrows contain preselected lists that can be viewed by clicking the arrows. You cannot alter the selections in the boxes with arrows. Figure 11.20 shows the Edit Number format dialog box, which is typical of the other secondary dialog boxes.

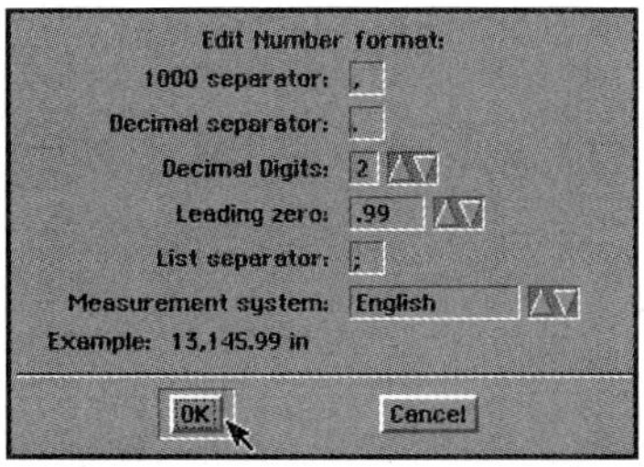

The Edit Number format dialog box.

4. Change the settings; then click OK to record your choices and return to the International dialog box.

5. Choose **C**lose to return to the Preferences window.

The PC/GEOS Option Button

The message at the top of the PC/GEOS dialog box sums up the situation with the PC/GEOS settings (see fig. 11.21). Do not change these settings unless you are advised to do so by a technician on the GeoWorks Pro support line. The default settings are fine under almost all normal circumstances.

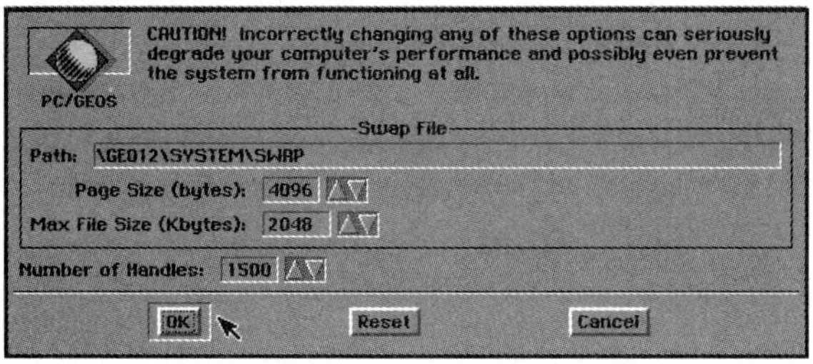

Fig. 11.21

The PC/GEOS dialog box.

Chapter Summary

This chapter is devoted to an explanation of the twelve sections of the Preferences desk tool from which you can change the default settings for many of GeoWorks features. The desk tool has far-reaching effects on many aspects of GeoWorks Pro.

The Look & Feel option controls screen text and safeguarding of documents. Other option buttons control the printer, keyboard, and mouse settings. The date and time formats can be reset through the Date and Time option button, and GEOS can be informed of a new memory or port configuration with the Computer option button. Buttons that change settings for video, modem, and sound also are available.

The newly-added International option button controls items such as default number of decimal places, units of measure, and date and time formats.

When GeoWorks Pro is installed, its default settings get you started. After you feel comfortable with the program, however, you can use the Preferences desk tool to tailor GeoWorks Pro to be distinctively yours.

Learning Other Desk Tools

In GeoWorks Pro, desk tools are small applications designed for specific purposes. Chapter 11, "Customizing with the Preferences Desk Tool," describes the Preferences desk tool in detail. This chapter explains the three remaining desk tools: the Notepad, the Scrapbook, and the Calculator. Although they are not nearly as complex or powerful as larger applications like GeoWrite or GeoDraw, the desk tools are as indispensable as staplers or scissors to an office desktop. You find that these desk tools fill a small, but vital, spot in GeoWorks Pro. Additionally, in GeoWorks Pro, an excellent Tetris game has been added, and the Solitaire and Banner appliances are duplicated from the Beginner workspace.

Launching Desk Tools

All GeoWorks Pro applications are visible as icons in the GeoManager WORLD view; you can launch these applications from the WORLD view. You can launch applications from the Express menu, which is available in any active window. You also can launch an application by double-clicking a text document. Each of these techniques can be useful at different times.

Launching Desk Tools with GeoManager

Launching an application from GeoManager is appropriate if you typically start your GeoWorks Pro work session from GeoManager. To open an application from GeoManager, you first must open GeoManager and display the WORLD directory window. This window contains icons representing the Notepad, the Scrapbook, and the Calculator (see fig. 12.1). Double-click the application icon you want to open.

Launching Desk Tools with the Express Menu

You can launch an application from the Express menu, which looks like a stylized letter E. This menu is available in the upper left of any active application window and furnishes a handy way to start an application if the WORLD window is not open, or if you are using another GeoWorks Pro application. To open an application from the Express menu, do the following:

1. Click the stylized E in the upper left of the window.

   The Express menu opens.

2. Choose **S**tartup.

   The cascade menu that lists the GeoWorks Pro applications appears (see fig. 12.2).

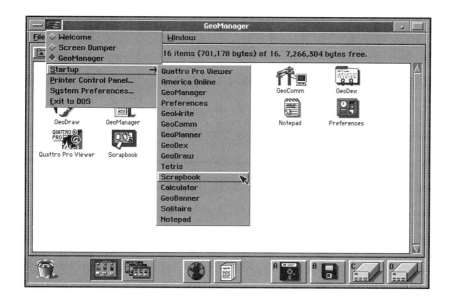

Fig. 12.2

The Express menu's
Startup menu.

3. Choose the application name.

   GeoWorks launches the program.

Launching Desk Tools with Document Icons

You also can launch an application by using the document icons found
in any folder that stores documents for the program you intend to
launch.

You can launch Notepad by double-clicking the icon for a DOS document, which resembles a stack of papers in a box marked DOS. You can
launch the Scrapbook by double-clicking the scrapbook icon, a stack of
three pages including a picture (is that an avocado?), some text, and a
graph (see fig. 12.3). *Note:* The DOS document name must end with the
file name extension TXT.

Understanding the Notepad

Although this desk tool is simple and handy for quick memos, the
Notepad possesses another property that distinguishes it from GeoWrite
and makes using the Notepad appropriate for certain files. The unique
property is that the Notepad is a simple text editor that works with
unformatted (ASCII) files.

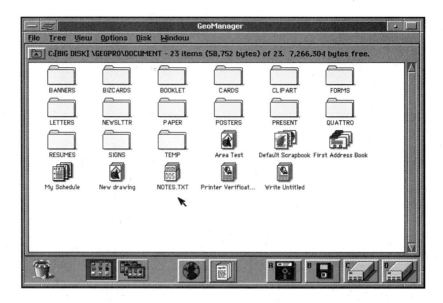

Fig. 12.3

The document icons in
the Document
directory.

To explain the distinction between the Notepad and GeoWrite, you must take an excursion into computer technology. The trip is as short as possible, but when you return you will have a clearer understanding of when and why you use the Notepad.

GeoWorks Pro uses a special file structure to save information about fonts, formatting, color, and the other enhancements you apply to GeoWorks Pro files. These files cannot be read by non-GEOS programs. In GeoWrite, you cannot load a file from another word processor unless you use an import filter that removes all formatting. Likewise, you cannot import a GeoWrite file into a DOS word processor without sacrificing the GeoWrite formatting. One type of file exists, however, that almost all word processors can read: the ASCII file.

The acronym ASCII stands for American Standard Code for Information Interchange (remember that for your next game of Trivial Pursuit). In practical terms, a file saved in ASCII code is in a standard format widely accepted and used throughout the personal computing industry. A large variety of programs can read and write ASCII files. The problem with ASCII is that as a sort of "lowest common denominator" of text files, ASCII cannot carry complex information about fonts, formatting, and graphics. An ASCII file contains text, spaces, punctuation, carriage returns, and sometimes tabs.

The Notepad is, fundamentally, an ASCII text editor. Consequently, the Notepad can read documents in ASCII format from either GeoWorks Pro or DOS-based programs; therefore, you cannot load a GeoWrite file into Notepad without first stripping the specialized formatting. Then you must turn the GeoWrite file into an ASCII file, using the Save as **T**ext File option in the GeoWrite File menu.

Of what use to you is an ASCII editor like Notepad? Most importantly, Notepad provides an easy medium for export and import between GeoWorks Pro and DOS. In addition, Notepad provides a simple, speedy text editor when you create simple documents that don't require elaborate formatting. Notepad also provides a way to read and edit DOS files saved in ASCII format. As you become more familiar with GeoWorks Pro, you find that the programs use several important DOS files to exchange information with the DOS operating system in GeoWorks. You can view and edit these files in Notepad.

Touring Notepad

When you launch Notepad, using any of the methods explained in "Launching Desk Tools," the Notepad window appears (see fig. 12.4).

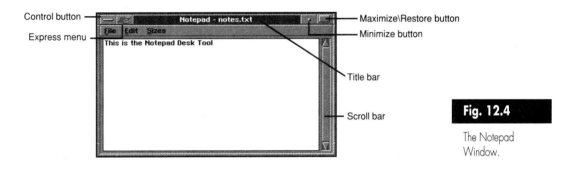

Fig. 12.4

The Notepad Window.

In Notepad, the focus is simplicity and efficiency. Notepad has only three menus, and those menus contain a limited number of commands. You can open, save, and print files; cut, copy, and paste text; and choose from five type sizes that apply to all text.

The Notepad window is similar to other GeoWorks Pro application windows. Table 12.1 describes the screen features.

Table 12.1 Notepad Screen Features

Feature	Function
Title bar	Displays application name and name of open file
Express menu	Provides options to open other applications or exit to DOS

continues

Table 12.1 continued

Feature	Function
Control menu button	Provides options to move and size window
Scroll bars	Enables viewing of documents larger than window
Maximize/Restore button	Switches between maximized window (fills entire screen) and standard window (can be moved and resized)
Minimize button	Reduces window to icon at the lower left corner of screen
Main window	Displays current document

Creating a Notepad Document

Creating a Notepad document is simple. The limited editing and formatting choices make the Notepad very useful for brief, uncomplicated documents.

When you open Notepad, the Notepad window automatically opens with the default file NOTES.TXT loaded. You can use NOTES.TXT as an electronic blackboard.

To create a document, open the Notepad and follow these steps:

1. To clean the NOTES.TXT blackboard, select all the text, open the **E**dit menu, and choose the Cu**t** command.

   Alternatively, you can delete the NOTES.TXT file from the Geo-Manager DOCUMENTS directory by selecting the file and choosing **D**elete from the **F**ile menu. Notepad creates a new, blank version the next time you start the program.

2. If you want a Notepad file you can name (other than NOTES.TXT), open the **F**ile menu and choose **N**ew.

   The new Notepad window has the default name Notes; however, when you open the **F**ile menu, only Save **A**s is available (**S**ave is grayed). Because the program already uses the name Notes for the default file, you must give your file a new name.

3. Enter text in the Notepad file.

   Standard GeoWorks Pro editing conventions work in Notepad. Use Backspace and Del for small errors. Drag the mouse to select larger blocks; then use Del or Cut, **C**opy, and **P**aste from the **E**dit menu to edit.

4. Select the **S**izes menu and choose a type size to apply to the entire document.

5. If you rely on the Document Safeguarding feature provided in the Preferences desk tool to save your work automatically, be aware that Notepad does not have this feature. If you are making significant changes in your text, use the **S**ave command frequently.

   Save the document in one of the following two ways:

■ To save a named document (such as NOTES.TXT) select the **F**ile menu and choose **S**ave.

■ To save an unnamed document or to change the name or location of a named document, select the **F**ile menu and choose the Save **As** command.

   Use the icons in the dialog box that appears to navigate to the directory in which you want to save the document.

   Type a new name for the file in the text field and choose **S**ave.

NOTE Because Notepad creates DOS files, you must name the file, using the DOS file name conventions. Give the file a name from one to eight characters in length; then type a period and the three letter file name extension **TXT**. Examples of appropriate file names are MYFILE.TXT, FILE.TXT, or MY_FILE.TXT. Notice that DOS file names cannot contain spaces.

Adding the TXT extension is not mandatory: however, the extension can help identify the files both in GeoWorks Pro or in DOS and provides the only means to open them by double-clicking the document icon.

You may find yourself using the Notepad for short memos and for documents being transferred in and out of GeoWorks Pro. The Notepad's capability of acting as a translator—to speak both DOS and GEOS— makes Notepad even more valuable.

Printing a Notepad Document

Notepad has access to the same printing resources used by other GeoWorks Pro applications. If you have printed from other applications, you are familiar with the procedure.

To print your Notepad document, follow these steps:

1. Select the **F**ile menu and choose **P**rint.

   The dialog box shown in figure 12.5 appears.

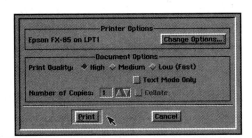

Fig. 12.5

The Notepad Printer
Options dialog box.

2. Click the Change Options button in the Printer Options area to change printer, paper size, or paper source.

   The dialog box shown in figure 12.6 appears.

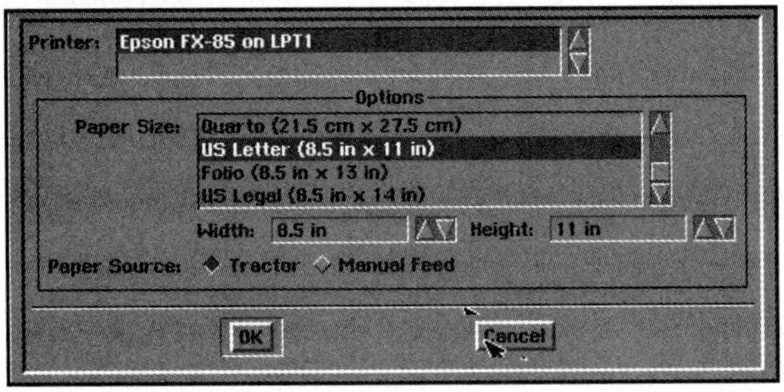

Fig. 12.6

The Change Options
dialog box.

3. In this dialog box, select a printer if you have more than one printer installed.

4. If necessary, scroll to select a different paper size or type in a custom size or in the Width and Height boxes.

5. Indicate the paper source by selecting Tractor or Manual Feed, as appropriate.

6. Click OK to enter changed settings and return to the Printer Options dialog box.

7. In the Document Options section of the Printer dialog box, select the print quality and number of copies. Click the Text Mode Only box to use your printer's internal fonts.

8. Choose **P**rint to begin the printing process.

9. Choose **Exit** to return to the GeoManager window. If you have unsaved material, a dialog box appears, enabling you to save any changes.

Understanding the Scrapbook

The Scrapbook is a tool you can use for permanent storage of small items of text or images. You can paste Scrapbook items into any GeoWorks Pro document. The name Scrapbook evokes the character of this electronic gallery. You can page through the Scrapbook, finding pictures, letterheads, scraps of frequently used text, and any other item you may have saved in the Scrapbook. Although the Scrapbook window resembles other GeoWorks Pro application windows, it does contain special features not found on other windows (see fig. 12.7).

The Scrapbook contains three menus: the File menu, the Edit menu, and the View menu. Although the Scrapbook File menu is similar to the File menus in other GeoWorks Pro applications, the Scrapbook File menu does contain an Import command that enables you to import images from DOS applications using the PCX and TIFF file formats. You can find the Import command, also found in the GeoDraw File menu, discussed in detail in Chapter 8, "Using GeoDraw."

Image name

Page buttons

Go to Page button

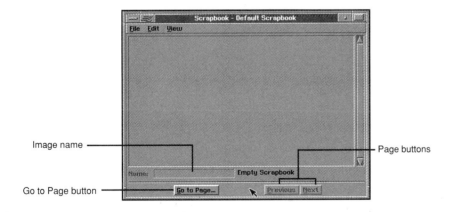

Fig. 12.7

The Scrapbook window.

The Scrapbook Edit menu (see fig. 12.8) contains the standard Cut, Copy, Paste, and Delete commands, as well as two other commands that you find only in Scrapbook: the Copy at View % command and the Paste at End command. The Copy at View % command works in tandem with scaling you can do with the View menu, enabling you to resize an image and copy it at its new size. The Paste at End command enables you to add a new image as the last page of the Scrapbook.

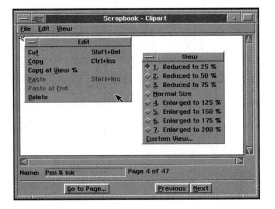

Fig. 12.8

The Edit and View
menus.

The View menu, also shown in figure 12.8, enables you to scale graphic
objects (not text) from 25 to 200 percent of normal size. Using the Custom View command in the View menu, you can change in one percent
increments from 1 to 337 percent of normal size. The size controls in the
View menu enable you to size images to fit your purpose.

After you size the image, you can use the Copy at View % command on
the Edit menu to copy the image at its Scrapbook size. If you use the
Copy command, the image reverts to its original size when you paste it
at its destination. Chapter 15, "Using Quattro Pro Viewer," includes a
demonstration of resizing a chart in Scrapbook and pasting the chart
into a GeoWrite document.

Using a Scrapbook

To practice using a Scrapbook, you use a prepared scrapbook furnished
with GeoWorks Pro. To open the prepared scrapbook, follow these
steps:

1. Open the Express menu and use the Startup menu to start
   GeoManager.

2. Click the DOCUMENT icon at the bottom center of the screen to
   open the DOCUMENT directory window.

3. Locate the folder called CLIPART and double-click it. Notice the
   three distinctive icons that indicate Scrapbook documents (see
   fig. 12.9).

Fig. 12.9

Scrapbook document icons in the CLIPART directory folder.

4. Double-click the icon named CLIPART to open the document. Click OK in the dialog box that tells you the file is a template.

The prepared Scrapbook of clipart is a template that you can read only, not alter. To work with the Scrapbook template, you must save it with a new name so that the original template file is left unaltered. You work with a *copy* of the original. Follow these steps to save the practice file:

1. Open the Scrapbook **File** menu and choose the Save **As** command.

2. In the dialog box that opens, type the name **My Scrapbook** and choose **S**ave to save the template as a new file.

You now have a practice file with which you can experiment. In the next steps, you copy an image from one page and paste a duplicate of the image at the end of the Scrapbook. Normally, you add images from another source, but working within the Scrapbook greatly simplifies the practice steps. Later, you easily can duplicate these steps to move material between another application and the Scrapbook.

To copy and paste a Scrapbook image, do the following:

1. Choose the **N**ext button to turn to the second page of the Scrapbook. You see an image named Telephone.

2. Open the **E**dit menu and choose the command **C**opy to copy the image into memory.

3. Open the **E**dit menu again and choose the command Paste at **E**nd. Notice that the number of pages shown next to the image name increases from 47 to 48.

4. Choose the **G**o to Page button.

5. In the dialog box that opens, scroll to the end of the list and double-click image 48—still named `Telephone`. Choose **C**lose to exit the dialog box. You see the copy of the telephone image in the Scrapbook window.

6. To end the demonstration, open the **F**ile menu and choose **E**xit. When asked whether you want to save changes, choose **N**o to discard the duplicate phone image.

Of course, duplicating images within the Scrapbook isn't the reason this tool is so popular. You can move images between GeoWorks Pro applications and the Scrapbook as easily as you did within the Scrapbook. You can use the Copy command on an Edit menu in a variety of applications, including GeoWrite, GeoDraw, and Notebook.

The Copy command puts an image of the selected item (text or graphics) in memory. You then can start Scrapbook and paste your image in place. Moving an image from Scrapbook to an application works the same way, using the Copy and Paste commands.

Using the Default Scrapbook

In the preceding section, you started Scrapbook by using a Scrapbook document. Double-clicking a Scrapbook document icon launches the Scrapbook application and opens the selected file; however, launching Scrapbook by using the application icon or the Express menu produces a different result.

You can find the Scrapbook application in the GeoManager WORLD window. The application resembles a cork board with notes tacked to it. Double-clicking this icon starts the Scrapbook application. Because you have not specified a document to open, Scrapbook looks for a file called Default Scrapbook. If Default Scrapbook cannot be found, Scrapbook creates one.

The first time you open Default Scrapbook, it is empty. You can add images, using the Copy and Paste techniques you practiced previously. If you do not change the name of the Scrapbook file, this file opens automatically when you start Scrapbook. If you save many images or different types of images, you may want to create multiple scrapbook files.

You can create as many scrapbooks as you want by using the File menu's New command (to open an unnamed empty scrapbook) and Save As command (to save the new files with different names). GeoWorks recognizes these files as Scrapbook files, regardless of the names you assign to them. For your convenience, you should use the word *scrapbook* in the file name (TEXT SCRAPBOOK or ART SCRAPBOOK, for example). The file name can be up to 32 characters in length.

If you have multiple scrapbooks, you may want one of the scrapbooks to open automatically when you start Scrapbook. You can use any scrapbook as your default scrapbook with a simple name switch. To change the default scrapbook, follow these steps:

1. Close any scrapbooks that are running.

2. Open the GeoManager DOCUMENT directory.

3. Single-click the left mouse button on the Default Scrapbook icon to select it (double-clicking opens the file).

4. Select the **F**ile menu, choose **R**ename, and type the new name (for example, Original Scrapbook) in the text field; then choose **R**ename to change the file name.

5. In the DOCUMENT window, select the Scrapbook file you want to make the new Default Scrapbook.

6. Open the **F**ile menu, choose **R**ename, and type **Default Scrapbook**. Type the name exactly, with the first letter of each word capitalized and one space separating the words. Choose **R**ename to change the name.

7. Restart Scrapbook.

   The program looks for the file named Default Scrapbook and automatically opens the file you renamed Default Scrapbook.

Using Multiple Scrapbooks

To transfer images between scrapbooks or to have a wider selection of images available, you can open more than one scrapbook at a time.

To use multiple scrapbooks simultaneously, you must have the Default Scrapbook open. See the "Launching Desk Tools" section of this chapter for instructions. Then follow these steps:

1. Click the Express menu icon of any active window and choose **S**tartup.

2. From the Startup cascade menu, click Scrapbook.

   An empty scrapbook and a dialog box that says the Default Scrapbook is in use appear (see fig. 12.10).

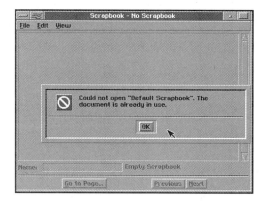

Fig. 12.10

Window to open a
second scrapbook.

3. Click OK in the Scrapbook-No Scrapbook window to acknowledge the message and dismiss the dialog box.

4. In the empty window, select the File menu and choose **O**pen.

   The Select Document to Open dialog box appears.

5. In the dialog box, double-click the name of the scrapbook you want to open.

   GeoWorks loads a second scrapbook.

6. To close any Scrapbook, open its **F**ile menu and choose **E**xit. If you have not saved changes, a dialog box appears, enabling you to save.

You can cut and paste between Scrapbooks, using the same procedures as moving Scrapbook items to and from another application. Refer to "Using a Scrapbook" in this section.

Understanding the Calculator

The Calculator is an on-screen version of a simple desktop calculator. In the same way a pocket calculator saves time and avoids mistakes, GeoWorks Pro's Calculator desk tool can prove very handy. GeoWork's Calculator has all the features of a standard small calculator, but you can keep this calculator on-screen while other applications are running. You also can copy the results of calculations into the other applications.

The Calculator is just like most pocket calculators (see fig. 12.11). You can run the calculator with the mouse pointer, the numeric keypad, or the number row on the keyboard.

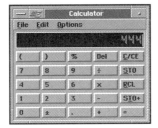

Fig. 12.11

The Calculator.

The Calculator has only three menus: the File menu, the Edit menu, and the Options menu. The File menu contains only an Exit command; the Edit menu contains Cut, Copy, and Paste commands; and the Options menu enables you to set the number of decimal places and switch between Standard and Reverse Polish Notation (RPN). For information on Reverse Polish Notation, see "Switching between Standard and RPN Operation" in this chapter.

Although you can enlarge the window boundaries, the calculator only enlarges to a limited degree. The best strategy for using the calculator is to keep the calculator window as small as possible, which enables you to use the Calculator adjacent to or on top of other application windows in which you may need to perform calculations. The window does not reduce less than a minimum size, but you can click the Minimize button in the upper right to convert the Calculator to an icon when you are not using it.

Making Standard Calculations

To use the calculator with the mouse, place the mouse pointer on the appropriate number and symbol buttons and click. The numbers you choose appear in the display window, and the results appear in the display when you click the operation buttons.

To operate the calculator from the keyboard, use the numbers across the top of the keyboard or press the Num Lock key to activate this feature and use the numeric keypad at the right end of your keyboard. You can find some underlined letters on the Calculator buttons, for example, the C on the C/CE button. Pressing the underlined letter on the keyboard operates the button. In this case, unlike in other GeoWorks Pro applications, you do not have to hold down the Alt key while you press the underlined letter.

Key	Function
/	division
*, X, x	multiplication
Enter, =	equals
Backspace, Del	delete

Using Memory Operations

The Calculator memory holds a single number that you can replace, recall, add to, or clear.

- ■ To store a number from the display, choose the **STO** button or press **S**.

- ■ To recall a stored number, choose the **RCL** button or press **R**.

- ■ To add the display amount to the number in memory, choose the STO+ button or press **T**. (You must press **RCL** to display the result.)

- ■ To clear the memory, enter a zero; then choose STO or press **S** to store the zero amount.

Copying to and from Applications

The process described in the following steps works either way in copying to or from an application. In the example provided, you copy information from the Calculator to an application.

To copy a number from the Calculator display to an application, follow these steps:

1. Drag or double-click the mouse in the Calculator window to select the number displayed in the results window (see fig. 12.12).

2. Select the Edit menu and choose Cut or Copy.

   The program stores the number in memory.

3. Switch to the application that you want to receive the number and position the insertion point in the location where you want the number to appear.

4. Select the Edit menu in the receiving application and choose **Paste**.

   GeoWorks pastes the number stored in memory into the application (see fig. 12.13).

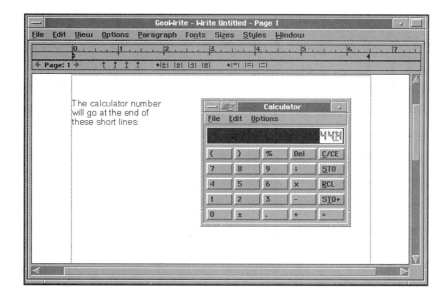

Fig. 12.12

Selected number to copy from the Calculator.

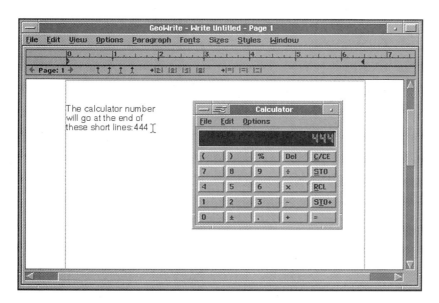

Fig. 12.13

Pasted number from the Calculator.

To move a number from an application to the calendar, do the following:

1. Drag or double-click the mouse in the application window to select the number.

2. Select the **E**dit menu in the application window and choose **C**ut or **C**opy. The program stores the number in memory.

3. Switch to the Calculator. Position the insertion point in the location where you want the number to appear.

4. Select the **E**dit menu in the Calculator and choose **P**aste. GeoWorks pastes the number in memory into the Calculator.

Using the Options Menu

With the Options menu, you can switch between Standard and RPN (Reverse Polish Notation) operation. You can also set the number of decimal points you want displayed in the results window.

Setting Decimal Places

To set the number of decimal points, do the following:

1. Select the **O**ptions menu and choose **D**ecimal Places.

   The Decimal Places dialog appears.

2. Type the number of decimal places in the text field or click the increase/decrease arrows until the correct number appears.

3. Click OK to record your choice and close the dialog box.

Switching between Standard and RPN Operation

Reverse Polish Notation is on the HP calculators widely used in science and engineering. Fundamentally, you enter numbers first, then apply an arithmetic function. The keys of the RPN Calculator work the same way as the Standard calculator with the following exceptions:

■ *The Enter button* separates one number from the next number.

■ *The Exchange button* switches the display number with the number previously entered.

■ *The C/CE button* clears a number if Enter hasn't been clicked.

To switch between Standard and RPN operation, choose the Standard or RPN (HP-Style) from the Options menu. The RPN-style calculator appears in figure 12.14. The keyboard changes to accommodate RPN operations.

Fig. 12.14

The RPN calculator.

Understanding Order of Operations

To know how the Calculator evaluates an equation involving multiple operations and parentheses, you must know the order of operations. If you enter the equation 3 + 2 * 2, for example, is the result 10 (addition performed first) or 7 (multiplication performed first)? The answer is 7 because, in the Standard Order Of Operations used by the calculator, multiplication is first. In the Calculator, operations take place in the following order:

Operations in parentheses performed

Multiplication and division performed

Addition and subtraction performed

Operations with the same precedence performed in order from left to right in the equation.

Closing the Calculator

You can exit the calculator in three ways: press the F3 function key, double-click the Control button in the upper left corner of the calculator window, or press Alt+F4.

Using the Fun and Games Tools

To give users of the Advanced Workspace equal time with those who enjoy the Solitaire and Banner appliances in the Beginner Workspace, GeoWorks Pro includes advanced versions that you can access from the GeoManager window—with the bonus of the popular Tetris game. The basic instructions for Solitaire and the Banner are found in Chapter 2, "Learning GeoWorks Appliances." Advanced Solitaire has additional scoring and dealing options for which you can find instructions by clicking the Help button on the Solitaire screen.

You can start the GeoWorks version of the widely available Tetris game by double-clicking the "St. Basil's" icon in the GeoManager window. Click the Help button on the Tetris screen for detailed instructions.

T I P   While playing Tetris, you can press P on the keyboard to pause and C to continue. These are undocumented features I use all the time. GWRep Rose

T I P   If you have a particular way to play Solitaire in GeoManager—level, scoring, or the number of cards drawn—you can save your defaults so that you don't have to reset them each time you start a new game.

Open Solitaire in GeoManager. Click on Options in the Solitaire menu bar and set your options; then click on the Game menu to "pin" it. Drag the menu along the Title bar next to the Minimize button. From your pinned menu, you now have the Undo and Re-deal game options available all the time.

Each time you leave Solitaire, you must use the Minimize button to "iconize" it. This practice stores your defaults, and a Solitaire icon will appear at the bottom left of the screen. Also, you must exit using the Exit to DOS command on the Express menu to save the state of the game and load it as an icon each time you run GeoWorks Pro. If you exit from the Welcome screen, the icon and your defaults will be lost. GWRepJohn

Chapter Summary

In this chapter, you learned to use three simple, but useful, GeoWorks Pro Desk Tools: Notepad, Scrapbook, and Calculator. The Notepad is a simple ASCII text editor used to move files between GeoWorks Pro and DOS. The Scrapbook can store text or graphics from many sources. You learned how to move items to and from the Scrapbook and how to create multiple Scrapbooks and designate a different Default Scrapbook.

The final section of the chapter introduces the Calculator, which can be kept available anytime you are working in GeoWorks Pro. This section explains the features of the calculator and the process for moving numbers to and from other documents.

Operating DOS Programs

The four buttons in the GeoWorks Welcome window are Beginner, Intermediate, Advanced, and DOS Programs. In this chapter, you learn how to use the DOS Programs area to manage DOS programs outside GeoWorks Pro. Using this feature, you can put GeoWorks Pro into suspended animation while you work in a DOS program. When you quit the DOS program, you can pop back into GeoWorks Pro or exit to the DOS prompt.

You also can set up a program *command post* in GeoWorks Pro to use as a location from which you move back and forth between DOS and GEOS. And you can create *batch files*, collections of DOS commands that perform a series of useful actions. The DOS Programs window is an excellent feature, enabling you to make your work on the computer easier and more productive.

Opening and Closing the DOS Programs Area

Entering the DOS Programs area is very similar to entering the Appliances area. From the GeoWorks Welcome screen, click the DOS Programs button (see fig. 13.1). The full-screen DOS Programs window opens (see fig. 13.2).

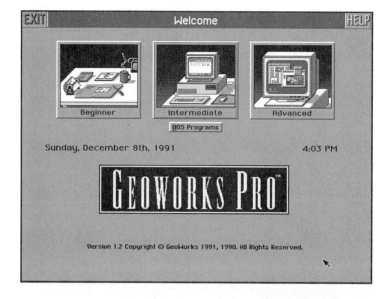

Because you will be working from the DOS Programs window throughout
this chapter, you don't need to exit this window until you have completed the operations that follow. When you are ready to close the DOS
Programs window, click the EXIT button in the upper left corner of the
window. GeoWorks returns you to the Welcome screen.

Touring the DOS Programs Area

The first time you enter the DOS Programs area, a single, lonely button sits in the middle of the screen. The window displays the EXIT and HELP buttons at the upper left and right corners and only one menu, **O**ptions, is available. What about this area, then, merits any special attention?

The hidden power of the area lies in the capability to add and activate buttons like the Enter DOS button in the center of the screen. You can attach actions to these buttons so that you can start programs and open files with a click of the mouse button. When you type **exit** from DOS or quit a program, you can quickly get back into GeoWorks Pro without hunting through directories or menus for the right command.

To get a sense of what you can do in the DOS Programs area, examine the Options menu (see fig. 13.3). Table 13.1 summarizes the commands and their actions.

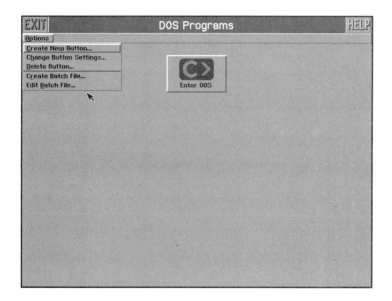

Fig. 13.3

The DOS Programs Options menu.

Table 13.1 DOS Programs Commands

Command	Function
Create New Button	Choose program to run and button image to represent it
Change Button Setting	Edit the actions activated by a button

continues

Table 13.1 continued

Command	Function
Delete Button	Remove a button from the DOS Programs screen
Create Batch File	Create a text file containing DOS commands
Edit **B**atch File	Change an existing batch file

Understanding Batch Files

A batch file is a special type of file that consists of DOS commands and commands that start programs. A batch file always has the three-letter file name extension BAT that DOS recognizes. When you type the name of a batch file on the command line and press Enter, DOS finds the file and runs the commands contained within the file.

Writing batch files is a type of programming. You first must be familiar with DOS commands and their effects because DOS commands are the main ingredients of batch files. To tap the power of batch files, you also must have some familiarity with programming concepts like branching and looping. The language of batch files contains commands that can enable these files to accept and process input from the keyboard.

This book's role is not to make you an expert in DOS or teach you batch file programming, but to intrigue you with the possibilities and get you started. In this section, you create a very simple batch file. The batch file you create displays a directory listing on-screen, announces your accomplishment, and returns you to GeoWorks Pro. Nothing to charge admission for, but enough to sense the possibilities.

Creating a Batch File

The DOS Programs Options menu includes the commands Create Batch File and Edit Batch File (refer to fig. 13.3). These commands open a simple, but elegant, text editor that has the tools needed to create and save batch files. Batch files must be saved as unformatted text files. The text editor opened with the Create Batch File command does just that.

In this exercise, you create a simple batch file that displays the contents of the root directory on the C drive of your computer. The program cannot harm your computer.

Having a basic familiarity with DOS commands helps. If you feel you are in the dark on the topic, a good book, like Que's *Using MS-DOS 5*, can clear up questions and give you much greater control of your computer.

A batch file accomplishes only the tasks you can accomplish by typing commands at the DOS prompt. The reason for putting batch files together is convenience. You are free from having to remember the complex syntax of DOS commands and you can run a long string of commands just by clicking a button.

Doing work on DOS in GeoWorks Pro may seem odd, but two powerful reasons exist for working on DOS through GeoWorks. The first reason is the text editor available in the DOS Programs area. Until a full-screen editor was furnished in DOS 5.0, most batch file editing in DOS was done with very crude tools, like the infamous *EDLIN*, an editor more cryptic than most programs it was used to write.

The second reason to *do* DOS from GeoWorks Pro is that you can attach a button to your batch file. You can create a graphic environment with the new buttons. You can name the buttons and assign significant icons so that you don't have to memorize the names of a large number of batch files; you just click the button you want.

To create a simple batch file, choose the **D**OS Programs button from the Welcome screen, if you have not already opened the DOS Programs window, and follow these steps:

1. Select the **O**ptions menu from the DOS Programs window and choose Create Batch File.

    The window shown in figure 13.4 appears, asking you to specify a name and a location for your file. For this example, you want to store the file on the root directory of the C drive.

2. To change drives, double-click the icon that resembles a floppy disk.

    GeoWorks displays a list of available drives.

3. Double-click the drive; you move to the root directory of the drive.

4. Type the name **list** in the Filename text box.

    Notice the .BAT extension to the right of the box. GeoWorks Pro automatically saves your file with a BAT extension so that DOS recognizes LIST.BAT as a batch file.

5. Click the Create button at the bottom of the dialog box.

    The Batch File Text dialog box appears (see fig. 13.5).

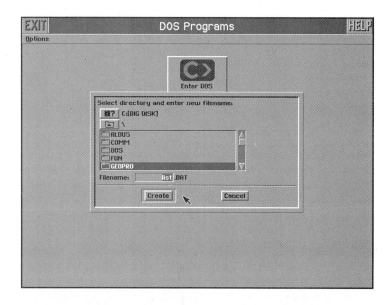

Fig. 13.4

The Select directory
and enter new
filename dialog box
for a batch file.

Fig. 13.5

The Batch File Text
dialog box.

The Batch File Text dialog box is a simple editor that produces the
unformatted ASCII files required for batch files. *ASCII* is a "bare-
bones" word processor. You enter the file text in this dialog box.

6. Begin your batch file by typing **echo off** on the first line of the
Batch File Text dialog box.

If you make a mistake as you enter the file, use the Backspace or Del keys to remove letters. If things get totally fouled up, click the Cancel button and start over. The text explains the commands you type after you complete the entries.

7. Press Enter to move to the next line.

8. Type **dir/p** and press Enter.

9. Type **echo my first batch file** and press Enter.

   When you finish, your file should look like the file in figure 13.6.

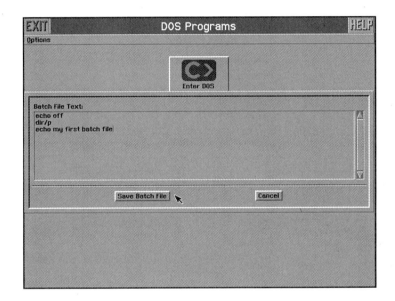

The completed batch file.

10. When your file is correct, click the Save Batch File button.

    Your batch file saves as LIST.BAT, the name you specified when you chose the file location.

Later in this chapter you create a button for your file and run the file. Before doing that, however, review the following list, which explains the effect of the commands you just typed:

■ The first command is ECHO OFF. This command tells DOS not to repeat on-screen the commands in the batch file. You do not see the next command (DIR/P) appear on-screen, for example.

■ The second command is DIR/P. DIR tells DOS to list the contents of the current directory on-screen. The /P (called a *switch* because it makes the command behave differently) makes the list of files pause every time the list fills the screen, and the message Press any key to continue appears.

■ The third command is ECHO, which tells DOS to display on-screen the words that follow, in this case, My First Batch File.

This example is a simple file, but fully developed batch files can be very powerful and convenient. Complex batch files can stop for input from the keyboard, choose different actions depending on user input, and start other applications. You find entire sections devoted to batch files in the DOS manual or in books like *Using MS-DOS 5* from Que.

Editing a Batch File

You may discover an incurable temptation to fiddle with batch files. After you create batch files, you will be forever tempted to make them just a bit better. GeoWorks Pro indulges this craving by making editing a batch file very easy. In this example, you edit the LIST.BAT file you just created. The steps can be easily adapted to fit any batch file.

To edit LIST.BAT, follow these steps:

1. Select the **O**ptions menu from the DOS Programs window and choose Edit **B**atch File.

2. In the dialog box that appears, scroll until LIST.BAT is visible; then select LIST. BAT.

3. Click the Edit File button.

   The Batch File Text window appears with the text of LIST.BAT displayed (refer to 13.6).

4. To place the insertion point at the location where you want to edit, click the mouse just left of dir in the second line. Press Enter to create an empty line as the second line in the file.

5. Click the mouse at the left side of the new line to move the insertion point; then type **tree** and press Enter to create another blank line.

6. Type **pause** on the blank line.

   The TREE command causes a graphic listing of the directory to appear on-screen. The PAUSE command stops the batch file to enable you to inspect the directory tree before the DIR command replaces the tree with a text directory.

The revised batch file should look like figure 13.7.

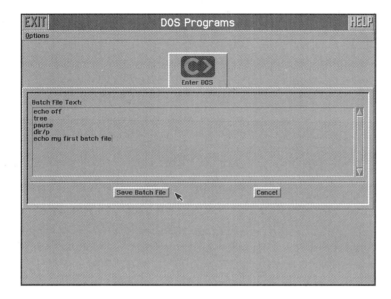

Fig. 13.7

The edited LIST.BAT
file.

7. When your changes are correct, click the Save Batch File button to save your changes.

You need to study to master batch files, but hopefully these examples give you an idea of what batch files can do. A thoughtfully developed DOS Programs screen with a useful mix of program and batch file buttons can automate your use of DOS in such a way that you rarely have to worry about the complexities of DOS commands.

Understanding Buttons

Buttons are a way to transfer from the GEOS environment to the DOS environment without shutting down and restarting GeoWorks Pro. To create buttons, you must be somewhat familiar with DOS programs and commands. If GeoWorks Pro is one of your first computer packages, you may want to enlist the aid of a friend or associate to help you set up buttons. After you establish the buttons, however, you can use the them without worrying about the operating system that lies behind them. To use buttons for more complex purposes, you must increase your knowledge of DOS. Many excellent books on DOS, including Que's best-selling *Using MS DOS 5*, are available.

Using Dialog Boxes to Create New Buttons

In the next section, you create a button for your LIST.BAT file. Before you create the button, however, you must be familiar with the dialog boxes used to create buttons. Resist the urge to actually create the button as you read through this section; when you have absorbed the information here, you will be better prepared to create buttons.

When you choose the **C**reate New Button command from the DOS **O**ptions menu, GeoWorks displays the Select DOS file for button dialog box that you use to create new buttons (see fig. 13.8).

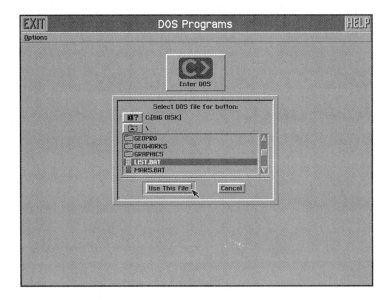

Fig. 13.8

The Select DOS file for button dialog box.

The items listed in the dialog box vary depending on the programs installed on your computer. Only DOS files ending with the three-letter extensions COM, EXE, and BAT are shown. These files are *executable* files, which are programs or collections of DOS commands called batch files. (All three file types are—in the broadest definition—programs. They all can be executed to carry out instructions. The batch file, however, is a simple type of program that belongs with COM and EXE program files.)

To install a button, you must navigate through the dialog box's scroll list to locate the program for which you are creating a button. When you locate the file and click the Use This File button, the Button Settings dialog box appears.

The Button Settings dialog box, which contains a complete set of tools to establish the appearance and behavior of a button, is the primary dialog box used to create buttons (see fig. 13.9).

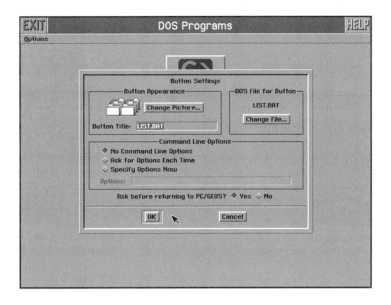

Fig. 13.9

The Button Settings
dialog box.

In the upper right of the Button Settings dialog box is the DOS File for Button area. The information in this area confirms that the file you choose in the Select DOS file for Button dialog box is *connected* to the button.

In the upper left of the Button Settings dialog box is the Button Appearance area. When you click Change Picture, a scroll list appears (see fig. 13.10). In this scroll list you find several images, or icons, you may assign to the button you create. GeoWorks Pro contains a wonderful selection of button images, both businesslike and whimsical. Be sure to scroll through the entire list so that you are aware of the range of options available to you when you create buttons.

Below the button image is the Button Title text box that displays the name which appears below the button. If you already have designated a file to be activated by the button, the file name appears here; however, you can type a new name.

In the Command Line Options section of the Button Settings dialog box, you have three options: No Command Line Options, Ask for Options Each Time, and Specify Options Now. To understand these options, you need to understand a command line.

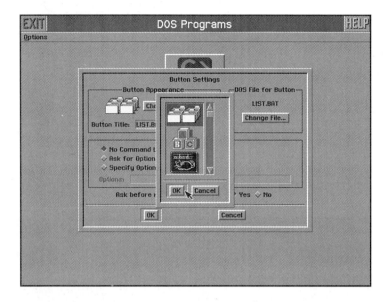

Fig. 13.10

The icon list in the Button Settings dialog box.

If you click the DOS Prompt button, which comes built into the DOS Programs screen, you see a typical DOS prompt (see fig. 13.11). The prompt (C:\>) appears at the left end of the line. You type DOS commands on the command line.

```
Microsoft(R) MS-DOS(R) Version 5.0
          (c)Copyright Microsoft Corp 1981-1991


Type "exit" to return to PC/GEOS.

C:\>
```

Fig. 13.11

The DOS command line.

Command line options contain additional information that makes a program behave differently. Some programs, for example, open a file if the file name is an option on the command line. To make use of the Command Line Options feature, you must be familiar with the features of the DOS program you are using.

The Command Line Options section gives you the following three options:

- *No Command Line Option.* Click this button if a command line option is not necessary.

- *Ask for Options Each Time.* Click this button if the command line option changes (a file name, for instance).

- *Specify Options Now.* Click this button to use a fixed command line option each time. The text box below the button activates, and you can enter your option.

The Button Settings dialog box also gives you the option to enable the Ask before returning to PC/GEOS? prompt. If you choose Yes, a message asking whether you want to return to GeoWorks Pro or exit to the DOS prompt (see fig. 13.12) appears at the bottom of the DOS screen displayed when you quit a program. If you choose No, no message appears; you automatically return to GeoWorks.

```
CONFIG    SYS        830 12-24-91    4:02p
NC        BAT         15 11-09-91    1:32p
DUMMY     BAT        102 01-01-92    1:01p
FINDBOOT  COM        162 02-21-91    1:10a
PM4           <DIR>      10-08-91    7:56p
AUTOEXEC  BAT        513 12-19-91    9:50p
VB            <DIR>      10-23-91    9:58p
TEMP          <DIR>      10-26-91    5:03p
SMAN      TXT        672 10-27-91   12:05p
CCMENU    DVD       1598 10-15-90   12:45a
MS        BAT        149 01-01-92   12:41p
Press any key to continue . . .

(continuing C:\)
CCPICK    COM        225 11-20-88    2:49a
GEOPRO        <DIR>      11-24-91    2:13p
        43 file(s)      361674 bytes
                       7397376 bytes free
my first batch file


Press ENTER to return to PC/GEOS, or ESC to return to DOS.

C:\>
```

Fig. 13.12

The DOS exit message.

After you finish the settings in the dialog box, you click OK to create the button. You also can click Cancel to abandon your work.

Creating a Button

To complete this exercise in mini-programming, you attach a button to your LIST.BAT file so that you can run this file with the click of a mouse from the DOS Programs screen. The process is identical to the one used to attach a button to a program. Indeed, a batch file is a small program composed of DOS commands.

1. Select the **O**ption menu and choose **C**reate New Button.

   The Select DOS file for button dialog box appears with LIST.BAT on the list (refer to fig. 13.8). You may have to scroll the list to see the LIST.BAT file.

2. Highlight LIST.BAT and click the Use This File button.

   The Button Settings dialog box appears (refer to fig. 13.9). The DOS File for Button area confirms that the file LIST.BAT is connected to the button.

3. In the Button Appearance area, click the Change Picture button and select a picture from the scroll list.

   The image you select will appear on the LIST.BAT button.

4. In the Button Title text box, type **List Directory**.

5. Click the No Command Line Options button because a command line option is not necessary in this batch file.

6. Click Yes to Ask before returning to PC/GEOS? to be asked whether to return to GeoWorks Pro or return to DOS.

7. When all your settings in the dialog box are correct, click OK.

   A button called List Directory appears on the DOS Programs Screen (see fig. 13.13).

> **NOTE** The number of buttons that fit on a screen depend on your computer's video. If you create more buttons than can fit on-screen, GeoWorks creates additional screens, and Next and Previous icons appear automatically, enabling you to page through the screens of buttons.

8. To use the new button, click it with the mouse or press the Tab key until a dotted border appears around the button; then press Enter.

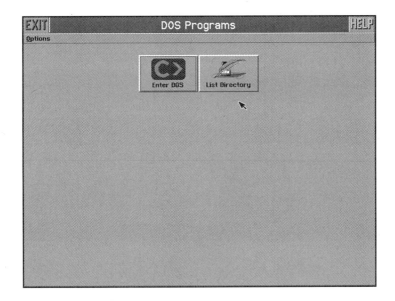

Enter DOS   List Directory

Fig. 13.13

The newly-created List Directory button.

The button starts the LIST.BAT batch file.

GeoWorks Pro shuts down while a directory listing appears. If the listing is more than one screen long, a prompt instructs you to Press any key to continue.

When the listing ends, your short message my first batch file echoes to the screen. Finally, a message appears asking you to press Enter to return to GeoWorks Pro or press Esc to go to DOS. Pause a moment to admire your work. You have written and run a program of your own!

Changing a Button

To change the settings that control a button, use the following steps:

1. Open the **O**ptions menu and choose the command **Ch**ange Button Settings.

    The Select button to change dialog box opens, displaying a list of the buttons in your DOS Programs window (see fig. 13.14).

2. Scroll to locate the button you want to change and click to select the button name.

3. Click the Change Settings button to open the Button Settings dialog box (refer to fig. 13.9).

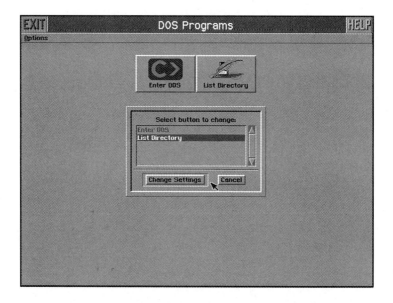

Fig. 13.14

The Select button to change dialog box.

4. In this dialog box, you have access to any element of the button's settings. Change these settings as necessary and click OK to record the changes and close the dialog box. The button acts according to the new settings.

Deleting a Button

Deleting a button does not remove the files associated with the button. Buttons are basically pointers that know where to find a program and what command to issue to make the program run.

To delete a button, use these steps:

1. Open the **O**ptions menu and choose the command **D**elete Button.

   The Select button to delete dialog box appears (see fig. 13.15).

2. In the scroll list, locate the name of the button you want to remove and select the button name.

3. Click Delete Button. The program immediately removes the button.

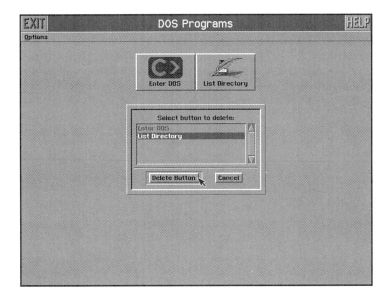

Fig. 13.15

The Select button to
delete dialog box.

Task Switching

If you frequently use DOS programs with GeoWorks Pro, you can free
yourself from the task of manually shutting down GeoWorks Pro and
starting up a DOS application. Using a technique known as *task switching*,
you can "open a door" in GeoWorks Pro and step through to a program
in the DOS environment. With task switching you can move between DOS
and PC/GEOS without losing your place in any of the programs you are
using. When you return to your work, you find it unchanged from when
you left it—and you return to exactly the same location that you left.

You can accomplish task switching by using either MS-DOS 5 or DR DOS
6.0. GeoWorks programmers have taken advantage of a DR DOS 6.0 feature called TaskMAX to produce smooth, tightly integrated task switching that uses the GeoWorks Pro menu. Task switching with MS DOS 5 is a
bit more "hands-on" and less efficient in memory management.

Task Switching with MS-DOS 5

The DOSSHELL program, furnished with MS-DOS 5, provides file and
directory management, including task-switching capability. The program
switches an application by taking a "snapshot" of its contents in
memory, writing the information to your hard disk for storage, then

starting another program. When you switch back to a program, the stored snapshot is written to memory, leaving you exactly where you were before you initially switched programs.

Because task switching creates an environment where many files may be open at the same time, you need to make provisions for the situation by modifying your CONFIG.SYS file. You need some familiarity with DOS to make the necessary changes. If you have not worked with CONFIG.SYS before, read the information on the topic in your DOS manual, consult Que's *Using MS-DOS 5*, or enlist the aid of a friend who is familiar with DOS.

Use these steps to prepare your CONFIG.SYS file for task switching in DOS:

1. Start GeoWorks Pro and open the Notepad application from the Express menu.

2. From the Notepad File menu, choose the **O**pen command.

3. Use the File Open dialog box to move to the root directory of drive C. Scroll through the list of files to locate CONFIG.SYS and double-click the file name to open the file in Notepad.

4. Scroll through CONFIG.SYS until you find a line that begins with FILES=. If the number following the equal sign is less than 100, change the number to **100**.

   If you do not find such a line, go to the end of the file, insert a line, and type **files=100**.

5. To activate the SHARE utility, insert another line in the CONFIG.SYS file and type

   install=c:\dos\share.exe/f:4096

   Note: The preceding line assumes that the DOS files are in the C:\DOS subdirectory. If not, change the path in the command to include the subdirectory in which you store DOS files.

6. From the Notepad File menu, choose **S**ave. Exit from GeoWorks Pro; then restart the computer to install the new CONFIG.SYS commands.

Activating Task Switching

You need to activate the task-switching capability before starting the programs you plan to switch. Use the steps below to activate task switching in DOSSHELL:

1. At the DOS command prompt, type **c:\dos\dosshell** to start the DOSSHELL program.

2. When the DOSSHELL screen appears, open the **O**ptions menu and click on the command **E**nable Task Swapper. A small symbol appears to the left of the command, indicating that Task Swapper is active. A new area labeled Active Task List appears at the lower right area of the screen (see fig. 13.16).

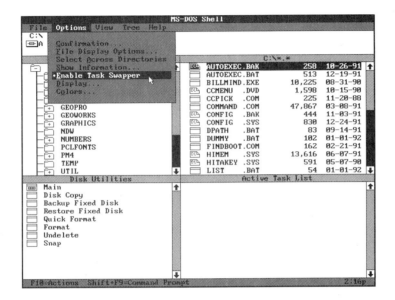

Fig. 13.16

The Task Swapper creates The Active Task List area of the DOSSHELL screen.

Starting GeoWorks Pro from DOSSHELL

Once DOSSHELL is running with task switching activated, you can begin opening the multiple applications with which you plan to work. This section details how to start GeoWorks Pro, but the procedure applies to starting any program from the DOSSHELL window.

To start GeoWorks Pro from the DOSSHELL, use the directory and file listings in the upper half of the DOSSHELL screen: move to the GeoWorks Pro directory and double-click the file GEOS.BAT.

To return to DOSSHELL (to switch to or start another program), press Ctrl+Esc. After a short wait while GeoWorks Pro is stored, the DOSSHELL screen appears.

Limited only by available memory and hard disk storage, you can start and switch to any other DOS application from DOSSHELL. The Active Task List lists any active DOS program. To switch to another running program, double-click its name in the Active Task List.

If you need assistance while using DOSSHELL, click the Help command to activate a series of help screens, including an index of topics. Pressing the F1 function key while a command or dialog box is highlighted opens context-sensitive help for your current action.

Task Switching with DR DOS 6.0

Task switching using DR DOS 6.0's advanced utility, TaskMAX, calls upon features of the operating system to achieve a more automatic and integrated swapping capability. Memory management features of DR DOS 6.0 enable programs to run simultaneously, so that switching between tasks is nearly instantaneous.

Loading DR DOS's TaskMAX Task Manager

TaskMAX is a memory-resident program that can be loaded either from the command line or at start up. Either way, TaskMAX must be active before you start GeoWorks Pro to take advantage of this powerful task-switching program.

Loading TaskMAX from the Command Line

If you seldom use TaskMAX, you probably don't want this program to load when you start the computer.

Before you load TaskMAX from the command line, you also must make sure that the SHARE command is active: at the DOS prompt, type **share**. If SHARE currently is active (this command may have been added to the AUTOEXEC.BAT or the CONFIG.SYS file when you initially loaded or reconfigured DR DOS 6.0), the message SHARE is already active appears; if SHARE is not active, DR DOS loads SHARE.

To load TaskMAX at the command line, at the DOS prompt, type **taskmax**.

Configuring TaskMAX To Load at Power Up

If you want TaskMAX to load when you start the computer, you first must reconfigure DR DOS. To load TaskMAX into memory when you turn on your computer, follow these steps:

1. In DR DOS, change to the \DRDOS directory and type **setup**. The DR DOS 6.0 SETUP screen appears.

2. Press Enter. The Reset Configuration screen appears.

3. Without changing the three settings on the Reset Configuration screen, press Enter again. The Area Configuration screen appears.

4. Using the up- and down-arrow keys, scroll down the list until the check mark appears in the box to the left of the line that shows TaskMAX and press Enter. The TaskMAX Task Switcher Configuration screen appears.

5. To accept the default settings on this screen, press Enter.

6. Press Enter repeatedly to cycle through the screens until the Area Configuration screen reappears.

7. Scroll down to the System Parameters option and press Enter repeatedly until the Buffers, Files, and FCBS screen appears. If the FILES entry is other than *120*, scroll up to the FILES text box, use the Del or Backspace key to delete the old number, and type **120**. Accept the current settings and press Enter until you return to the Area Configuration screen.

8. Save Changes, Exit, and press Enter. Press Enter repeatedly to cycle through the rest of SETUP's screens until you again arrive at the DR DOS command line.

NOTE When you use SETUP to reconfigure DR DOS 6.0 so that the TaskMAX task switcher loads when you power up the system, SETUP adds both SHARE and TaskMAX (in this order) to the AUTOEXEC.BAT file. You no longer type these commands at the command line. SETUP adds the line *FILES=120* to the CONFIG.SYS file as well.

These steps complete the procedure that enables DR DOS to load TaskMAX when you start the computer. To use this new configuration, turn off and then restart the computer. TaskMAX now loads by default and is ready to use.

For more information about changing TaskMAX defaults in the SETUP program, refer to the *DR DOS 6.0 User Guide*.

Activating TaskMAX

Before you can switch tasks within DR DOS 6.0 and PC/GEOS, you must first display the TaskMAX menu. Although the procedures differ greatly, you can accomplish this step in either operating system.

Using the TaskMAX Menu from DR DOS 6.0

Activating the TaskMAX menu from DR DOS is simple. With the DR DOS command line displayed on-screen, press the Ctrl+Esc key combination (also known as the TaskMAX activation keys). The TaskMAX menu appears. This menu consists of two boxes named Tasks and Functions.

The Tasks box lists all applications that you select for task switching. Note that only COMMAND, followed by a 1, appears in this list box.

Using the key presses shown in the Functions box, you control the various options that TaskMAX provides: Creating (Ins) or Deleting (Del) tasks, Copying (F5) and Pasting (F6) information between applications, displaying help screens About TaskMAX (F3), and (if no tasks are in the Tasks list box) removing TaskMAX from memory (Del).

Your next step is to load applications while TaskMAX is active, which adds tasks to the Tasks list box.

To load applications, follow these steps:

1. With the DR DOS 6.0 command line displayed on-screen, press Ctrl+Esc. The TaskMAX menu appears.

2. To start the Create New Task option, press the Ins key. The DR DOS command line replaces the TaskMAX menu.

3. At the command line, type the name of an application you want to add to the Tasks menu, such as **editor** if you plan to switch to the DR DOS Editor at some point in the current work session. Press Enter to load the application you typed.

4. Without exiting the application, press Ctrl+Esc again. The TaskMAX menu reappears, and you see EDITOR, followed by a 2 in the Tasks list box.

5. Enter each application that you plan to use during the TaskMAX controlled task-switching session by repeating steps 1 through 4. The TaskMAX Tasks list box can hold a maximum of 20 applications.

To select a task from the Tasks list box, use the up- and down-arrow keys, or press the related numeric key, for example, *2* to switch to the *DR DOS Editor* program.

You also can use switches and commands at the command line level to further manipulate TaskMAX from DR DOS, such as renaming the way programs appear on the Tasks list box. To learn more about renaming and other features, refer to the *DR DOS 6.0 User Guide*, or Que's *DR DOS Quick Reference*.

Using the TaskMAX Control Option in GeoWorks Pro

If you use the TaskMAX menu to load GeoWorks Pro, you can access this program while in GeoWorks Pro. GeoWorks programmers designed GeoWorks Pro to recognize the presence of—and to use—TaskMAX from both the Advanced Workspace and DOS Programs. This integration makes switching from GeoWorks Pro to a running DOS application extremely easy.

After TaskMAX is running, start GeoWorks Pro as you usually do. If you added any DOS programs to the TaskMAX Tasks menu (using the previous procedure to add programs, such as Editor, to the Tasks list box), before you started GeoWorks Pro, the names of the programs appear in capital letters at the top of the Express menu (see fig. 13.17).

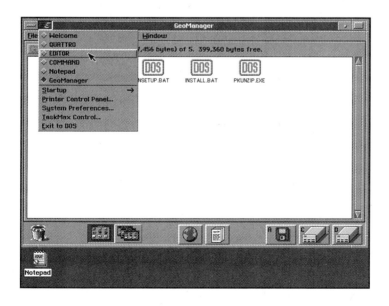

Fig. 13.17

Active DOS program names in the Express menu.

Switching from GeoWorks Pro to an active DOS program is easier than opening a door between two rooms. On the Express menu, click the name of the desired program. All GeoWorks Pro operations are suspended and the DOS program appears, displaying the same screen as when you last used the program.

To return to GeoWorks Pro, open the TaskMAX dialog box by pressing Ctrl+Esc. Use the arrow keys (or press the appropriate numeric key) to highlight GeoWorks Pro in the active programs list that appears. Press Enter to return to GeoWorks Pro.

Using the TaskMAX Dialog Box

When TaskMAX is running, a new command option named TaskMAX Control appears on the Express menu. Choosing this command opens the dialog box shown in figure 13.18. Using this dialog box, you can change TaskMAX settings while still in GeoWorks Pro.

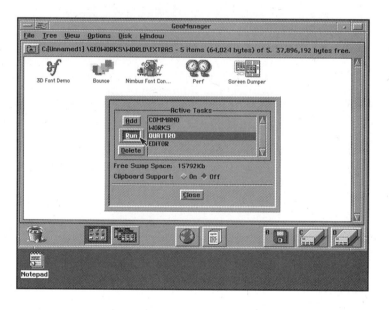

Fig. 13.18

Active DOS programs in the Active Tasks dialog box.

Table 13.2 lists the elements and related functions of the Active Tasks dialog box.

Table 13.2 The TaskMAX Dialog Box

Element	Purpose
Active Tasks list	Lists active DOS programs
Add button	Switches to DR DOS prompt for starting another program
Run button	Activates the selected program on the Active Tasks list
Delete button	Ends the selected program on Active Tasks list (see following caution)
Per task EMS limit	Displays maximum expanded memory available to each active DOS program
Free Swap Space	Displays free space on the hard disk available for swap files
Clipboard Support	Swaps GeoWorks Pro clipboard contents to DOS clipboard (and DOS clipboard contents to the GeoWorks Pro clipboard); turn off to protect the data in the GeoWorks clipboard before you work in DOS

CAUTION The Delete button forces a program to close without giving the program an opportunity to close files or relinquish memory. Shutting down a program by using its own Quit or Exit command is the preferred—and safer—method to remove the selected program from the Active Tasks list.

Using TaskMAX from the GeoWorks Pro DOS Programs Area

If you activated TaskMAX (by using Ctrl+Esc) before loading GeoWorks Pro, you also can switch to DOS programs from the GeoWorks Pro DOS Programs area. Unlike in the Active Tasks dialog box called by the TaskMAX Control option in the Express menu, however, you cannot add new tasks with the DOS Programs' Active Tasks dialog box. The options here are Run or Delete only. To use this feature, follow these steps:

1. If you are in a workspace, click the Express menu and select the Welcome option. The GeoWorks Pro Welcome screen appears.

2. Choose the **DOS** Programs button. The DOS Programs work area appears.

3. At the bottom center of the screen, you see the Task Activation button (see fig. 13.19). This button is the DOS Programs equivalent of the Express menu's TaskMAX Control command option described previously. When you click on this button, the DOS Programs Active Tasks dialog box in figure 13.20 appears.

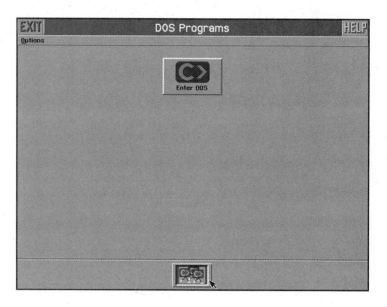

4. To use the Active Tasks dialog box for switching from GeoWorks Pro to a DOS program, move the mouse pointer over the program name, click on the name, and click the Run button. You also can double-click the name with the mouse button to switch from GeoWorks Pro to the DOS program.

5. (Optional) To remove a DOS program from the Active Tasks dialog box, click the task name that you want to remove and then click **D**elete. This action, however, *is not recommended*; for more information about Delete, see the Caution in the preceding section.

Using the capabilities of task switching, you can use GeoWorks Pro as a central workplace from which you can easily use both PC/GEOS and DOS-based applications.

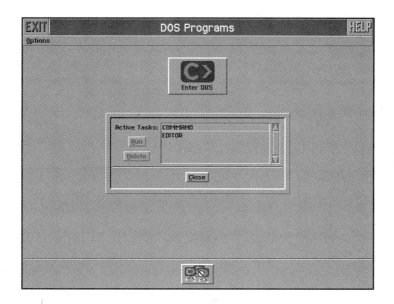

Fig. 13.20

The Active Tasks
dialog box in the DOS
Programs area screen.

Starting DOS Programs From GeoWorks Pro

While TaskMAX is running in memory, you can use the facilities of
GeoManager to easily launch DOS programs. If you installed a DOS program to a button in the DOS Programs area, you can click the button.
With TaskMAX, GeoWorks Pro does not have to shut down before
launching a DOS program. DOS Programs and GeoWorks can run together, which makes switching between GeoWorks Pro and DOS programs much faster. Remember that when TaskMAX is running and you
add a DOS Program from GeoWorks, GeoWorks automatically adds the
DOS program as a task.

Chapter Summary

In this chapter you learned to use the DOS Programs area to control
programs outside GeoWorks Pro. By attaching buttons to programs and
batch files, you learned how to establish a control center that enables
you to use every program on your computer without opening and closing GeoWorks Pro.

You also learned to change and delete a button. In a short excursion into DOS, you wrote a simple batch file, and learned the purpose of the commands included in it, and attached a button to your batch file to run it from the DOS Programs area.

The last half of the chapter covers the task-switching capabilities for GeoWorks in conjunction with MS-DOS 5 and DR DOS 6.0. You learned the techniques for using the Task Swapper in MS-DOS 5 and TaskMAX in DR DOS 6.0 so that you easily can switch from GeoWorks to any other program on your computer.

Using Spreadsheets

PART

V

OUTLINE

Learning about Spreadsheets

The principal new feature distinguishing GeoWorks Pro from GeoWorks Ensemble is the addition of Quattro Pro SE, a Borland spreadsheet that combines outstanding power with ease of use. The electronic spreadsheet was the application that made businesses view early PC's as more than hobbyists' toys. The spreadsheet's importance continues today; spreadsheet applications rank second only to word processors as the most-used type of software.

Quattro Pro SE is excellent for the home and small business. If you have had any experience with PC spreadsheets, you will enthusiastically embrace the advanced features that Quattro Pro SE provides. If you are a new spreadsheet user, you will appreciate how Quattro Pro SE combines simplicity with effectiveness.

With this chapter you learn to create a simple spreadsheet and chart. Although you can learn a great deal more about Quattro Pro SE, the head start this chapter provides enables you to begin work with the program. This chapter also prepares you for the following chapter, "Using Quattro Pro Viewer," which discusses the integration of Quattro Pro SE and GeoWorks Pro.

Starting Quattro Pro

Although closely linked to GeoWorks Pro, Quattro Pro does not run under PC/GEOS. Quattro Pro is a DOS application; therefore, when you use GeoWorks Pro, you must start Quattro Pro from the GeoWorks Pro DOS workspace. Chapter 13, "Operating DOS Programs," includes instructions for installing a button that can start Quattro Pro SE in GeoWorks Pro.

A third method of starting Quattro Pro is to exit GeoWorks Pro and start Quattro Pro SE from the DOS prompt. To start Quattro Pro SE from DOS, use the GeoWorks Pro Express menu and choose the command **E**xit to DOS. When you see the DOS prompt, switch to the Quattro Pro SE directory by typing **cd qpro**; then type **q** to start the program. (If you have installed Quattro Pro SE on another drive or in a directory with a different name, enter the appropriate path information.)

Understanding the Quattro Pro Work Area

When Quattro Pro opens, a *spreadsheet*—or worksheet—appears on-screen (see fig 14.1). Like its paper counterpart, the on-screen spreadsheet is a grid of vertical columns and horizontal rows. Unlike a paper spreadsheet, you cannot see the grid that defines the rows and columns; however, you can see the row and column position by looking at the labels along the left edge and across the top of the spreadsheet area. Letters of the alphabet designate columns; numbers designate rows.

The section of the spreadsheet that you can see on-screen is actually a small portion of the entire spreadsheet. The complete sheet is 256 columns wide and 8,192 rows deep. Few users ever use more than a portion of this vast area, but the potential for this large spreadsheet does exist.

Understanding Cell Addresses

A *cell* is the intersection of a row and a column. Each cell is a unique working area that Quattro Pro SE can track and manipulate. Remarkably, the full spreadsheet contains over two million cells! With so many possible cells to use, a method for giving a distinct address to each cell must exist. To determine a cell's address, you combine the column letter and row number of the cell. The cell in the tenth row of column B has the address B10, for example. Because the spreadsheet is 8,192 rows long, the last cell in column B has the address B8192.

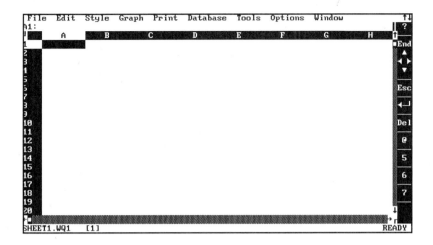

Fig. 14.1

The Quattro Pro SE
screen.

Quattro Pro SE has 256 vertical columns designated by letters of the alphabet. When Quattro Pro passes Z, it begins again with AA, BB, CC, and so on. Beyond ZZ, Quattro Pro begins BA, BB, BC, and so forth. Using this strategy, the 256th column is IV (not the Roman numeral four, but the letters I and V).

Before you get the impression of unmanageably vast spreadsheets, remember that the maximum number of cells you can use in a single spreadsheet depends on the amount of memory in your computer. The memory capacity is usually far smaller than the total number of cells in the Quattro Pro SE spreadsheet. In fact, a majority of spreadsheets you create will probably fit on a single screen (about 160 cells).

Using the Active Cell

As you work on a spreadsheet, the cell in which you are working is the *active cell*. Quattro Pro identifies the active cell with a red highlight on a color screen or a light grey highlight on a monochrome screen. The active cell's address also appears on the input line (just below the menu). Another way to identify the active cell is to note the active row and column markers along the edge of the spreadsheet and track the intersection. Figure 14.2 shows the cell selector at address C10. You must know the location of the active cell as you enter data or create formulas.

Using the Menu

The menu occupies the top line of the spreadsheet screen. The nine menu names access pull-down menus of commands for spreadsheet actions. You can activate the menus from the keyboard or with the mouse. Because of the strong mouse orientation of GeoWorks Pro, this chapter emphasizes using the mouse to access Quattro Pro SE commands, explaining keyboard techniques and shortcuts where they are more efficient or the only way to accomplish an activity.

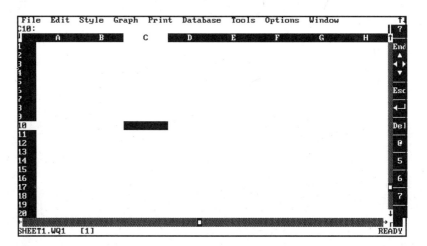

Fig. 14.2

The cell selector at the C10 address.

Commands from the Keyboard

To demonstrate how to use the menu and to prepare for the short demonstrations provided throughout this chapter, load a sample spreadsheet installed during a standard installation of Quattro Pro SE. If Quattro Pro SE is not running, start the program now. (Refer to "Starting Quattro Pro" earlier in this chapter for instructions on starting the program.)

To use the keyboard to access menus and commands, follow these steps:

1. Press the forward slash (/) key to activate the menu. Quattro Pro highlights the first menu item, **File**.

2. Press Enter. The File menu opens (see fig. 14.3). Notice the highlighted letters you can press to activate the commands.

3. Press **O** to activate the Open command. A dialog box appears.

4. Use the right-arrow key to highlight the file name, SAMPLE.WQ1.

5. Press Enter to load the sample file (see fig. 14.4).

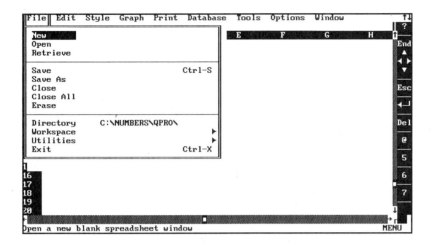

Fig. 14.3

The File menu.

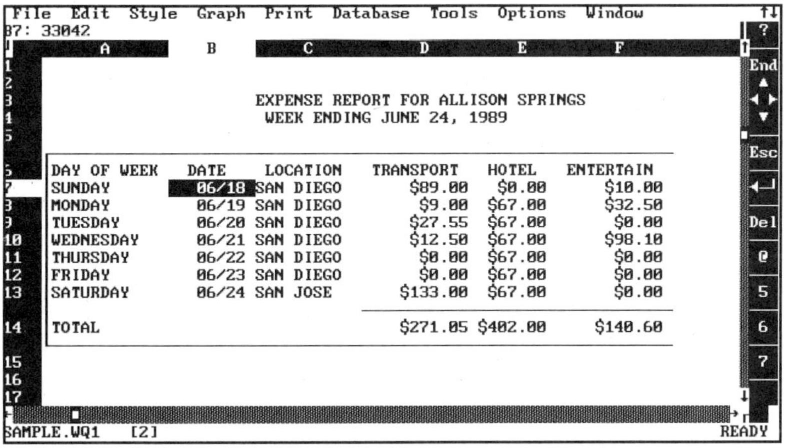

Fig. 14.4

The SAMPLE
spreadsheet.

You can type a highlighted letter, as you did to activate the Open command, to choose a command; Quattro Pro executes the command immediately. Many beginners find this method helpful.

If you are not sure what a command does, use the up- or down-arrow keys to move the highlighted bar on the menu to the command. At the bottom left of the screen, you can see a short description of the command's purpose. To use the highlighted command, press Enter.

Quattro Pro SE provides two techniques for abandoning a menu activity. To back out of an activity step-by-step, press the Esc key until you have returned to the desired command level. To completely abandon a command activity and jump directly back to a closed menu, press Ctrl+Break. *Note:* "Break" is often printed on the front side of the key rather than the top.

Function keys, numbered from F1 to F10 (F12 on some keyboards), are special purpose keys. Programmers assign varying actions to the keys depending on the design of the program. Quattro Pro SE has four particularly useful function keys as follows:

Key	Function
F1 (Help)	Opens the help window
F2 (Edit)	Switches to Edit mode, enabling you to edit the input line
F5 (GoTo)	Jumps to the cell you specify
F9 (Calc)	Recalculates all formulas if automatic calc is turned off

Commands with the Mouse

The menus in Quattro Pro SE work like the menus in GeoWorks Pro. To open a menu, place the mouse pointer on a menu and click the left mouse button. To activate a command, click the command. To close the menu, move the mouse pointer to an empty area away from the menu and click the mouse button.

Quattro Pro SE provides one mouse feature not found in GeoWorks Pro: the mouse palette (see fig 14.5). You can use this convenient menu, running down the right side of the screen, with a mouse only. Table 14.1 lists mouse palette items and their purposes.

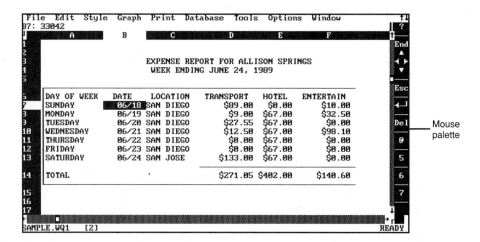

Mouse palette

Fig. 14.5

The Mouse palette.

Table 14.1 Mouse Palette Items

Item	Purpose
?	Opens help menu
End	Moves cell selector to last occupied cell in direction of the arrow you click
Esc	Backs out of current action (Same as keyboard Esc)
Enter	Same as pressing Enter
Delete	Deletes highlighted material
@	Opens list of functions
5,6,7	Can be customized to run any command

Navigating around the Spreadsheet

You can use two methods to move around a spreadsheet. You can move the cell selector from cell to cell within a spreadsheet, or you can move a large spreadsheet so that you can view portions outside the window. Quattro Pro SE provides several methods for the essential activity of moving in spreadsheets. As you become experienced at viewing and creating spreadsheets, you learn which methods are most efficient for particular tasks. This section covers a variety of movement tools, both mouse- and keyboard-centered.

Moving with the Keyboard

As you enter or edit material, you must move the *cell selector*, the highlight that indicates the active cell. The easiest way to move the cell selector is to use the arrow keys on your keyboard. Each keystroke moves the highlighted cell selector one cell in the direction of the arrow key.

Your keyboard may have one or two sets of arrow keys. If you use the arrow keys on the numeric keypad, you must make sure that you have turned off the Num Lock feature. If Num Lock is on, you type numbers, and the cell selector does not move.

To move farther distances, other keys become useful. The PgUp and PgDn keys move the cell selector up or down one full screen. Pressing Tab and Shift+Tab move the cell selector right or left, respectively, one full screen.

The F5 function key enables you to jump to any location. When you press F5, Quattro Pro displays a message on the input line, asking you to enter a cell address. When you enter an address and press Enter, the cell selector jumps immediately to that address.

If the cell selector is inside an area of filled cells, you can press the End key and an arrow key to make the cell selector move to the last occupied cell in the direction of the arrow. Pressing the End key and an arrow key provides a quick way of going to the top, bottom, left, or right edge of a sheet. In an empty area, the selector moves until it finds a filled cell or reaches the edge of the spreadsheet. Experiment with this method.

The Home key always moves the cell selector to cell A1. By pressing the Home key, you can return to a known location if you unexpectedly wind up in the outer reaches of a spreadsheet.

Moving with the Mouse

To use the mouse to move the cell selector, place the mouse pointer in a new location and click the left mouse button. The cell selector jumps immediately to the designated cell. For larger moves, Quattro Pro provides scroll bars at the right and bottom edges of the screen. Dragging the small scroll box inside each scroll bar moves the spreadsheet under the window as if you were looking through a porthole at passing scenery. Clicking the scroll arrows at either end of the scroll bars makes smaller moves. If you are not familiar with scroll bars, Chapter 4, "Mastering GeoManager," explains their use. You also can use the End arrows in the mouse palette for large moves. Pressing End+arrow moves the cell selector to the last occupied cell in the arrow's direction.

Understanding the Input and Status Lines

You can find two important items just above and below the spreadsheet: the input line and the status line. The input line is between the menu and the spreadsheet, and the status line is at the bottom of the window. These two lines play an important role in your spreadsheet file (see fig. 14.6).

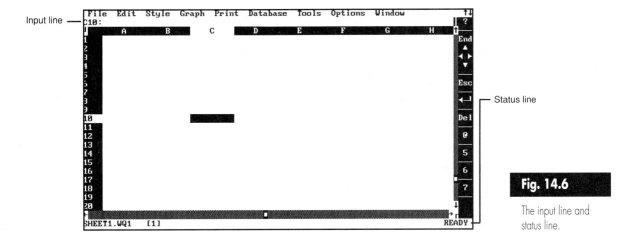

Input line

Status line

Fig. 14.6

The input line and
status line.

The Input Line

When you enter data into a cell, your entry appears in the input line. This line also contains important information about the current active cell.

If you highlight a cell that has been filled previously, the contents of the cell appear on the input line, where you can review or edit the contents of a cell. If you need more than the standard 74 character length, the input line expands to four lines to display complex entries. Any numeric format, column width, or font settings that have been changed from the defaults also appear at the left end of the input line.

The Status Line

At the left end of the status line, the name of the currently displayed spreadsheet appears. Next to the name, Quattro Pro displays the window number in brackets. *Note:* If you have multiple files open at the same time, Quattro Pro assigns each file window a different number. Using the Window menu, you can switch quickly between open windows.

At the right end of the status line is the mode indicator. Knowing the mode is important because you may be prevented from accomplishing certain actions in some modes. The key mode is READY. If the mode indicator displays READY, you can use any command or work on the spreadsheet. If you see WAIT, the program is performing some action, such as printing or sorting, and is not available. Table 14.2 lists other mode indicators.

Table 14.2 Mode Indicators

Indicator	Purpose
CALC	Manual recalculation on; must recalculate a changed formula
EDIT	The active cell available for edit
ERROR	Error you must correct before you can proceed
HELP	Using the Help system
LABEL	Entering text
MACRO	Quattro Pro executing a macro
POINT	Pointing to a block of cells while using a command or creating a formula
READY	Ready to perform any spreadsheet or menu activity
VALUE	Entering a number
WAIT	System temporarily in use

If your screen does not behave as expected, check the mode indicator first. If you start typing a cell entry and nothing appears on the input line, for example, you should look at the mode indicator. If you see POINT in the mode indicator, you know that the program thinks you are pointing to a block of cells as you carry out a command or formula. To type input, press Esc until READY appears in the mode indicator.

The status line also has indicators that show the status of keyboard keys like Ins, Caps Lock, Num Lock, and Scroll Lock. You see NUM near the bottom right of the status line when you activate the Num Lock key, for example.

Getting Help

Quattro Pro SE has excellent help resources. If you have not highlighted a command and Quattro Pro does not display an error message, you can press F1 to move to a general help screen, shown in figure 14.7. You can move from this help screen through a network of linked topics identified by boldfaced words with small chevron symbols next to them. With the keyboard, use arrow keys to highlight a keyword and press Enter. Using the mouse, place the mouse pointer on the keyword and click the left mouse button.

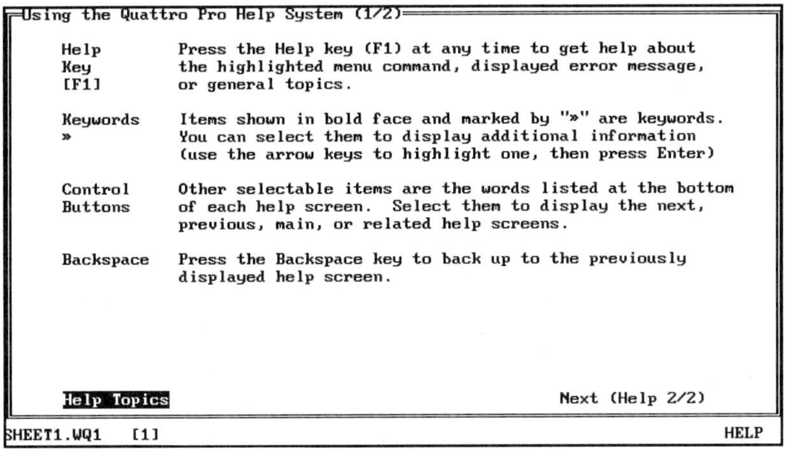

```
┌─Using the Quattro Pro Help System (1/2)══════════════════════════╗
│                                                                  │
│   Help         Press the Help key (F1) at any time to get help about
│   Key          the highlighted menu command, displayed error message,
│   [F1]         or general topics.                                │
│                                                                  │
│   Keywords     Items shown in bold face and marked by "»" are keywords.
│   »            You can select them to display additional information
│                (use the arrow keys to highlight one, then press Enter)
│                                                                  │
│   Control      Other selectable items are the words listed at the bottom
│   Buttons      of each help screen.  Select them to display the next,
│                previous, main, or related help screens.          │
│                                                                  │
│   Backspace    Press the Backspace key to back up to the previously
│                displayed help screen.                            │
│                                                                  │
│                                                                  │
│                                                                  │
│                                                                  │
│   Help Topics                              Next (Help 2/2)       │
└──────────────────────────────────────────────────────────────────┘
SHEET1.WQ1   [1]                                          HELP
```

Fig. 14.7

The general help screen.

If a command is highlighted or an error message is present before you press F1, you get *context-sensitive help*—help related to the specific command or error. To get context-sensitive help, highlight a command. Be careful not to activate the command, however. To highlight a command without activating it, select a menu and use arrow keys to move the menu highlight to the command. Do not press Enter; press F1 instead. A help screen for the command appears.

For aid on using Help and an index of help topics, press F1 to start the help system. In the help screen, press F1 again. Quattro Pro takes you to the first of two screens titled Using the Quattro Pro Help System. Every screen in the help system has a Help Topics button. If you press this button, Quattro Pro takes you to a primary index of help topics. Press the down arrow on your keyboard until you highlight Help Topics; then press Enter.

Click the Help Topics button. The Quattro Pro Help Topics screen appears (see fig. 14.8). This screen contains a list of the major help categories.

To sample a screen of additional topics, choose Basics. You see a screen that lists basic Quattro topics, such as menus, that you can explore by clicking the highlighted words.

Choose the Help Topics command at the bottom of the screen to return to the Help Topics screen. Press Esc to return to the spreadsheet screen.

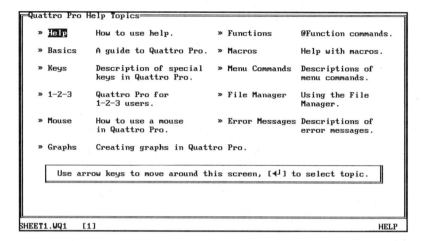

Fig. 14.8

The Quattro Pro Help
Topics screen.

Entering Information

When you enter information into cells to create a spreadsheet, you must understand how Quattro Pro SE interprets the data you enter. Quattro Pro can interpret an entry of *1992* to be a value or text. If you intend 1992 to be the number of dollars in your paycheck, you may want Quattro Pro SE to add 1992 to your bank balance. In this example, Quattro Pro must view 1992 as a *value*. If you intend for 1992 to represent the year, you may want to use it as a title for your spreadsheet. Quattro Pro should interpret the title 1992 as *text* rather than a number and exclude 1992 from spreadsheet calculations.

Quattro Pro SE distinguishes between cell entries that are numbers or formulas and cell entries that are text. Normally, the distinction is fairly clear, but, as illustrated in the 1992 example, situations occur in which Quattro Pro can interpret an entry as text or a value. If this is the case, you must indicate whether the entry is text or a value by using Quattro Pro SE rules.

The term *label* is used sometimes to indicate cell contents that may contain numbers, but that should be excluded from computations. *Label* is a broader term than *text* but has a similar meaning.

Text

For Quattro Pro to view 1992 as a label, for example, you must indicate that the entry is text. Quattro Pro treats any entry that starts with a letter or an apostrophe as text. If you enter *'1992* in the spreadsheet, for example, Quattro Pro treats the entry as text.

To experiment with text in the SAMPLE spreadsheet, follow these steps (if Quattro Pro SE is not running, start Quattro Pro by changing to its directory and typing **q**):

1. Open the **File** menu and choose the **New** command to create a new blank spreadsheet.

2. Type **label** and press Enter. Quattro Pro places `label` in the cell. Notice that the program puts an apostrophe on the input line in front of the entry to indicate the entry is a label.

To prepare for the next section, press the right-arrow key or click the cell to the right of `label` to move to a new cell.

Values

In Quattro Pro, a cell entry is a value if the entry starts with any of the following:

A number

A decimal point

The signs + – $ # @ (

Using these rules, Quattro Pro SE interprets the entry 1992 as a number.

Quattro Pro SE divides values into two types: numbers and formulas. *Numbers* are digits or groups of digits. To enter numbers, use decimal points when appropriate. Do not use commas to divide a number. When you get to the section of this chapter on formatting, you find that the appearance of a number depends on the formatting of the cell the number occupies rather than the way you typed the number.

The second type of value is a formula. *Formulas* are a combination of data and symbols, called *operators*, that produce a result. 2+2 is a formula; the twos are data and the plus sign is the operator. The result, of course, is 4. When you enter a formula in a spreadsheet, you type the entire formula, but only the result appears in the cell.

To practice using values and formulas in the SAMPLE spreadsheet, do the following:

1. Type the formula **2+2** on the entry line and press Enter. The result (4) appears in the active cell. Notice that the input line still shows the formula.

2. Move right to the next cell and type **1,234**; then press Enter. Quattro Pro SE displays the error message `Invalid character`, reminding you that a comma is an invalid character.

3. Press Esc twice to remove the message and the entry.

4. Type **12.34** and press Enter. The decimal point is appropriate and necessary in some value entries.

Leave your work on the screen while you read the next section in which you use the same material for practice.

Editing the Input Line

If you make a typing mistake or want to change data in a cell, use the input line and the available input line editing keys. Table 14.3 lists keys you can use for editing:

Table 14.3 Editing Keys

Key	Function
Ins	Switches between insert and overwrite modes
Esc	Erases input line if used before pressing Enter
Del	Erases character at cursor
Backspace	Erases character to left of cursor
Home	Goes to beginning of input line
End	Goes to end of input line
Left and Right arrows	Moves cursor on edit line

In this lesson, you use different Quattro Pro methods to edit a cell. Follow these steps:

1. Use the right-arrow key to move to a new blank cell.

2. Type **Press Esc before Enter**.

3. Press Esc to delete the entire input line contents.

4. Type **Enter puts this in the next cell** and press Enter to put input line contents in the cell. Notice that the Mode indicator at the lower right changes from LABEL to READY, anticipating that you are ready to work in the spreadsheet area.

5. Press the F2 function key to activate the input line. Notice the mode indicator changes to EDIT.

6. Use the left-arrow key to move the cursor to the space between the next and cell.

7. Press the Backspace key to erase next and press Enter. The edited text replaces the original text.

Leave your work on the screen. You learn how to save your work in the next section.

Understanding File Storage

A file, which is a named collection of information, is the basic unit of storage a computer uses to identify stored programs, documents, or data files. On the Quattro Pro SE screen, the file name appears in the left corner of the status line. If you have not named and saved a new spreadsheet, Quattro Pro SE uses generic names (SHEET1, SHEET2, etc.) to identify the document.

Saving Files

Quattro Pro provides two commands to save files. The Save command from the File menu saves the active file, using its current name and location. The Save As command enables you to enter a file name and a location other than the default directory.

To save a file, do the following:

1. Select the **F**ile menu and choose **S**ave. A dialog box showing previously named files and asking you to enter a name for your new file appears. Figure 14.9 illustrates a typical Save dialog box.

2. Type **MYFILE**. As you begin to type, a second dialog box appears to accept the name (see fig. 14.10).

3. Press the Enter button to save your file.

Closing Files

After you have saved a file, you can close it. Close MYFILE by selecting the **F**ile menu and choosing the **C**lose command. Quattro Pro removes the sheet from the screen. If you have not saved changes, Quattro Pro prompts you to save the file. (Closing a file after saving it is not necessary.)

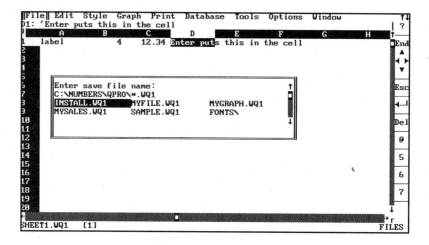

Fig. 14.9

The Save dialog box.

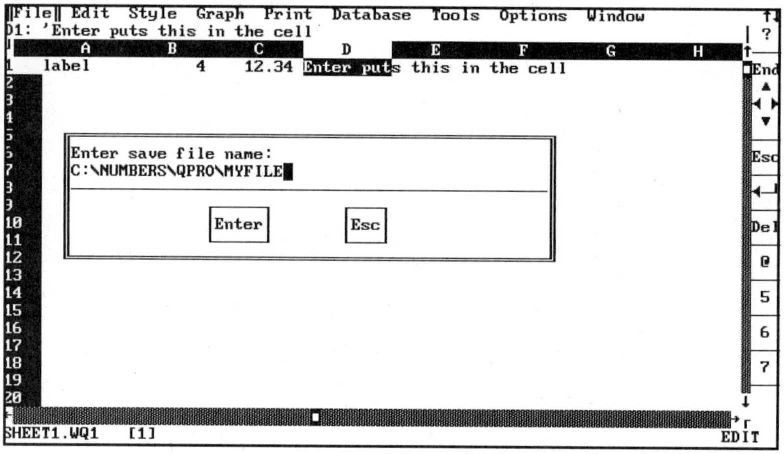

Fig. 14.10

The File name dialog box.

Retrieving Files

If you select the **File** menu and choose **O**pen, the program presents a list of files in the default storage location. Highlighting a file and pressing Enter opens the selected file. To start a new blank spreadsheet, open the **File** menu and choose **N**ew.

To reopen your file, choose the **O**pen command from the **File** menu. A dialog box containing the name of files in the default directory appears. Then locate MYFILE, use arrow keys or the mouse to highlight the name, and press Enter. Quattro Pro retrieves the file.

You can inspect open files that are stacked on-screen by selecting the **W**indow menu and choosing **P**ick. A dialog box listing open worksheets appears (see fig. 14.11). To bring a file to the top of the stack, click the file or type the file's number.

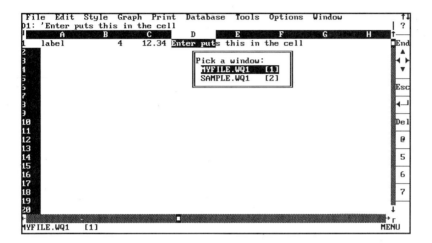

Fig. 14.11

The Pick a window dialog box.

Using Blocks

In spreadsheets, blocks—sometimes called *ranges*—are rectangular groups of cells. If you define a block of cells, you can apply a command to the entire block rather than the individual cells. To delete the contents of several cells, for example, define a block of cells from the keyboard or with the mouse (as shown in the following) and apply the Delete command to the block. Because you are likely to spend a great deal of time working with blocks, Quattro Pro provides several tools you can use to streamline block management.

Defining Blocks with Addresses

Specifying a block of cells in a formula is often necessary. To specify a block of cells, you use the starting and ending addresses of the cells in the block. Separate the addresses with two periods. (A block must be continuous and cannot be L-shaped, and you cannot skip cells within a block boundary.) To describe a block that begins at cell A1 (upper left) and ends at D6 (lower right), type A1..D6, for example.

Selecting Blocks

To select a block with the mouse, you place the mouse pointer at one corner of the block, hold down the left mouse button, and drag the pointer to the corner diagonally opposite the beginning cell. Quattro Pro SE highlights the area.

Selecting a block with the keyboard is more complex. You use the cell selector in conjunction with arrow keys. Begin by *anchoring* the cell selector at one corner of the block. To anchor a cell, position the cell selector; then press Shift+F7 (Select). An EXT indicator appears near the right end of the status bar, indicating that you can extend your selection with arrow keys. Use arrow keys to extend the selection to cover the block (see fig. 14.12).

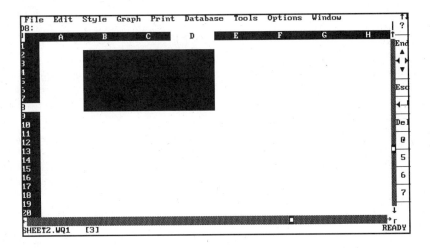

Fig. 14.12

A selected block.

After you select a block, you can choose a command. The command applies to the entire block. To remove the block selection, press Esc and move the cell selector in any direction.

To select a block of text with the mouse, do the following:

1. Enter the word **BLOCK** in cells B4, B5, C4, and C5 of the MYFILE spreadsheet.

2. Place the mouse pointer in cell B4, hold down the left button, and drag the mouse pointer diagonally to C5.

3. Click anywhere outside the block to remove the highlight.

To select a block of text with the keyboard, do the following:

1. Move the pointer to B4 and press Shift+F7 to anchor the highlight.

2. Use the arrow keys to extend the selection to C4 and C5.

3. Select the **E**dit menu and choose **E**rase Block to erase the block.

Understanding Formatting

You control the appearance, or *format*, of a cell with settings in the spreadsheet, not with what you type as you enter data. Quattro Pro SE has default (built-in) settings that control the appearance of cell contents. You can change the way information appears in any cell or block of cells. You also can change settings for an entire sheet, as well as alter system settings that affect all spreadsheets. This brief introduction, however, deals only with *global formatting*, which changes the format of all cells in your current spreadsheet, and *local formatting*, which changes only the blocks you specify.

Using Numeric Formats

Numeric formats control the number of commas, percent signs, and zeros to the right of the decimal point. You can apply formats to an entire spreadsheet by opening the **O**ptions menu and choosing **F**ormats. From the cascade menu that appears, choose **N**umeric Format. Applied globally, the selected format becomes the default for numbers entered in any cells on the sheet. To apply different formats to selected blocks or cells, you can use the Numeric Format command from the Style menu, which applies local formatting to the cells you select and overrides any global formatting. Table 14.4 lists the seven numeric formats.

Table 14.4 Numeric Formats

Format	Effect
Fixed	Fixed number of decimals
Scientific	Scientific notation for large numbers
Currency	Dollar signs and commas
Comma	Commas indicate thousands
General	Default format; two decimal places, no commas

continues

Table 14.4 continued

Format	Effect
+ and −	Number represented by symbol (5 shown as +++++)
Percent	Percent sign; two decimal places

If you use the Fixed, Scientific, Currency, Comma, or Percent formats, you can change the number of decimal places displayed.

NOTE Keep in mind that although the display may be rounded, the program retains the underlying number entered in the cell. If you enter 4.5 and then format the entry with no decimal places, for example, the cell displays the number 5; however, any formulas using the cell use 4.5—the number you entered originally.

To practice numeric formatting, follow these steps:

1. Choose the **N**ew command from the **F**ile menu to open a new blank spreadsheet.

2. Starting at cell A1, type the following numbers across row A: **12345**, **123.45**, **.123**. Quattro Pro initially displays these numbers in General format with no commas and the number of decimal points you entered when you typed the entries.

3. Select the **S**tyle menu and choose **N**umeric Format.

4. Choose the style comma (,) and press Enter. A dialog box asking for the number of decimal places appears.

5. Type **0** and press Enter.

6. Type **A1** on the input line to specify the block of cells to format; then press Enter. The entry 12345 is now 12,345.

For more practice in formatting cells, repeat steps 3, 4, 5, and 6. Substitute cells A2 and A3 for A1. Apply the **C**urrency format to cell A2 (with two decimals) and the **P**ercent format (with 0 decimals) to A3.

NOTE When you format cell A3, the cell contents appear as 12%. Highlight the cell and examine the input line. The value is actually .123 or 12.3%. Changing the number of decimals causes rounding to be applied.

Formatting Text

With Quattro Pro SE, you can use a variety of fonts to enhance the appearance of text in your spreadsheet. A *font* is a family of typefaces. Quattro Pro SE builds a standard set of typefaces when you install the program or creates fonts as needed. The exercise in the section on printing includes a simple example of changing fonts.

Understanding Functions

Functions are pre-programmed calculations. Quattro Pro SE has 113 functions. Quattro Pro uses these functions for a variety of purposes, from statistical analysis to data manipulation. To add a column of numbers, you can type A1+A2+A3+A4; however, if the list becomes long, this method is inefficient. You can use the SUM function to add a specified range of cells. In this example, you type @SUM (A1..A4). Quattro Pro automatically adds the specified range of cells. Keep in mind that you must precede a function with the @ symbol; otherwise, Quattro Pro doesn't recognize the entry as a function.

A function needs a cell or a block address on which to work. In the preceding example, you specify a block of values (A1..A4). These items, always enclosed in parentheses, are *parameters*. In most cases, the parameters consist of a cell or block address. You can use text values and special keywords as parameters in advanced function applications.

You can use functions to create extremely powerful, highly automated spreadsheets. In this brief introduction, you examine the use of SUM, undoubtedly the most commonly used function. As you become an experienced spreadsheet user, spend time extending your knowledge of functions. The return in speed and convenience is great.

To examine the use of the SUM function, follow these steps:

1. If necessary, open the **File** menu and choose **O**pen to retrieve the SAMPLE spreadsheet. If you think SAMPLE is open but hidden, open the **W**indow menu, choose **P**ick, and select SAMPLE from the list.

2. In the totals rows at the bottom and column at the right edge of the spreadsheet, highlight the cells one at a time. Examine the formulas that appear on the input line.

3. Leave the spreadsheet open for use in the next section on printing.

Previewing and Printing

Quattro Pro SE is noted for its advanced printing capabilities that enable you to enhance text and graphics in a variety of ways. Quattro Pro also enables you to use a wide range of printers. This short section deals only with the rudiments of printing. To realize the full power of Quattro Pro SE's graphic enhancement capabilities, you must do additional study.

Understanding Print Preview and Settings

To explore basic on-screen preview and printing techniques, do the following:

1. Open the SAMPLE spreadsheet (if SAMPLE is not already on your screen).

2. Open the **Print** menu and choose the command **B**lock to set the area to be printed.

3. Type **A1..I16** on the input line and press Enter. After you set the block, Quattro Pro remembers the block for future printing.

4. Choose the **D**estination command. A dialog box appears (see fig. 14.13).

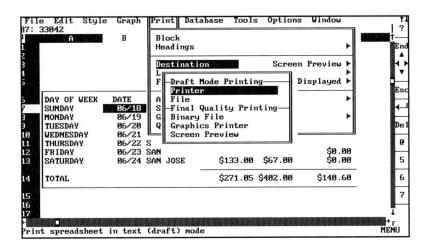

Fig. 14.13

The Print Destination dialog box.

5. Choose **S**creen Preview, which directs printer output to the screen for examination.

6. Press Enter to save the change, which sends output to the screen.

7. Open the **P**rint menu and choose the **S**preadsheet Print command. A screen preview appears. If you choose not to have fonts generated during installation, you may have to wait briefly for font creation.

   When the preview appears, notice that the program does not show the right edge of the image (see fig. 14.14). You can modify the margins to include the right edge. The continuing steps explain this technique.

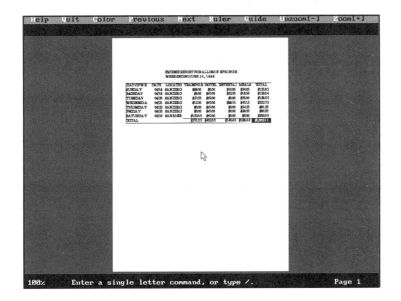

Fig. 14.14

Print Preview of
SAMPLE.

8. Press Esc to leave the preview.

9. Open the **P**rint menu and choose **L**ayout; in the box that appears, choose **M**argins.

10. Choose **L**eft, type **0** to set the left margin, and press Enter.

11. Choose **R**ight, type **80** to set the right margin, and press Enter.

12. Choose **Q**uit twice to close dialog boxes, record settings, and return to the Print dialog box.

13. Open the **P**rint menu and choose **S**preadsheet Print. This time the preview shows both edges of the sheet.

You can quit the exercise at this point or continue with instructions for actually printing your sample. If you close the spreadsheet, save your changes to preserve the print settings.

Printing

In the preceding steps you made all the settings for printing and checked the settings, using an on-screen preview. Before printing, you must choose between draft and final output. *Draft* output uses the fonts built into your printer. Using draft output is fast, but the results may not resemble the preview because draft does not use special fonts and sizes.

You can produce Final or Graphics output by downloading fonts from your computer to your printer. In this way, you can duplicate on paper the fonts seen in the preview. In the exercise that follows, you print both Draft and Graphics output.

To print in Graphics and Draft mode, do the following:

1. Open the SAMPLE spreadsheet if necessary.

2. Open the **P**rint menu and choose **D**estination. A dialog box appears.

3. In the destination dialog box, choose **P**rinter and press Enter.

4. With your printer turned on and on-line to the computer, choose **S**preadsheet Print.

   If the sheet prints but does not eject from the printer, select the **P**rint menu and choose **A**djust Printer. In the box that appears, choose the **F**orm Feed command to send an eject command to the printer.

5. When printing is complete, select **P**rint and choose **D**estination to reopen the dialog box.

6. Choose **G**raphics Printer as the destination and press Enter.

7. Choose **S**preadsheet Print to print the spreadsheet, using fonts generated by Quattro Pro SE.

   If the sheet prints but does not eject from the printer, select the **P**rint menu and choose **A**djust Printer. In the box that appears, choose Form Feed to send an eject command to the printer.

Using Fast Graph

Quattro Pro SE has powerful graphing capabilities. With Quattro Pro, you can display and print complex graphics. This section introduces you to the Fast Graph feature, a tool for making quick, simple graphs; however, you also should become familiar with advanced graphing options.

Creating a Graph

For this section, you create a simple spreadsheet that you turn into a graph. To create the spreadsheet, open a new blank spreadsheet and type the following information in the specified cells:

Cell	Data
A2	**Month**
A3	**Jan**
A4	**Feb**
A5	**Mar**
A6	**Apr**
B2	**Sales**
B3	**5000**
B4	**6000**
B5	**8000**
B6	**12000**

Open the **File** menu and choose the **S**ave command to save your work as MYSALES. Your spreadsheet should resemble the spreadsheet in figure 14.15.

To convert your data to a graph, following these steps:

1. Highlight the range A2..B6

2. Select the **G**raph menu and choose the **F**ast Graph command. With default settings, a bar graph similar to figure 14.16 appears.

3. Press Esc to switch from graph to spreadsheet.

4. From the **G**raph menu, choose the **G**raph Type command.

5. To create a pie chart, choose **P**ie in the dialog box that appears.

6. Choose **V**iew to see the change in the graph (see fig 14.17).

7. Press Esc to return to the spreadsheet.

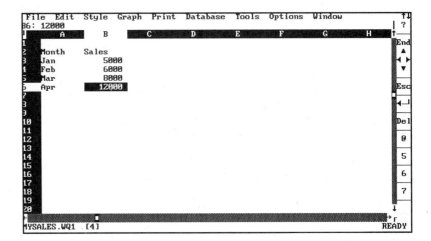

Fig. 14.15

The MYSALES spreadsheet.

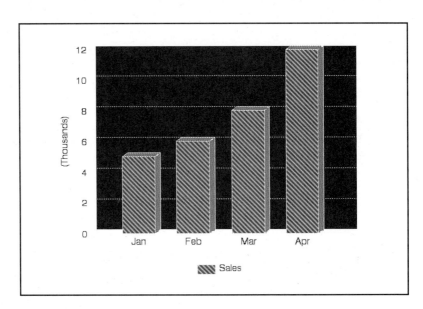

Fig. 14.16

Bar graph from MYSALES.

Saving a Graph

When you save the spreadsheet, Quattro Pro saves a single graph associated with a spreadsheet. To create a second graph, however, you must save the first graph; otherwise, the new graph overwrites the first graph's settings.

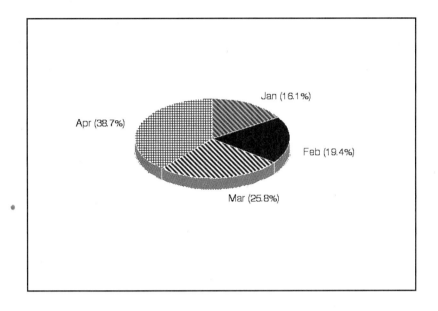

Fig. 14.17

Pie chart from
MYSALES.

To name and save a the graph, follow these steps:

1. Select the **Gr**aph menu and choose **N**ame. In the box that appears, choose **C**reate.

2. Type the name **SALESPIE** and press Enter. Remember that you cannot use a name longer than eight characters.

3. Choose **Q**uit from the **Gr**aph menu.

4. To locate and display the named graph, open the **Gr**aph menu and choose **D**isplay. In the box that appears, choose **N**ame.

To preview how your graph will print, open the **P**rint menu and choose **G**raph Print. In the box that appears, choose **D**estination. In the second box that appears, choose **S**creen Preview. Press Enter; then choose **G**o. To print a graph, change the destination to **G**raph Printer, press Enter, and choose **G**o.

You can learn a great deal more about graphs. Quattro Pro SE makes embedding graphs in a spreadsheet, enhancing graphs with color, dimensional effects, elaborate labels, and lettering easy.

Chapter Summary

In this chapter you learned the basics of working with the Quattro Pro SE spreadsheet. You learned screen layout and terminology, how to navigate around the spreadsheet, and how to use the help features. Through a series of exercises, you learned to enter formulas and functions and edit information. You also learned methods of selecting and using blocks. You practiced changing a worksheet's appearance with formatting. Finally, you previewed and printed a spreadsheet and a Fast Graph derived from a spreadsheet.

You still have a great deal to learn about Quattro Pro SE! The manual that accompanies the spreadsheet is nearly the length of this book. You may never use every facet of Quattro Pro SE, but to use the program with efficiency, you should be prepared to invest time in detailed study.

Using Quattro Pro Viewer

The Quattro Pro Viewer does a remarkable job of integrating the DOS-based Quattro Pro SE spreadsheet with the graphics power of GeoWorks Pro. Using the Viewer, you can switch rapidly between the two applications and use the features of both applications to enhance the effectiveness of your spreadsheets and graphs.

With the Quattro Pro Viewer, you can operate Quattro Pro SE by "remote control." GeoWorks includes commands that suspend GeoWorks Pro, switch to Quattro Pro SE, and—when you complete your work with Quattro—return to GeoWorks Pro. This *task switching* blends Quattro Pro SE into the GeoWorks Pro environment. In this chapter, you learn the commands you need to use the task switching feature.

Quattro Pro SE, which is capable of printing full-page spreadsheets and graphs, is not capable of directly integrating its output into other documents. Quattro Pro SE also has a limited capability for manipulating the size, placement, and fonts used in graphs. By copying spreadsheets and graphs into GeoWorks Pro, however, you can apply all the tools available in GeoWrite, GeoDraw, and the Scrapbook to enhance Quattro Pro SE output; you can develop sophisticated documents and presentations in GeoWorks Pro.

Understanding the Viewer Window

The Quattro Pro Viewer is an application similar to GeoWrite or GeoDraw. You can see the Quattro Pro Viewer icon in the WORLD window, which is the default opening screen for GeoWorks' Advanced Workspace (see fig. 15.1).

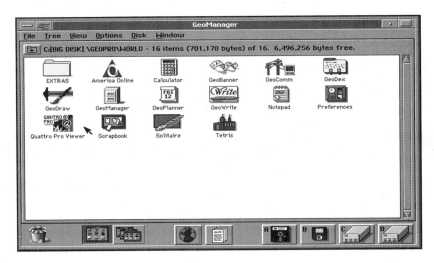

Fig. 15.1

The Quattro Pro Viewer icon in the WORLD directory window.

You can double-click the Quattro Pro Viewer icon to start the Viewer. You also can start the Viewer by opening the Express menu, choosing **S**tartup, and selecting Quattro Pro Viewer from the list of applications in the cascade menu. When you start Quattro Pro Viewer, the screen shown in figure 15.2 appears.

Because the Viewer window shares a common structure with other GeoWorks Pro windows, you may discover that many of the features of this window are familiar. Table 15.1 explains the components of the Viewer window.

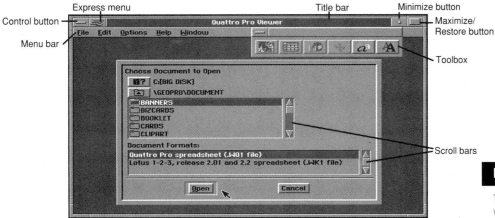

Express menu · Title bar · Minimize button
Control button · Maximize/Restore button
Menu bar
Toolbox
Scroll bars

Fig. 15.2

The Quattro Pro
Viewer window.

Table 15.1 The Viewer Window

Part	Purpose
Title bar	Contains the names of the application and any document that is currently open; turns dark if the window is active
Express menu	Enables you to switch rapidly to other active applications, launch other applications, move to the Welcome screen, and exit to DOS
Control button	Opens a special menu that contains commands which control the position and size of the Viewer window
Menu bar	Displays the Quattro Pro SE menus that you use to access various features and commands of the Quattro Pro Viewer
File	Controls selecting, opening, and closing of files you place in the Viewer
Edit	Enables you to select and copy screen contents
Options	Sets printer type and controls the display of warning messages
Help	Opens a scrolling window that contains help topics
Window	Switches between single and overlapping displays and switches documents in the window
Toolbox	Contains six buttons that represent frequently used commands

Understanding the Viewer Toolbox

Unique to the Viewer is a Toolbox, which consists of six buttons (see fig. 15.3). The buttons represent frequently used commands. From left to right, the buttons are Edit Spreadsheet, View Matching Spreadsheet, View Matching Chart, Set Spreadsheet Range, Set Font, and Set Point Size. The grayed buttons are inactive with the current window contents.

You can turn off a Toolbox by double-clicking its Control button. If you turn the Toolbox off, you can reactivate it by opening the **O**ptions menu and choosing the Show **T**ool Box command. You also can drag the Toolbox to a new location by its Title bar.

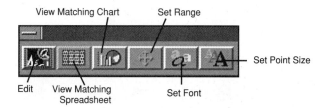

Fig. 15.3

The Viewer Toolbox.

Launching Quattro Pro SE from the Viewer

Although you can launch Quattro Pro SE from the Viewer, the method you use to launch Quattro Pro SE may depend on your purpose. The following sections summarize the necessary steps for the methods you can use to open the program.

To launch Quattro Pro SE from the menu, use these steps:

1. Select the **F**ile menu and choose **O**pen. A dialog box appears.

2. Click the spreadsheet file type in the Document Formats box (see fig. 15.4).

3. Scroll through the file list to locate the file.

4. Choose **O**pen. Quattro Pro SE opens with your selected file loaded.

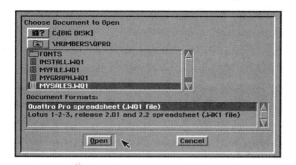

Fig 15.4

The Choose Document
to Open dialog box.

Launch To Create a New Spreadsheet

To launch Quattro Pro SE so that you can create a new spreadsheet,
follow these steps:

1. Double-click the Viewer icon in the WORLD directory.

2. Click Cancel to close the dialog box that opens existing files.

3. In the Viewer window, select the **File** menu and choose **New**.
   A dialog box appears (see fig. 15.5).

4. Choose the directory in which you want to save the new
   spreadsheet.

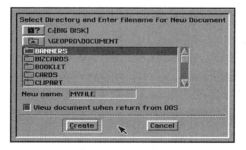

Fig 15.5

The save as dialog
box.

5. Type the new file name in the New name text field and choose
   Create. *Note:* If you do not disable the View document when you
   return from DOS feature, you see the file in the Viewer when you
   exit Quattro Pro SE.

6. In the dialog box that appears, click OK to launch Quattro Pro SE.

Launch To Edit the Spreadsheet in the Viewer

To launch Quattro Pro SE so that you can edit a spreadsheet loaded into the Viewer, follow these steps:

1. Select the **W**indow menu and choose **E**dit Spreadsheet. A dialog box appears, asking whether you want to edit the document currently displayed in the Viewer (see fig 15.6).

2. Click OK to launch Quattro Pro SE with the Viewer document loaded.

NOTE The Edit Spreadsheet button in the Toolbox is a convenient way to edit a spreadsheet in the Viewer. Clicking the button is equivalent to choosing the Edit Spreadsheet command in the Window menu.

Working With Spreadsheets

In this section, you learn how to manage spreadsheets you loaded into the Viewer. The spreadsheet is re-created in the Viewer, using GeoWorks Pro's graphics resources to create a document that you can edit, move, and paste within other GeoWorks Pro documents. Remember, you are not changing the original spreadsheet; you are working on a replica.

Viewing Selected Areas

GeoWorks Pro can import approximately 26 columns by 60 rows. Although most spreadsheets fit within this matrix, sometimes you may need to view portions of a larger spreadsheet that does not fit in GeoWorks Pro. This section explains the tools and techniques you use to view large spreadsheets.

To select an area of the spreadsheet smaller than the 26-column-by-60-row matrix that the Viewer imports, you must specify the block of cells you want to display. To select a small portion of the standard Viewer window, use the following steps:

1. Select the **O**ptions menu and choose the **S**preadsheet Range command. The dialog box shown in figure 15.7 appears.

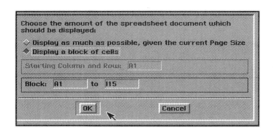

Fig. 15.7

Dialog box used to specify the portion of a spreadsheet to display.

2. Click the Display a block of cells button.

3. In the Block text fields, type the addresses of the upper left and lower right cells of the block you want to display.

4. Click OK to display the specified block.

NOTE Clicking the Set Spreadsheet Range button in the Toolbox is equivalent to choosing the Spreadsheet Range command from the Options menu.

Viewing Large Spreadsheets

If a spreadsheet exceeds the 26-column-by-60-row limit, you can use one of four techniques to view the spreadsheet. The first technique simply views another portion of a large spreadsheet; the other three methods actually pack more information into the Viewer.

Specifying a Starting Cell

Moving to another portion of the spreadsheet enables you to see important areas without altering the spreadsheet's appearance. To specify a different viewing location, follow these steps:

1. Select the **O**ptions menu and choose the **S**preadsheet Range command.

2. Click the Display as much as possible, given the current Page Size radio button.

3. In the Starting Column and Row text field, type the cell address of the upper left corner of the area you want to view and click OK.

The Viewer displays as much of the spreadsheet as possible, with the address you specified in the upper left corner of the screen.

Removing Borders

Each vertical line in a spreadsheet requires part of the Viewer's limited space. You can turn off borders to gain room in which to display more numeric information. To remove borders, follow these steps:

1. Select the **O**ptions menu and choose Cell **B**orders.

2. From the cascade menu that appears, choose **N**one to remove cell borders (see fig. 15.8).

   You can restore borders by choosing As In **F**ile from the same cascade menu.

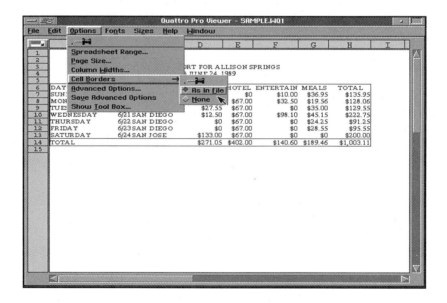

Using Fixed Column Widths

Using a single column width enables the Viewer to include more information; however, GeoWorks Pro limits you to three selections for width. Any text wider than the fixed width is cut off. Any number wider than its cell appears as a row of asterisks. This technique also strips all cell boundary lines. To set a single column width, use the following steps:

1. Open the **O**ptions menu and choose Column **W**idths. The dialog box shown in figure 15.9 appears.

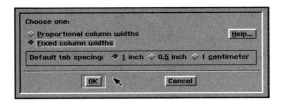

Fig 15.9

The Column Widths
dialog box.

2. Choose **F**ixed column widths.

3. Choose a tab spacing option from the Default tab spacings box and click OK.

   You can restore the default one-inch spacing by choosing **P**roportional Column Widths.

Changing Page Size

The default page size displayed in the Viewer window is 17-by-22 inches. Although few computer users can print such a large spreadsheet, displaying the spreadsheet in the window enables you to view a large spreadsheet. Larger and smaller sizes are available. (The page size feature is not available if you view a chart.)

You do not print directly from the Viewer. GeoWorks moves the spreadsheet or graph into GeoWrite or GeoDraw, and the application's printer settings control the printed size. You use Size settings in the Viewer to control how much you see on-screen and to help you roughly size the sheet before moving it.

To change page size, follow these steps:

1. Open the **O**ptions menu and choose **P**age Size.

2. In the dialog box that appears, use the scrolling list to choose a size.

3. Click OK to apply the new size. You may see a warning indicating that some cells cannot be seen (see fig. 15.10).

Fig 15.10

The dialog box
warning that some
cells will not be visible
in the Viewer.

Changing the Image

Changing font and font size is another technique for modifying spreadsheet size. Given the rich assortment of fonts and sizes, you can select a font that not only modifies the size of your spreadsheet, but also enhances its appearance and legibility.

The technique for changing font size is simple. Open the Sizes menu and choose a new font size. GeoWorks Pro changes the entire spreadsheet. Use the same steps with the Fonts menu to change fonts for the entire spreadsheet.

NOTE   Instead of using the Size and Fonts menu, clicking the Set Font or Set Point Size buttons in the Toolbox may be more convenient. Whether you use the menu or the Toolbox, the results are identical.

Transferring Spreadsheets

If you move a spreadsheet into GeoWrite or GeoDraw, you must use the Viewer's Page Size command from the Options menu to set the page size to match the page size of the receiving document. Although viewing a larger page so that you can see more of a large spreadsheet may seem sensible, when you copy a section or an entire spreadsheet, GeoWorks Pro redraws the spreadsheet in its new location based on the page size you specify. If the page size of the Viewer and your destination do not match, the results are unusable.

Moving to GeoWrite

If you copy into GeoWrite, the copy appears as a table of fixed size, matching what you see in the Viewer. Although you can edit the spreadsheet data, the document is no longer *interactive*—if you change cell values, totals do not change; formulas do not work. Conceptually, you have a text replica of the original spreadsheet. You can add GeoWrite text above or below the spreadsheet and choose where to paste the spreadsheet, just as you choose where to insert new text.

Follow these steps to transfer a spreadsheet from the Viewer to GeoWrite:

1. Create a GeoWrite document to receive the spreadsheet from the Viewer.

2. Switch to the Viewer, open the **O**ptions menu, and choose the **P**age Size command.

3. Set the Viewer's page size to match your document's page size.

4. Select the Viewer **E**dit menu and choose **S**elect All to highlight the entire spreadsheet or click the Select All button at the intersection of the row and column borders.

5. Select the **E**dit menu and choose **C**opy.

6. Switch to GeoWrite, using the Express menu. Place the text cursor in the location where you want the spreadsheet to appear.

7. Select the GeoWrite **E**dit menu and choose **P**aste to insert the spreadsheet in the selected location.

Moving to GeoDraw

In GeoDraw, you can treat the spreadsheet image like a piece of art, changing its size and proportions. You also can draw borders and add annotations in various fonts. You can use the Fuse objects command to bind the spreadsheet and any enhancements into a single graphics unit you can save or paste into another document. Remember, you cannot edit the cells of the spreadsheet in GeoDraw. The spreadsheet has become a graphics object rather than a text document, as in GeoWrite.

To move a spreadsheet into GeoDraw, follow these steps:

1. Open a blank GeoDraw document.

2. Switch to the Viewer, select the **O**ptions menu, and choose the **P**age Size command.

3. Set the Viewer's page size to match your document's page size.

4. Open the Viewer's **E**dit menu.

5. Choose **S**elect All to highlight the entire spreadsheet or drag the mouse to highlight the part of the spreadsheet you want to copy.

6. From the **E**dit menu, choose **C**opy.

7. Switch to GeoDraw, using the Express menu, and choose the **P**aste command from the GeoDraw **E**dit menu to insert the spreadsheet.

Working With Graphs

A graph is often the most effective way to present spreadsheet results. The Viewer enables you to insert graphs created by Quattro Pro SE into GeoWorks Pro documents.

As you work with graphs, you may need to switch the Viewer between a graph and the spreadsheet from which it was created. The Window menu contains two commands for this purpose: View Matching Spreadsheet and View Matching Chart. For convenience, you also can activate these commands with the second Spreadsheet and third Chart buttons in the Toolbox.

Despite similarities between the way you use Viewer with graphs and with spreadsheets, differences also exist. You cannot resize graphs in the Viewer; however, you can use GeoDraw or the Scrapbook for resizing. Later sections in this chapter discuss techniques for resizing with GeoDraw and the Scrapbook.

Preparing Graphs for the Viewer

The program normally stores the graphs you create and view with Quattro Pro SE in a format that the Viewer cannot read. To prepare a chart for use in the Viewer, you must use the Quattro Pro SE Print menu to save the graph in *EPS (Encapsulated PostScript)* format. After you complete your graph in Quattro Pro SE, follow these steps to save the graph for use in the Viewer:

1. Select the **P**rint menu and choose **G**raph Print.

2. In the cascade menu that appears, choose **W**rite Graph File. A small box of file types appears.

3. Choose **E**PS Files. A dialog box appears.

4. Enter the name of the spreadsheet that contains the chart. (GeoWorks Pro automatically adds the EPS extension.)

5. Press Enter. The `Now Printing` message indicates that GeoWorks Pro is creating the EPS file.

Seeing Accurate EPS Color

Your color EPS charts may appear only blue or black in the Viewer. For Quattro Pro SE to record the proper information in the file, you must set the default printer to Postscript. Having an actual PostScript printer is not necessary; however, you must set the default printer to Postscript in the Hardware menu. You change this setting only once to cure the false color problem.

To trick Quattro Pro SE into thinking it is preparing the EPS file for a PostScript printer, follow these steps:

1. Select the **O**ptions menu and choose **H**ardware.

2. Choose **P**rinters.

3. In the cascade menu that appears, choose **2**nd Printer.

4. Choose **T**ype of Printer in the cascade menu.

5. Scroll through the printer list. Highlight Postscript and press Enter to select it.

6. Choose PostScript again in the small dialog box (see fig 15.11).

7. In the Mode dialog box, choose Normal.

8. Choose Quit to close menus until you are back to the menu headed by the Hardware command.

9. Choose **H**ardware; then choose Printer.

10. Choose **D**efault Printer.

11. Choose **2**nd Printer; then choose **Q**uit.

12. On the **O**ptions menu, choose Update.

13. Choose **Q**uit to save changes.

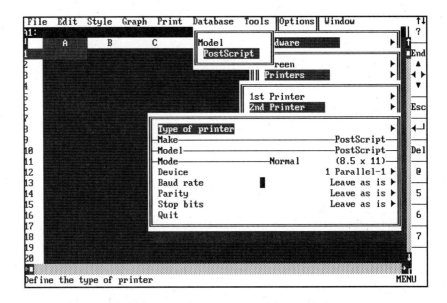

Fig 15.11

The second PostScript
dialog box.

Viewing EPS Charts

To start the Viewer and load a specific chart, follow these steps:

1. Double-click the Viewer icon in the GeoManager WORLD directory to start Viewer.

2. Select the Viewer's **File** menu and choose the **View** command. A dialog box appears.

3. Select the document format for Quattro Pro SE Charts (EPS).

4. Scroll through the file list to locate the directory containing the graph.

   The file list displays directory folders and the file names of any EPS charts in the current directory. To load a chart, double-click it. (You also can double-click a folder to open it and continue looking.)

5. Select the chart and click OK to load it.

You can load a chart into Viewer by locating the file in the GeoManager DOCUMENT window. Notice the distinctive icon of Quattro Pro SE documents (see fig 15.12). Double-click the icon to launch the file in Viewer.

EPS Chart icon   Spreadsheet icon

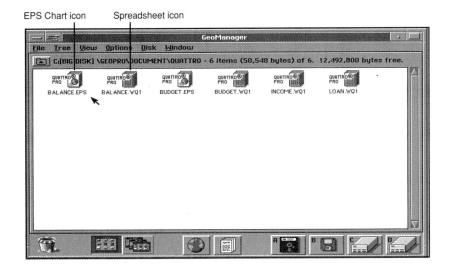

Fig. 15.12

A Quattro Pro SE chart
and spreadsheet
icons.

NOTE You can view several Quattro Pro SE spreadsheets and charts at the same time. Open the spreadsheets and charts by repeatedly using the **View** command from the Viewer **F**ile menu. After you open the documents, use the **W**indow menu's **O**verlapping command to array the windows so that you can move and size them as necessary.

Using the Fit in Window Option

GeoWorks Pro initially loads charts at the size in which you create them, often more than filling the Viewer window. If you cannot view all of a graph, select the Options menu and activate the Fit in Window check box. The program automatically sizes the graph to be completely visible in the window.

The graph appears smaller if you use the Fit in Window option; however, you can copy the graph into other GeoWorks Pro applications at its original size. You can use GeoDraw to resize a graph permanently. You also can resize the graph proportionally with the Scrapbook. For more information about GeoDraw, refer to Chapter 8, "Using GeoDraw."

Using Scrapbook To Resize Graphs

Although the Scrapbook may seem an odd place to work with graphs, the Scrapbook has the capability to resize images proportionally—something you cannot do anywhere else in GeoWorks Pro. Proportional resizing retains the ratio of height to width, avoiding the distortion that frequently occurs if you resize in GeoDraw. The resized Scrapbook graph retains its new size when you paste the graph to other applications.

To use the Scrapbook to resize a graph, follow these steps:

1. Start the Scrapbook from the Express menu or from GeoManager.

2. In the Viewer, open the Edit menu and choose Copy.

3. Switch to the Scrapbook and choose Paste at End from the Edit menu.

4. To resize the graph, open the Scrapbook's View menu and select one of the enlargement or reduction percentages (see fig 15.13).

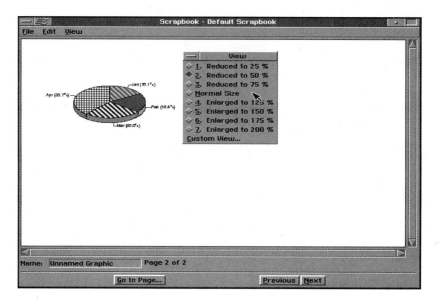

5. Select the Scrapbook Edit menu and choose Copy at view % to preserve the image size.

6. Switch to the desired destination (such as GeoWrite, or Clipboard) and paste the reduced or enlarged graph.

Preparing To Print a Graph

You must make a small, but significant, choice for any graph you plan to print. The Options menu contains two printing choices: **P**ostScript Printer and **N**on-PostScript printer (see fig 15.14). To include the appropriate printing information with the image, be sure to click the appropriate command, which depends on the printer you use, before moving the graph image to another application.

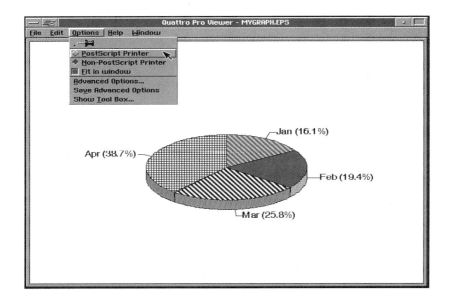

Fig. 15.14

Printer selection buttons.

Remember that to print graphs from within Quattro you must select a printer type other than PostScript (unless you own a PostScript printer) because this printer is now the default printer.

Customizing the Viewer

You can customize several settings in the Viewer. The Advanced Options dialog box, which appears when you choose the Advanced Options command from the Viewer's Options menu, contains the settings you can customize (see fig. 15.15).

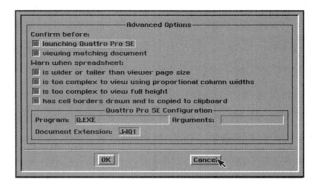

Fig. 15.15

The Advanced Options
dialog box.

The Advanced Options

In the Advanced Options dialog box, you determine which dialog boxes
appear as you work with the Viewer. In Viewer, dialog boxes open to
confirm your intention to launch Quattro Pro SE, to view the chart that
matches the current graph, and so on. These dialog boxes, which draw
attention to what you are doing, help you avoid performing certain tasks
by mistake. After you are familiar with the Viewer, you can turn these
dialog boxes off. To deactivate the dialog boxes, click to turn off the top
two boxes in the Advanced Options dialog box.

The remaining Advanced Options check boxes are warnings. The dialog
boxes warn you if the spreadsheet is larger than the page or if the complexity of your spreadsheet can prevent Viewer from fully re-creating the
spreadsheet, for example. Keep these warnings active until you are a
skilled user of Viewer.

Other Spreadsheet Files and Programs

The Quattro Pro SE Configuration box at the bottom of the Advanced
Options dialog box contains text fields that you use to modify the commands given to launch Quattro Pro SE. In the Arguments box, for example, you can include the name of a macro that Quattro Pro SE runs at
start-up. You also can include a file to be loaded automatically when you
start Quattro Pro SE.

The Program text field and the Document Extension text field enable you
to use a spreadsheet program other than Quattro Pro SE or to read compatible spreadsheets created by other programs. The Viewer reads any
spreadsheet format equivalent to the 1-2-3 WK1 file type. Many spreadsheet programs support this file type. If you type the spreadsheet file

extension in the Document Extension text field, the Viewer looks for files with that extension. If the files are fully compatible with the WK1 and WQ1 file format, they load into the Viewer when you press Enter.

You also can start another spreadsheet from the Viewer by typing its path and file name in the Program text field. Although you have no guarantee of compatibility with programs other than Quattro Pro SE, advanced users with large numbers of WK1 files in another spreadsheet may want to experiment with this feature.

After you change any of the Advanced Options, close the dialog box. Then choose the Save **A**dvanced Options command on the Viewer's **O**ptions menu. Click OK to record your changes and exit.

Chapter Summary

In this chapter, you learned how to link Quattro Pro SE and GeoWorks Pro through the Quattro Pro Viewer application. Using this tool, you learned to start and switch to Quattro Pro SE from the Viewer. You learned methods of working with spreadsheets larger than the capacity of the Viewer and methods for moving spreadsheets and graphs into GeoWrite and GeoDraw.

This chapter also explains how to prepare, scale, and enhance charts for the Viewer. The chapter concludes with an explanation of the Advanced Options setting and suggestions for loading other types of spreadsheet files into the Viewer.

The Quattro Pro Viewer provides an excellent way to combine powerful spreadsheets from Quattro Pro SE with the exceptional formatting and enhancement capabilities of GeoWorks Pro. If you have ever wanted to merge spreadsheet information into presentation documents, you now have the full "tool kit" to undertake the challenge.

Installing GeoWorks Pro

Installing some computer programs can be a major struggle, requiring stacks of disks and arcane settings. Right out of the box, however, GeoWorks demonstrates how program power can be approachable. Although you do some very sophisticated work with GeoWorks and your computer, you don't have to use every part of the program immediately.

Most GeoWorks Pro installations proceed flawlessly; you can get the software up and running without realizing what a remarkable array of power is at your disposal. In this appendix, you can do a "dry run" installation by reading through the steps. The appendix anticipates and answers questions you may see during the installation and should help you to approach the installation comfortably, even if you have never installed a computer program.

This appendix begins by outlining the equipment and information you need before beginning installation, then describes the installation procedure step-by-step and explains the configuration phase. Finally, with GeoWorks Pro running, you learn how to start and quit GeoWorks Pro. With the program installed and properly configured, you are ready to move to the body of this book, where you can learn the dimensions of this extraordinary program.

Preparing for Installation

Although GeoWorks Pro is very flexible, the program requires certain basic hardware and suggests some optional equipment for best performance. One of the program's major virtues is its capability to work well on older or less-powerful equipment. You may think twice about running Microsoft Windows without an 80286 computer, substantial memory, and plenty of disk storage; however, GeoWorks Pro is a pleasure to use even on older XT-type machines. Sorry, you can't run GeoWorks Pro without a hard disk, but with a basic hardware configuration, you can enjoy many of the benefits of the latest graphical user interface technology. The sections that follow describe both required and recommended equipment.

The Computer

GeoWorks Pro runs on every personal computer built by IBM, from the original PC through the PC/XT, AT, and the PS/2 series, in addition to any computer that is fully *IBM-compatible*. Compatibility can be a subtle issue, but basically for your computer to be IBM-compatible, it must be able to run any software that runs on IBM equipment. Today, a PC *clone* that isn't fully-compatible usually is rejected by the marketplace; if your machine is of recent vintage and doesn't need any special preparation to run IBM PC software, you should be able to run GeoWorks Pro.

The Disk Operating System

Your computer must have MS-DOS, the Disk Operating System for personal computers, installed. GeoWorks Pro recognizes any version of DOS from 2.0 through the recently released MS-DOS 5.0. At your DOS prompt, you can type the DOS command **ver** to get a message showing which version of MS-DOS your computer uses.

NOTE If you are using MS-DOS Version 5.0 with GeoWorks Version 1.0, type the following command at the DOS prompt:

setver geos.exe 4.0

Version 1.0 does not recognize MS-DOS 5.0. This command "tricks" GEOS into believing it is running an earlier version of MS-DOS. You need to enter the command only once. The program stores the change permanently. GeoWorks Pro 1.2 recognizes MS-DOS 5.0 and does not require use of SETVER.

Memory Requirements

Your computer needs a minimum of 512K of memory installed. This figure is remarkably low, considering that the common memory standard for many computers is 2M due to memory-hungry graphics programs. The designers of GeoWorks Pro packed a great deal of performance into a very small package.

GeoWorks Pro can use additional memory: conventional, expanded, or extended. GeoWorks can draw and redraw large documents and graphics more rapidly with added memory.

If you install more memory after installing GeoWorks Pro, you need to tell the program about the additional memory by using the Computer option button in the Preferences Desk Tool, described in Chapter 11, "Customizing with the Preferences Desk Tool."

Disk Storage Requirements

Your computer must have a hard disk storage device. GeoWorks Pro gives you the option of installing a *minimal* package (2.7M free disk space), a *medium* package (3.9M) and a *standard* installation (4.7M). In addition, you need about .5M for temporary use during the installation.

GeoWorks Pro offers the options of a standard installation (6.5M) and a minimal installation (4.0M). An additional .5M is required for temporary use during installation.

If you have enough space, the standard installation is recommended. (No matter which level you choose, you get the complete functionality of all major elements of GeoWorks Pro.) Table A.1 describes the results of each type of installation:

Table A.1 Installation Options

Type of Installation	Disk Space	Items Excluded
Ensemble		
Standard	4.7M	Includes all applications, samples, clip art, and fonts
Medium	3.9M	No Screen Dump, Perf,or Spintext No business or personal document templates No GeoWrite or GeoDraw clip art No sample docs for GeoWrite or GeoDraw No background pictures

continues

Table A.1 continued

Type of Installation	Disk Space	Items Excluded
Minimal	2.7M	No Screen Dump, Perf or Spintext No business or personal document templates No GeoWrite or GeoDraw clip art No sample docs for GeoWrite or GeoDraw No background pictures No spelling checker dictionaries Only a few outline fonts No America Online or Solitaire applications
Pro		
Standard	6.5M	All documents, clip art, and backgrounds
Minimal	4.0M	Partial documents, clip art, and backgrounds

After you select an installation type, the screen shown in figure A.1 appears. The message on this screen, though a bit obscure, indicates that in the future you cannot run Setup again, select a smaller installation type, and have Setup remove *excess* files from your disk as it installs a smaller version.

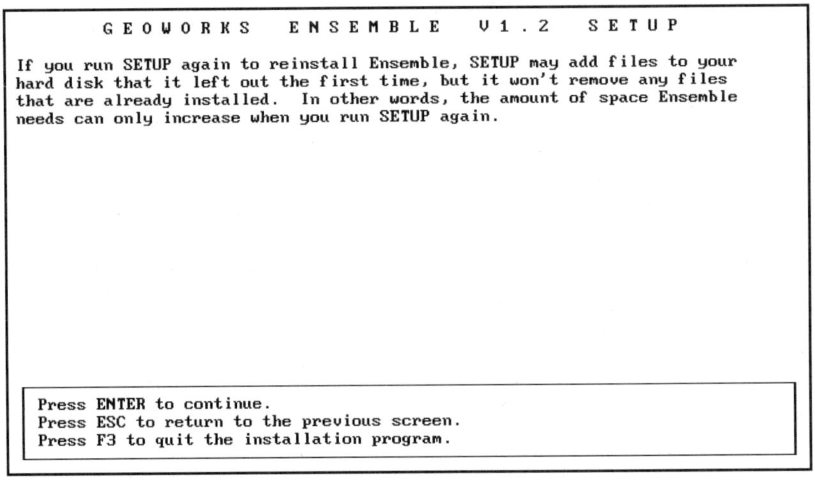

```
         G E O W O R K S     E N S E M B L E     V 1 . 2     S E T U P

If you run SETUP again to reinstall Ensemble, SETUP may add files to your
hard disk that it left out the first time, but it won't remove any files
that are already installed.  In other words, the amount of space Ensemble
needs can only increase when you run SETUP again.




 Press ENTER to continue.
 Press ESC to return to the previous screen.
 Press F3 to quit the installation program.
```

Fig. A.1

A message about installation sizes.

To move from a larger to a smaller installation, you must use DOS to delete the GeoWorks Pro files from your disk before beginning again. If you delete GeoWorks Pro to reinstall, be sure that you first save your data files.

The Video System

GeoWorks works with a variety of video standards, including EGA, VGA, SVGA, CGA, MCGA, and Hercules. If you don't have a color system, you see lovely shades of gray; however, GeoWorks Pro makes such excellent use of color to clarify and decorate that you may be tempted to upgrade your system.

The Mouse

To use GeoWorks, you need a mouse. If you have not yet used a mouse, or if you have sworn you will never touch one of those mechanical rodents, GeoWorks Pro gives you reason to rethink your position.

One of the greatest advances that graphical interfaces like GEOS have brought to personal computing is the capability to move objects on-screen with a mouse—a process that has come to be known as *drag and drop*. After you experience the convenience of dragging an item from one location to another on-screen, adjusting the size of a picture, or selecting a word to delete with two quick clicks, you may well be ready to join the legions of happy, rodent-wielding computer users.

Because the mouse listing on the GeoWorks Pro setup screen offers 79 choices, you probably can find one right for you and your computer. Your mouse should be compatible with Microsoft, Logitech, or Mouse Systems mice.

A number of three-button mice exist. GeoWorks Pro doesn't use the middle button; you can use the right and left buttons normally, but you don't get any "bonus" from the third button.

The Printer

GeoWorks Pro doesn't require a printer, but you probably will want to print the excellent documents and graphics you produce with the program. GeoWorks supports a variety of printers; you can use dot-matrix printers, laser printers, and, in Version 1.2, PostScript printers. The program's advanced printing features enable you to produce excellent graphic output and text characters of any size, free of the jagged edges that distinguish the output of less-sophisticated programs.

Answering Installation Questions

During the automatic installation process, GeoWorks Pro checks your equipment to determine type and capabilities. In most installations, the program makes the right choices; however, if you have an unusual configuration or if the installation program makes a wrong choice, you may need to choose an alternative.

To make the installation process as easy as possible, make sure that you have the following information available before you begin the installation:

■ *The name of the drive and directory where you want to install the program.* The default drive and directory suggested by the installation program is C:\GEOWORKS, which is fine for most installations. If your disk space or computer configuration requires a different location, plan for the alternate path and check available space *before* you start the installation.

Type the DOS command **dir** to get a directory listing of the drive you plan to use. The bottom of the listing displays the free space on the hard drive (see fig. A.2). Using DIR, you can ensure that you have the free space required for a standard installation, or you can decide on a medium or minimal installation if you can't gain more free space.

■ *The display type.* Do you have EGA, VGA, SVGA, CGA, or MCGA graphics? If you aren't certain, check your hardware literature, particularly the information that accompanied your video board.

■ *The printer make and model, and the port where the printer attaches.* (Most printers use *parallel* cables attached to the port called LPT1.) If necessary, check your printer literature or physically inspect the printer connection.

If you have a printer that uses a *serial* port, you need to know the port and the settings for *baud rate*, *stop bits*, and *parity*. These settings are listed in the printer manual.

```
C:\GRAPHICS>dir

 Volume in drive C is STACKER
 Directory of C:\GRAPHICS

 .             <DIR>      04-30-91  11:08p
 ..            <DIR>      04-30-91  11:08p
 COREL         <DIR>      05-20-91   8:51p
 NEWPS         <DIR>      04-30-91  11:08p
        4 file(s)             0 bytes
                      74596352 bytes free

C:\GRAPHICS>
```

Fig. A.2

The amount of free
disk space displayed
in response to the
DOS DIR command.

■ *The mouse type and the port where the mouse attaches.* Check the
label on the bottom of the mouse for the mouse type. (One of the
mouse brands and models shown in the installation list is No Idea,
which you can choose if you don't find your mouse listed.) Check
which port on your computer is attached to the mouse (usually one
of the serial ports: COM1, COM2, and so on).

■ *Your program serial number.* The Customer Support Handbook that
came with your original GeoWorks Pro package contains this number, which you need to complete the installation.

After gathering this information, you can proceed with the installation
process.

Installing with Setup

The GeoWorks Pro installation process is highly automated. In this section, you learn how to start the installation process and some important
points to consider when installing the program.

Running the Setup Program

Retail versions of GeoWorks Pro come with a complete set of 5 1/4- and 3 1/2-inch disks. The Version 1.2 upgrade is shipped on 5 1/4-inch disks with a card you can use to request 3 1/2-inch disks. Use the appropriate disk size for your equipment (or the size you prefer if you have both drive sizes). The files on the disks are compressed to save storage space. You must run the Setup program to decompress the files with the GeoWorks installation program.

To install GeoWorks Pro, follow these steps:

1. Make an archive copy of your master disks, using the MS-DOS DISKCOPY command to make exact duplicates (see your MS-DOS manual for instructions); then write-protect your installation set.

   With 5 1/4-inch disks, use a write-protect tab on the notch at the edge of the disk. On 3 1/2-inch disks, open the write-protect slider at the top edge of the disk.

2. Start your computer and go to the DOS prompt. Shut down any programs that are memory-resident or that load automatically when you start your computer.

3. At the DOS prompt, type **a:setup** (or **b:setup** if the installation disk is in drive B) and press Enter.

   The first Setup screen appears, as shown in figure A.3.

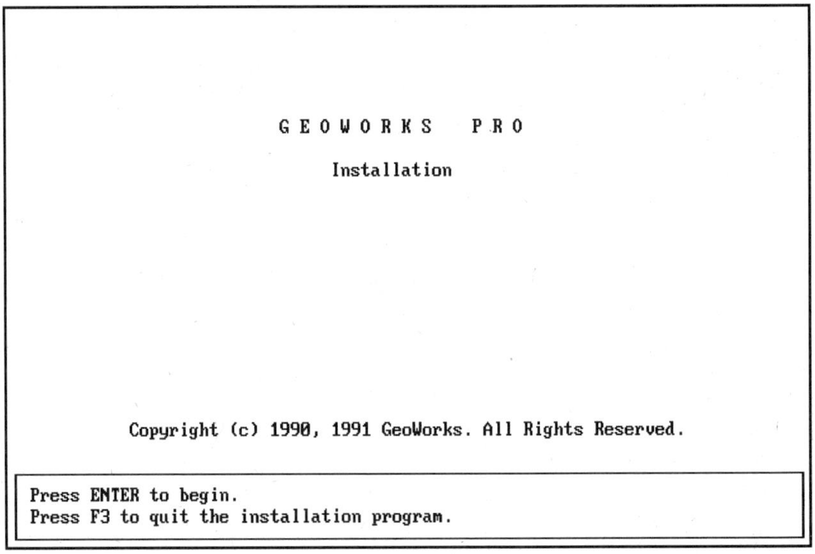

```
                    G E O W O R K S   P R O
                        Installation












        Copyright (c) 1990, 1991 GeoWorks. All Rights Reserved.

  Press ENTER to begin.
  Press F3 to quit the installation program.
```

Fig. A.3

The first Setup screen.

You can stop the installation process at any time by pressing F3. As the installation progresses, you also can use the Esc key to return to previous screens.

4. Press Enter to continue the installation.

The second screen contains information to reassure you about the installation process and explains that you can change options if your choice doesn't work correctly. Read all screen messages carefully. Take your time; GeoWorks Pro waits as long as necessary.

5. Press Enter to continue to the third screen (see fig. A.4) for designating the directory where you want GeoWorks Pro installed.

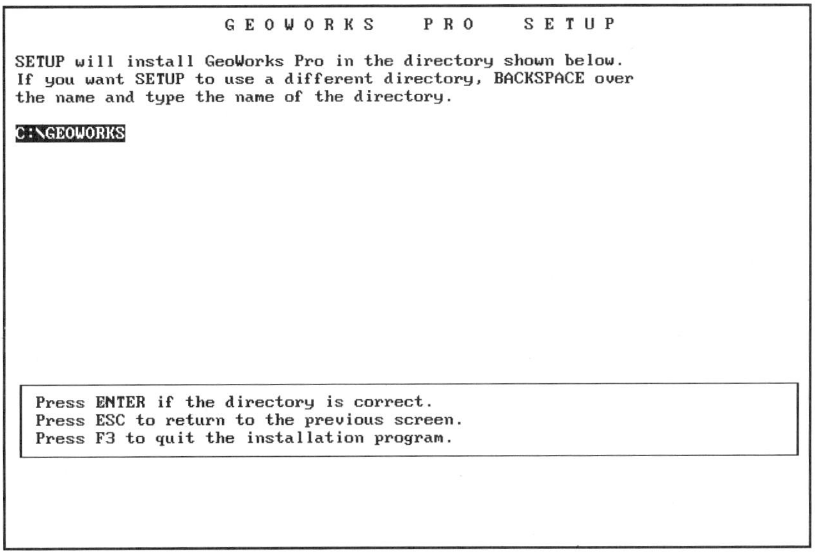

```
              G E O W O R K S    P R O    S E T U P

SETUP will install GeoWorks Pro in the directory shown below.
If you want SETUP to use a different directory, BACKSPACE over
the name and type the name of the directory.

C:\GEOWORKS




    ┌──────────────────────────────────────────────────────┐
    │ Press ENTER if the directory is correct.             │
    │ Press ESC to return to the previous screen.          │
    │ Press F3 to quit the installation program.           │
    └──────────────────────────────────────────────────────┘
```

Fig. A.4

The third Setup screen.

The default installation directory is C:\GEOWORKS. To load the program in another location, use the Backspace key to delete the default directory and then type the full path name of the desired directory.

6. When the directory choice is correct, press Enter to continue.

7. Using the up- or down-arrow key, select the type of installation you want: standard, medium (Ensemble only), or minimal (see fig. A.5).

```
          G E O W O R K S     P R O     S E T U P

GeoWorks Pro, with all its applications, sample documents, clip art, and
outline fonts, takes up a lot of hard disk space.  You can, however, save space
by leaving certain parts out during the installation process
(although you won't get to use those items when you run GeoWorks Pro).

Choose one of the options listed below to learn more about and install that
configuration of Pro on your hard disk. Should you decide to install a
different configuration, press ESC to return to this screen. Note that
in addition to the sizes listed below, Pro requires 0.5 Meg of free space
on your hard disk for working files.

Options:
      Standard Install (needs 6.5 Meg)
      Minimal Install  (needs 4 Meg)



    Press ENTER if the highlighted answer is OK.
    Press ESC to return to the previous screen.
    Press the UP and DOWN arrows to change the answer.
    Press F3 to quit the installation program.
```

Fig. A.5

Installation type
options.

8. Press Enter to confirm your installation selection. The next screen describes the installation type you selected.

9. Press Enter to continue, Esc to return to the preceding screen and change the installation type, or F3 to terminate the installation process. If you press Enter, the next screen (shown in fig. A.6) asks whether you want to be able to start GeoWorks Pro from any directory.

```
          G E O W O R K S     P R O     S E T U P

Would you like to be able to start GeoWorks Pro no matter
what directory you are currently working in?

If you say "Yes", the path in your AUTOEXEC.BAT file will be changed
to contain C:\GEOPRO.  A copy of the original file will be
kept in C:\GEOPRO\SYSTEM\AUTOEXEC.OLD.

Changes to the AUTOEXEC.BAT file don't take effect until the next
time you restart your machine.

Options:
      Yes
      No




    Press ENTER if the highlighted answer is OK.
    Press ESC to return to the previous screen.
    Press the UP and DOWN arrows to change the answer.
    Press F3 to quit the installation program.
```

Fig. A.6

Prompt to start
GeoWorks from
any directory.

Choose **Yes** if you want the installation program to add the Geo-Works Pro directory to the *PATH command* in the AUTOEXEC.BAT file. (With this modification, you can type **geos** at any DOS prompt to start GeoWorks Pro.)

Choose **No** if you don't want the installation program to modify the PATH command. If you choose No, GeoWorks displays another screen with the commands you must type to start GeoWorks Pro (see fig. A.7).

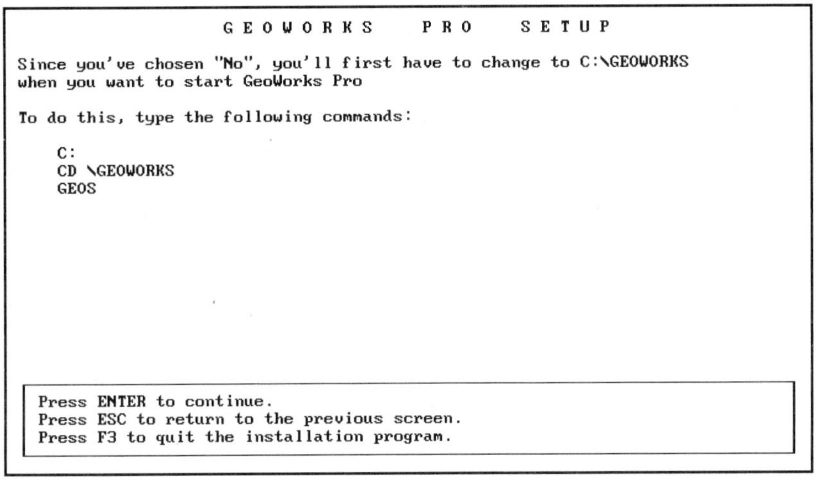

```
               G E O W O R K S     P R O     S E T U P

Since you've chosen "No", you'll first have to change to C:\GEOWORKS
when you want to start GeoWorks Pro

To do this, type the following commands:

   C:
   CD \GEOWORKS
   GEOS




   Press ENTER to continue.
   Press ESC to return to the previous screen.
   Press F3 to quit the installation program.
```

Fig. A.7

The start-up commands if the GeoWorks directory is not in the DOS directory path.

Copying the Disks

At this point, the Setup program has the necessary information to copy the files to your computer. When you press Enter, GeoWorks requests that you insert the first disk and press Enter again.

From this point, the program creates the GeoWorks Pro directory structure and copies files onto your hard disk. Because the files must be decompressed, the installation may take 15 to 20 minutes (see fig. A.8).

Occasionally, a file may not decompress correctly, and you may see the message File size mismatch.... If this problem occurs, retry the decompression a couple of times. If the problem continues, remove the disk when the disk drive light is off, reseat the disk in the drive, and try again (sometimes a slight misalignment of the disk can cause problems). If these techniques don't work, contact GeoWorks Customer Support, by phone or using America Online, for a replacement disk. Keep the suspect disk with you; you need the information on the disk label when you contact GeoWorks.

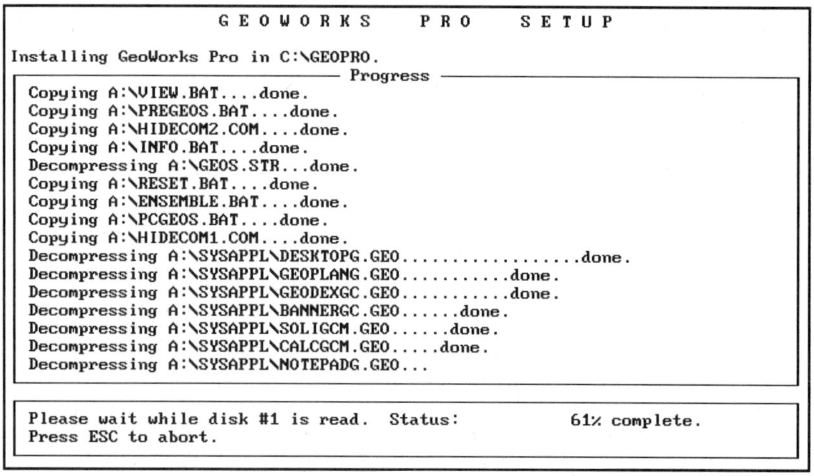

```
                    G E O W O R K S    P R O    S E T U P
Installing GeoWorks Pro in C:\GEOPRO.
                          ──── Progress ────
 Copying A:\VIEW.BAT....done.
 Copying A:\PREGEOS.BAT....done.
 Copying A:\HIDECOM2.COM....done.
 Copying A:\INFO.BAT....done.
 Decompressing A:\GEOS.STR...done.
 Copying A:\RESET.BAT....done.
 Copying A:\ENSEMBLE.BAT....done.
 Copying A:\PCGEOS.BAT....done.
 Copying A:\HIDECOM1.COM....done.
 Decompressing A:\SYSAPPL\DESKTOPG.GEO.................done.
 Decompressing A:\SYSAPPL\GEOPLANG.GEO..........done.
 Decompressing A:\SYSAPPL\GEODEXGC.GEO..........done.
 Decompressing A:\SYSAPPL\BANNERGC.GEO......done.
 Decompressing A:\SYSAPPL\SOLIGCM.GEO......done.
 Decompressing A:\SYSAPPL\CALCGCM.GEO.....done.
 Decompressing A:\SYSAPPL\NOTEPADG.GEO...

 Please wait while disk #1 is read.  Status:        61% complete.
 Press ESC to abort.
```

Fig. A.8

The Setup Copy
Progress screen.

After the Setup program copies the files to your disk, you see the message Press Enter to run GeoWorks Pro, Press F3 to exit to DOS. At this point, you can exit the installation by pressing F3; then return later to start GeoWorks Pro and configure the program for your hardware. To start GeoWorks Pro, press Enter.

Configuring the Program

This section begins at the point where you start GeoWorks Pro for the first time. Whether you continue the installation after files have been copied to the disk or quit and start again by typing **geos** from the DOS prompt, the procedures described in this section are identical.

Changing the Video Configuration

The first screen you see when you start GeoWorks Pro after installation evaluates the video selection made by the installation process (see fig. A.9). If the installation program made the correct selections and you can read the screen clearly, press Enter and skip the next section on changing the video setup.

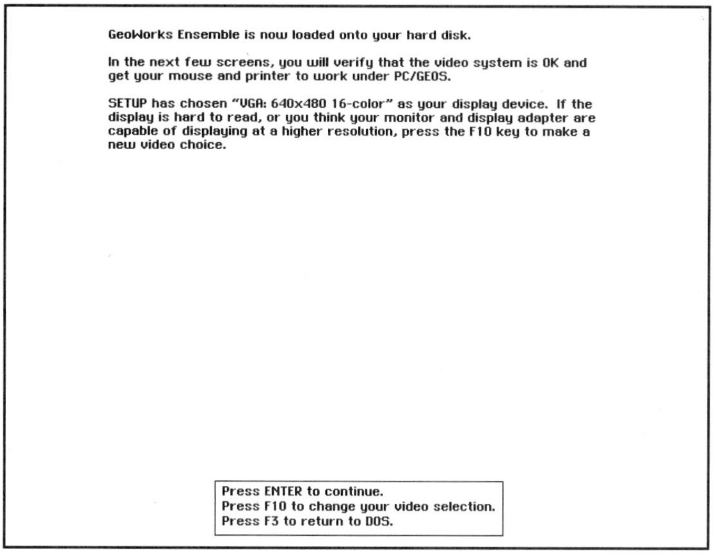

GeoWorks Ensemble is now loaded onto your hard disk.

In the next few screens, you will verify that the video system is OK and get your mouse and printer to work under PC/GEOS.

SETUP has chosen "VGA: 640x480 16-color" as your display device. If the display is hard to read, or you think your monitor and display adapter are capable of displaying at a higher resolution, press the F10 key to make a new video choice.

Press ENTER to continue.
Press F10 to change your video selection.
Press F3 to return to DOS.

Fig. A.9

The video selection evaluation screen.

Consider changing the video selection if the screen is hard to read or scrambled or if you think your system is capable of higher resolution than the video setup chosen by the installation program.

To select a different video display type, press F10 to access a list of video adapters. Scroll through the list using the up- and down-arrow keys and highlight the selection you want to try. Press Enter to restart the program with the new video selection.

If the new selection doesn't work, you can use the clever "escape hatch" provided by the designers of GeoWorks. Press F10 to reload the preceding video driver and restart GeoWorks with the preceding video settings. Then continue trying video selections until you find an acceptable setting. When you finish selecting the video settings, press Enter.

The next video screen, shown in figure A.10, evaluates the screen size settings. A white arrow appears at each corner of the screen. If the arrows are not visible or are more than a half-inch inside the boundaries of your screen, adjust the screen height and width settings until the arrows are properly positioned.

If you cannot adjust the screen properly, select another video setting. (You may need to consult the documentation for your computer, video adapter, or monitor for specifications on the type of video produced by your display adapter and supported by your monitor.) When the screen size is properly adjusted, press Enter to continue.

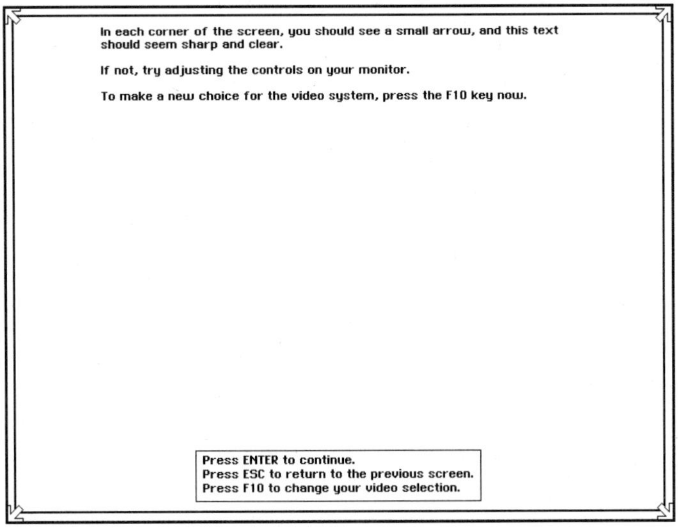

In each corner of the screen, you should see a small arrow, and this text should seem sharp and clear.

If not, try adjusting the controls on your monitor.

To make a new choice for the video system, press the F10 key now.

Press ENTER to continue.
Press ESC to return to the previous screen.
Press F10 to change your video selection.

Fig. A.10

The screen size
adjustment screen.

The final video test screen presents either a color or patterned panel, depending on whether you use a color or monochrome monitor. Use this test screen to adjust brightness and contrast.

Adjust the monitor's contrast setting until you can distinguish a difference between each of the sixteen boxes in the test pattern. Adjust the brightness setting until colors are neither washed out nor too dark. With a monochrome monitor, adjust for the best detail in the patterns.

Press Enter to complete your video configuration. The next screen that appears configures the mouse.

Configuring the Mouse

Mouse configuration is straightforward; select the mouse type you use and check the mouse's on-screen behavior. The first mouse screen (see fig. A.11) shows a scrolling list with 79 mouse types. Find the correct mouse brand and model using the up and down arrows, and then press Enter to install the mouse.

Figure A.12 shows the second mouse configuration screen. Test for successful mouse installation by pointing to the test button and pressing the left mouse button. If the installation is correct, the button flashes and your computer beeps. If you have a problem (usually no mouse pointer on-screen), work through the three suggested solutions presented on this screen.

What kind of mouse do you have? Choose one from the following list.

If you're not sure, check the box the mouse came in, or look at the label on its bottom. If you have no idea, choose "No idea."

Press the UP and DOWN arrows to scroll through the list one item at a time. Press PgUp and PgDn to scroll more items at once. Typing a letter will position the list at the first mouse whose name begins with that letter.

Kensington Serial Trackball
Kraft Serial Mouse (Microsoft Mode)
Laser 3-button (Microsoft Mode)
Laser 3-button Serial (Mouse Systems Mode)
Logitech 2-button Serial
Logitech Bus Mouse

Press ENTER to continue.
Press ESC to return to the previous screen.
Press F3 to return to DOS.

The first mouse configuration screen.

Move the mouse until the pointer (the small arrow) is over the box that reads "Click here to test" and press and release the left mouse button. The box will flash and the computer will beep.

Possible problems: If your mouse is hooked up, but there is no pointer on the screen, or the pointer does not move, you may have:
1.   Selected the wrong type of mouse. Press F10 to make another choice. If you have installed the mouse driver software supplied with your mouse, try choosing "MOUSE.COM or MOUSE.SYS."
2.   Chosen the wrong COM port or interrupt level for your mouse. Press ESC to go back and change your selections.
3.   Selected "No idea" but have not yet installed the driver software. Press F3 and install the software. When you are done, type "geos" to proceed with this setup.

Click here to test

Press ENTER to continue.
Press ESC to return to the previous screen.
Press F10 to change your mouse selection.
Press F3 to return to DOS.

The second mouse configuration screen.

When the mouse installation is satisfactory, press Enter to continue. The printer selection screen appears, as shown in figure A.13. The next section describes how to specify your printer.

```
What kind of printer do you have connected to your computer?  Choose one
of the models from this list.

The list is quite long; press the UP and DOWN arrows to scroll through it
one item at a time. Press PgUp and PgDn to scroll more items at once.
Typing a letter will position the list at the first printer whose name begins
with that letter.

  NEC P2200
  NEC P2200XE
  NEC P5200
  NEC P6
  NEC P6300
  NEC P7

Press ENTER to continue.
Press ESC to return to the previous screen.
```

Fig. A.13

The printer selection screen.

Specifying a Printer

The final step in the initial installation is to specify the type of printer you use and the port to which the printer is connected. Locate your printer on the scrolling list using the up and down arrows or the mouse. Press Enter to continue.

If your printer is not listed, select a printer similar to yours. Alternate choices usually are mentioned in the printer documentation. You also can experiment with some of the generic choices in the list. With non-specific choices, however, some special features of your printer may not be available.

After you specify the printer, you must indicate which port the printer uses so that GeoWorks Pro can direct printing output to that port. You must know whether your computer uses a parallel or serial connection and which parallel or serial port is used for the connection.

Your printer documentation indicates the type of connection required by the printer. You can determine the port name by examining the back of your computer to see the label where the cable is connected. Parallel ports usually are labeled LPT1, LPT2, and so on; serial ports are COM1, COM2, and so on. Parallel ports are used exclusively for printing, but you may find other devices, such as mice and modems, connected to some of the serial ports. After you specify your printer and its connections, press Enter to continue.

The final window in the configuration process (figure A.14) enables you to check your printer setup. Clicking the button marked Click here to test, with your printer turned on and on-line, should cause a printer test page to print successfully. Press Enter to end the printer setup process.

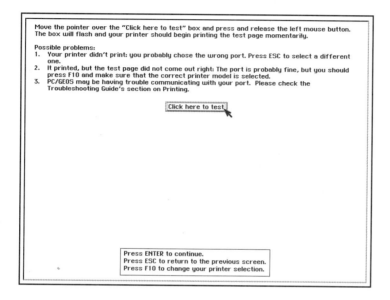

The printer test screen.

Entering Your Serial Number

When you leave the printer setup screen, GeoWorks displays a window where you enter your program serial number. Press Enter to complete the registration process. You can delay entering the serial number by clicking the button marked Wait till later, but the program will present the screen each time you start GeoWorks Pro until you enter the serial number.

You can find the serial number inside the front cover of the Customer Support Manual that comes with your original copy of GeoWorks Pro.

When you click either of the buttons in the serial number window, GeoWorks displays the Welcome screen, the starting point for GeoWorks Pro. The lessons in this book begin from this screen.

Starting GeoWorks Pro

The installation process automatically starts GeoWorks Pro the first time through, but to repeat the process, you must know how to launch the program on your own. The process is simple, with only two variations, depending on how you chose to specify the installation.

If you specified that your AUTOEXEC.BAT file should be modified during the installation, you can start GeoWorks Pro by typing **geos** at any DOS prompt. By default, the program opens with the Welcome screen, shown in figure A.15.

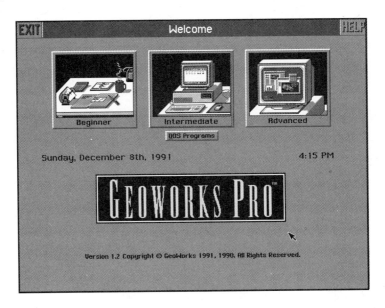

Fig. A.15

The Welcome screen.

If you did not direct the installation program to modify AUTOEXEC.BAT, you need to change to the GeoWorks directory and then launch the program. Assuming that the program is in the directory called C:\GEOWORKS, you type the three following lines, pressing Enter after each line to execute the command:

```
c:
cd \geoworks
geos
```

If the program is on another drive or in another directory, substitute the appropriate names in the preceding commands.

Quitting GeoWorks Pro

You discover, as you learn more about GeoWorks Pro, that you can quit the program in several ways, depending on your current task. One way to quit the program is to click the Exit button in the upper left corner of the Welcome screen. A confirming dialog box appears, asking whether you want to exit PC/GEOS. Choose **Yes** to quit.

You also can quit GeoWorks from any location in the program. Press the F3 function key. Each time you press F3 one *layer* of GeoWorks Pro closes down. Keep pressing F3 until you see the message asking whether you want to exit to PC/GEOS; choose **Yes** to return to DOS.

The instructions in this appendix guide you through the first installation of GeoWorks Pro, the configuration of your video, mouse and printer, and how to start and exit from GeoWorks Pro.

Installing Quattro Pro SE

Now that you have GeoWorks Pro installed on your hard disk, your next steps should be to install Quattro Pro SE on your hard disk, start Geo-Works, and add Quattro Pro SE as a DOS Program in GeoWorks. The following sections outline the steps necessary to accomplish these tasks.

Putting Quattro Pro SE on Your Hard Disk

Find the Quattro Pro SE disks that you get in the complete GeoWorks Pro package. There are four 5-1/4 inch disks or two 3-1/2 inch diskettes. Make sure that you have the disks in order and follow these steps to install Quattro Pro SE:

1. Turn on your computer. When you have the DOS prompt on–screen (normally C> or C:\>), place disk 1 in disk drive A.

2. Change drives to drive A by typing **a:** and pressing Enter.

3. At the DOS prompt (either A> or A:\>), type **install** and press Enter.

   The QUATTRO PRO SE Installation Utility screen appears. Press Enter to continue.

4. On-screen, you see the prompt Enter the SOURCE drive to use: A. Press Enter.

5. The next prompt asks for the directory on your hard disk to which you want to install Quattro Pro SE. The default directory is C:\QPRO. Press Enter to accept the default, or type a new directory name and press Enter.

The installation program begins copying files from the program disks to your hard disk. When the installation program prompts you for the next program disk, remove the current disk, insert the disk requested, and press Enter. Copying the files from the program disks to your hard disk takes just a few minutes.

Completing the Quattro Pro SE Installation

Once all Quattro Pro SE files are on the hard disk, you will see prompts to answer a few questions. The questions enable you to do the following:

■ Select a display type

■ Add the Quattro Pro SE subdirectory to the DOS path

■ Install a printer

As you complete the installation, be sure to read each screen completely. Press the F2 key to change a selection, and press Enter to continue. When you answer all the questions, the DOS prompt reappears on-screen. Type **c:** and press Enter to return to the hard disk.

Adding Quattro Pro SE as a DOS Program

You may start Quattro Pro SE from GeoWorks in one of two ways. With the first method, you change to the C:\QPRO directory, using Geo-Manager, and double-click on Q.EXE, the program that starts Quattro Pro SE. The second method, a more elegant way to start Quattro Pro SE, is to add a button in DOS Programs that starts Quattro. Follow these steps to add Quattro Pro SE to a button in DOS Programs:

1. Start GeoWorks by typing **geos** at the DOS prompt and pressing Enter.

2. From the Welcome screen, click the **D**OS Programs button.

3. Select the **O**ptions menu and choose **C**reate New Button. The Select DOS file for button dialog box appears.

4. Change to the directory to which you installed Quattro Pro SE. Use the Drive and Directory buttons and scroll through the file list using the scroll bars. To open a directory in the file list, double-click on the directory.

5. Click the file name Q.EXE—the file that starts Quattro Pro SE.

6. Click the Use This File button.

7. When the Button Settings dialog box appears on-screen, you can choose the following options:

   ■ Use the Change Picture button to change the button image (a Quattro Pro image is available).

   ■ Double-click in the Button Title text box and change the title of the button.

   ■ Add any command line options.

   ■ Enable the Ask before returning to PC/GEOS? option.

8. Click OK to exit the dialog box. The button appears on the DOS Programs screen. Click the new button to start Quattro Pro SE.

Troubleshooting Tips

G eoWorks Pro is a well-built, well-tested program that is not prone to frequent crashes or unpredictable failures. Most users experience no problem with normal installation or operation of the program. Problems that do arise are frequently related to memory conflicts or incorrect settings in areas such as video and printers. You easily can correct most of these problems. When GeoWorks Pro is up and running correctly, you can expect consistent, solid performance.

The following sections summarize the most frequent problem areas and common solutions. Suggestions for steps to take if you cannot solve a problem are included at the end of this appendix.

Installation Problems

The first part of any GeoWorks Pro installation consists of copying files from the distribution disks to the new GEOWORKS directory. Unless you do not have the necessary amount of space on your disk, this process should proceed smoothly.

After you copy all files to your disk, GeoWorks asks you to start the program and then presents a series of screens used to configure such features as the video, mouse, and printer. Appendix A, "Installing GeoWorks Pro," describes the normal installation process.

If the program fails to work after being installed according to the instructions, you should exit to DOS. You can press the F3 function key repeatedly to return to DOS if GeoWorks is running but not visible because of video problems. If pressing F3 doesn't work, you can return to DOS by restarting your computer. At the DOS prompt, you may want to use GeoHelp to diagnose your problem.

To access GeoHelp, follow these steps:

1. At the DOS prompt, to change to the GEOWORKS directory, type **cd geoworks** and press Enter.

2. Type **geohelp** to start GeoHelp.

   GeoHelp, new with Version 1.2 and GeoWorks Pro, methodically leads you through troubleshooting procedures for both software and hardware conflicts. Some elements of GeoHelp can get quite technical, but other elements offer suggestions and information useful at any level of technical skills.

3. If GeoHelp doesn't get you started, call the help line listed at the end of this appendix.

Running but Frozen

If you see a screen message that GeoWorks Pro is running, but the screen is frozen, that is, unaffected by mouse movements or keyboard commands, check the back of your keyboard for a switch designating an AT or PC setting. Set the switch to the other position and reboot.

If your computer has a Turbo switch on its front panel, turn the switch off and restart the program in nonturbo mode.

Video Problems

If your screen is illegible, GeoWorks Pro may be running properly, but the video setting may be wrong. Press F3 until you return to DOS. (If GeoWorks Pro is working normally, each press of F3 closes an application; two or three presses may be required to return to DOS.) If pressing F3 returns you to DOS, the program is working, but the video setup is wrong. The first step toward correcting this problem is to change your video setting to a mode that almost all video boards support.

When you are back at the DOS prompt, you can change the video setting by doing the following:

1. Type **setup cga** to run a subset of the installation program using monochrome CGA screen graphics.

2. Continue through the setup screens, following the on-screen instructions until you are able to restart GeoWorks Pro.

3. After the program restarts, select the Express menu and choose **S**tartup.

   The Startup cascade menu appears.

4. Click Preferences.

5. When the Preferences window opens, click the Video option button. In the Video dialog box that opens, you can select the correct video mode.

   The internal video setup procedure has provisions for reverting back to the preceding video choice if a new selection does not work.

Memory Problems

One of the most frequent reasons GeoWorks Pro fails to start is a collision with a type of memory-resident program running in extended or expanded memory on your system. These programs, called *TSR*'s (for Terminate and Stay Resident), may be used by DOS or started by another program.

If you suspect that this problem exists, type **geos /nomem** to start GeoWorks. *Note:* Be sure that you type the space and the forward slash in this command. This command makes GeoWorks Pro run entirely in standard memory. If the program starts properly, then search your AUTOEXEC.BAT or CONFIG.SYS files to find memory resident programs that conflict with GeoWorks Pro. If you are using DOS versions 4.X or 5, the mem command profiles memory usage and assists in finding any offending TSR's. GeoWorks, which contains its own memory managers and device drivers, does not need or use any TSR's.

If GeoWorks Pro starts correctly using geos /nomem, examine your AUTOEXEC.BAT and CONFIG.SYS files and remove the lines that start the TSR programs. You should then be able to start GeoWorks Pro without the /nomem command.

Mouse Problems

With more than 40 mouse drivers from which to choose, you are likely to find a mouse driver that works. If you cannot find a suitable mouse driver, you can correct the problem with the following steps:

1. Install the driver software that comes with your mouse.

2. Click the Preferences desk tool and choose the Mouse option button. A list of mouse drivers appears.

3. Choose the Nothing Else Works option from the list of mouse drivers.

   GeoWorks looks for and uses the driver that comes with your mouse.

Printing Problems

The default settings for GeoWorks Pro use the computer BIOS for printing services; however, some machines do not work with this setting. To change the BIOS setting, do the following:

1. Select the Express menu and choose Startup.

2. From the cascade menu that opens, click Preferences.

   The Preferences window appears.

3. Choose the Computer option button.

4. In the Parallel Ports section of the window, next to the name of the port you use for printing (probably LPT1), choose the button marked DOS.

Another common printer problem is the wrong port specified for connections. The most common problem situation with PCs involves a parallel printer connected to the computer port LPT1. If your printer is not responding, check your manuals or inspect the labels on the hardware to be certain that you have specified the right port and port type.

During program installation, be sure that you choose the right printer from the Printer Setup list. The list covers nearly every popular printer. If the Printer Setup list does not contain your printer, you may be able to specify a compatible printer. Refer to your printer manual to find information on compatible printers.

If your printer manual contains a recommendation for a compatible printer, open the Preferences window, choose the Printer desk tool, choose Install New in the Printer dialog box, and select the recommended printer from the displayed list.

Crashes

Occasionally something happens that causes GeoWorks Pro to freeze completely or *crash* and return to DOS. Whether Pro freezes or crashes, a message indicating that the program did not shut down normally appears when you restart the program. This message prompts you to Start PC/GEOS Normally or Reset Advanced Workspace.

Restarting normally returns you to the configuration you were using when you crashed. You lose any work you did not save recently or that had not been automatically protected by the timed save feature found in the Preferences Look and Feel desk tool.

Resetting the Advanced Workspace starts the session with only GeoManager running. Use this option if you want to clean up the previous configuration—particularly if you suspect that the crash was caused by running too many applications or windows simultaneously.

America Online

Most America Online problems revolve around modem settings. You must specify the right port for connection, the proper modem speed, and modem start-up commands. Chapter 10, "Using America Online," addresses these topics in detail. You should check your modem settings again as the first step in diagnosing communication problems.

America Online may collide with programs running in extended or expanded memory. If you cannot get America Online to run, remove any TSRs from memory and restart AOL.

Modem setting priorities can be confusing. The Preferences desk tool contains a Modem option button. The settings for ports and modem setup strings you enter in the Preferences desk tool become the default when using GeoComm. America Online also contains a modem setup window in which you establish settings used while America Online is running.

The Computer desk tool, activated from the Preferences window, displays a serial port setting box. Normally, you don't need to worry about the serial port setting; however, GeoWorks Pro turns COM3 and COM4 ports off by default. To use them, open the Computer desk tool, click On for each port to turn it on, and use the arrow boxes for each port to specify which interrupt level each one uses.

An interrupt is an instruction that halts processing momentarily so that input or output operations can take place. The computer must know which interrupt setting is used by the port to which your modem is attached. If you use COM3 or COM4, consult your computer hardware manual to determine the interrupt settings for the serial ports on your machine. Changing the interrupt settings is not a job for the faint-hearted or technically timid. Do not worry about changing interrupt settings unless you use COM3 or COM4.

The End of Your Rope

Occasions arise when your troubleshooting skills just aren't equal to the task. If, after prolonged effort, you and your computer still stare blankly at one another, take heart; or more precisely, take phone. GeoWorks provides an excellent staff on the Customer Service Hotline. As of this writing, the Hotline number is (510) 644-3456. The Hotline hours are 9:00 a.m. to 5:00 p.m. Pacific time (except Wednesday when the Hotline closes at 3:00 p.m.). Although you pay for the call, you are not charged for the service.

If you can run America Online, your best bet for technical support is found in the GeoWorks Forum. Post a note outlining your problem in the Beginner's Room, and you may well have an answer overnight. You also can learn a great deal by following the messages posted in the Frequently Asked Questions section of the main GeoWorks Forum menu or by browsing the GeoWorks Product Message Boards, which contain sections for each major GeoWorks Pro application. A wonderful collection of talent is available in the Forum. You can be virtually certain that someone else has encountered and probably solved your problem.

If you are having trouble setting up America Online, you can get specialized help by calling the help line for First-Time Installation. The number is 1-800-227-6364.

New Features in Versions 1.2 and Pro

Version 1.0 of GeoWorks Ensemble, released in November 1990, proved to be remarkably bug-free. A few minor bug fixes were nothing that prevented most users from enjoying a trouble-free program. Still, enthusiastic users flooded GeoWorks with requests for additional features and improvements.

In late August, 1991, GeoWorks released Version 1.2, providing many small—but highly-desired—improvements and one large improvement: the spelling checker. Late in 1991, GeoWorks Pro (technically Version 1.2.8) emerged. This new version includes all the Version 1.2 features, as well as Quattro Pro SE, Borland's excellent spreadsheet that comes "bundled" with GeoWorks Pro. The Pro version also reorganizes the workspace areas into Beginning, Intermediate, and Advanced.

This book includes all features from GeoWorks Ensemble 1.0, 1.2, and GeoWorks Pro. (Version 1.1, a specialized maintenance release, is not distributed widely.) To assist users who may not use or know about some of the excellent program enhancements, this appendix explains the new features added to Versions 1.2 and Pro. Each of the following sections provides references to the *Using GeoWorks Pro* chapter that fully explains the topic.

Version 1.2 Enhancements

Version 1.2 was a major step forward for GeoWorks Ensemble. The upgrade included the much desired spelling checker and many other bonuses, such as PostScript printer drivers and a greatly expanded Preferences application.

Spelling Checker

If you used GeoWorks Ensemble Version 1.0, you probably understand why a GeoWorks newsletter headlined Version 1.2 as the "Spellchecker Upgrade." A spelling checker for GeoWrite was the most requested improvement in the program. Chapter 7, "Using GeoWrite," explains using the robust 100,000 word spelling checker, added to the GeoWrite Edit menu.

Installation and Removal

A DOS application called GEOHELP.EXE, found in the program directory, helps troubleshoot installation problems. Typing GEOHELP from the DOS prompt starts a menu-driven help program. An improved installation program enables you to choose different installation sizes if you have limited hard disk space. Appendix A, "Installing GeoWorks Pro," explains both features.

DOS 5 Compatibility

Version 1.0 of GeoWorks Ensemble had to be "tricked" into recognizing DOS 5.0. The upgrade recognizes the new DOS version and can utilize the task swapping feature of DOS 5, which enables the user to switch quickly from one program to another, thus suspending the unused programs.

You can run GeoWorks Ensemble, together with other DOS programs, under the task swapper. See Chapter 13, "Operating DOS Programs."

Printing Enhancements

PostScript printers (both color and black-and-white) have been added to the printer selection. Paper size settings have been expanded to accept heights and widths from 2 to 45 inches. The new Printer Control Panel (on the Express menu) enables you to send several documents to the printer and monitor their status while you continue with other work.

If you are a "font junkie," you can get more fonts to use with GeoWorks Ensemble by converting Nimbus Q fonts from the German type foundry URW using a Font Converter appliance stored in the EXTRAS folder of GeoManager. GeoWorks also sells new font packs that contain assortments of ready-to-run fonts for different purposes. Contact Customer Support at (510) 644-3456 for details. Chapter 7, "Using GeoWrite," covers these features.

Customization

The Preferences desk tool has been expanded to include three new buttons, and the original buttons, still present, contain new features. In particular, don't ignore the International button, which controls settings for the number of digits in decimal entries. The International button also controls date and time formats and several other settings that may be useful to you.

Chapter 11, "Customizing with the Preferences Desk Tool," covers the new Preferences features.

DOS Programs

An excellent selection of new icons has been added to the DOS Programs screen. You can set the buttons to return automatically to GeoWorks Ensemble after exiting the DOS program. Chapter 13, "Operating DOS Programs," explains this feature.

The EXTRAS Folder

The upper left corner of the GeoManager WORLD screen displays an EXTRAS folder. The material inside this folder indicates the dedication, skill, and craziness of the crew at GeoWorks. For starters, you can see a spinning word display, whose only evident purpose is to look great and chew up computer resources so that you can see what happens with the amazing Perf (short for "Performance") tool.

Words fail to describe Perf. Perhaps the closest approximation is a brain scan of your computer. If you are a technical whiz, read the help screens that accompany Perf. Each of the vivid little charts analyzes an aspect of program or computer performance. If you are not technically inclined, enjoy the show, browse the help screens, and admire the skills of the team at GeoWorks.

If you need to capture GeoWorks screens, you can find Adam de Boor's excellent screen dumper utility in EXTRAS. In the EXTRAS folder, you also can find the Nimbus font converter referred to previously (notice the great icon).

Although you may not need to venture into the EXTRAS folder for day-to-day work, find some excuse to explore the EXTRAS folder. You will return a changed—well, at least an entertained—person. Although no specific chapter covers the EXTRAS folder, the components of this folder are mentioned, where appropriate, throughout the book.

New Features of GeoWorks Pro

Old features have been reorganized and new ones added to GeoWorks Pro. The result is a sleeker, more powerful package that should please previous users and be even easier to work with for new users.

Workspace Reorganization

The Welcome window presents a new face in GeoWorks Pro. Where earlier versions had buttons for Appliances, Professional, and DOS Programs Workspaces, Pro now shows Beginning, Intermediate, and Advanced buttons.

The new name for the Appliances Workspace is *Beginning* and the previous Professional Workspace is now *Advanced*; otherwise, these two workspaces remain essentially the same in structure. The Intermediate Workspace, however, is an entirely new concept designed to bridge the gap between Beginning and Advanced.

The Intermediate Workspace is document-oriented. The main screen for the new workspace is the File Cabinet. Rather than finding icons that represent programs like GeoWrite and GeoDraw, you find folders containing document templates. Double-clicking the template icons launches the associated programs.

Another feature of the Intermediate Workspace eliminates the need to learn DOS commands for common procedures like copying files or formatting disks. Buttons that carry out file and directory management tasks by means of simple dialog boxes surround the File Cabinet window.

The Quattro Pro Viewer

In the GeoManager window, you find a new application: the Quattro Pro Viewer. This program provides a smooth, automatic link between GeoWorks Pro and the Quattro Pro SE spreadsheet that comes with the program. Using this feature, you can look at spreadsheets and charts and copy them to other applications without leaving GeoWorks Pro. You also can switch smoothly to Quattro Pro SE to create and modify spreadsheets and charts. When you quit Quattro Pro SE, GeoWorks Pro automatically reopens and displays in the Viewer the spreadsheet you were using.

This book devotes two chapters to the new spreadsheet features. Chapter 14, "Learning about Spreadsheets," is a primer on using Quattro Pro SE. Chapter 15, "Using Quattro Pro Viewer," shows how to use the Viewer to link GeoWorks Pro with the spreadsheet program.

Enhanced Task Switching

GeoWorks Pro improves its previous task-switching capability by adding compatibility with TaskMAX, the task switcher contained in DR DOS 6.0 from Digital Research. Using TaskMAX and sufficient memory, you can run GeoWorks Pro and DOS programs side-by-side in memory, switching rapidly from one to another. Chapter 13, "Operating DOS Programs," explains this feature.

Other Changes

GeoWorks Pro also provides other beneficial changes. Because of the heavy use of templates in the new Intermediate Workspace, users of the Advanced Workspace in GeoWorks Pro have access to these excellent added documents whenever they enter the DOCUMENT directory. See Chapter 3, "Learning File Cabinet," for details. In addition, you now can import TIFF images and Quattro Pro EPS charts into GeoDraw and the Scrapbook. See Chapter 8, "Using GeoDraw," for additional information.

GeoReps on America Online

The GeoWorks GeoRep program is a unique means for a software company to provide customer service. The program is made up of volunteers from across the country, authorized by GeoWorks to speak with authority on behalf of the company. These representatives assist GeoWorks' customers to overcome any problems they have in using the software. Daily, these GeoReps sign on to America Online to answer the various questions raised on the boards (see Chapter 10, "Using America Online").

The GeoReps vary in age and are located as far apart as Maryland, New Brunswick, and California. All the Reps are fully familiar with the GeoWorks products as a whole; however, each also has an area or areas of expertise.

The Reps are assigned to message boards on America Online according to these special areas of support. Some Reps serve as hosts, making themselves available nightly in a "chat room" so that those customers with questions (or who just want to talk) can get prompt answers. The list of GeoReps, with their screen names and expertise, appears in table D.1.

Table D.1 GeoReps on America Online

GeoRep	America Online Screen Name	Responsibility
Kenneth L. Bell, Sr.	GWRepKenny	Wednesday Chat Host
Kenneth Bell, Jr.	GWRep Ken2	Friday Chat Host
Timothy Bereman	GWRep Tim	GeoManager
Doug Blair	GWRepDougB	Hardware Configuration
Robin Bush	GWRepRobyn	The Beginners Area
Bruce Cole	GWRepBruce	Education
Jim Collette	GWRep JimC	PC/GEOS Technical Information
Derek Cooper	GWRepDerek	Suggestions & Impressions, Librarian, Frequently Asked Questions
Robert DaCunta	GWRepBobby	Graphics
Clark Jay Degn	GWRep Jay	GeoDraw
John Ezike	GWRep John	DOS Programs, Saturday Chat Host
Dave Gibson	GWRep Dave	GeoComm, Librarian, Newsletter
John Knox	GWRepJohnK	Other Applications
Marshall Kragen	GWRep MK	Online Assistant to Manager, Librarian
Mike Kumin	GWRepMike1	General Questions
Peter Lerten	GWRepPeter	Installation & Setup
Steve Main	GWRepSteve	Monday Chat Host, Newsletter
Randy Padawer	GWRepRandy	GeoWrite, Sunday Chat Host
Chris Russo	GWRepChris	Thursday Chat Host
Rosemarie Sterchie	GWRep Rose	Tuesday Chat Host, Newsletter
Donald L. Stewart	GWRep Don	Printers & Printing, Tech Notes
Ken Tomb	GWRep Ken	America Online Reports
Tony Cuozzo	TCuozzo1	Provides GeoWorks support on GEnie

Feel free to contact these Reps with any problems you are having using GeoWorks products. You may contact them on their message boards or by E-mail. You will find each of them is on-line nightly, ready to assist you. You get a prompt answer to your question, and if it is detailed, the answer is in writing so that you can print it out and follow it properly. This service is a benefit you don't get when you use the telephone technical service lines of GeoWorks.